# A HISTORY OF THE
# JEWS IN ENGLAND

# A HISTORY OF
# THE JEWS
# IN ENGLAND

BY

CECIL ROTH

THIRD EDITION

JOHN TROTTER PUBLISHERS

ISBN 1 871840 00 7

*Reprinted by arrangement
with Oxford University Press*

© *Oxford University Press 1964*

*First edition 1941*
*Second edition 1949*
*Third edition 1964*
*Reprinted 1978, 1979, 1980*
*1989*

*Printed and bound in Great Britain by
Antony Rowe Ltd, Chippenham, Wiltshire*

# PREFACE TO THE THIRD EDITION

THE changes in this new edition of this work have been substantial: for it has been necessary to take into account the further research of the past fifteen years, including in particular the significant contributions of Mr. H. G. Richardson on the medieval period. For serious study and correct information this entirely supersedes the previous editions. I have done my best to combine accuracy with a sense of proportion and appreciation of permanent and human values. But, during the long years since this volume was written, I have become more and more painfully conscious of my inadequacy to cope satisfactorily with every aspect even of the limited subject with which it deals.

C. R.

*Oxford, January 1964*

# PREFACE TO THE FIRST EDITION

IT is curious that none of the great Jewish communities of the western world found an historian so early as the numerically unimportant nucleus in England. The first formal history of the Jews in this country was, in fact, published more than two centuries ago—the *Anglia Judaica* of Dr. D'Blossiers Tovey, like myself a member of Merton College, Oxford ('by me never to be mentioned without terms of *Affection* and *Respect*', if I may be permitted to repeat his words). This comprehensive work, which can still be consulted with profit, was itself based on the researches of the Exchequer historian Madox and the anti-Semitic pamphleteer Prynne, the latter having published his findings eighty years earlier as a contribution to the debate under the Commonwealth on the readmission of Jews to England. The results of this early interest in the subject have not been altogether good; for the general histories of Anglo-Jewry, produced in a more scientific age and with access to vast new stores of information, have tended to be based upon their remote forerunners with a fidelity which is often noteworthy and sometimes regrettable. This is the reason for the present attempt to furnish a completely new work on the subject, summing up the results of the voluminous and exceptionally important researches of the last half-century.

So far as the medieval period is concerned, down to the reign of John, one illustrious scholar, Joseph Jacobs, laid the foundations in his remarkable work, *The Jews of Angevin England*, a pioneering attempt of astonishing maturity. While some of his incidental hypotheses were at once disputed with considerable vigour, his general conclusions have been accepted by subsequent writers without examination. But there are some serious flaws in the work. Jacobs claimed to bring together every scrap of information that could be assembled on the life of Anglo-Jewry until 1206. He included, indeed, a great deal of dubious material. But his omissions, though less patent, are perhaps more striking. Thus, in the first Pipe Roll of Henry I, which embodies the oldest official record of Jews in England, he omitted one entry out of six, confused another, and introduced mistakes into two more. For that of the first year of Richard I, he gives only ten entries of Jewish interest, out of a possible thirty-four in the printed text even then available; for the first year of John (for which he had recourse, with typical zeal, to the original manuscript) he gives only four entries out of a possible sixty-six. His translations too, whether from the Latin or the Hebrew, are extremely unreliable, and sometimes ludicrously misleading.[1]

What has been said here is not intended to be in disparagement of Jacobs's remarkable work. But it is enough to indicate that he is not to be relied upon implicitly, and that at every turn it is necessary to have recourse to the original authorities, the published mass of which has moreover increased enormously since his day. From the beginning of the thirteenth century, where Jacobs left off, the Calendar of the Plea Rolls of the Exchequer of the Jews, three volumes of which have now appeared, constitute an inexhaustible but hitherto imperfectly utilized source. There is, too, a very great amount of material,

---

[1] Thus, *cum equis et armis* becomes 'with horses and asses'; *de obol. musce* ('for an obol of musk') is suggested to be an indication of Muscovite origin: and the phrase *judaei legales* ('law-worthy Jews') is repeatedly rendered as 'Jewish lawyers'.

out of all proportion to the slight numerical importance of those involved, in the long series of Patent and Close Rolls and similar record-sources, which have been drawn upon only sporadically in the past. If those of my chapters which deal with this period may appear sometimes to be imperfectly digested, it is because the volume of new material has necessitated public deglutination.

For the 'Middle Period' of three and a half centuries after the Expulsion of 1290 (during which, contrary to the general belief, there were few interludes when no Jew was to be found in the country) the sources of our information are quite different. Use has not been made hitherto in any general work of the remarkable recent discoveries bearing upon this, which have revolutionized our knowledge of the Jews in Shakespeare's England in particular. Moreover, there is still much to be revealed in this field. The present volume contains, for example, the first account of an illustrious group of crypto-Jewish physicians under Henry VIII, whose distinction exceeded that of Roderigo Lopez a generation later. In dealing with the Resettlement, I have drawn lavishly and at times verbally on my *Life of Menasseh ben Israel*, which, though based to a large extent on original sources, has remained unknown in this country owing to the fatal accident of Transatlantic publication. I have, however, been able to take advantage of later and riper investigations here as well, at some points with important results. Attention may be drawn to the completely new account of the premature attempt by Gentile enthusiasts to secure the recall of the Jews to England in 1648, and the drastic restatement of the part played by Cromwell in the negotiations of the following decade.

For the subsequent period, an attempt has been made to compress into a hundred and fifty pages the numerous monographs and articles published during the last forty years. But I have endeavoured to eschew the parochial and personal aspect which has hitherto monopolized attention and to write the history of the Jews in England rather than the *memorabilia* of the community of London, which have engaged the attention of previous writers. Here and there, moreover, I have been able to make use of unexplored manuscript material and ephemeral publications, which correct or supplement the accepted account. I have concluded my work with the Parliamentary Emancipation of the Jews in 1858/9, with which English Jewry entered definitely into English life; but an Epilogue gives an outline of the most important subsequent developments. Throughout, I have tried to stress the social side and to describe, not only what happened to the Jews in England, but also what manner of men they were and what part they played in the life of the country. Perhaps as much as one-half of the data given in this volume have not appeared in any previous work devoted to the subject: but it is rather this approach which, I venture to believe, makes the story I have told virtually a new one.

It is a pleasant duty for me to acknowledge the great debt I owe to Mr. J. M. Rich, who generously placed at my disposal his abstracts of medieval English records relating to the Jews, prepared for a work of his own which I trust will see the light in the future. His liberality enables me to parade a maximum of erudition with a minimum of effort, and to him is due a great part of the credit for any special quality in my first chapters. I am deeply grateful, too, to the Rev. Michael Adler, formerly President of the Jewish Historical Society of England; to Mr. Christopher Cheney, Reader in Diplomatic in the University of Oxford; and to Mr. Max Beloff, Lecturer in Modern History in the University of Manchester, who between them read the typescript, gave me the benefit of their criticisms and suggestions, and saved me from many egregious displays of ignorance. Finally, I am happy to have this opportunity of expressing my thanks to Mr. Harry Sacher and the associated founders of the Readership in Post-Biblical Jewish Studies in the University of Oxford, which provided me with the opportunity of carrying into effect a project that had long remained in the limbo of unfulfilled hopes.

This Preface is dated on the six hundred and fiftieth anniversary of the Banishment of the Jews from England in 1290.

C. R.

*Oxford, 1 November 1940*

# CONTENTS

# BIBLIOGRAPHICAL NOTE

A COMPLETE Bibliography of Anglo-Jewish history, containing upwards of 2,000 entries, has been published under the editorship of the present author (*Magna Bibliotheca Anglo-Judaica*, London, 1937; to be referred to in the following pages as *Bibl.*, with the section and number of the entry in question). It is therefore superfluous to give here any detailed bibliographical indications, which by comparison must be inadequate and incomplete. The list that follows contains only the titles of some subsequent works and those cited most frequently in the succeeding pages.

ABRAHAMS, B. L. *The Expulsion of the Jews from England in 1290* (Oxford, 1895)      = *Expulsion.*

ABRAHAMS, I., and STOKES, H. P. *Starrs and Jewish Charters Preserved in the British Museum*, with additions by H. Loewe (3 vols., Cambridge, 1930–2)      = *Starrs.*

ADLER, M. *Jews of Medieval England* (London, 1939)      = *J.M.E.*

BARNETT, L. D. (ed.). *El Libro de los Acuerdos* (Oxford, 1931)      = *Libro.*

—— *Bevis Marks Records* (Oxford, 1940, &c.)      = *B.M. Records.*

DAVIS, M. D. *Shetaroth: Hebrew Deeds of English Jews before 1290* (London, 1888)      = *Shetaroth.*

HENRIQUES, H. S. Q. *The Jews and the English Law* (Oxford, 1908)

JACOBS, J. *The Jews of Angevin England: Documents and Records* (London, 1893)      = *J.A.E.*

RIGG, J. M. *Select Pleas, Starrs, and other records from the Exchequer of the Jews, 1220–1284* (London, 1902)      = *P.E.J.*

—— *Calendar of the Plea Rolls of the Exchequer of the Jews* (3 vols., London, 1905–29; third volume edited by H. Jenkinson)      = *E.J.*

ROTH, C. *Life of Menasseh ben Israel* (Philadelphia, 1934)

—— (ed.). *Magna Bibliotheca Anglo-Judaica: a Bibliographical Guide to Anglo-Jewish History* (London, 1937)      = *Bibl.*

—— (ed.). *Anglo-Jewish Letters, 1158–1917* (London, 1938)

STOKES, H. P. *Studies in Anglo-Jewish History* (Edinburgh, 1913)      = *Studies.*

WOLF, L. *Menasseh ben Israel's Mission to Oliver Cromwell* (London, 1901)

—— *Essays in Jewish History* (London, 1934)      = *Essays.*

*Transactions of the Jewish Historical Society of England* (20 vols., London, 1895–1964) = *Trs. J.H.S.E.*

*Miscellanies of the Jewish Historical Society of England* (6 vols., London, 1923–62) = *Misc. J.H.S.E*

*Publications of the American Jewish Historical Society* (52 vols., 1893–1963) = *Pub. A.J.H.S.*

Books and articles on the subject published between 1937 and 1960 are now listed in *Nova Bibliotheca Anglo-Judaica*, ed. R. P. Lehmann, London, 1961 (to be referred to in supplementary notes in these pages as *Nov. Bibl.*). The following major contributions, published since this work originally appeared, have been extensively used:

HYAMSON, A. M. *The Sephardim of England* (London, 1951) = *Sephardim.*

LIPMAN, V. D. (ed.). *Three Centuries of Anglo-Jewish History* (London, 1961) = *Three Centuries.*

RICHARDSON, H. G. *English Jewry under Angevin Kings* (London, 1960) = *J.A.K.*

ROTH, C. *The Jews of Medieval Oxford* (Oxford, 1951) = *Oxford.*

—— *The Intellectual Activities of Medieval English Jewry* (British Academy supplemental papers, No. viii, London, 1949) = *Int. Act.*

—— *The Rise of Provincial Jewry* (London, 1950) = *Prov. Jewry.*

—— *Essays and Portraits in Anglo-Jewish History* (Philadelphia, 1962) = *Essays and Portraits.*

## OTHER ABBREVIATIONS

C.R.    Close Rolls.*
P.R.    Patent Rolls.
Pp.R.   Pipe Rolls.
F.R.    Fine Rolls.
Obl.R.  Oblate Rolls.
Ch.R.   Charter Rolls.
C.R.R.  Curia Regis Rolls.
Lib.R.  Liberate Rolls.
S.P.D.  State Papers, Domestic.
S.P.V.  State Papers, Venetian.

* These and the similar series, whether Calendared or otherwise, are referred to for the sake of convenience and clarity by year and page, not by volume.

| | |
|---|---|
| H.O. | Home Office. |
| *H.M.C.* | *Historical Manuscripts Commission.* |
| *J.Q.R.* | *Jewish Quarterly Review* (N.S. = New Series). |
| *R.E.J.* | *Revue des Études Juives.* |
| *J.C.* | *Jewish Chronicle.* |
| *A.J.H.E.* | *Anglo-Jewish Historical Exhibition* [of 1887: *Papers* and *Catalogue*]. |

# I

# SETTLEMENT AND CONSOLIDATION

## *To* 1189

### § 1

THERE can be no doubt that the Jews began to be associated with England and the British Isles later than with any other country of western Europe that received them in the Middle Ages. Fantasy has indeed attempted to carry the story back to a remote antiquity, to the period of the fall of the kingdom of Judaea and the destruction of Jerusalem by Nebuchadnezzar; while some sober students do not consider it improbable that, with the Phoenician traders who reached Cornwall in the seventh or eighth century before the Christian era, there may have come a few adventurous Hebrews from the maritime territories of the Holy Land.[1] But it is more likely that the connexion began centuries later, in Roman times, when merchants or captives from Palestine reached every province of the Empire.

The legendary missionary journey of St. Paul, which led to the foundation of the British church, presupposes the existence of a Jewish community—always the initial object of his propaganda—even before the capture of Jerusalem by Titus in the year 70.[2] After that catastrophe, the entire Roman world was flooded with Palestinian slaves, and there is no reason to imagine that Britain was excepted. Tangible proof of intercourse between the two lands at this period has been provided by the discovery, during the course of excavations in England, of coins minted in Judaea in the first and second centuries.[3] Whoever

---

[1] The discovery during excavations at Gaza of ornaments made of Irish (?) gold proves that there was indirect intercourse between the British Isles and Palestine even before the Israelite conquest, and renders this hypothesis somewhat less improbable.

[2] The first Bishop of Britain was legendarily Aristobulus, brother of Barnabas.

[3] For details see now S. Applebaum, *Were there Jews in Roman Britain?* in *Trs. J.H.S.E.* xvii. 189–205, where all the archaeological evidence is carefully examined,

brought them—Roman legionaries or Jewish captives—it is probable that trade and traders went between the two provinces by the same route that was followed by these insignificant relics. There is accordingly good reason to believe that the greater urban centres in Britain harboured, if not organized Jewish communities, at least some nucleus of Jewish population. St. Jerome, in the fourth century, certainly thought so; and, in more than one passage of his writings, he specifically referred to the extension of the Diaspora as far as this remote island province, and to the conviction of the Jews of his day that their co-religionists would be gathered even thence at the time of the great final Deliverance.[1]

If such a community existed it must have been wiped out in the anarchical interlude of the Teutonic invasions, when the Romanized Celts yielded to the Anglo-Saxons, and Britannia became England. In the Saxon period the Jewish traders, then so important in the Mediterranean world and on the Continent of Europe, may have extended their activities as far as the British Isles, but all the evidence formerly adduced in support of this hypothesis is apocryphal.[2] Whether or no individuals visited the country, it may be stated with confidence that no permanent settlement was formed, no community established, and no synagogue built.

## § II

This is not the place to describe in detail how the normally constituted Syrian people known as the Jews were dispossessed of their ancestral home, scattered to every corner of the known world, and driven overwhelmingly into an urban existence. Though before the fall of the Roman Empire even those of the Diaspora in Europe continued to be interested in agriculture, as their brethren in Palestine and Mesopotamia had been, they

---

without wholly conclusive results. An iron wall-sconce reminiscent of a Jewish seven-branched candelabrum has recently been found at Silchester.

[1] Commentary to Isaiah lxvi. 20, Amos viii. 12, and Zephaniah ii. 8 (9) (Migne, *Patrologia Latina*, xxiv. 672, xxv. 1083, 1364). The phrasing makes it clear that Jerome believed Jews to be living in Britain and even to have attained positions of dignity there: he mentions the province together with Spain, Italy, Gaul, &c., where they were indubitably settled in his day.

[2] See Note I (*a*), p. 270.

were gradually excluded from this. The rise of Christianity undermined their economic and social life. The Church (and its over-ready disciples, the Christian emperors) frowned on their intercourse with true believers on equal terms, hampered their ownership of land, and flatly forbade them not only to have Christians in their employment, but even to acquire moral authority over them in a professional capacity. Slowly, they were driven out of ordinary activities, and restricted to those for which their international connexions, their adaptability, and their acumen gave them perhaps special qualification.[1]

In the Dark Ages, the terms 'merchant' and 'Jew' were sometimes used, in western Europe, virtually as synonyms: and certain branches of trade and manufacture were almost exclusively in Jewish hands. But, as time went on, Gentile competition in these spheres became increasingly strong. The Italian maritime republics embarked upon commercial activities with a degree of cohesion, reinforced by political backing, which the Jews could not emulate. Trade was everywhere organized on a co-operative basis, and impregnated with a feeling of religious solidarity which left few loopholes for the unbeliever. Accordingly, the Jew was driven to employ his capital in the only manner that remained open. Unable to engage in personal enterprise, he had to finance that of others—to lend out his capital, that is, at interest. This tendency became all the more marked since an impossible idealism backed by faulty exegesis was causing the Church—oblivious of the fact that credit is a necessity in any society which has progressed beyond its most rudimentary stage—to oppose the lending of money at interest in any circumstances whatsoever. Not until the Middle Ages were drawing to their close did the change become anything like general. Nevertheless, in some parts of Europe, the process had made great progress as early as the eleventh century, when the Jewish financier or money-lender(the terms are interchangeable)

[1] The process described here in a few lines was of course a long and gradual one, extending over some centuries. For a fuller account see the present writer's *Short History of the Jewish People* (London, 1959) or, in greater detail, H. Graetz, *Geschichte der Juden* (preferably in the German original: latest edition, Leipzig, 1890–1911); S. Dubnow, *Weltgeschichte des jüdischen Volkes* (Berlin, 1925–9); and two basic works by James Parkes, *The Conflict of the Church and the Synagogue* (London, 1934) and *The Jew in the Medieval Community* (London, 1938), with the authorities listed in them, and especially S. W. Baron's *Social and Religious History of the Jews* (2nd ed., 1952, &c.).

was already a familiar figure. Particularly was this the case in north-eastern France, with which (as we shall see) medieval Anglo-Jewry, as England generally, was to be most intimately associated.

With the Norman Conquest of 1066 England became an integral part of the European system for the first time since the Roman evacuation. Thus it entered at last into the cognizance of the Jewish communities of the Continent, hitherto barely aware of its existence.[1] The virtual absence of a middle class and the scarcity of money (now rendered more necessary by new social and economic developments) gave enterprising capitalists a unique opportunity. In the continental possessions of William the Conqueror, considerable Jewish communities were already to be found (at Rouen, for example, they had been settled from about the year 1,000 at the latest).[2] It was natural for some of the more adventurous spirits to follow their duke to the new field of enterprise that offered itself, even if (as is sometimes reported) he did not specifically invite them.[3] Within a short period, con-gregations—probably consisting in no case of more than a hand-ful of persons—were to be found in a few of the greater cities, that of London of course predominating. The earliest settlers originated almost exclusively from northern France, on which the English communities remained to a very large degree dependent culturally, linguistically, and economically. From the beginning there were also a few individuals from the Rhine-land, which at that time formed a single *bloc* with Champagne in the geography of the Jewish world. Subsequently, isolated individuals or families arrived from further afield.

The influx was slow, but its effects were important. While the face of England was being Normanized, while the adminis-tration was being reformed on the continental pattern, and while feudalism in its widest sense was being established, England gave its tardy welcome to a band of Jewish wanderers,

---

[1] The earliest explicit mention of England in Hebrew literature appears to be in the pseudo-Josephus ('Josippon'), probably composed in south Italy in the ninth century.

[2] There is a semi-legendary record of a persecution at this place in 1007, when the Pope is said to have intervened to prevent the massacre of those Jews who refused to accept baptism. However questionable the details, the account pre-supposes the existence of a fairly numerous Jewish community.

[3] See Note I (*b*), p. 270.

and the most narrowly feudal of all the Jewish communities of
the Middle Ages came into existence.

§ III

Of the history of the English Jews under the first two Norman
monarchs, hardly anything is known. From the scanty glimpses
that we are afforded, it would seem that they were treated with
favour—contemptuous, perhaps, but solid. Except for the incidental statement that Jews had been brought over from Rouen
to England by William the Conqueror, there is no authentic
reference to them during his reign. William Rufus encouraged
the exotic strangers somewhat too exuberantly, in words at
least, if we are to believe contemporary accounts. On a certain
solemnity when the Jews of London brought him a gift, he
persuaded them to enter into a religious discussion with bishops
and churchmen present at court. Not content with the scandal
caused by this, he jestingly swore, by the Holy Face of Lucca,
that if they were victorious he would himself embrace Judaism
—an impiety which can hardly have enhanced their popularity
in ecclesiastical circles.[1] Not, indeed, that there was any objection on the part of the Church to religious discussion as such.
About the same time, a certain Jew who had studied at the
famous Talmudic academy of Mainz entered into a friendly
argument on matters of faith with Gilbert Crispin, abbot of
Westminster, with whom he had business dealings. The tenor
of the conversation, far more amicable in tone than most medieval encounters of the sort, was afterwards committed to writing
by the abbot and communicated to St. Anselm, the learned
archbishop of Canterbury.[2] In consequence of these arguments
(so at least the ecclesiastical champion claimed) a Jew was

---

[1] William of Malmesbury, *Gesta*, iv. 317.
[2] *Gisleberti Crispini abbatis Westmonasteriensis Disputatio Judaei cum Christiano* in
Migne, *Patrologia Latina*, clix. 1034 ff.: cf. J. Armitage Robinson, *Gilbert Crispin,
Abbot of Westminster* (Cambridge, 1911), pp. 60–67, I. Lévi, *R.E.J.* v. 238–45, and,
most recently, A. Lukyn Williams, *Adversus Judaeos* (Cambridge, 1935), pp. 375–80.
The probable historicity of the account appears from the meticulousness of some
of the details: e.g. the statement that Crispin's interlocutor had studied in Mainz,
which was in fact one of the great centres of Rabbinic learning at the time, and
the reference to business relations (for which we have documentary evidence)
between the Abbot of Westminster and London Jews. The latest edition is by
B. Blumenkranz, *Gisleberti Crispini Disputatio Judei et Christiani* (Utrecht–Antwerp,
1956).

converted to Christianity and became a monk; and he was followed to the font not long afterwards by another, who was earnestly commended by Anselm to the charity of zealous Christians.[1] This is absolutely all that is known with any degree of assurance of the Jews in England until 1100.

It was at this period that there took place the great massacre of the Jews of Rouen by the crusading knights in 1096—a prelude to the atrocities on the Rhineland—when all who refused to accept baptism were butchered forthwith. Those who managed to escape would naturally have sought refuge in their duke's domains across the Channel, as yet untouched by the crusading frenzy. It is likely that a settled and relatively numerous Anglo-Jewish community owes its origin to this event, though there is no documentary evidence to support the assumption.

With the reign of Henry I (1100–35) we begin to be on surer ground. It is likely that he issued a charter of protection to the Jews, or at least to certain individuals. The text of this is now lost, but it was so important that it continued to be referred to and imitated for nearly two centuries as a model document, and it may be regarded as the fundamental charter of liberties of medieval English Jewry. It guaranteed, above all, liberty of movement throughout the country, relief from ordinary tolls, protection from misusage, free recourse to royal justice and responsibility to no other, permission to retain land taken in pledge as security, and special provision to ensure fair trial. It confirmed the community, in short, in a position of privilege as a separate entity—existing for the king's advantage, protected by him in all legitimate transactions and answerable to him alone. This charter was confirmed by succeeding rulers after their accession, though not gratuitously.[2]

Protected by these privileges, English Jewry slowly gathered strength.[3] For some years an illustrious ex-Jew was prominent

---

[1] *S. Anselmi Epistolae*, iii. cxvii.

[2] The original grant of this charter by Henry I is suggested in the preamble to John's confirmation of 1201 (*Rot. Cart.* i. 93): 'to hold all that from us which they held from King Henry our father's grandfather'. For its various confirmations see below, pp. 10, 19, 31–32, 66. On the other hand, the new Borough Charters of the twelfth century refer similarly to 'Henry our Grandfather', suggesting that it was a conventional phrase: see also Richardson, *J.A.K.*, p. 111.

[3] There is, however, no justification for the former statement that in this reign preachers were dispatched to the principal cities of the realm to serve as a corrective to the growing Jewish influence.

as royal physician—the Spaniard Petrus Alfonsi (*c.* 1062–1110), an important figure in the history of the transmission of the Hellenic legacy of the Arabs to medieval Europe, author of the homiletic collection known as the *Training School for Clergy*, and a welcome visitor at Malvern Abbey.[1] The first mention of the 'Street of the Jews' in London is found about 1128, in the 'Terrier' of St. Paul's;[2] while references to Jewish activities in finance are recorded three years later in the earliest extant record of the Exchequer, the Pipe Roll of the 31st year of Henry I (1130).

This invaluable document shows us a community centred in London. At its head is a certain Rabbi Joseph, popularly known as Rubi Gotsce[3]—obviously a person of considerable reputation in the intellectual world and presumably the outstanding scholar in Anglo-Jewry in the first half of the twelfth century.[4] He appears to have originated in Rouen, with which city his children retained their associations. His descendants continued to play an important part in Anglo-Jewish life for more than a century. Besides being a notable scholar, Rubi Gotsce was also a capable financier. Three or four other prominent London business men are also mentioned, especially Manasser (Menasseh) and Jacob, who was assisted in his business affairs by his wife. Their transactions were on a large scale, and mainly, it seems, with the nobility (Jacob has dealings also with the Abbot of Westminster). As always in later history, the Crown was acquisitive rather than benevolent, and would impartially accept a promise of money from a noble to exert pressure on the Jews to remit his debts, or a gift from the Jews to exert pressure on the other side to pay them. Rubi Gotsce and his associates were on the other hand making advances to the Crown also, though of relatively small amounts. A ruthless method of evading payment was found, as will be seen later; so ruthless indeed as to qualify

[1] *Legacy of Israel*, pp. 208–9, &c.
[2] See Note I (*c*), pp. 270–1.
[3] Pronounced *Yotsce* or *Josce*, the *G* being equivalent to *Y*.
[4] Jacobs's identification (*J.A.E.*, pp. 15, 23) with the Talmudist and exegete R. Joseph Bechor-Shor of Orleans is untenable, the latter having been a disciple of R. Jacob Tam of Ramerupt and belonging therefore to the second half of the century. He is probably to be identified with the scholarly Joseph of Moreil (below, p. 126).

the accepted view, that this was in every respect a halcyon period for English Jewry.[1]

Indeed, from the few glimpses that we are afforded it does not appear that the condition of the community, though generally tranquil, was enviable. During the civil war between Stephen and the 'Empress' Matilda, they clearly suffered more than the rest of the population. The case of Oxford was no doubt typical. In 1141, during her occupation of that city, Matilda imposed a levy on the Jews. When the place was recaptured by her rival, he demanded from them, by way of punishment for their complaisance, three and a half times as much. Since the victims were unwilling, he sent incendiaries bearing lighted torches with instructions to set fire to all the Jewish houses. Only when one of the finest had been consumed by the flames (it was that of the communal magnate, Aaron fil' Isaac, the earliest known Oxford Jew) did his co-religionists provide what was asked.[2]

Though the Crusading movement had as yet gained only a slight footing in England, the fanatical spirit which it engendered was not altogether absent. About 1130 the London Jews were accused of killing a sick man, who perhaps had gone to one of them for medical treatment—an anticipation of the cruder accusations which were to make their appearance not long after. This charge seems to have given rise to a persecution of some sort—how virulent cannot be determined. But, like most vicissitudes of Jewish life, it was turned to the advantage of the Exchequer. The London community, with Rubi Gotsce at its head, was fined the enormous sum of £2,000. Out of this the claims of Jewish financiers on the Crown were satisfied, or rather cancelled, the credit balance being thus turned into a debit balance of a far greater magnitude and a considerable cash payment being made besides. The timeliness of the accusation, from the point of view of the Exchequer, was such as to

[1] Another entry of the earliest Pipe Roll for Norfolk and Suffolk (Pp.R. 1130–1 p. 91: reference should in every case be made to the original, as Jacobs's excerpts are both defective and inaccurate) refers to a certain Benjamin who accounts for £4. 5s. 'ut custodiat placita quae coronae regis pertinent'—apparently an early anticipation of the office of Coroner. Maitland suggests that 'a Benjamin who has no surname looks uncommonly like a Jew, and perhaps the pleas that he wishes to "keep" are pleas concerning the Jews'. But it now appears that he was King's Serjeant: Richardson and Sayles, *Governance of Medieval England*, 1963, pp. 186–7.

[2] There are elements of doubt in the story : cf. Roth, *Oxford*, pp. 2–3.

make one suspect that the coincidence was not altogether accidental.[1]

In 1144 the conception implicit in this charge received a terrible extension. On Easter Eve of that year, the dead body of a young skinner's apprentice, named William, was found in a wood near Norwich. Modern inquirers, after careful examination of the facts, have concluded that the child probably lost consciousness in consequence of a cataleptic fit, and was buried prematurely by his relatives. It was bruited about, however, that he was a victim of the Jews, who had enticed him away from his family and crucified him after synagogue service on the second day of Passover, in mockery of the Passion of Jesus. This was the first recorded instance in the medieval world of the infamous Ritual Murder accusation, which subsequently caused the Jews throughout Europe untold misery. A wave of religious exaltation swept through the city; and the child's body was buried with all solemnity in the Cathedral, where miracles were said to be wrought at the grave-side. The civil authorities did not indeed give any encouragement to this outbreak. The Jews were protected to his utmost ability by the sheriff, who permitted them to seek refuge in the Castle, and would not allow them to be taken to the bishop's court for a biased trial. Nevertheless, after they ventured into the open, one of the leaders of the community was murdered by the followers of a lawless knight who was in his debt; and this was not conceivably the only case. Down to the time of the Reformation, the relics of William of Norwich were venerated as those of a saint and martyr, and he remained a popular figure in the hagiology of the eastern counties.[2]

It is not recorded that these allegations had any wider repercussions. That there were none is hardly to be credited: in 1146, indeed, during the Second Crusade, Bernard of Clairvaux thought it necessary to address his famous appeal against the

---

[1] Pp.R. 1130-1, p. 149. The amount of the fine, £2,000, must be multiplied by perhaps 100 times to get an idea of its significance in modern currency. It represented something like one-tenth of the total royal income, estimated for this period at £20,000.

[2] A. Jessopp and M. R. James, *St. William of Norwich* (Cambridge, 1896). It may be added that on this occasion (as in subsequent cases, in England) the essential element of the continental *blood* accusation was lacking, as no suggestion was apparently made that the blood was required for ritual purposes.

molestation of the Jews to England, as well as to Germany and France. A few individuals resident in England found it advisable at this period to return to Cologne, near which place one of them, Simeon the Pious of Treves, was murdered by the Crusaders on refusing to be baptized. Nevertheless, a contemporary Hebrew chronicler gratefully records how Stephen, king of England, was inspired to protect the Jews of his realm, not allowing them to be molested in their persons or property. Thus safeguarded, the Anglo-Jewish communities were able to consolidate themselves, attaining in the next generation the zenith of their prosperity.

§ IV

During the long reign of Henry II (1154–89) they and the country enjoyed peace. The crusading spirit had as yet gained little hold. There was no pretext therefore for Englishmen to imitate the massacres which intermittently continued on the Continent. The king mulcted the Jews, indeed, to the utmost; but at the same time he protected and to a certain extent even encouraged them. He not only confirmed, but even extended, his grandfather's charter of protection, formally granting the Jews of England the privilege of internal jurisdiction in accordance with Talmudic law, except in the case of offence against public order.[1] Contemporary chroniclers speak bitterly (if with palpable exaggeration) of the favour with which the sovereign treated his Jewry. 'By an absurd arrangement', writes one of them, 'they were happy and renowned far more than the Christians, and, swelling very impudently against Christ through their good fortune, did much injury to the Christians.'[2] Jews

---

[1] This concession was renewed by John in 1201 (below, p. 32) apart from his confirmation of Henry I's charter, with specific reference to the grant by Henry II. The original issue may be dated *c.* 1164, when the position of the Jews was put forward as an argument in favour of the autonomy of the clergy (J. C. Robertson, *Materials for the History of Thomas Becket*, iv. 148).

[2] William of Newburgh, *Historia rerum anglicarum*, ed. Howlett, i. 280. For the position of the Jews, cf. *St. William of Norwich*, ed. Jessopp and James, p. 100: 'We are thy Jews. We are thy tributaries year by year, we are necessary to thee continually . . . since we are always faithful to thee and highly useful to thy realm. Thou rulest us leniently and gently. . . .'

The story once used to illustrate the favourable position of the Jews in the twelfth century, that the Norwich capitalist Jurnet (= Eliab) of Norwich married almost with impunity a Christian heiress who became converted to Judaism, has

held property as tenants-in-chief of the Crown, though the
world would have been scandalized had they attempted to discharge their obligations by performing military service.[1] Even
churchmen treated them with marked tolerance. Notwithstanding the laws which forbade it, Jewish financiers lent money
to abbeys and minsters on the security of plate, vessels used in
divine worship, and—worst scandal of all—relics of the saints.[2]
They were allowed to place their womenfolk and children in the
monasteries for safety at times of disturbance. They kept their
business-deeds in the cathedral treasuries, then generally used
for safeguarding valuables in emergency. In Canterbury and
Bury St. Edmunds, they even took sides in monastic politics
when a fresh abbot was elected, and prayed in their synagogue
for the success of the candidate whom they favoured. They were
familiar figures in St. Paul's Cathedral in London, to which
they resorted to seek their debtors. Jews and clerics rode together
on journeys, and jested together in bad French.[3] In London,
Lincoln, and York, the Jewish financiers aroused comment by the
stone houses—almost fortress-like in their strength—which they
built for their security at a time when the majority of the population had to content themselves with flimsy constructions of wood.[4]

At the beginning of the reign of Henry II, according to the
official Treasury records, there were Jewish nuclei not only in
London but also in Norwich, Lincoln, Winchester, Cambridge,
Thetford, Northampton, Bungay, Oxford, and Gloucester (the
order given is that of financial, and presumably in most cases
numerical, importance).[5] In addition, isolated families were

been shown by Richardson (*J.A.K.*, pp. 33–39) to have arisen from a confusion of
names on the part of the eighteenth-century Norfolk historian Blomefield.

[1] Below, p. 15. Jacobs (*J.A.E.*, p. 204, &c.) grossly exaggerates the implications.
[2] Benedict Abbot, ed. Stubbs, i. 106: a general statement interestingly confirmed in Pp.R. 1169–70, p. 8, and 1182–3, p. 14, which show Jews paying a fine
for having taken church vessels in pledge, and in the story (Wharton, *Anglia Sacra*,
i. 645–6) that Bishop Nigel of Ely (1133–69) pledged relics with the Jews of
Cambridge.
[3] Giraldus Cambrensis, *Itin. Camb.* ii. xiii. (Many of these points are reverted to
below, in Chap. V.)
[4] In the accounts of the London and York massacres, the strength of the houses
in the Jewish quarter is accentuated, while in Lincoln actual specimens dating
from this period are extant. For a stone house built at Canterbury in 1190, see
Adler, *J.M.E.*, p. 69. (Cf. also p. 123, below.)
[5] For these Jewish centres, cf. Pp.R. 1158–9, pp. 1, 3, 12, 17, 24, 28, 35, 46, 53,
65. The amounts specified would suggest that the London community was at this
time three times as large as that of Norwich. But too much stress should not be laid

living in Worcester and Leicester, and from other sources we know communities to have existed in Bristol and York. In consequence of favourable conditions, there seems to have been during the course of the reign a veritable influx from the Continent—stimulated without doubt by the expulsion of the Jews from the Île de France in 1182, and facilitated by the immense extension of the Angevin possessions overseas. The area of settlement expanded, the records showing further groups before the end of the reign at Exeter, Stamford, Lynn, Bury, Bedford, Devizes, Ipswich, Canterbury, Hereford, Dunstable, Chichester, Newport, and some smaller places. New arrivals may sometimes be traced in literary sources. Abraham ibn Ezra, the wandering Spanish scholar, was in London in 1158; and there are indications that he returned to England to die.[1] Rabbi Yomtob of Joigny, an eminent pupil of the famous Jacob of Ramerupt ('Rabbenu Tam'), settled at York. His contemporary and fellow disciple, Jacob of Orleans, migrated to London. The influx from Germany was so great that an embassy sent to England in 1168 by Frederick Barbarossa protested (as it seems) at the loss of these profitable subjects, over whom the emperor claimed special rights. As a result, some of them were forced to return overseas, while a fine of 5,000 marks was exacted from those who remained.[2] In a roll of the community of London in 1186, we find Jews deriving from Spain and France (Étampes, Joigny, and Pontoise). This was paralleled in other cities of the kingdom. Jews from Paris and elsewhere in France were settled at York; Jews from Italy (known as 'Lombard') in Lincoln, Nottingham, and Winchester; and there is recorded even an individual from Russia, where the Rabbis of Kiev and Novgorod were already famous. The official records at the close of the reign show scattered about the country some 300 Jewish business men and householders, whose contributions to the Exchequer were worth recording.[3]

---

on this; Oxford, for example, is shown as paying only 20 marks as against London's 200, but it had been mulcted 100 marks only a short while previous (Pp.R. 1155, p. 36). The importance of Thetford may be due to the fact that, like Norwich, it had a mint: the name of David the moneyer is suggestive.

[1] *Bibl.* A. 11. 41; below, p. 126.

[2] This seems to be the most rational interpretation of a highly obscure passage (Gervase of Canterbury, ed. Stubbs, i. 205).

[3] See the lists in *J.A.E.*, pp. 345–69. But the Moroccan Jew, p. 89, is fictitious.

Hitherto, the burial-ground in London had to serve for the whole kingdom. When a death occurred, the body was transported thither by wagon, even from places as far away as Exeter or York. The toll-lists specified the charge to be made for a dead Jew; and we read gruesome accounts of how the dogs would bay after the corpse on the road.[1] With the increase of population, such an arrangement was out of the question; and, in 1177, each community was permitted to purchase a place for interring its dead outside the city walls.[2]

Few known episodes disturbed the tenor of Anglo-Jewish life during the reign, but it was not invariably smooth. Before the terrible precedent set at Norwich in 1144 was imitated abroad (the first Ritual Murder accusation on the Continent was that of Blois, in 1171) a similar case took place in the city of Gloucester, where a number of Jews assembled in March 1168, at Passover-time, in honour of a circumcision in the family of a prominent member of the community. It was alleged that they took advantage of this to seize upon a Christian child named Harold, whom they martyred with unspeakable tortures, afterwards throwing the body into the River Severn. In 1181 a similar incident was reported at Bury St. Edmunds, where a certain Robert was the alleged victim; and there was yet another in Bristol by 1183.[3] The relics of these youths, like those of 'St.' William of Norwich, were subsequently venerated as those of martyrs. None of these cases apparently entailed any serious consequences upon the Jewish community at large, safe in the royal protection. It is true that the Assize of Arms of 1181 (which ensured the possession by every Englishman of adequate weapons) forbade Jews to retain 'mail or hauberk', which were to be sold or given away; but this clause was clearly prompted

[1] *Acta sanctorum* (Brussels, 1853), viii. 576; cf. Neubauer in *Collectanea* of the Oxford Historical Society, ii (1890), pp. 282 ff.

[2] It does not follow that all availed themselves of the permission, or that those which did acted immediately: the York cemetery (at what is still called 'Jewbury') was originally shared with the communities of Lincoln and Northampton, which, however, acquired their own burial-grounds in due course. As on the Continent, the Jewish cemetery was generally called the Jews' Garden (e.g. in London, Norwich, and Oxford). Jewin Street, &c., mark the area of the former London burial-ground, for which see now M. B. Honeybourne in *Trs. J.H.S.E.* xx.

[3] *Historia monasterii S. Petri Gloucestriae* (Rolls Series), p. 21; Jocelin de Brakelond (ed. Camden Society), p. 13; *Chronicle of Melrose*, ed. Anderson, p. 43; Adler, *J.M.E.*, pp. 185–6.

by the desire to have all weapons deposited where they would be most usefully employed, rather than by any wish to leave the Jews unprotected.[1]

## § v

The favour and protection enjoyed by the Jews under the first Plantagenet ruler were not due (as was the case, with certain reservations, later on) simply to their importance as tax-payers. This was of course considerable; and when the king went abroad, he often raised large sums by fine or loan from leading members of the community. But they were at the same time what might be termed Treasury agents, advancing large sums to the Crown to defray day-to-day expenditure or unexpected calls, and being repaid by drafts on the sheriffs, secured on the 'ferm of the Shire' or county revenue. Already in the time of Henry I, as we have seen, Rubi Gotsce of London and certain of his associates had dealings with the Crown. These were greatly extended under Henry II when, for convenience as well as security, certain capitalists found it convenient to pool their resources and to work together. Hence, after the middle of the reign, we find a few prominent *consortia* of Jews dealing with the Treasury, the heavy advances that they made being reflected in orders for repayment in due course out of the county revenues. Brun of London, Josce Quatrebuches, and the brothers Jurnet and Benedict of Norwich form one group, providing the Crown on a single occasion, in 1177, with as much as 5,750 marks (£3,833. 6s. 8d.) in one payment. This was displaced in due course by another group made up of Deodatus Episcopus,[2] Vives of Cambridge, and the brothers Moses and Benedict fil' Sara whose names are noted in at least thirty Treasury transactions in the course of a single year.[3] In the west of England, Moses of Bristol and Belaset his wife acted as Crown agents. Isaac fil' Rabbi, son of Rubi Gotsce and the principal member of the London community, worked in loose

---

[1] That this clause of the Assize of Arms was enforced is shown by Pp.R. 1185–6, p. 78—a Jew fined 40 marks on account of the hauberk that his wife had taken in pledge 'against the prohibition'.

[2] Probably = Nathaniel haCohen: see below, p. 94.

[3] Pp.R. 1176–7, introduction, p. xxiii. Another outstanding Anglo-Jewish financier of the period was Josce of Gloucester, who advanced money to the adventurers who raided Ireland in 1169. (Jacobs's conclusion, *J.A.E.*, p. 51, that he 'financed' Strongbow's expedition, is not justified by the evidence.)

association with the first group, having been officially authorized to enter into partnership with Jurnet of Norwich. Such was his status that he and his family were granted the manor of Ham by the Crown for services rendered.[1] For some years his financial supremacy was unquestioned. After 1166, however, he began to be outdone in financial importance by his occasional associate, Aaron of Lincoln, who for some years occupied the leading place among the Jews of England, and was among the outstanding European financiers of the twelfth century. Between the two of them, English Jewry was organized to a certain extent into a great co-operative banking association, spread throughout the country.

Like the other Jewish financiers, Aaron of Lincoln periodically made advances to the Crown on the security of the local taxation; in 1166 (when his transactions are first mentioned) these amounted to over £600. He advanced money to private individuals on corn, armour, estates, and houses, acquiring thus important interests in twenty-five counties (especially in the east and south-east of England), in at least seventeen of which he maintained his agents. Loans were contracted with him to assist in the building of no less than nine Cistercian abbeys, as well as the cathedrals of Lincoln and Peterborough. So considerable was his assistance in the construction of the famous conventual church at St. Albans, that he used to boast, with more outspokenness than tact, that it was he who had made the great window in the church, and had prepared a home for the saint when he had been without one.[2]

When he died, about 1186, Aaron of Lincoln was probably the wealthiest person in England, in liquid assets. The king therefore did not scruple to vindicate his legal rights (seldom exercised to the full) and to declare all the property of the

---

[1] Rymer, *Foedera*, i. 51: the family also owned the manor of Thurrocks, acquired by purchase from the Earl Ferrers (ibid.) and sold in 1199 to Henry de Gray (Pp.R. 1199, p. 6b). Abraham of Felmingham, who received a grant of land for bringing Henry II a report that the King of Scotland had been captured (*Book of Fees*, i. 130) was contrary to appearances (his son's name was Isaac!) not a Jew, as is clear from other references. For some reason, Isaac fil' Rabbi never paid the fee for his partnership-licence.

[2] The 'traditional' association with Aaron of the house in Lincoln bearing his name dates only from the nineteenth century. Richardson (*J.A.K.*, pp. 90–91) suggests that the indebtedness of the Cistercian abbeys resulted from loans for acquiring encumbered estates: cf. also J. C. Holt, *The Northerners* (Oxford, 1961), p. 166.

deceased usurer escheated to the Crown. The bullion and
treasure was sent over to France to assist in the war then in
progress against Philip Augustus. The vessel in which it was
conveyed was lost with all it contained while crossing the
Channel from Shoreham to Dieppe, in February 1187. The
outstanding credits amounted to £15,000, being equivalent to
three-quarters of the royal income in a normal year, owed by
some 430 persons distributed over a great part of England. To
deal with the collection of these amounts, it was found necessary
to establish a special branch of the Exchequer, the *Scaccarium
Aaronis*, with two treasurers and two clerks, whose labour of
sorting out the debts and ascertaining what was due to the
Crown took nearly five years. This bureau continued in existence until 1205, when (notwithstanding the chancellor's annual
exhortation to debtors to compound with him for their dues)
one-half of the total was still outstanding. Among those with
whom the dead financier was found to have had dealings were
the King of Scotland, the Count of Brittany, the Archbishop
of Canterbury, the earls of Northampton, Arundel, Aumale,
and Leicester, the bishops of Bangor and Lincoln, the Abbot of
Westminster, the Prior of the Knights Hospitallers, and the
towns of Winchester and Southampton.[1] Such transactions
never failed to be turned to the advantage of the Exchequer.
It has been estimated that an average of £3,000—that is, something like one-seventh of the total revenue—was derived at this
period from the Jews every year in the normal course of
taxation, without taking into account occasional windfalls
when individual or community were amerced for some real or
imaginary trespass. In 1159, moreover, there had been a fresh
departure in the financial administration. On the occasion of
the king's expedition against rebellious Toulouse, the cost of the

---

[1] A detailed study of the activities of Aaron of Lincoln, by Joseph Jacobs, is in
*Trs. J.H.S.E.*, vol. iii; see also Mrs. Stenton's informative introduction to Pp.R.
1191–3. For Aaron's very important transactions with the King of Scotland see
A. C. Laurie, *Annals of Malcolm and William*, p. ccxix. Jacobs's date for Aaron's
death, 1187, is too late: cf. J. H. Round, Pp.R. 1185–6, p. xxx. The amount of
his debts in Lincolnshire and Yorkshire was so great that a special membrane
dealing with them had to be added to the Pipe Roll. But it should be noted that
William Cade, the Flemish Christian usurer, who died about 1166, had worked on
similar lines: see Jenkinson in *Studies Presented to R. Lane-Poole*, pp. 190–210:
Richardson, *J.A.K.*, pp. 51–61: and for Aaron, ibid. 61–76, 247–53, &c., and J. C.
Holt, *The Northerners*, pp. 164–5.

expeditionary force was defrayed in part by an arbitrary levy, or 'tallage', on the towns of the country, and on the Jews.[1] The amounts involved on this occasion were not excessively heavy. But, especially as far as the infidel financiers were concerned, it was a particularly dangerous innovation. Instead of having their ability utilized, as hitherto, they could henceforth be exploited, by a facile method which was to end in their ruin.

It was not indeed until the close of the reign that the full potentialities of the new instrument were realized. In 1188, in order to finance the king's proposed Crusade, the Saladin Tithe —the first English tax on personal property—was ruthlessly levied throughout the kingdom. The Jews had been assessed separately at Christmastide 1186 at Guildford, their contribution being fixed not at one-tenth of their property, as was the case with the other inhabitants of the country, but at one-fourth. It is significant that this was expected to bring in no less than £60,000, as against £70,000 from the general levy. Thus, the Jewish capital was estimated to constitute more than one-third of the mobile wealth of the nation—certainly an exaggeration, yet at the same time indicative of their relative importance to the Exchequer.[2] The collection of this vast sum—the equivalent of perhaps £6,000,000 in modern values—had not been completed when, in 1189, Henry Plantagenet ended his long life of struggle, leaving the throne to his worst-hated son.

Fresh light is thrown upon the succession to the claims of Aaron of Lincoln by the sections devoted to his credits in Pp.R. 1208, pp. 80–81 (Lincoln), 143–4 (York). For a payment of 200 marks, his son Elias secured £400 'of the worst of the charters of Aaron his father which are not paid off and are worth little to the Lord King': later, he gave 3 marks of gold to have further charters 'such as may bear fruit to him'. He was now at liberty to exact what he could, and is unlikely to have been light-handed.

[1] Pp.R. 1158–9, pp. 46, 53, &c. This was anterior to the tallage of 5,000 marks in 1168, said by Rigg (*P.E.J.*, p. xvi) to be the earliest.

[2] For the levy, see Pp.R. 1186–7, p. 44. It was expected to be so profitable that the Crown suspended the collection of debts from leading Jews, to the amount of some £6,500. Richardson (*J.A.K.*, p. 162) states that £60,000 was a symbolic figure used to denote an enormous sum. Even so, this was immediately followed by a levy of 10,000 marks on the Jews at the time of the Saladin Tithe. These impositions marked the beginning of a new Exchequer policy which had a profound influence on English Jewry. Hitherto the king had financed himself largely by raising loans from the Jews. This system inevitably broke down because of the difficulty of repaying money lent for unproductive purposes. At the end of his reign, therefore, he began to impose heavy taxation in place of this: but this system similarly broke down in the end owing to the unpopularity which accrued to the royal instruments and their ultimate exhaustion.

# II

## THE BEGINNING OF PERSECUTION AND THE ORGANIZATION OF JEWRY

### 1189–1216

### § 1

DURING the course of the past few years the tide of religious feeling had been rising. The recent exactions had been occasioned by the fact that Henry II himself had 'taken the Cross', pledging himself thus to go on Crusade to deliver the Holy Land from the infidel. He had died without being able to fulfil his vow; but his son and successor, Richard Lion-Heart, ascended the throne pledged to the great enterprise, and determined to carry it into effect.

For the first time Crusading enthusiasm—hitherto at a low ebb—spread throughout England among all classes, from highest to lowest. It was inevitable that the feeling against the Jews was accentuated. The heavy exactions of the previous reign, of which they had been to some extent the instruments, were not forgotten, and there was little prospect that the policy of the government would change. Increasing numbers and prosperity were a prolific cause of jealousy. In 1179 Pope Alexander III had felt obliged to exhort the king to protect the monks of St. Augustine's, Canterbury, in their business dealings with the Jews, which must have been of considerable volume.[1] The anti-Jewish legislation of the Third Lateran Council of that same year had applied to England as to other countries. The recent succession of Blood Accusations marked the direction and intensity of the current. The ground was thus fully prepared for an outbreak in the continental style, which England had hitherto escaped. It was an unfortunate coincidence, if nothing more,

---

[1] Thomas Elmham, *Hist. Monast. Sancti Augustini*, p. 431. It is suggestive that, less than ten years later, in 1187, the Jews of Canterbury were zealously supporting the monks of Christchurch in their struggle against their rivals of St. Augustine's, praying for them in Synagogue and smuggling in supplies of food and wine for their use (Adler, *J.M.E.*, p. 52). The complaint of 1179 probably had an inner history.

that the Assize of Arms had left the Jews helpless, without the prospect of defending themselves as other men could when the storm broke.

A trivial episode at the coronation of the new king proved to be the spark which set the tinder ablaze. The proceedings at Westminster were long and stately, and the solemnity of the occasion was emphasized by a proclamation ordering that no woman, and no Jew, should be admitted.[1] Nevertheless, on the afternoon of the coronation day (Sunday, 3 September 1189), while the festivities were at their height, a deputation from the Jewish communities of the kingdom presented itself at the gateway of Westminster Hall, bearing rich gifts—probably in the hope of obtaining a renewal of the charter of privileges granted originally by Henry I. Some of them, eager to see the magnificence, took advantage of a momentary disorder to slip in, and were driven out by a zealous doorkeeper with unnecessary brutality. This was enough to arouse the crowd at the palace gates. Several members of the deputation were beaten or trampled to death before they could escape. The wealthy Benedict, who had come as one of the representatives of the community of York, saved his life by consenting to embrace Christianity, and was immediately baptized in the adjacent Church of the Innocents by a priest from his own city.

Exaggerated rumours of what was happening at Westminster soon spread to London, where it was reported that the king had given orders for the Jews to be exterminated. In their well-built stone houses, the inhabitants were able to resist for some hours until, towards nightfall, one of the mob threw up a lighted torch which set fire to a thatched roof. The flames rapidly spread, and before long the whole of the Jewry was in a blaze. Though some of the inhabitants found refuge in the Tower of London or under the protection of friendly neighbours, several perished in their houses, and others were done to death when they ventured into the street. Thirty persons lost their lives, amongst them being the eminent Rabbi Jacob of Orleans, not long since arrived from the Continent.

---

[1] 'Because of the magic arts which Jews and some women notoriously exercise at royal coronations', according to Matthew Paris (*Hist. Angl.* ii. 9). It may be observed that Jewish custom prescribes a special benediction on seeing a monarch, the recital of which might conceivably give rise to a suspicion of this sort.

The news was reported to the king as he sat banqueting. He immediately dispatched the justiciar, Ranulph de Glanville, to check the disorders, but he was unable to make any impression. The outbreak had indeed been of so universal a character, and enjoyed such general sympathy, that it was not considered advisable to take serious measures against those who had participated. Nevertheless, some of the ringleaders were arrested and three were hanged—one for robbing a Christian and two because the fire they had kindled burned down a Christian house. Little else was done except to dispatch letters to all parts of the kingdom ordering the Jews to be left in peace. The day after the riot Richard sent for Benedict of York, who admitted that he had adopted Christianity only in order to escape death. Turning to the Archbishop of Canterbury, the king inquired how he should be dealt with. 'If he will not serve God, let him serve the devil', replied the prelate: and his contemptuous advice was followed.[1]

## § 11

The royal proclamation was sufficient to secure the maintenance of peace only so long as the king was in the country. In December he crossed to the Continent, and for six months remained in France gathering his forces. Meanwhile, in every town in England, Crusading detachments were assembled in readiness for departure overseas. Their reasoning was similar to that of Crusaders everywhere: that it was not right to allow Jewish infidels to enjoy their ill-gotten riches undisturbed at home, while the soldiers of the Cross were facing untold dangers to combat Moslem infidels overseas: the redemption of the Holy Sepulchre, and the avenging of the Crucifixion, should begin in England itself. There was a widespread impression that the slaughter of a single paynim would gain Paradise even for the most hardened sinner. Unhappily, the assembly of the Crusaders coincided with the season of Lent, when the deepest-rooted

---

[1] William of Newburgh, ed. Howlett, i. 294; Matthew Paris, *Hist. Angl.*, ii. 9 (Rog. Wend. iii. 7); R. Howden, ed. Stubbs, iii. 14; Ephraim of Bonn in Neubauer-Stern, *Hebräische Berichte über die Judenvervolgungen während der Kreuzzüge* (Berlin, 1892), pp. 69–70 (translation in *Trs. J.H.S.E.* v. 78; that in Jacobs, *J.A.E.*, pp. 107–8, is grotesquely inaccurate). The fact that the charter of John (not of Henry I or II), was confirmed by Henry III suggests that the original may have been destroyed during the coronation riots.

religious passions were aroused and the most inflammatory recollections revived.

Early in February the first outbreak took place at the port of Lynn, in Norfolk (subsequently King's Lynn). Here, a recent apostate from Judaism took refuge from the insults of his former co-religionists in a church, where the latter had the imprudence to follow him.[1] The consequent uproar developed into a riot, in which foreign sailors in port took a leading part. The community was all but exterminated, the houses being stormed and pillaged, and the inhabitants butchered or burned in the flames which destroyed a good part of the city.[2] A few days after, the news reached Norwich, the principal town in the eastern counties, where the example was followed (6 February), though most of the Jews took refuge previously in the royal castle. Large numbers of Crusaders and others meanwhile assembled at Stamford for the Lent Fair. 'Indignant that the enemies of the cross of Christ who dwelt there should possess so much when they had not enough for the expenses of so great a journey',[3] they made a similar attack, putting to the sword all who did not get to the castle in time. The houses in the Jewry were pillaged, and a large amount of property was seized (7 March). At the populous city of Lincoln, most of the Jews were able to put themselves and their valuables under the protection of the royal officers in good time, but much havoc was effected nevertheless. Further attacks appear to have taken place in Colchester, Thetford, and Ospringe.[4] At other places, not mentioned in the records, there may also have been outbreaks, for a contemporary tells us that it was only at Winchester, thanks to the phlegmatic nature of the citizens, that the Jews were unscathed; but, as if to compensate, this city was the scene of a ritual murder accusation

---

[1] This contemporary story does not carry conviction: the medieval Jew may not always have been tolerant, but experience had taught him to be circumspect.

[2] But the great *incendium de Lenna* took place before this: cf. Pp.R. 1186–7, p. 55.

[3] William of Newburgh, i. 310.

[4] These attacks are not mentioned by the chroniclers, but may be inferred from the entries relating to recent murders of Jews at these places in Pp.R. 1191–2, pp. 147, 203, 313; Pp.R. 1193, p. 145, and in C.R.R. 1194, pp. 15, 16. It has been suggested (Pp.R. 1190–1, p. xxii) that some converts from Judaism shared the fate of their former co-religionists, since two of them, Nicholas and John, who had formerly enjoyed a pittance of one penny daily from the counties of Essex and Surrey, henceforth disappear from the records and are replaced by born Gentiles. In the Pipe Rolls for 1191–2 about 200 Jewish names only occur, as against 300 in Jacobs's lists for the close of the reign of Henry II.

two years later.[1] At Dunstable it is reported that the entire
diminutive community saved itself from massacre by submitting
to baptism. Jewish tradition preserved the memory of one place
containing a small congregation of twenty-two souls, who were
exterminated without exception.[2]

The worst outbreak of all, which has survived in the recollec-
tion of both the English and the Jewish peoples as a classical
example of stark tragedy, took place at York. Here, the existence
of a community is first recorded in the year 1130, but in such
terms as to make it evident that it had already been established
for some years and was of considerable importance. Under
Henry II it had grown in wealth and numbers. It was one of
the principal seats of Aaron of Lincoln's activity, and had apparently attracted some distinguished settlers from the Continent. The local baronage was heavily indebted to the Jews—
particularly Richard Malebysse (Malbis), whose fierce temper
led him to be nicknamed by his creditors 'the Evil Beast'. On
hearing the news of the southern outbreaks, he and various
members of the Percy, Faulconbridge, and Darrel families determined to seize the opportunity to wipe out their indebtedness.
One stormy March night, when an outbreak of fire caused
confusion in the city, a number of the conspirators broke into
the house of Benedict of York (who had died of his wounds on
his way back from London), murdered his widow and all the
other persons whom they found there, seized all the movable
property and set the building in flames. The next morning, the
other Jews (headed by Benedict's colleague Josce, who had been

[1] Richard of Devizes, ed. Howlett, pp. 383, 435. The chronicler's sarcastic
account, which has led to the suspicion that the whole story is fictitious, is grimly
confirmed by a record of the expenses for escorting the Jews of Winchester to
Westminster (Pp.R. 1193-4, p. 134). There was an alarm of the same nature
at Lincoln in 1202, when the discovery of a child's body outside the walls brought
the Jews under suspicion (*Earliest Lincoln Assize Roll* (Lincoln Record Society),
§ 996), and in the same year a Jew of Bedford was accused of causing the death of
a Christian child by 'ementulating' him (Tovey, *Anglia Judaica*, p. 66; *Select Pleas
of Crown*, Selden Society, i. 26; Fowler, *Roll of Justices in Eyre at Bedford*, i. 133, 247).

[2] This place is possibly to be identified with Lynn, where according to the
English sources the slaughter seems to have been comprehensive. Ephraim of
Bonn and the chroniclers who derive from him, followed by all modern authorities,
speak of this as a 'community of proselytes'. This is highly unlikely, and the reading
is plainly due to a faulty passage in the chronicle of Ephraim of Bonn, where *Gerim*
('proselytes') was read for *Garim* ('inhabitants'): a subsequent copyist fixed the
confusion by adding the Talmudic gloss 'a community of proselytes is considered
a community'.

one of the principal agents of Aaron of Lincoln) sought refuge
with their more precious belongings in the castle, leaving only
a few subordinates behind as caretakers. Following the example
set at Norwich and Lincoln, the Warden did what he could to
protect them, allowing them to take up quarters in the keep
subsequently called Clifford's Tower, which stood isolated on
an artificial mound. A few nights later, an assault was delivered
on Josce's residence, those left in it being butchered. Popular
feeling and greed were now thoroughly aroused, and the few
Jews who remained in the city were given the alternative of
baptism or death.

The refugees in the castle became more and more apprehen-
sive, and in the end, anticipating treachery, refused admittance
even to the Warden. The latter applied for help to the sheriff,
John Marshall, who rashly summoned the armed forces of the
county to assist in recovering the stronghold. That evening (it
was Friday, 16 March 1190—the eve of the 'Great Sabbath'
before Passover, and two days before Palm Sunday according
to the calendar of the Church) a terrible scene occurred. The
venerable Rabbi Yomtob of Joigny (a poet and legalist, one of
whose hymns is still chanted in most Synagogues on the Eve of
Atonement) urged his co-religionists to anticipate their inevitable fate in heroic fashion. Fire was set to their valuables, and
by the light of the flames, which soon set the whole building
in a blaze, the proposal was carried into effect. The number of
victims was reported to exceed one hundred and fifty, besides
those who met their death in the town: among them being the
learned R. Elijah of York, whose opinions were cited with
respect by the Rabbinical authorities on the Continent. The
last to die were Josce and Rabbi Yomtob, who killed the former
before making away with himself.

Next morning at daybreak, when the besiegers gathered to
deliver the final assault, the few who had not succumbed were
persuaded to throw open the gates, with a promise of clemency
if they embraced Christianity. As they ventured out, they were
set upon and massacred to a man. Immediately the butchery
was over, the ringleaders went to the Cathedral and forced the
sacristan to give up the bonds which the Jews had deposited
there. These they burned on the floor of the Minster, kindling
the flames from the light on the High Altar. All the attendant

circumstances go to indicate that the outbreak was at least as much economic as religious in origin.[1]

Not long afterwards, the majority of those responsible left for the Crusade. The handful of survivors were removed to London as soon as order was re-established (their transport cost only eight shillings).[2] It was many years before any community was re-established at York, and it never again attained the importance which it had enjoyed before that fiery night.[3]

The communities of Lynn and York were not the only ones which came to an end at this time. Under the walls of the great monastery of Bury St. Edmunds a relatively considerable Jewish community had grown up in the twelfth century. During the loose rule of the Abbot Hugh (1173-80) the house fell deeply into their debt. This was largely owing to the improvidence of the sacristan and cellarer, who borrowed on their own responsibility sums which increased at interest with startling rapidity: though the greatest individual creditor was, as it appears, a Christian. The sacristan, William, was on friendly terms with the local Jews, allowing them to deposit their deeds and money in his charge, and to lodge their wives and children in the refectory in time of disorder. In return, they strenuously favoured his claims to be elected abbot on the death of Hugh in 1180. One of the first actions of Abbot Samson, the successful candidate, was to depose the sacristan from office. Immediately afterwards, he set about freeing the monastery from the burden of debt in which it had become involved.[4]

The rapid growth of anti-Jewish feeling in the little monastic town is indicated by the ritual murder accusation which took place there, with the connivance of the monks, in the interregnum before Abbot Samson's election, when the child Robert was alleged to have been murdered (10 June 1181). The ground was thus amply prepared for more violent manifestations. The day after the tragic occurrences at York, on Palm Sunday, 1190,

[1] See Note II (a), p. 272.
[2] Pp.R. 1189-90, p. 75.
[3] In the Northampton Donum of 1194, York does not figure. By 1221 it was sufficiently recovered to contribute more than any other city to the Aid to marry the king's sister (below, p. 44 n.); but this unprecedented tribute was probably raised in York itself. Not all the community perished in the massacre: Aaron of York, the great thirteenth-century capitalist, was one of Josce's sons.
[4] The details of the episode are familiar to English readers from Carlyle's account (based on Jocelin of Brakelonde) in his *Past and Present*.

a massacre took place, fifty-seven Jews being killed. Shortly afterwards, Abbot Samson procured a writ from the Sovereign, authorizing the survivors (there cannot have been many) to be expelled from the town, on the ground that all its inhabitants ought to be vassals of St. Edmund. An armed escort was provided to conduct the exiles to their new places of residence. Henceforth, they were allowed to stay in the town for no longer than two days at a time for the purpose of collecting their debts, a sentence of excommunication being pronounced against any person who should give them further hospitality.[1]

The news of these tragic happenings was not long in reaching the Continent; and it was soon substantiated by the splendid manuscripts pillaged at York, which were brought to Cologne for sale. For the first time Jewish historians incorporated the sufferings of the communities of England in their martyrologies, and synagogal poets, such as Joseph of Chartres and Menahem of Worms, bewailed what had taken place in heart-broken elegies.[2]

## § III

The news of the outbreak at York reached the ears of the king (who was still in France completing his preparations) through a special messenger dispatched on Easter Monday.[3] The impression made on him and his advisers was profound. Any breach of the peace was manifestly against public policy, even if

[1] Richardson, *J.A.K.*, pp. 43–44, 80–81, has some pertinent information on the Jewish transactions with the Monastery. He points out that a prominent London citizen held a bond for the sum of £1,040, which would be unlikely to include any overt usury, whereas the amount owed to the principal Jewish creditor, including interest, was no more than £1,200. This strikingly demonstrates the fact that Christian financiers lent money as well as the Jews, and sometimes on a larger scale.

[2] In the earlier editions of this work there was incorporated here a translation of part of the Hebrew elegy by Menahem ben Jacob of Worms, of some literary but little historical significance, first published by S. Schechter in *Trs. J.H.S.E* i. 8–14. I subsequently traced and published in *Trs. J.H.S.E.* xvi. 213–20 a more important and more poignant commemorative poem by the French synagogal poet Joseph of Chartres, embodying some hitherto unknown details. Several of the martyrs are mentioned by name, including the scholars of Yomtob of Joigny, Elijah (already known in Rabbinical literature) and Joseph—obviously Josce of York, whose liberality towards students of the Law is spoken of with warm commendation. The author calls down imprecations on 'The King of the Islands', unaware that Richard did what he could to suppress the disorders. The English massacres are referred to also in another elegy by Menahem of Worms published by A. M. Habermann, *Gezeroth Ashkenaz veZarphath* (Jerusalem, 1936), pp. 147–151.

[3] Pp.R. 1190–1, p. 3.

infidels only were concerned: and the Jews had been specifically taken into the royal protection not many months before. Moreover—and this was more important—the Exchequer stood to lose heavily, both by the impoverishment of the Jews who survived and by the despoiling of those who had perished, part at least of whose property would normally have escheated to the Crown on their demise. Accordingly, when William Longchamp (bishop of Ely, and chancellor and co-justiciar of the kingdom, who happened to be with the king at the time) returned to England after the holyday, he was instructed to take vigorous proceedings against the culprits. Early in May he sent his brother Osbert north with an armed force to stamp out any embers of disorder, following him a little later to administer justice. The panic-stricken citizens of York denied complicity in the outrages, while the baronial ringleaders fled to Scotland before they could be touched. However, the estates of seven fugitives were confiscated (though subsequently restored), fines were inflicted upon some fifty prominent burghers, and hostages for future good conduct were sent in custody to Northampton. The sheriff was punished by removal from office, being replaced by Longchamp's brother. Not a single capital penalty was indeed inflicted, but few outbreaks against the Jews in medieval times gave rise to proceedings so drastic. On the other hand, it was observed that punishment fell most heavily on the adherents of the Percies, the relatives and allies of Longchamp's rival and co-justiciar, the Bishop of Durham.[1] For the restoration of the destroyed keep, in which the tragedy had occurred, an expenditure of over £200 was necessary in the course of the year.[2] From York the chancellor proceeded to Lincoln, taking with him sixty pairs of fetters to secure the prisoners whom he anticipated. But he under-estimated, for in the event no fewer than eighty persons belonging to all classes in the city were arraigned, though punished only by fine.[3]

---

[1] Stubbs, Introduction to Roger Howden in *Historical Introductions to the Rolls Series*, p. 218; Pp.R. 1190–1, *passim*. It is interesting to note the callings of some of those punished—e.g. Daniel *le bouvier* (drover) and Galfridus *carnifex* (butcher). In some cases the culprits appear not to have been inhabitants of York. Some Lincoln citizens were also fined—one as much as £100: J. W. F. Hill, *Medieval Lincoln* (Cambridge, 1948), pp. 390, 392.

[2] Pp.R. 1191–2, p. 61; *Archaeological Journal*, 1934, p. 296.

[3] See the list in Pp.R. 1191–2, pp. 242–3.

By now Richard was immersed in the final preparations for his Crusade, which officially opened at the beginning of July. The enterprise was brilliant as a military achievement, though not peculiarly successful in its object. It was brought to a conclusion in 1192 by a three-year truce with Saladin, which protracted the life of the attenuated Frankish kingdom in Palestine for a little longer, and secured Christian pilgrims access to Jerusalem.[1]

On his return journey (it is a familiar story) Richard was captured by his old enemy, the Duke of Austria, who in turn handed him over to the Emperor Henry VI. A humiliating treaty and a ransom of £100,000 were the price of his release. In England every fibre was strained in order to raise the amount. The Jews, as always, contributed disproportionately, being assessed at 5,000 marks, or three times as much as the burghers of London (incomparably the wealthiest city of the realm). Their representatives were summoned to meet at Northampton on 30 March 1194 to decide what amount each community should pay towards this sum.[2] The *Northampton Donum*, as it is called, which records the outcome of their deliberations, is a particularly valuable record of medieval English Jewry. It reveals the presence of Jews in about twenty major communities, as well as in a number of minor places scattered throughout the country. The most important centres were London, Lincoln, Canterbury, Northampton, and Gloucester, each with from twenty to forty contributors, these being the most affluent men of affairs in each place. The concentration of the greater capitalists in London is indicated by the fact that its contribution easily exceeded that of Lincoln and Northampton combined, whereas the number of direct contributors mentioned is less than half of their total. York, Stamford, Dunstable, Lynn, and Bury, where the worst of the outbreaks of four years previous had occurred, are conspicuous by their absence.[3] The amount

---

[1] The story that Richard invited Moses Maimonides to enter his service as his body-physician has now been disproved.

[2] The assessment was apparently made on the occasion of the King's Council at Northampton that Easter (Richardson, *J.A.K.*, p. 164). Subsequently, the representatives of the communities were summoned to him at Laigle in Normandy, where they agreed to contribute 3,000 marks towards his ransom (May 1194): cf. *Memoranda Roll, I John* (Pipe Roll Society), p. 71: 'Quidam Judei dicunt quod Judei Anglie finaverunt apud Aquilam cum R. Riccardo de quodam tallagio de 3,000 m.'

[3] The lists, which are among the most important sources for the condition of

actually raised was only about one-half of what was demanded—
a fact in which it does not seem unreasonable to see a reflection
of recent tribulations.

## § IV

The king and his advisers had not forgotten the flouting of his
authority by the rioters and the loss to the Exchequer that had
ensued. It was the administrative genius of Hubert Walter,
archbishop of Canterbury, that devised a means for preventing
a repetition of the disaster. When the justices went 'on eyre'
that autumn, for the administration of justice in the various
parts of the kingdom, they were enjoined to conduct an inquiry
into the events of 1190. Any person who had been implicated
in the attacks and had not yet compounded for his offence was
to be arrested. A diligent inquiry was to be made into the state
of the affairs of the victims before their death—what had been
in their possession, what sums had been owing to them, and
what pledges they had held. All this was to be 'taken into the
king's hands', so that those responsible should be prevented from
profiting from their crime.[1]

Finally, provision was made to safeguard the royal rights in
case of future disorder. Two Exchequer officials (the first were
William of Sainte-Mère-Église, future bishop of London, and
William de Chimillé) were designated to supervise the affairs
of the Jews, among other duties. Orders were given for all Jewish possessions and credits to be registered, and for six or seven
cities (probably London, Lincoln, Norwich, Winchester, Canterbury, Oxford, and either Northampton, Cambridge, Gloucester, Nottingham, or Bristol) to serve as centres for all business
operations in the future. In each of these places a bureau comprising two reputable Jews, two Christians, and two clerks
was to be set up, under the supervision of a representative

---

the Jews in England at the close of the twelfth century, and have been drawn
upon to a considerable extent in the course of the present study, are published
in full in *Misc. J.H.S.E.*, part i. The relatively small number of London contributors is possibly due to the presence there of the headquarters of the great
*consortia* and to the fact that the community was called upon for assistance at more
frequent intervals.

[1] See Stubbs, *Select Charters* (ed. Davis), p. 253, for the text. The inquiry seems
to have remained part of the regular functions of the Justices in Eyre: cf. *Annales
Monastici*, i. 330, 338.

of the newly established central authority. All deeds and contracts were to be drawn up in duplicate, in the presence of these
officials, the counterparts being deposited in a chest (*archa, huche*)
provided with three locks and seals. As a final precaution every
Jewish financier was to take a solemn oath upon the Hebrew
Pentateuch, or Scroll of the Law, that he would register his
transactions without concealment, and denounce to the authorities all forgeries or evasions that came to his notice.[1] Thus,
however the Jews might be maltreated in future, the Treasury and its claims were safe; for the death of their creditors
would merely place the debtors in the hands of the king, who
was informed exactly of all outstanding claims. Thus also it
became possible to control the affairs of the Jews themselves
without leaving any loophole for evasion, thereby making the
new system of arbitrary taxation temptingly simple.

This organization rapidly developed. The central authority
reorganized in 1194 became extended into the institution of
Wardens, or Justices, of the Jews.[2] When this office first emerged
in 1198 it was filled by three Christians working in collaboration with one Jew (the first were Simon of Pateshall, Henry of
Whiston, and Joseph Aaron on the one side, with Benedict of
Talmont on the other).[3] After April 1200 this group ceased to
figure: no Jewish name is included thereafter, the Justices of the
Jews being exclusively Christian.[4] Their number varied between
two and eight, though it was seldom that there were so many.
The office was considered to be one of dignity as well as
profit, and later on persons of the highest importance in the

---

[1] Stubbs, op. cit., pp. 256–7; and, for a more detailed account of the system
in its final development, below, pp. 110–11. These innovations seem to have been
imitated in France, where in 1198 the *Produit des Juifs* was established as a department of the Exchequer and after 1206 notaries were appointed in every town to
register Jewish debts. For the *custodes judaeorum* in Normandy, see P.R. 1204,
p. 39b, and Richardson, *J.A.K.*, pp. 206 ff.

[2] Below, pp. 112–13.

[3] Notwithstanding his name, Joseph Aaron was a Christian and in minor orders,
holding a prebend at St. Chad in Shrewsbury (C.R. 1212, p. 116b: it is possible,
however, that he was a convert). Benedict of Talmont (the royal residence near
La Rochelle, to which centre he belonged) is mentioned as a Jew in P.R. 1202,
p. 14, &c. He also had a Jewish clerk, Peter, possibly identical with Peter the Scribe
mentioned in Pp.R. 1185–6, p. 182.

[4] The Jewish Arch-presbyter (below, pp. 30–31) and the Assessors at the
Exchequer of the Jews were, however, sometimes styled 'Justices'; cf. C.R. 1249,
pp. 163, 165, 177, 179, and 1252, p. 271.

administration were sometimes appointed to fill it, though without giving up their other functions.

The institution over which these officials presided became known as the Exchequer of the Jews—a department of the Great Exchequer of the realm. By degrees it expanded into something a good deal more important than the original plan had implied. There was a natural tendency for the financial departments of the central administration in England to develop judicial functions, as was the case with the Great Exchequer itself. In precisely the same way the activities of the *Scaccarium Judaeorum*, as it finally evolved, were not purely fiscal but at the same time administrative and judicial, though restricted to matters in which some Jewish transaction or activity was ultimately (though in some cases very remotely) involved. It naturally had complete control over the local centres. The half-dozen specified in the ordinance of 1194 were found insufficient —more by reason of the slowness of communications than pressure of business. Accordingly, a chirograph-chest was ultimately established in each of the principal Jewish centres in the country, some twenty-seven in number, including a few which were very small and owed their importance to the activity of a single individual. At times of popular unrest in subsequent years, the first object of the rioters would be to seize the *archa* and destroy the records of indebtedness that it contained.[1]

In connexion with this organization there evolved the office of *Presbyter Judaeorum*. This was not (as was once held) a 'Chief Rabbi', or spiritual head of the Jews of the country, but an officially appointed expert on Jewish affairs and activities— generally a wealthy magnate—who was selected without any necessary regard to the general desire.[2] The first incumbent

---

[1] The best account of the Exchequer of the Jews is still that by C. Gross in *Papers A.J.H.E.* (London, 1888); but there are important additions and amplifications by Rigg and Jenkinson in the prefaces to the *Exchequer of the Jews* and *Trs. J.H.S.E.* viii. 18–54, ix. 185 ff., and by Richardson, *J.A.K.*, 135–60, &c. See also below, pp. 111–13.

[2] There has been a great deal of discussion with regard to the exact significance of this office. H. Adler, in *Papers A.J.H.E.*, championed the older view put forward in the seventeenth century by Coke and Selden, that the office was ecclesiastical: while Prynne and, two and a half centuries later, H. P. Stokes (*Studies*, pp. 23–43) and M. Adler (*J.M.E.*, pp. 137–9) have maintained that it was essentially secular. Though this is certainly true, the title *Presbyter* and the occasional alternative *Sacerdos* clearly indicate something more than lay functions (the office was sometimes filled indeed by persons of recognized scholarship) and the incumbent's

known (1183) was apparently a certain Jacob of London, who immediately after Richard's death followed the new king to Normandy in order to urge his claim to office. In July 1199 he received at Rouen formal reappointment to the Presbyterate, together with a safe conduct home. Little is known as to his career, whether before or after confirmation, though the terms of his appointment are indicative of cordial relations at Court.[1] He was succeeded in 1207 by a person of more eminence—Josce fil' Isaac, a grandson of Rubi Gotsce. His father, Isaac fil' Rabbi, the great financier of his day, survived his rival Aaron by some years and in 1190 secured from Richard I a confirmation for himself and his household of the Charter of Privileges which the tragic events of the previous year had prevented the communities of the realm from obtaining as a collectivity. His son, the new Archpresbyter, inherited his father's position as a leader of London Jewry. He was, however, deposed some time before his death, being succeeded in turn by Aaron of York (1236), Elias le Eveske (1243), Hagin fil' Rabbi Moses of Lincoln (1258), and lastly Cok Hagin fil' Deulecresse (1281). To all of these we shall have occasion to return. With the development of this office, the organization of medieval English Jewry in its relation to the state was completed.

§ v

The benefits of the mechanism for the exploitation of the Jews, perfected by the ministers of Richard I, were enjoyed by his successor. The ruling passion of John's nature, his rapacity, was the key too to his attitude towards the Jews. At the outset of the reign their contributions to the Exchequer were considerable,

opinion must occasionally have been consulted in matters of religious as well as financial practice. (The continental 'Court Rabbi', &c., furnishes a close parallel.) Cf. now also Richardson, *J.A.K.*, pp. 120 ff.

[1] Recent research has made it virtually certain that as Jacobs conjectured Jacob of London's nomination in 1199 was a reappointment; he may thus be identical with the Jacob Presbyter mentioned in Pp.R. 1183, p. 15 in connexion with Exchequer activities. In the Memoranda Roll of I John he is associated with Benedict of Talmont: hence it is incorrect that the Presbyterate derived from the latter's office. A Christian officer in charge of Jewish transactions (Hugh Bishop of Coventry) is mentioned before 1194, while the practice of keeping separate Jewish accounts was already followed by 1186. It thus appears that the essential part of the structure of the Jewish Exchequer antedates the re-organization of 1194. For details of the successive occupants of the office see the chapter in Stokes, *Studies*, pp. 23–43, and below, pp. 51, 79–80, 112.

but not beyond their means. They paid therefore with good grace, and were rewarded by various privileges. Later, when his treasury was empty, the king set about extorting money from them by a series of desperate expedients which betray his short-sightedness. Thus he set the example of extortion which was followed with such fatal results, and over a far longer period, by his successor. The rebellious baronage moreover resented the assistance that the king derived from his Jewish chattels, who became identified more and more in their minds with the royal oppression. Hence the reign of John marks the beginning of the political, as distinct from the religious, reaction against the Jews amongst the English people.

At the outset, there was no reason to anticipate this. Though the first acts of the new sovereign included the pardon and restoration to his possessions of Richard Malebysse (the ring-leader of the York massacre of nine years before)[1] and the ap-pointment of new Justices of the Jews,[2] this did not indicate the inauguration of an anti-Jewish policy. A Jew, Leo of Norwich, was royal goldsmith;[3] others received special grants of protec-tion and favour;[4] and, in appointing Jacob of London *presbyter judaeorum* in 1199, John referred to him as 'well-beloved' (*dilectus et familiaris noster*)—a phrase generally reserved for the great officers of state. Two years later, on 10 April 1201, the old exem-plary charter of liberties for the Jews of England and Normandy was reissued, confirming their right to dwell in the country and to enjoy all the rights and liberties granted by previous sove-reigns.[5] This concession cost the Jews of the realm 4,000 marks —a sum so great in their reduced circumstances that they were compelled to pay it in four instalments.[6]

[1] Obl.R. 1199, p. 41 (Jacobs's version, *J.A.E.*, p. 190, is very inaccurate: for Norwich hawks read Norway hawks; for two leashes of leopards read two leashes of greyhounds). But Malebysse (ancestor of the Yorkshire family of Beckwith) had made a nominal composition some years before: see Pp.R. 1192, p. 221, and Stubbs, *Historical Introductions to the Rolls Series*, p. 218. It is curious to find Jews giving him further opportunity to default on his debts: C.R. 1205, p. 58*b*. By 1202 he was a Justice! (*Earliest Lincoln Assize Roll*, p. xxiv).

[2] Ch.R. 1200, p. 61.

[3] Ch.R. 1199, p. 62*b*; P.R. 1208, p. 81*b*.

[4] P.R. 1208, p. 27.

[5] Ch.R. 1201, p. 93. The alleged additions in John's reissue, from which Dr. J. Parkes draws significant conclusions (*The Jew in the Medieval Community*, London, 1938, pp. 169–70), are non-existent.

[6] Obl.R. 1201, p. 133.

This was only a minor detail of the revenue extracted by John from the Jews over and above their customary dues. He continued on a vast scale the example of exempting certain debtors, obviously for a monetary consideration, from the necessity of paying the Jews interest or even the capital of their debts; and he would generously make over to his favourites lands which had fallen into the hands of the mortgagees. The fines imposed on individuals rose to a fantastic level, the unfortunate Isaac of Norwich, for example, being mulcted in 10,000 marks, to be paid off at the rate of one mark daily over a period of nearly thirty years.[1] The cost of the French wars was in part defrayed by cancelling the debts due to the Jews by those willing to serve overseas.[2] When in 1205, in order to honour his mother's memory, John ordered a general release of all persons incarcerated in the kingdom, the Jews were among those expressly excluded from its scope.[3] This was presumably in connexion with an extraordinary levy recently made on them. Two high officials, including one of the Justices of the Jews, had been appointed to supervise it; peremptory instructions were sent to the sheriffs, urging them to greater efforts in their exactions, under dark threats that otherwise they would themselves be held responsible;[4] and the possibilities of evasion were minimized by an order forbidding the Jews to place their chattels in churches for safe-keeping.[5] The assistance derived by the king so ostentatiously from his Jewish subjects bore its inevitable fruit in a deterioration of the relations between the latter and their Gentile neighbours. In London, in 1203, feelings ran so high as to necessitate a peremptory communication from the king to the mayor, taking the Jews under his protection ('If I give my peace even to a dog', he wrote contemptuously, 'it must be kept inviolate'), and threatening summary vengeance in case any attack on them should take place.[6]

[1] P.R. 1218, p. 180. He was son of the Jurnet of Norwich mentioned above, pp. 10, 14. See for this fine below, p. 35, and for its payment (£604 for 3¾ years) C.R. 1221, p. 459.          [2] Lib.R. 1203, pp. 44, 48 ff.

[3] P.R. 1205, p. 54.

[4] P.R. 1204, p. 38b.

[5] C.R. 1205, p. 20b.

[6] P.R. 1203, p. 33 (29 July 1203; not 22 July 1204, as in Jacobs). It is made clear in the communication that elsewhere in England the Jews were unmolested.

## § VI

In 1206 there came a turning point in Anglo-Jewish history, as in that of England as a whole. From the moment of the Jewish settlement, a century and a quarter before, the country had been closely connected—politically, culturally, and linguistically— with northern France. It was thence that the Jewish settlers had come in the first instance, and they remained bound to it by manifold ties. Like the nobility, English Jewry was to a certain extent Anglo-Norman in character. In fact, the Charters of Privileges conceded by successive sovereigns, from Henry I onwards, were issued to the Jews of England and Normandy, implying an association of organization as well as of interest between the communities of the two countries. However, in the years 1204–6, Normandy was lost through John's military incompetence. Once more England became, politically, an island —a fact of importance in English history.

To the Jews the consequences were no less momentous than to the country at large. They, too, were henceforth cut off to a considerable extent from the great centres on the Continent. It was no longer easy for a Jewish family, like that of Rubi Gotsce, to carry on business simultaneously on both sides of the English Channel.[1] The influx from abroad was checked, the names of native scholars are henceforth more prominent, and England had to become intellectually self-supporting. The civil authorities accentuated this tendency, forbidding the Jews to appeal to continental scholars against the decisions of their own Rabbis.[2] On the other hand, it was his endeavours to recover Normandy which led John to weigh down the country with arbitrary taxation, and thus to hasten the decline of medieval Anglo-Jewry.

In 1207 there was demanded from the Jews, in addition to a tallage of 4,000 marks, a levy of one-tenth of the value of their bonds, of which they were ordered to furnish precise details.[3]

---

[1] Cf. Lib.R. 1203, p. 72, and Ch.R. 1203, p. 105*b*, for indications of the family's continental interests: Abraham, a grandson of Rubi Gotsce, had to sell his houses and lands in England and in Normandy to pay his debt to the Crown.

[2] Below, pp. 55, 116–17.

[3] J. C. Holt, *The Northerners: a Study in the Reign of King John* (Oxford, 1961), suggests that in this year the Exchequer began also to tighten the screw in respect of debts which had been owing to Aaron of Lincoln.

This proved the preliminary to the confiscatory operations of
1210—a black year in the history of medieval English Jewry.
On the king's return to Bristol after his fateful campaign in
Ireland, he issued instructions for the arrest of all the Jews of
the kingdom (at least, that is, the men of substance), their charters being meanwhile seized and investigated.[1] There was thus
obtained sufficient evidence of the withholding of information to
justify widespread condemnations accompanied by confiscations
on a very large scale and the imposition on All Saints' Day
(1 November) of a tallage of unprecedented magnitude,[2] which
was exacted with the utmost barbarity. Jewish officials were
nominated in each county to distrain on debtors,[3] while the
property of those who could not pay was confiscated outright,
their houses being sometimes demolished so that something
could be realized on the building-materials. Even those of the
poorest class had to pay a levy of 40s. each or else abjure the
realm: thus in effect all who did not belong to the capitalist
element were expelled from the country.[4] Meanwhile, proceedings were pressed forward ruthlessly against those accused
of concealing their assets. Some were hanged:[5] while Isaac,
son of Jurnet of Norwich, purchased his pardon with the enormous fine spoken of above, which was still being collected so
many years later.[6]

In the circumstances, England ceased to be a land of security
and of prosperity, as in previous reigns. There was a considerable exodus from the kingdom, attaining such proportions that
one chronicler actually speaks of a general expulsion in 1210; and
in the following year several scholars joined a great pilgrimage
of three hundred French and English Rabbis to Palestine—
possibly to attend a synod on the writings of Maimonides.[7]

[1] The details are straightened out by Richardson, *J.A.K.*, pp. 167-71, where
references are given.
[2] Contemporary writers speak of 66,000 or 60,000 marks (confirmed by *E.J.* i. 4)
but according to Richardson this is only a term denoting an incalculable sum of
money. B. L. Abrahams in *Trs. J.H.S.E.* viii. 179-80, also questions the amount and
many details in the traditional account.
[3] That these officials were given the title of 'Sheriff' is an unwarranted detail
of the English version in *E.J.* i. 4, cf. H. Cole, *Documents Illustrative of English
History*, pp. 287-8.
[4] Cf. C.R. 1215, p. 186b.
[5] e.g. Isaac of Canterbury (Adler, *J.M.E.*, p. 64).
[6] Richardson, *J.A.K.*, p. 170; cf. above, p. 33, and below, pp. 41, 101.
[7] For the organization of this, it may be, Joseph ben Barukh of Clisson crossed

The arrears of the Bristol Tallage were inexorably levied in the ensuing period, together with fresh exactions. Hardly had there been time for the Jews to recover a little from their losses when in 1213 a further inquiry into their property was ordered.[1] In the following year the sheriffs again brought pressure to bear upon them to pay their arrears. On this occasion those who pleaded penury were imprisoned at the other end of the country: thus, the recalcitrant members of the few Hampshire communities were dispatched to Bristol to be shut up in the castle, while the wealthiest member of Bristol Jewry was sent to the Tower of London.[2] Throughout the country the houses of Jews were confiscated and made over to royal favourites.[3] Large numbers fled the realm, none being allowed back unless he could give security that he would pay his dues.[4] So reduced were the once wealthy Jews of London that in the words of the chronicler 'they prowled about the city like dogs'.[5]

The outbreak of civil war not long after made their position even worse. Violence became rife; and the barons, seeing in the Jews not only creditors but also the royal agents, considered them doubly deserving objects of attack. When London was occupied on 17 May 1215, the Jewry was the first objective of the insurgents. It was ruthlessly sacked, the houses being demolished and the stone used to repair the City walls.

When the Magna Carta was extorted from the king a short time later, the part which the Jews were forced to play as passive instruments of the royal exactions, and the unpopularity which they earned in consequence, was indicated by the tenth and eleventh clauses. In these it was stipulated that debts due to them or other usurers should bear no interest during the minority of the heir of a deceased debtor, and that if they fell into the king's hands in such circumstances (as might be the case, for example,

---

to England, where he was arrested and his precious burden of books seized (MS. Mich. Add. II in Bodleian Library, Oxford, f. 11; *MSS. Codices Hebraici Biblioth. I.B. De-Rossi*, ii. 111; cf. *Bibl.*. A. 4. 60). The *Flores Historiarum*, ii. 139, specifically mention an exodus of Jews from England *prae maxima afflictione* as a result of the financial extortions of 1210; on the other hand, J. de Oxenedes, in the place above, suggests the expulsion of those unable to pay.

[1] P.R. 1213, p. 97.
[2] Adler, *J.M.E.*, pp. 200–5; cf. P.R. 1213, p. 102*b*, and Davis, *Shetaroth*, p. 371.
[3] Ch.R. 1214, p. 200*b*, &c.; C.R. 1213, pp. 152, 161 ff.; Roth, *Oxford*, pp. 14–15.
[4] C.R. 1216, p. 186*b*.
[5] *Chronicle of Lanercost*, p. 7; cf. J. de Oxenedes, ed. Ellis, p. 125.

if the creditor died) the capital only, without any interest, should be exacted. Similarly, a widow's dowry and the support of children under age was to be a first charge on every estate, debts contracted by the father being payable out of the residue only. These clauses, with the burning sense of grievance which underlies them, give some idea of the animosity with which the royal satellites were now regarded by those with whom they transacted their principal and most lucrative business. Had the reign continued, they would inevitably have known further attacks by the one side and further spoliation by the other. John's death in 1216, as he was preparing for his revenge, unquestionably saved them from much fresh suffering.[1]

[1] A most important new source for the organization of English Jewry at the close of the twelfth century is Benedict of Talmont's *compotus de debitis et finibus Judaeorum Anglie* for 1198–1200 included in the Memoranda Roll of I. John (Pipe Roll Society, 1943), pp. 69–72, which gives a detailed picture of the working of the new financial arrangements and of the structure of English Jewry at the period of John's accession.

# III

## THE ROYAL MILCH-COW

### 1216–72

### § 1

THE beginning of the long reign of Henry III, an infant of nine at the time of his father's death, brought an immediate respite for all sections of his subjects. William Marshal and Hubert de Burgh, the successive regents, set themselves to restore order and stability, and in this they had the fullest support of the nation at large, which realized the necessity of reasserting the legitimate prerogatives of the Crown. There was still some suffering in store for the Jews while the embers of disorder were being stamped out,[1] but otherwise they immediately felt the change for the better. As part of the policy of re-establishing the financial system, everything possible was done to renew their confidence and rescue them from the deplorable condition into which they had fallen. Thus, in the confirmation of Magna Carta which took place at Bristol almost immediately after John's death, the clauses relating to the Jews were omitted, as prejudicial to the interests of the Exchequer; and they were not reinserted in any of the many reissues in subsequent years.[2] Instructions were given for the release of those Jews imprisoned at the close of the previous reign or in the subsequent unrest, and in some cases their sequestered bonds were restored and they received safe-conducts.[3] In the following year, when preparations for the Crusade proclaimed by the Pope in 1215 renewed the bitter memories of the last reign but one, precautionary steps were taken in good time. In every city in which Jews were to be found in any number, the royal officers were instructed to select as sureties twenty-four burgesses who would be held responsible

---

[1] C.R. 1217, p. 313, &c. For the Jews under Henry III, see especially Adler, *J.M.E.*, which deals mainly with this period, and *Bibl.* A. 4. 1.

[2] They were, however, re-enacted separately later on: see below, p. 53.

[3] P.R. 1217, pp. 59, 95, 98, 105.

for any outrage on those placed under their care. By this means, a repetition of the murderous outbreaks of York and London was effectively prevented.[1] The right of the Jews to live in Hereford, Worcester, York, Lincoln, Stamford, Gloucester, Bristol, Northampton, and Winchester was expressly confirmed, the local officials being enjoined not to molest them or to permit unauthorized persons to interfere with them in any way.[2]

In consequence of the improved conditions, there was a renewal of immigration from abroad, some of those who had fled in the previous reign doubtless returning to their former homes. Difficulties were encountered by many on their arrival owing to the unfriendly attitude of the Wardens of the Cinque Ports, which controlled communications with the Continent. When this became known, the latter were peremptorily instructed to liberate those whom they had thrown into prison and to admit intending immigrants freely in future. No formality was to be required from them henceforth except to give a guarantee that they would present themselves before the Justices of the Jews to be enrolled. On the other hand, no Jews were to be allowed to leave the realm without licence—renewed testimony to their importance to the State.[3]

§ II

The policy of the ecclesiastical authorities was less liberal. Stephen Langton, archbishop of Canterbury, had been one of the leading spirits at the Fourth Lateran Council of 1215, which affected the Jews profoundly. Considering their influence to have been responsible for the alarming spread of heresy in Europe, it renewed all the degrading restrictions that the Church had postulated academically in its first flush of triumph, with some even more stringent additions. Moreover, it attempted to extend to them the obligation to pay church tithes and—particularly where the borrowers were Crusaders—to restrict their 'usury' (the practice of which by Christians had been a principal

---

[1] C.R. 1218, pp. 354*b*, 357, 359.

[2] P.R. 1218, p. 157. 'Suhamtonia' implies Hampshire—i.e. Winchester.

[3] P.R. 1218, p. 180. The last important influx seems to have been in consequence of the expulsion from Brittany in 1239 (*R.E.J.* xiv. 86). The *Flores Historiarum*, ii. 218, speak of Italian (and Spanish?) Jews seeking refuge in England in 1236, but the persecution alleged to be responsible for this immigration is recorded nowhere else.

preoccupation of the Third Lateran Council of 1178-9). Transgression in these matters was to be placed, moreover, under the jurisdiction of the church courts. The English authorities, particularly subservient to Rome at this period, had no objection against the first part of this policy; and England was thus the first country in Europe to enforce consistently the restrictive and humiliating clauses in the new anti-Jewish code. But it was impossible for them to tolerate the attempt to drive the Jews out of the activities that proved so useful to the Treasury, or to permit the extension over them of the power of the ecclesiastical tribunals. This therefore was stoutly resisted; and the conflict that resulted between the secular and spiritual authorities continued intermittently throughout the first half of the reign.

The conflict of policy began to manifest itself as soon as order was restored. The most novel and least palatable of the recent Lateran regulations was that which introduced into the Christian world for the first time the obligation for all the unbelievers to wear a distinguishing badge—ostensibly in order to prevent the scandal of unwitting sexual intercourse between the adherents of different faiths. This was introduced into England as early as 1218, when a royal decree enjoined every Jew to wear at all times a mark on his outer garment (the form was carefully prescribed) by which he might be differentiated from Christians.[1] At the same time, the Church was beginning to enforce other innovations of the same sort, without any objection being raised.[2] But matters were different when it embarked upon a campaign to

[1] C.R. 1218, p. 378b. Tovey, Anglia Judaica, p. 79, followed after two centuries by modern historians (Norgate, Minority of Henry III, p. 97, and, with further deductions, Gibbs and Lang, Bishops and Reform, 1215-1272, pp. 134-7, &c.), states that the innovation was intended to save the Jews from molestation; but there is no authority for this curious interpretation. Richardson, J.A.K., pp. 178-80, shows that from the beginning very many exemptions were purchased both for individuals and for communities: it was thus only after 1253 that the Badge was consistently enforced. See also below, pp. 96, 71.

[2] The most zealous of the English bishops was apparently William de Blois, bishop of Worcester, who as early as 1219 forbade the Jews to employ Christian nurses or servants, to take sacred objects in pledge, to lend out on usury moneys received from non-Jews, or to continue to deposit their property in churches for safe-keeping (Wilkins, Concilia Magnae Britanniae, i. 570-1). These constitutions were repeated by the same prelate ten years later (ibid., p. 626) and by his successor Walter de Cantelupe in 1240 in much the same form, with an additional clause forbidding resort to Jewish soothsayers (ibid., pp. 671, 675). But it is not easy to understand why there should have been such interest in the Jews in this diocese: see below, p. 130.

undermine the economic position of the Jews and bring them
under the discipline of its own courts. This could not be tolerated,
and in reaffirming the right of undisturbed residence for the Jews
the civil authority specifically repudiated all clerical claims to
interference 'as the Bishops have no concern with our Jews'.[1]
The all-powerful papal legate, Pandulph, could not remain indifferent. In a peremptory letter of complaint addressed to the
justiciar, he voiced his indignation at what he considered the
excessively favourable position of the Jews. Above all, he objected
to the conduct of Isaac of Norwich (the wealthiest English Jew
of the age, whose caricature executed by a playful Exchequer
clerk is still extant, and who was still paying off at the rate of one
mark daily the fantastic fine imposed on him by King John); and
he requested that the proceedings pending between the financier
and the Abbey of Westminster should be postponed until he was
himself at liberty to be present.[2]

The reaction was strengthened by a dramatic episode that
took place at this period. At the Council of the Province of Canterbury, held in Oxford in 1222, the most violent passions were
aroused by the trial of a certain deacon who had been induced
through the study of Hebrew to adopt Judaism and had married
a Jewess.[3] He was degraded and handed over for punishment to
Fawkes de Breauté, the sheriff of Oxfordshire. The latter, swear-
ing 'by the throat of God' that he would be avenged on the
blasphemer, and expressing his regret that he would go to Hell
without his paramour, immediately had him burned.[4] (This
incident served as the common-law precedent for the punishment of heretics by burning, for which the notorious statute 'De
Heretico Comburendo' passed in 1401 was in fact unnecessary:

[1] P.R. 1218, p. 157. The clerical antagonism is not likely to have been minimized by an alleged attempt of a Jew to defraud the Prior of Dunstable (who had
recently permitted a few of them to live within his lordship on payment of a nominal
tribute) by forging a bond for £70—in bad Latin, it appears, which added insult
to injury. The forger's co-religionists saved him from the gallows by a payment
of £100, levied in 1221: see Tovey, *Anglia Judaica*, pp. 85 ff., and *Trs. J.H.S.E.*
xi. 97–99.

[2] *Royal Letters*, i. 35. For some transactions of Isaac of Norwich see C.R. 1218,
p. 367; 1219, p. 180, and *passim*; Davis, *Shetaroth*, pp. 2–4 and 24–26; and Adler,
*J.M.E.*, frontispiece and pp. 20, 146. Cf. also Bracton's *Note-Book*, 1376 and 1445.

[3] *Bibl.* A. 4. 67.

[4] The Deacon of Oxford is sometimes identified with Robert of Reading, about
whom a similar tale is told; but the latter seems to have belonged to a later
generation. See below, p. 83, and Roth, *Oxford*, pp. 19–20.

accordingly, it was the occasion for many executions both before the passing of this law and after its repeal.) Thoroughly stirred by this episode, the Council went on to reiterate the anti-Jewish regulations decreed at the Lateran seven years before, with a few elaborations. Jews were forbidden to employ Christian servants, to enter churches or store their property in them, or to build new synagogues; they were enjoined to pay tithes to the priests of the parishes in which they resided not only on their real estate but also on their usurious profits; they were once more ordered to wear a distinguishing badge, the size of which was stipulated for the first time; and they were submitted to the ecclesiastical authority in cases of neglect.[1] But this was not enough. In over-meticulous obedience to the Lateran canons which ordered those who practised 'immoderate' usury or exacted it from Crusaders to be cut off from intercourse with Christians, the Archbishop of Canterbury apparently determined to apply this drastic discipline to all Jews without discrimination. Zealously supported by the bishops of Norwich and Lincoln, he published an injunction threatening with excommunication those who entered into familiar relations with Jews or even sold them provisions. Obedience to this would have resulted in the annihilation of the Jewish communities in a large part of the country by starvation. Accordingly, Hubert de Burgh, now justiciar, issued an order forbidding the king's subjects under pain of imprisonment to refuse to provide Jews with the necessities of life.[2] But the English Church remained stubbornly set on this plan, and at intervals during the reign the central authority had again to be exerted to prevent its execution.

Against minor ecclesiastical annoyances, on the other hand, there was no protection—least of all in the pious young king, who had shown his prejudices by having the Jews of London shut up in the Tower during his recoronation ceremony in 1220. In 1221 the Black Friars, to be followed three years later by the Franciscans,

---

[1] Wilkins, *Concilia*, i. 591-2 (§§ xxxix, xl).

[2] C.R. 1223, p. 567. There seems to have been unpleasantness elsewhere in England at this time. In the spring of 1221 the Jews of York once more requested the royal protection (P.R. 1221, p. 290); and, the next year, those of Stamford were arrested on a charge (which the authorities in London do not seem to have taken too seriously) of making a game in mockery of the Christian faith (C.R. 1222, p. 491: from the dates, it seems probable that a misinterpretation of a Purim masquerade was responsible). Two Jews were killed in an attack at Lincoln in 1220 (*E.J.* i. 46).

acquired a tenement in the immediate neighbourhood of the Oxford Jewry, certainly not by chance. About this time (the exact date is unknown, but it was before 1243) a synagogue newly erected in London, and alleged to be of great magnificence (though this is most unlikely) was confiscated, later being made over to the Brethren of St. Anthony.[1] In 1232, moreover, there was set up under the royal auspices, outside London, an establishment known as the 'Domus Conversorum', for the reception of those Jews who abandoned their ancestral faith: and proselytization was henceforth carried on more systematically.[2]

§ III

Ecclesiastical vexations notwithstanding, the condition of the Jews remained tolerable during the royal minority, and so long as the old ministers were entrusted with authority. However, on the fall of Hubert de Burgh in 1232, a new spirit prevailed. The Court, thronged with alien favourites, was extravagant to a degree. The king's intensely artistic nature, his love of the beautiful, his passion for building, proved a constant strain on his resources, being no less a source of misery for his subjects than of delight for their posterity. His foreign policy, which culminated in a series of unsuccessful wars, was ruinously expensive. Extreme piety led him to support implicitly the schemes of a succession of popes against the Holy Roman emperor, which were largely financed by the people of England. Taxation became oppressive, and of all the king's subjects (as was deemed natural and proper) the Jews were made to suffer most. The old system, under which they had been permitted to amass wealth as the financial agents of the Crown, was now superseded. Henceforth they were regarded

---

[1] The site is now occupied by the Westminster Bank in Threadneedle Street, nearly opposite the Royal Exchange. The building was long known as St. Anthony's Hospital.

[2] Adler, *J.M.E.*, pp. 279 ff. Legally, converts from Judaism forfeited to the Crown all their property, as having been acquired by the sinful means of usury. Destitute as they were, a hostel was indispensable. Generally, however, the Exchequer waived part of its rights in such cases. The account repeated by most historians, of the establishment of a similar Home for Converted Jews at Oxford in 1221, is based on a misinterpretation (*Misc. J.H.S.E.*, ii. 29 ff.): and the same applies according to Richardson to that which is said to have existed from 1154 at Bristol (Adler, *J.M.E.*, pp. 183, 281). The institution for 'conversi' set up in Southwark in 1213 by the Prior of Bermondsey was not for Jewish converts, as so often stated, but for lay-brethren.

only as a source of revenue—an object of pitiless excoriation, regardless of the ultimate result. From an extraordinary expedient resorted to only in case of emergency, the raising of money by arbitrary tallage became a regular source of income, exploited with every circumstance of cruelty.

During the minority, the extraordinary amercements on the Jews had been comparatively mild.[1] With the beginning of the king's personal rule in 1227, conditions changed, and during the next ten years alone tallages were exacted to the combined value of at least 65,000 marks—nearly four times as much as the total exacted during the previous decade. This was, however, far from representing the total burden. The cost of the foreign campaigns from 1230 onwards was defrayed to a considerable extent by the remission of the interest on, or sometimes the principal of, the debts owed to the Jews by those who participated—whether the whole or part, temporarily or for good.[2] In 1237, in the interval between two heavy tallages, the communities of the realm were commanded to make a gift of 3,000 marks to the Earl of Cornwall, the king's brother, for the purpose of his intended Crusade, and this became a precedent henceforth whenever a member of the royal family announced his intention of going to fight the Saracens. One debtor after another obtained from the sympathetic ruler an order for the extension of time and more reasonable terms for the repayment of his debt. The burden of tallage was made more serious on the general body by the exemption from participation, for special considerations, of some of the wealthier;[3] and the administration of the Exchequer of the Jews passed into the hands of the king's foreign ministers, who were alleged to use it as a means of patronage and extortion. The only possible

[1] Apart from an intermittent attempt which continued till 1221 to collect the remnants of the Bristol Tallage (Adler, *J.M.E.*, p. 205: cf. F.R. 1235, p. 174) and the levy of an unspecified amount in 1219, when sureties were sent to London for imprisonment (Stokes, *Studies*, pp. 250–1), the tallages in these years consisted of 1,000 marks in 1221 towards the dowry of the king's sister, 3,000 in 1223, 5,000 in 1224–5 (when the rest of the realm paid the king one-fifteenth in return for the confirmation of Magna Carta), 3,500 in 1225, and 4,000 in 1226: the gradual increase is significant.

[2] See the repeated examples in Gascon Rolls, vol. i.

[3] e.g. Isaac of Norwich (P.R. 1231, p. 453; *Rot. Fin.* 1232, p. 226) or Aaron of York (P.R. 1235, p. 93). A promise that on his return from Gascony the king would make provision for lightening the burden on certain hard-pressed members of the community (C.R. 1230, p. 439) does not seem to have had any practical outcome.

method of evasion was by flight, and the exodus from the country seems to have reached considerable proportions.[1]

As long as Henry's authority was supreme, there was no break in the record of spoliation. From the close of the royal minority down to 1259, a total of over 250,000 marks in tallages was extorted from English Jewry, without reckoning other wholesale levies of unspecified amount.[2] The methods of exaction became more and more cruel and rapacious. In 1236 ten of the richest Jews of the realm were taken into custody as security for the sum of 10,000 marks to be contributed by their co-religionists. Three years after, an alleged murder in London was punished by the confiscation of one-third of their property.[3] 1240 witnessed a census of every Jew and Jewess in the country above the age of twelve, presumably with a view to assessing the levies of the following year.[4] On this occasion, the so-called 'Parliament of Jews' consisting of from two to six members of each of the twenty-one communities of the realm then recognized, was summoned to meet at Worcester to apportion among themselves a fresh tallage of 20,000 marks, nominally equivalent to one-third of their property, for the collection of which they were personally held responsible. Appalled at the amount, unprecedented hitherto in the reign, some of the London community set out after the Court to expostulate.[5] The king was unaffected and ordered drastic steps to be taken. Many Jews from all parts of the country, unable to raise their full assessment, were arrested with their wives and children and imprisoned in the Tower, the deficiency being presumably made up by the seizure of their property.[6]

The success attending the experiment was so great that the king was emboldened to repeat it on yet a larger scale. In 1244 a fine of the stupendous sum of 60,000 marks was assessed on the Jews on the pretext that they had been guilty of a ritual crime.[7] Somehow the amount was raised, though it was six years before the last arrears were collected. Meanwhile, the same year, a

[1] Adler, *J.M.E.*, p. 211.
[2] See Note III (a), pp. 272-3.
[3] M. Paris, *Chron. Maj.* iii. 543; *Misc. J.H.S.E.* ii. 17-19; below, p. 55.
[4] C.R. 1240, p. 238.          [5] C.R. 1241, p. 268.
[6] In this year, too, donations were obtained from wealthy individuals to defray the expenses of the queen's childbed (C.R. 1241, p. 290).
[7] M. Paris, *Chron. Maj.* iv. 377-8; see below, p. 55, and for the mechanism of the levy, *E.J.* i. 74 ff.

minor levy of 4,000 marks was extorted in order to repay a loan to the Italian merchants,[1] and in the next a fresh tallage of 8,000 marks was imposed to meet the emergency expenditure of the Welsh war. On this occasion, payment was secured by a threat that, in case of undue delay, the wealthiest of the Jews would be dispatched to Ireland to be imprisoned. It was only natural that some, fearing a repetition of the wholesale arrests of 1241, placed their wives and children in hiding: a precaution for which they and their families were outlawed and their property confiscated.[2] On the king's safe return from Wales that autumn, a thank-offering of forty gold marks was exacted, though it is question-able whether those who paid it in fact appreciated the event.[3] When in 1250 Henry was compelled by the pressure of debt and poverty to take the Cross, and proclaimed his contrition by beg-ging the forgiveness of the people and ordering a reduction in his household expenditure, he consoled himself by a further raid on the Jews. First, an official inquiry was made throughout the king-dom into concealed Jewish property: and in the following year a new levy of 10,000 marks was ordered, instructions being issued that no Jew was to be spared, and the community of Wilton at least being imprisoned *en masse*.[4] The commissioners to whom the assessment was entrusted were accompanied by an unprincipled Jew, Abraham of Berkhamsted, who urged them to greater severity and threatened to denounce them if they showed the slightest moderation.[5] When in 1253 Henry crossed to Gascony, the Jews had to 'pacify' him with a payment of 5,000 marks.[6]

Next year the Treasury was again empty. The king sent home urgent instructions to his brother, Richard of Cornwall, who had already shown himself the only competent financier of the family, to raise money by any expedient to meet the anticipated invasion. Barons, prelates, and Commons were all unhelpful, and the brunt of the attack fell on the Jews, whose represen-tatives were assembled at Westminster to hear the royal com-munication. After being kept waiting about for three weeks,

[1] P.R. 1244, p. 445; *P.E.J.*, p. 74.
[2] C.R. 1244, p. 275.                                    [3] C.R. 1244, p. 371.
[4] C.R. 1251, p. 544; M. Paris, *Chron. Maj.* v. 114-16, *Hist. Angl.* iii. 76.
[5] P.R. 1250, pp. 64, 71. (M. Paris dates this levy in 1253.)
[6] C.R. 1253, p. 386. The amount included 1,000 marks advanced by Richard of Cornwall, who from this date became more and more interested in the financial administration of Jewry.

they were summoned before the earl and told what was wanted. Elias le Eveske of London, who had been appointed *Presbyter Judaeorum* in 1243,[1] and was at the head of the Jewish representatives, was aghast at the magnitude of the sum demanded. In a pathetic speech, he intimated that his co-religionists had no more left to give and begged in their name for permission to leave the country. Richard was sufficiently moved by what he said to modify his demands, exacting only an amount which was within the bounds of possibility. The licence to emigrate was of course refused. However, after his return from Gascony in the following year, when he was in desperate straits to find money in order to obtain the throne of Sicily for his son Edmund, the king repeated the experiment, demanding from the unhappy Elias immediate payment of 8,000 marks under the penalty of hanging. He was met once more by a blank confession of inability to pay, and a further request for permission to leave the realm. This he angrily refused ('I am a mutilated and diminished king', he exclaimed. 'It is dreadful to think of the debts in which I am involved, and I am under the necessity of obtaining money from every quarter'); and the Wardens of the Cinque Ports were enjoined to arrest any intending emigrants.[2]

It was now obvious that all immediate possibilities for raising revenue were exhausted. Henry, over head and ears in debt, now exercised his rights as suzerain by mortgaging the whole of the community as security for a loan of 5,000 marks to his wealthy brother, who (in the words of the chronicler) 'was thus permitted to disembowel those whom the King had flayed' (1255). This amount, with an additional 1,000 marks by way of douceur, was to be paid by the detested usurers in instalments over a period of two years, during which two adroit Jewish financiers were appointed to administer the affairs of their co-religionists—for all the world like an estate in bankruptcy.[3] In fact, Richard (whose relations with the Jews had been

[1] Elias le Eveske (for whom see Stokes, *Studies*, p. 30) has been confused with Magister Elias fil' Magister Moses (i.e. Rabbi Elijah Menahem: below, pp. 125, 127) of London, whose brother Hagin was the other's successor. But the two are mentioned individually in the same document (Stokes, p. 6).
[2] M. Paris, *Hist. Angl.* iii. 334; C.R. 1255, pp. 227, 233. Already in 1250 inquiry had been made about the assets of the Jews in the Cinque Ports, presumably for the same reason.
[3] M. Paris, *Hist. Angl.* iii. 115; P.R. 1255, pp. 400, 439.

consistently good, and whose candidature to the Imperial Throne in Germany they are said to have favoured) proved himself a comparatively mild master. But immediately this period was at an end, the Jewish communities were made over in a similar manner for three years, with the whole mechanism of the Jewish Exchequer, to the king's son Edward, the heir to the throne, to secure his loyalty, in return for an annual revenue of 3,000 marks from his estates; and he was even allowed to maintain his own prison for incarcerating them in case of need (1262).[1] The latter in turn assigned them after a little more than twelve months to their business competitors, the Cahorsin merchants (who were acquiring an increasingly evil reputation for their usurious activities) in security for a loan.[2] (The comparatively small amounts which were in question at this period indicate how far the victims had been impoverished.)

Meanwhile, unprecedented sums were exacted from individuals. In 1250 the king put forward a claim to succeed to the possession of all houses owned by Jews on their demise, though he did not carry it into execution. Nevertheless, when any wealthy capitalist died, vast reliefs were exacted, in accordance with custom, from his heirs; and in 1257 a loan of 10,000 marks was raised from the Florentine merchants in London largely on the security of the Escheats of Jewry.[3] On the rebuilding of Westminster Abbey in 1245, the Jews were forced to contribute both in their corporate capacity and as individuals. Licoricia, widow of a wealthy Oxford financier, was made to give over £2,500; Moses of Hereford furnished £3,000; Elias le Eveske had to provide a silver-gilt chalice; others defrayed the cost of internal embellishments.[4] (It was a needless aggravation of insult by injury to sell the Hebrew scrolls of the Pentateuch used by the Justices of the Jews for administering oaths, so as to defray the cost of a new chasuble and other appurtenances.)[5] The worst individual sufferer was Aaron of York, son of the Josce of York martyred in 1190 and *Presbyter Judaeorum* before Elias le Eveske. With dealings extending over at least fourteen English counties,

---

[1] P.R. 1262, p. 233; C.R. 1262, p. 79; *Selected Cases before the King's Bench, Edward I* (Selden Society), vol. ii, pp. cxlvi f.

[2] P.R. 1263, p. 263.        [3] P.R. 1257, p. 562.

[4] P.R. 1246, p. 474. But the payments by Licoricia and Moses were death duties.

[5] C.R. 1245, p. 292.

and with some twenty co-religionists serving as his local agents, he was the greatest Anglo-Jewish financier of the thirteenth century, as Aaron of Lincoln had been of the twelfth. His importance to the Treasury must have been as high, though different in type. At every exigency of the reign, it was to him that recourse was had by the Court. In 1243, on the occasion of Richard of Cornwall's marriage to the queen's sister, Sanchia of Provence, he had to provide 400 gold and 4,000 silver marks to defray the expenses, as against a bagatelle of 100 levied from the remainder of English Jewry; and contemporary observers were shocked at the spectacle of the King of England demeaning himself to accept the gold (though not indeed the silver) with his own hands. Five years later Aaron was fined 1,000 gold marks, and he was mulcted in a further 4,000 marks in 1250 on a charge of forging a deed, apart from his contributions to the general burden of taxation in the interval. The next year he was assessed for tallage at 2,000 marks. Meanwhile, Henry, unable to restrain his greed, had begun to wring from the financier's family the estate-duty which they were expected to pay on his death—a presumption not in fact justified, as, worn out by incessant exactions, he ended his days in penury. In seven years only, he complained to Matthew Paris, the historian of the reign, the court had received from him upwards of 30,000 marks in silver and 200 in gold, without reckoning the *aurum reginae* that he had to pay to the queen.[1]

Meanwhile, as the king pressed forward with his unpopular policy of setting up a centralized administration, the alleged abuses at the Jewish Exchequer reached a climax. The Treasurer, Peter des Rivaulx, who concentrated in his hands an unprecedented accumulation of offices, was given in 1232 custody of the Jewry, 'so that all the Jews of England should be intendant and accountable to him'.[2] The Deputy Treasurer, Robert Passelewe, was Justice of the Jews: while the Justiciar, Stephen Segrave, worked in collusion with them. The Jewish Exchequer

---

[1] For the career of Aaron of York (d. 1268) see Adler's very full study, *J.M.E.*, pp. 127–73. He is believed to have provided the money for the Five Sisters window in York Minster.

[2] Ch.R. 1232, p. 163 (June 28th). He was not himself Justice of the Jews, as formerly stated, and the implications of his appointment are not quite clear. He also had custody of the Jews of Ireland (P.R. 1232, p. 494: cf. also C.R., p. 102).

was among the government departments included in their
drastic administrative reorganization, figuring as well (so at
least their enemies alleged) as an inexhaustible opportunity for
personal enrichment. They imprisoned their charges to obtain
ransom, manipulated their taxes, made them pay exaggerated
sums for licences to live where they wished, compelled them to
reduce debts and return pledges, charged a commission for
nominal assistance in collecting dues, extorted free-will gifts in
money and jewels on the slightest pretext or none at all, even
held the *archa* to ransom and abstracted the bonds, which were
publicly offered for sale in West Cheap. The Exchequer itself
was alleged not to be safe from their audacity: on one occasion,
when the Jews were to pay a tallage of £500, they were assessed
for no less than £700, of which, however, the king received
only £462.

When in 1234 the Archbishop of Canterbury forced the king
under menace of excommunication to dismiss these unpopular
administrators, their conduct at the Exchequer of the Jews constituted one of the long series of charges against them. The
palace revolution took place with dramatic suddenness: on
3 May the Jewish communities had been enjoined to give Passelewe implicit obedience: on 30 May they were told to obey him
no longer, and the Justices of the Jews were directed to report
all matters of importance direct to the king, and not to Des
Rivaulx as hitherto. In the subsequent inquiry, eighteen London
Jewish business men gave damning evidence of the manner in
which they and their co-religionists had been fleeced by the
disgraced trio—especially Passelewe—for their own enrichment.
They were nevertheless restored to favour two years later, Des
Rivaulx having the opportunity later on of imposing his authority once more as Treasurer.[1]

The struggle was by no means at an end, and the control of
the Exchequer of the Jews remained a point of contention in the
stormy years that followed. In November 1239 a clean sweep
was made of the chirographers and clerks of the *archae* throughout the country, and new arrangements were made for the
preparation and custody of bonds.[2] In 1244-5, in consequence

[1] M. Adler, 'The Testimony of London Jewry against the Ministers of Henry III',
in *Trs. J.H.S.E.* xiv. 142-85.
[2] Richardson, *J.A.K.*, p. 147.

of the constitutional demands of the barons, the entire staff of
the Exchequer, Jewish as well as Christian, was suspended.[1]
When in 1249 the king renewed his attempt to set up a bureau-
cracy, the Jewish Exchequer was among the administrative
bodies placed under the control of Philip Lovel, who had rapidly
been advanced from a simple clerkship to the highest offices
of state. In 1251, however, he and his clerk Nicholas of St. Albans
were charged with corruption in tallaging the Jews in the north
of the country and were suspended from their functions, while
in the following year Robert de la Ho, another of the Justices,
was cashiered for forging a charter.[2] Nevertheless, before six
months had passed Lovel was back in office again, continuing
to serve as before for several years.[3] The Jewish officials at the
Exchequer were no safeguard to their co-religionists; and one
arch-presbyter after the other—Josce fil' Isaac of London (1207–
36), Aaron of York (1236–43), and Elias le Eveske (1243–57)—
was removed from office. The last named was driven in the end
to become converted to Christianity, and tried to reinstate himself in favour by bringing wild accusations against his former
co-religionists. So obnoxious had the institution of the arch-
presbyter become during his oppressive period of office that an
undertaking was obtained from the king not to make any further
appointment except by election of the Jewish community, whose
nominee would receive official sanction. Their choice fell upon
Vives, or Hagin, son of Master Moses of Lincoln, member of a
family outstanding for its scholarly reputation.[4] Needless to say,
this privilege also was granted only at the price of a considerable
payment.

The consequences of such rapacity should have been obvious
to any intelligent being. The king was like a spendthrift with a
cheque-book, drawing one amount after the other in utter indifference to the dwindling of his resources. Even as regards his

[1] C.R. 1246, p. 416: see below, p. 59.
[2] The confused sequence of Justices of the Jews in the reign of Henry III has
been straightened out by C. A. F. Meekings in *Bulletin of the Institute of Historical
Research*, xxviii. 173–88. For the reorganization of personnel at the Exchequer in
1249, see C.R., pp. 163, 165, 175, 177, 179, 180.
[3] M. Paris, *Chron. Maj.* v. 261, 320, 345. The example of the central administration of the Jewish Exchequer was naturally followed at the local *archae*, where
every now and again suspected chirographers had to be removed—e.g. at Wilton
in 1256 (C.R. 1256, p. 15).
[4] Stokes, *Studies*, pp. 3–11; P.R. 1257, pp. 570–1; Ch.R. 1258, p. 8.

personal interests, the policy was foolish. It progressively impoverished the English Jewries, rendering them less and less
remunerative to the Exchequer as time went on. Moreover, in
order to support these constant calls upon their purse, they were
compelled to exercise still greater acquisitiveness in their business affairs, grinding desperately out of their clients the amounts
that they would be compelled so inexorably to surrender to the
Crown. Never was it more true that the Jews were like a sponge,
sucking up the floating capital of the country, to be squeezed
from time to time into the Treasury; while the king, high above
them and sublimely contemptuous of their transactions, was in
fact the arch-usurer of the realm.

Paradoxically, measures were taken at the same time which
tended to restrict their activities. In 1234 Crown tenants were
forbidden to borrow money from Jews on the security of their
estates;[1] and four years later the provision was extended to all
who held their property by military service. Thus, it was ensured that failure to redeem their lands (very frequently followed, or else forestalled, by sale to the Church) would not have
any untoward effect upon the feudal levies of the realm, or make
it difficult for the tenants-in-chief to raise their quota.[2] The
outcome of other regulations was similar. As a concession to
religious houses, it was ordered that estates given to them should
be exempt from any liability on account of the debts of the
original donor; henceforth, therefore, an impoverished layman
who raised a loan from the Jews and was unable to repay could
present the security to the Church (perhaps in return for a slight
monetary compensation) and thereby both ensure the felicity
of his soul and deprive the Jewish creditor of his dues.[3] The
papal decree that interest could not be taken from a Crusader
was enforced, and even extended to intending crusaders who
supported the king with money instead of going in person;[4] and

[1] C.R. 1234, p. 592.
[2] C.R. 1238, p. 119. It should be remembered that such regulations did not
necessarily mean that the practices stopped; the same complaints and restrictions
periodically recur until the Jews were expelled.          [3] C.R. 1241, p. 505.
[4] P.R. 1251, p. 75; 1252, p. 164. Hitherto, the ecclesiastical regulations had not
been enforced consistently, unless the debtor were on good terms with those in
authority. So at least Master Robert of Gloucester (not Glover, as in the English
translation in Grayzel, *The Church and the Jews*, pp. 231–3) asserted in 1237 to
pope Gregory IX among his other complaints against the Archbishop of Canterbury (Auvray, *Régistres de Grégoire IX*, § 3419).

the provision of the Magna Carta, that it could not be charged on the property of a minor on account of his late father's debts, was re-enacted separately.[1] In order to safeguard the Church's right to tithes, the acquisition of further land or tenements in the capital was forbidden. New, particularly harsh, regulations issued on 4 April 1233 (which ordered the expulsion from the realm of all Jews who could not be of financial profit to the king) severely restricted Jewish business activities and limited the rate of interest anew to twopence weekly on every pound.[2]

## § IV

Theological odium meanwhile was increasing more and more: a current perhaps fostered by, and expressed in, the legend of the Wandering Jew, the earliest medieval literary expression of which is connected with the visit of an Armenian archbishop to England in 1228.[3] Feelings ran especially high in the eastern counties, where medieval English anti-Semitism was always most acute. At Norwich it was noted with resentment how the Jewish community had swollen in consequence of recent expulsions elsewhere in the neighbourhood, and the popular hatred was unconcealed. Here, accordingly, in 1234, certain Jews were accused of having seized and forcibly circumcised four years previously the son of a certain Benedict, a physician—possibly a converted Jew, whose offspring they considered to belong by right to their community. Though the alleged offence had happened so long before, and the traces of the operation had been partly effaced, the consequences were most serious. Ten persons were arrested and sent to London for trial. The case was heard before the king himself, in the presence of the Archbishop of Canterbury and many bishops and barons of the realm. They decided that, as an offence against the Church, it should be tried by ecclesiastical law, and it was remitted accordingly to the Ordinary of Norwich for decision. In the end, after long delays and a vain attempt (reinforced by lavish gifts) to secure trial by a mixed jury, in which Jews too would have been included, some of the prisoners were condemned to be drawn and

---

[1] C.R. 1235, p. 214.

[2] Richardson, *J.A.K.*, pp. 293-4. The limitation of interest was confirmed in 1248; C.R., pp. 64, 65, 114, 216.

[3] M. Paris, *Chron. Maj.* iii. 161-3, v. 341.

hanged, while one, who had fled the realm, was outlawed.[1] Meanwhile, repeated rioting took place: several Jewish houses were set on fire; and there was a clash between the mob and the soldiers sent from the castle to protect them.

When in the following year the king passed through Norwich, he was met by a throng of citizens and priests, headed by the mayor, vociferously complaining of the increase in the Jewish population and of the severity of the sheriff in punishing those implicated in the recent disorders.[2] Though these complaints did not lead to any drastic action, proclamation was made not long after throughout the eastern counties once again forbidding Christian women to enter Jewish employment as nurses or domestic servants.[3] Elsewhere conditions were not very different. Royal intervention was periodically necessary to ensure that the unbelievers should not be starved out by a boycott on the sale of food:[4] and during the festivities at the time of the king's marriage to Eleanor of Provence in 1236 the entire London community took the precaution of seeking refuge in the Tower.[5] There is some evidence[6] that at this stage the Jews appealed to the Holy See for protection; but there were certainly no positive results. The Church Synods held at Worcester (1240), at Chichester (c. 1246), and at Salisbury (c. 1256) renewed the prohibition to employ Christians, with the rest of the old anti-Jewish regulations: in the diocese of Lincoln Bishop Grosseteste took steps to prevent friendly intercourse between Jews and their neighbours; and in the Council of Merton in 1258, and of Lambeth three years later, it was ordered that those who transgressed in matters ecclesiastical should be forced to appear before the Church authorities and, in case of contumacy, be

---

[1] *Bibl.* A. 8. 179; M. Paris, *Chron. Maj.* iv. 30; Roger of Wendover, iii. 101; Rigg, *P.E.J.*, pp. xliv ff.; C.R. 1240, pp. 168–75. F. Liebermann (*E.H.R.* xvii. 554) observes that the deposition against the Jews shows at least one gross lie and three self-contradictions.

[2] *Bibl.* A. 8. 179. It seems that there were further anti-Jewish riots at Norwich three years later, unless the Inquisition of 1238 about the fire raised in the Jewry (op. cit., p. 331) refers to the earlier disorders.

[3] C.R. 1234, p. 13.

[4] C.R. 1235, p. 329; 1245, p. 378.        [5] C.R. 1236, p. 334.

[6] J. de Oxenedes, p. 164; Bart. de Coton, p. 118. It is possible that this should be connected with the publication of the benevolent papal edict of September 1235 (Grayzel, op. cit., pp. 228, 231), which, however, was not specifically addressed to England. Cf., however, the undated bull 'Regi Anglie illustri quod rex iudeos teneat recommendatos' published by Grayzel in *J.Q.R.*, N.S. xlvi. 56–57.

cut off from all association with the faithful.[1] The king readily
followed the lead set by the Church. On the first Saturday of
Lent in 1240, while the Jews were at service in their synagogues,
their books were seized in obedience to a papal decree, and all
copies of the Talmud were subsequently burned.[2] In 1241 a
pretext was found to qualify the autonomy of English Jewry in
internal matters.[3] In 1246 the lending of money on the security
of ecclesiastical vestments or appurtenances was made a capital
offence;[4] and in 1251 Jews were forbidden to eat meat on Fri-
days or during Lent, when Christians had to do without it.[5]

The episode at Norwich proved to be the first of a fresh series
of accusations of ritual outrage, now made with the connivance
or even the encouragement of the civil authorities.[6] On the
Feast of St. Alban (22 June) 1239, a bloody riot was started in
London when a Jew was accused of murder. Henry's principal
minister at this time was Brother Geoffrey of the Temple, recently appointed Keeper of the Wardrobe, who combined the
religious zeal of a Churchman with the jealousy of what was in
effect a rival body of bankers. Accordingly, he avidly seized the
opportunity offered him. A number of Jews were thrown into
jail, several were put to death, and a tax of one-third of their
property (for the collection of which the Knights Templars
themselves acted as agents!) was levied collectively from the
entire community as a punishment for the crime.[7] Five years
later, in 1244, another accusation—this time wholly preposterous—was made in the capital. It was alleged that the body of
a child found in the churchyard of St. Benet's bore an incrim-
inating Hebrew inscription cut into the flesh, proving that it
had been done to death for ritual purposes. Absurd though the
tale was, the corpse was claimed by the canons of St. Paul's
Cathedral and buried near the High Altar, and it cost the

---

[1] Wilkins, *Concilia*, i. 671, 675, 676, 693, 719, 739, 751; Grosseteste, *Epistolae*,
ed. Luard, pp. 317–18 (1244?).

[2] The papal instructions concerning this were specifically addressed also to
Henry III and the English ecclesiastical authorities (Grayzel, op. cit., pp. 240–3)
and it is improbable that they were neglected, though positive evidence is lacking.

[3] C.R. 1242, p. 464; below, p. 116.

[4] C.R. 1246, p. 475.

[5] M. Paris, *Hist. Angl.* iii. 103; *Flor. Hist.* ii. 376, iii. 274.

[6] See Note III (*b*), pp. 273–4.

[7] Above, p. 44. The tax brought in 60,000 marks, according to Matthew Paris;
see Adler, *J.M.E.*, pp. 142–3.

Jewish communities of the country a payment of a further 60,000 marks to the Treasury to escape worse consequences.[1] In 1250, Abraham of Berkhamsted, who has been mentioned above as one of the wealthiest financiers of his time, was arrested on a charge of maltreating an image of the Virgin and murdering his wife for her refusal to imitate him. On the intervention of Richard of Cornwall, his patron, he was released without further punishment than the payment of a heavy fine (in itself it would seem testimony of his innocence).[2]

The reaction culminated in the most famous case of all the fantastic and tragic series. In Lincoln, at the end of August 1255, large numbers of Jews from all parts of England had assembled perhaps for the marriage of Belaset, daughter of Magister Benedict fil' Moses (without doubt identical with Berechiah ben Moses of Nicole, who figures in the Rabbinic literature of the time). On the day after the wedding there was discovered in a cesspool near the house of one of the community the body of a little Christian boy, Hugh, the son of a widow named Beatrice. He had been missing for over three weeks, and there is every reason to believe that he fell in accidentally while running after his ball at play. To the thirteenth-century mind, however, there could be only one explanation. The corpse was removed to the cathedral, to the accompaniment of miraculous manifestations which made it obvious, to those who wished to believe so, that it was that of a martyr. It was escorted by the dean and canons, and a long procession of officials bearing crosses, candles, and censers, amid chanting and weeping. The Jew Copin, near whose house it had been found, was seized and tortured until he 'confessed' that the child had been put to death for ritual purposes at a representative gathering of his co-religionists.

The king himself, who was in the neighbourhood, heard the news and hurried to Lincoln to inquire into the matter in person. He immediately ordered Copin to be hanged, after being dragged up and down the precipitate streets of the city tied to a horse's tail. The rest of the Jews implicated, to the number of nearly one hundred, were brought to London, followed by a 'jury' of twenty-four burgesses and twenty-four knights to try the case. Eighteen of those accused preferred not to submit to

---

[1] Adler, *J.M.E.*, p. 287; above, p. 45. But these vast figures cannot be taken literally.          [2] See Note III (*c*), p. 274.

the judgement of this biased tribunal, and demanded a mixed jury of Jews and Christians. This was taken as a confession of guilt, and they were immediately hanged. The remainder (with the exception of one acquitted and two pardoned before the case came on) were convicted and sentenced. So far were popular passions aroused in London that the intervention of the Franciscans,[1] whose learned teacher Adam Marsh pleaded eloquently for moderation, was generally ascribed to bribery and brought so much unpopularity upon the Order that for some time the common people of London withheld their customary alms. Material considerations carried greater weight, and thanks to the intervention of Richard of Cornwall (to whom the Jewry of the kingdom had recently been mortgaged, and who was naturally anxious to safeguard his property) the surviving prisoners were ultimately released.[2]

The case of 'Little' St. Hugh of Lincoln (as he was called, to distinguish him from the bishop of the same name, benign even towards the Jews, who had died half a century before) was of more than temporary importance. The body was buried in a splendid shrine in the Cathedral, where the relics were venerated down to the time of the Reformation as those of a martyr, working miraculous cures. The legend entered into the folk-lore of the English people: it was cited and imitated by Chaucer in his *Canterbury Tales*: it formed the inspiration of many ballads, in English, in French, and in Scots, which were handed down for centuries in the mouth of the peasantry. Thus, in after generations, when no Jew was left in England, it was from the poetical descriptions of this half-legendary event that a large part of the population received its impressions of the despised race.

All these episodes contributed to increase the unpopularity of the Jew in the eyes of the English people. Many places, not content with restrictions, began to demand exclusion. In consequence there was a complete reversal of the tolerant policy of the early years of the reign, when the settlement of the Jews in every part of the country had been so sedulously encouraged. The lead in the reaction was taken by Simon de Montfort, son

---

[1] According to the Burton Annalist (*Ann. Monast.* i. 346–7) the Dominicans intervened.

[2] For the Lincoln Blood Accusation, see the works listed in *Bibl.* A. 8. 157–63, and more especially J. W. F. Hill, *Medieval Lincoln*, pp. 224–32.

of the warrior of the same name who had harried the Jews and
Albigensians in Provence, and of the fanatical Lady Alice de
Montmorency, who in 1217 had given the Jews of Toulouse the
alternative of baptism or death. His personal religious prejudice
was heightened by the realization that the Jews were in a large
measure the instrument of the royal absolutism, of which he was
so determined an opponent; and in addition (it can hardly have
been without effect upon his mind) he was himself heavily indebted to them. His prejudice found expression in 1231, when
he issued an edict expelling the Jews from his city of Leicester—
the first measure of the sort recorded since the expulsion from
Bury St. Edmunds forty-one years before.[1]

The example was readily followed. In 1233 an inquiry was
held in the diocese of Lincoln, and perhaps elsewhere, to dis-
cover whether any Jews were now living in places from which
they had previously been absent. This was a prelude to a whole
series of local expulsions—from Newcastle, Wycombe, the entire
county of Warwick and parts of East Anglia in 1234, from
Southampton in 1236, from Northamptonshire (outside the
county town) in 1237, from Berkhamsted in 1242, from Newbury with Speenhamland in 1243.[2] The tendency culminated
in 1253, in an order forbidding settlement, except by special
licence, in any place where no recognized community was to be
found. Hitherto the Jews were permitted to live in any place
from which they were not expressly excluded; now they were
excluded from all places where they were not expressly permitted to live. The consequent influx into the few major
centres left open caused much resentment among the general
population. It was natural for Canterbury Jewry to make an
attempt at this period to exclude further immigration likely to
prejudice its interests.[3]

The restriction of the area of residence was the conclusion
and culmination of the 'Mandate to the Justices assigned to the
Custody of the Jews' issued on 31 January 1253, which crystal-
lized Henry's policy. The first of the thirteen paragraphs was
typical of the whole, stipulating as it did that no Jew should

---

[1] The edict is reproduced in facsimile in *Trs. J.H.S.E.* v. 41.
[2] *C.R.* 1234, pp. 466, 515; 1234–7, pp. 20, 225, 425; 1243, p. 149. These
expulsions were not necessarily final: there was an *archa* again at Warwick in 1261.
[3] Adler, *J.M.E.*, p. 83; *Misc. J.H.S.E.* iii. 76–79.

remain in England unless his presence were of benefit to his
sovereign. Subsequent clauses re-enacted in excruciating detail
all the restrictions embodied in the current papal legislation—
from building new synagogues, contaminating Christian ears by
over-loud psalmody in those which already existed, entering a
church and disputing on matters of religion or impeding conversions to the true faith, down to the scandalizing of Christians
by eating meat during Lent, employing Christian servants and
nurses or daring to discard the Jewish badge of shame.[1]

Meanwhile, popular dislike continued to express itself in intermittent local outbreaks. Thus in 1244 the Oxford students
had attacked the Jewry (mostly in and about what is now St.
Aldate's) and sacked the solidly constructed houses of their
creditors.[2] In 1261 there was a similar onslaught, in which many
monks and priests participated, at Canterbury, where a determined attempt was made to set fire to the Jewish quarter.[3] It
will be recalled that here, in the previous century, relations
between Jews and monks had been especially cordial.

## § v

From the outset of the constitutional struggle between Henry III
and his barons, led by Simon de Montfort, the Jews formed one
of the objects of dispute. The lesser baronage was particularly
involved with them, and therefore desired some check to be
placed upon their activities. At the same time it was bitterly
realized by the more far-sighted that they were, in fact, merely
an instrument in the hands of the Crown. In the period of
agitation and unrest which preceded the Civil War one of the
reforms demanded from time to time was 'that the Exchequer
of the Jews should be amended'; and it was proposed in 1244
that the Council of the Realm should be allowed to nominate
at least one of the Justices of the Jews and thus share in the
control of this important branch of the Exchequer.[4] Plainly this
could touch only the fringe of the problem, which was essentially
economic. One of the complaints specifically ventilated at the

---

[1] Rigg, *P.E.J.*, pp. xlviii f.
[2] See Roth, *Oxford*, pp. 127-8, for full details and references. Though forty-five
of the rioters were arrested, the episode resulted in the regulation of the interest
chargeable to students and the recognition of the right of the chancellor to jurisdiction in cases arising out of such transactions.          [3] Adler, *J.M.E.*, pp. 78-79.
[4] M. Paris, *Chron. Maj.* iv. 367; *E.H.R.* lxv. 215; above, p. 51.

Parliament of Oxford in 1258 was that the Jews sold lands pledged to them to the great magnates of the realm, who took possession and subsequently refused to accept payment of the debt if it were offered. Thus, if the debtor died leaving an infant child as his heir (when, in accordance with provision of Magna Carta re-enacted in 1235, the interest on debts was cancelled and the rights of inheritance safeguarded) the latter entirely lost his rightful due. (It may be noted that the Jews are mentioned here only incidentally; in the following clause they do not figure with the Cahorsins among those whose usury was complained of.) Moreover, even when.payment was accepted, the magnate often prolonged the negotiation unnecessarily on the pretext that he could do nothing without the knowledge of the Jew who had made the loan in the first place.

The Provisions of Oxford, which were forced on the king's acceptance by the 'Mad Parliament' in 1258, embodied an undertaking in general terms to cope with the problem, in particular by reforming the Exchequer of the Jews and appointing new Justices. The autumn of the following year saw the presentation of a further, more precisely formulated set of requirements, one of which stipulated that the Justiciar and Treasurer of the realm should appoint 'honest men' to ensure that the Exchequer of the Jews was rid of its abuses.[1] Philip Lovel had in fact already left office: now Simon Passelewe, his coadjutor for so many years, was also removed, though only temporarily, and two inconspicuous judges were appointed to take their place. For a little while they continued to administer its affairs efficiently, the king chafing against their incorruptibility. Unable to replace them, he found a means to render them impotent: and in 1261, when he made a violent attempt to rid himself of baronial control, he appointed his faithful instrument, John Maunsell, chancellor of St. Paul's and noted pluralist, over the head of the Justices of the Jews, who in May 1261 were enjoined to obey him in all things—like Des Rivaulx thirty years earlier.[2]

The Jews thus remained an integral part of the financial system of an unpopular government. Accordingly, on the out-

---

[1] Petition of the Barons, in Stubbs's *Select Charters*, § xxv; Provisions of Oxford, ibid. tit. *De vescuntes*; *Ann. Mon.* i. 451, 478

[2] P.R. 1261, p. 156. Simon Passelewe was reappointed in September 1259, continuing in office until 1262.

break of the Civil War, they suffered terribly at the hands of the
baronial party, recruited as it was largely from the class most
heavily in their debt, and led by a man who had already given
frequent testimony to his extreme anti-Jewish bias. In every city
that the barons entered, the Jewry formed their first objective,
and its business records were at once destroyed. The example
had been anticipated in London even before the outbreak of
hostilities. In November 1262 a dispute in Candlewick Street
between a Jew and his debtor who claimed that he was being
charged excessive interest developed into a vicious riot, which
culminated in the sack of the Jewry. The Mayor and Sheriffs,
acting with exemplary firmness, managed to suppress the disturbances, and even took proceedings against the ringleaders.[1]
Nevertheless, resentment smouldered, breaking out again with
renewed violence after the Barons took up arms. When in the
spring of 1264 Simon de Montfort fell back on London after
receiving the bitter news of his son's capture by the royalists
at Northampton, he allowed his disappointed followers a free
hand, and they found ready help from the city mob who poured
out in their support. A preposterous rumour somehow obtained
currency that the Jews, besides providing the king with money,
were plotting to betray the city to his forces, having prepared
duplicate keys to open the gates and Greek fire to set the buildings in flames.[2] On Saturday, April 12th (it was Passover eve,
the classic occasion for such outrages), a fresh attack took place
on the Jewry, led by John Fitzjohn, one of the most ruthless of
Earl Simon's henchmen. Even contemporaries were shocked by
the brutality that he displayed, but he betrayed his real motives
when he pillaged the house of the wealthy Cok (Isaac) fil'
Aaron after killing him with his own hands.[3] The synagogues
were looted and defiled. De Montfort himself did not disdain
to share in the plunder, sparing only those whose resources he
wished to investigate with a view to more exhaustive spoliation.

[1] Liber de Antiquis Legibus (R.C.S.), pp. 50–51.
[2] Ann. Mon. iii. 230.
[3] Ann. Mon. iv. 141–3. It is perhaps significant that among those who owed
money to Cok fil' Aaron (who had recently paid 2,000 marks to enter into his
father's estate) was the baronial leader Robert Ferrars, Earl of Derby. For the
vicissitudes of Cok's family at this time, see *P.E.J.*, pp. 73 ff.
  There are further references to the London massacre (often confused with that of
1262) in Ann. Mon. ii. 101; iii. 230; iv. 450: G. of Canterbury, ii. 235: Fl. of
Worcester, ii. 192. There is some uncertainty about the exact date.

The number of victims would have been greater but for the fact that many accepted baptism in their terror, or were given refuge in the houses of Christian neighbours, or were again escorted to the Tower by the Mayor. Nevertheless, the casualties were estimated—certainly with much exaggeration—at some hundreds. For the first time for three-quarters of a century, the report of English events impressed the continental Jewish martyrologists, who long afterwards commemorated this tragedy in their synagogues.[1]

The example set in London was followed shortly afterwards by Gilbert de Clare, the Earl of Gloucester, when he captured Canterbury. Here many Jews were killed and the *archa* in which the record of their debts was preserved was seized and conveyed to Dover. At Worcester, Lincoln, Bristol, and Bedford similar outbreaks took place, the chirograph-chests being burned or carried off. Isolated families in rural centres were fortunate if they escaped with their lives.[2] Henry de Montfort, one of Simon's sons, despoiled the few Jews at Kingston. The community of Northampton was forced to take refuge in the castle.[3] Large numbers of fugitives from other towns sought refuge in Oxford, their lack of visible means of sustenance causing the authorities serious preoccupation. After the baronial victory at Lewes (May 1264) there were disorders in Winchester, Lincoln, and Nottingham, and many householders, despairing of a restoration of order, fled to the Continent. In the last phase of the struggle (1266–7) a further wave of disturbance was caused by the so-called Disinherited (the last residue of the anti-Royalist party), who carried off the *archa* from Cambridge to the Isle of Ely and sacked the synagogue at Lincoln. The remnants of the community of London were driven, in the incongruous company of the papal legate Ottoboni, to take refuge in the Tower, which they manfully assisted to defend against the assailants (1 February 1266/7).[4]

---

[1] S. Salfeld, *Das Martyrologium des Nürnberger Memorbuches* (Berlin, 1898), p. 153.

[2] e.g. at Sittingbourne in Kent: *E.J.* i. 132–3.

[3] C.R. 1264, pp. 82–83; 1265, p. 66; Rymer, i. 441; P.R. 1264, p. 363. After the storming of Worcester on 29 March 1264 (*Ann. Mon.* iv. 449), the *archa* was carried off by the Earl of Derby to one of his castles. The ringleader of the disturbances at Northampton was arraigned a considerable time afterwards, but the Jews preferred not to prosecute: Hunter, *Rotuli Selecti*, p. 210.

[4] Rigg, *P.E.J.*, pp. xxxvii, 2, 76; Holinshed, *History*, iii. 272; *Flor. Hist.* iii. 14; Stokes, *Studies*, pp. 160–2. There seems to have been violence at Bristol also:

During the course of the sixteen months (May 1264–August 1265) when he was personally in control of the government of England, Simon de Montfort seems to have been sobered by the responsibilities of office, and his attitude towards the Jews changed. At last (late though it was) he realized their importance to the Exchequer, and attempted to restore their confidence. The London Jews were persuaded to leave their refuge and were taken under the king's nominal protection; those of Northampton had to evacuate the castle and return to their homes; the refugees in Oxford were ordered back to their places of origin. Letters patent were addressed to the authorities in the principal cities where the disorders had taken place, bidding proclamation to be made that the Jews might return and resume their activities peaceably, with twenty-four citizens in each place as guarantors responsible for their protection from further molestation. The Jewish chirographs were as far as possible re-assembled and the Jewish *archae* renewed; and instructions were given for those records which were still extant to be consulted to see whether it was feasible to retrieve the heavy losses suffered. Towards the end of the winter, normal conditions were so far re-established that it was possible for Justices of the Jews to resume their sessions (February 1265).[1] Yet at the same time the dangerous and uneconomic precedent was followed of rewarding zealous adherents of the new régime by cancelling their debts. When the Lord Edward, the king's son, to whom the Jewries of the realm had been pledged in 1262, joined the opposition to Montfort, Henry was forced by the latter to resume his nominal control, forbidding any money to be paid to his son's representatives or obedience given to the Justices whom he had recently appointed.[2]

De Montfort's defeat in the summer of 1265 initiated a more settled state of affairs. A new effort was now made to strengthen the position of the Jews—not from altruistic motives so much

Adler, *J.M.E.*, p. 220. The Winchester massacre was perpetrated at the beginning of his march through the Midlands by Simon de Montfort the younger: Ann. Mon. ii. 102, 363.

[1] P.R. 1264, pp. 322 (London), 323 (Winchester), 421 (Lincoln); C.R. 1265, pp. 19, 42, 82–83. After the disorders the Jews failed to re-establish themselves in some of the smaller centres. Thus in 1272 the sheriff of Sussex reported that the Jews of Arundel and Lewes 'have nothing save empty houses, and are no longer in his bailiwick' (Gross in *Papers, A.J.H.E.*, p. 190). See too Powicke, *Henry III and the Lord Edward*, pp. 516–17.        [2] C.R. 1265, pp. 32, 62.

as in anticipation of the benefit which would accrue. Persons who had fled overseas were encouraged to return. Edward was permitted to resume control of the Jewries, which were restored in matters regarding business transactions to the position that had obtained before the Battle of Lewes. All Montfort's acts of pardon to Christian debtors were revoked, the Jews being enabled to claim their debts as before (notwithstanding the destruction of the *archae*) if reasonable proof were forthcoming. A clerk was appointed to supervise their writs and records. Special protection was given to the communities of Wilton, Cambridge, and London in view of. the very heavy losses which they had recently sustained, a number of citizens in each place being again nominated to safeguard them. Those of Bedford as a body, as well as many individuals elsewhere, received a promise that none of their Christian debtors should be pardoned by the royal authority for five years. In consideration of a cash payment of £1,000 in 1269, the king pledged himself that no further tallage should be imposed for the next three years, unless he or his son should go on crusade. At the same time, several individuals who had been of service during the recent troubles were given special protection, and others impoverished in the wars had their debts to the Crown remitted. Thus the Jewries of the realm were afforded a breathing-space in which to recuperate.[1]

## § VI

The partial recovery was automatically followed by a recrudescence of complaint. For a long time past, discontent had been rife (as has been seen) in connexion with the loans made by Jews on the security of land. If the debt were not repaid, their simplest course was to dispose of the claim to some Christian magnate, who did not scruple to foreclose. Thus there was a tendency for private estates, and therewith military power, to become more and more concentrated in the hands of the great landowners, the increase in whose influence was highly unwelcome to the Crown. Alternatively, either debtor or creditor might seek the assistance of the Church by selling or surrendering his title. The reasons would, of course, be diametrically opposite: in the one case it was to evade repayment, in the other

[1] C.R. 1265, p. 147; 1269, p. 345; P.R. 1265, p. 431; 1266, pp. 13, 21.

to secure it. But so far as the interests of the State were concerned the result was identical—the loss of feudal dues and above all of military service.

Hence the mere fact of the lending of money by Jews to improvident landowners constituted, through no fault of theirs, a national problem. At intervals during the past thirty years or more, half-hearted attempts had been made to cope with it.[1] The restoration of peace brought the question forward again in an accentuated form. The Jews, on the verge of ruin, pressed their legal claims with a determination hitherto unusual, because impolitic: the Crown, determined to assist their financial recovery, abstained from granting debtors those concessions which had formerly served as a safety-valve. Edward, the heir to the throne, whose influence in affairs of state had come to be preponderant, realized that if the monarchy were to be strong, and the power of the great magnates curbed, steps must be taken to cope with this problem. With his brother Edmund he placed himself at the head of those who demanded reform, thereby attaining much popularity among the lesser baronage. The result was the enactment of the Provisions of Jewry, which were delivered at the Exchequer by Walter de Merton in January 1269. No debts whatsoever might be contracted in future with Jews on the security of lands held in fee; all obligations of the sort already registered were cancelled; the transference to a Christian of a debt thus secured was to be treated as a capital offence; and debts of any other nature could henceforth be disposed of to a third party only by special licence, and on condition that the principal only, without any interest, was exacted.[2]

Thus prevented from realizing loans made on the security of land, the Jews sought compensation in a different direction, so as to be able to liquidate past transactions without loss. Hitherto, when a mortgage fell in, they had often held property in their own name for a short while. Now they attempted to regu-

---

[1] Above, pp. 52–53, 60.

[2] Text in Rigg, *P.E.J.*, p. xlviii; P.R. 1269, p. 376; C.R. 1269, p. 101; Red Book of Exchequer, iii. 978: the preamble specifically mentions that the Provisions had been decided upon by the king 'par le conseil Sire Eadward, son fuiz esnee'. But his attitude was highly inconsistent: the first recipients of a licence to acquire Jewish debts, notwithstanding the Provisions, were a yeoman of Edward's, his wife's tailor, and his agent Stephen Penchester (P.R. 1269, p. 359; 1270, p. 440). A fresh inspection of the Chirograph Chests at this time (P.R. 1269, p. 382) was probably intended to prevent evasion of the new regulations.

larize and extend this practice. They accordingly presented a petition requesting permission to hold manors, with all the customary feudal 'incidents' enjoyed by Christian landowners. At the same time they secured a re-confirmation of their traditional Charter of Privileges first granted a century and a half before, in which the right to hold land was expressly guaranteed.[1] The matter came to a head contemporaneously in an actual case, when the financial magnate and subsequent arch-presbyter, Cok Hagin fil' Deulecresse of London, was formally enfeoffed by one of his debtors with the manor of Childewick, in spite of the efforts of the monastery of St. Albans to obtain possession. He was prevented from entering into occupation, and a lawsuit followed, in which the monastery was successful. In the royal council a strong body of opinion—influenced, as it was inevitably alleged, by bribery—favoured the application. Nevertheless, in the end (largely through the influence of a minorite friar, Henry of Wodstone) the opposition triumphed.[2] Not only was the petition of the Jews rejected, but it was determined to clarify the position and to curtail the privileges which they had enjoyed in virtue of their traditional Charter for the past century and a half. A new law was enacted forbidding them to have free holdings henceforth in any manor or lands, whether by charter, by gift, or by enfeoffment. Even in cities they might in future possess no houses except those in the personal occupation of the owner, or let by him to other Jews. In the event of any dispute arising out of property thus held, proceedings were allowed only before the Justices of the Jews, and not as in other cases by writ of Chancery. Lands already in Jewish occupation were to be vacated immediately, on the payment of the capital of the loans for which they served as security, without any interest (25 July 1271).[3] As a result of these measures, the economic activities of the Jews were greatly restricted. Forbidden to lend money at interest on landed security, whether to nobles or to citizens (who could at that time offer little else), they could no longer engage in any major transaction. A few Jews were permitted to hold property subsequently, but not for long: the day of the Jewish landlord, for example in Oxford, was over.

[1] Ch.R. ii. 164 (23 February 1271).
[2] Little in *Collectanea Franciscana*, ii. 150–7: cf. P.R. 1272, p. 644; *E.J.* ii. 17 ff.
[3] Text in Rigg, *P.E.J.*, pp. l–lv.

Even before this, their impoverishment had gone far. It had
not been so easy for them to recover from the succession of blows
which they had received at the time of the Barons' Wars and
during the previous misrule. On the departure of Edward on
his crusade in 1271, as his father's deputy, a comparatively
moderate tallage of 6,000 marks towards the expenses had been
imposed on them. The amount they could raise fell short by
one-third of this total. The remainder was advanced by Richard
of Cornwall, king of the Romans, to whom the Jews were assigned once more for one year as security: on the last occasion
when they had been pledged with him it had been for nearly
three times as much.

On Richard's death, not long before his own, Henry took the
Jews again into his own hand and laid upon them a tallage of
5,000 marks, of which one-fifth was assigned to the king's purveyor for his disbursements for the royal table.[1] After a little
time fierce measures were adopted to exact the arrears of this
levy. All who could not furnish security to pay within four
months (they included the entire community of Hereford) were
thrown into jail. When the time-limit had elapsed, those even
part of whose dues were still outstanding were held 'at the
King's mercy', with their families and chattels—reduced, that
is, to beggary and serfdom.[2] Large numbers were imprisoned
in the Tower and elsewhere, in the hope that their sufferings
would help them to recollect some untapped reserve. Even the
Jews' opponents, the Friars, and their rivals, the Cahorsins, are
said to have pitied their lot on this occasion. Yet hardly was this
transaction completed when they were re-entrusted to Edmund
of Almain, Richard of Cornwall's son, so that the residue of the
2,000 marks due to him might be extracted.[3] This typical
measure was one of the last in Henry's long reign. He died in
November 1272, leaving his successor, instead of the prosperous
Jewry which he himself had found on emerging from his minority, a ruined community, the condition of which was one of the
most serious problems of the following years.

---

[1] Ibid., p. xxxviii.            [2] Ibid., p. 70; P.R. 1272, p. 660.

[3] P.R. 1272, p. 671; *E.J.* ii. 24. The burden was increased by the conduct of the
Justices of the Jews, Sir Robert of Fulham, William of Watford, and William of
Orlaveston, who were removed from office this year: the temptations seem to have
been irresistible. Two years later, the Cahorsins were to be employed to exact the
tallage from the Jews: *E.J.* ii. 135.

# IV

# THE EXPULSION

## 1272-90

### § 1

A T the time of his accession Edward I was still in the East,
engaged in his crusade against the Saracen. He returned
to England two years later, in 1274, to find himself confronted with the problem of the Jew. The consequences of the
policy of his father's last years were by now apparent. The communities of the realm were all but ruined. Constant exactions had
begun the work: it had been completed by the recent enactments
which made impossible financial operations on a large scale.
Many debtors, who could well afford to pay what they owed, had
been emboldened to evade their dues, with so little concealment
that the government had to intervene.[1] A tallage of a third of
their property—the largest since 1241, expected to realize 25,000
marks—imposed by the Council of Regency during the new
king's absence, with the severe methods that had become recognized as normal, had failed to realize the amount anticipated, notwithstanding the inspection of chirograph-chests
which as usual had preceded it. Several once affluent financiers
had to sell their houses in order to meet their obligations. Even
so, the arrears were so great that, on 1 November 1274, it was
found necessary to appoint a special commission to exact them.
Those unable to pay were banished, in conformity with the old
idea that Jews were tolerated in England only if they could be
of benefit to the Crown.[2] Such desperate methods could not be
repeated indefinitely. It was obvious that the general condition
of the Jewish communities called urgently for reform.

Contemporary events abroad indicated one manner in which
this might be effected. In the year of the king's return, the

---

[1] C.R. 1274, p. 103. The audit ordered at this period of all payments made by
sheriffs since 1266 on account of Jewish debts (*E.J.* ii. 64-65) seems to suggest widespread corruption in addition.

[2] P.R. 1274, p. 63.

Council of Lyons, under the stimulus of Pope Gregory X, urged the Christian world to greater efforts against the sin of usury, and peremptorily demanded that no community, corporation, or individual should continue to tolerate those who followed this heinous practice, whether they were native-born or foreign. Edward, loyal son of the Church that he was, took immediate steps to put this policy into execution, ordering an inquiry to be made into the usurious activities of the Florentine bankers, who had been carrying on their activities in the kingdom since 1223.[1] Next he turned his attention to the Jews—with an austerity that most of his contemporaries would have regarded as excessive since, as 'infidels', they were not considered to be bound by canon law in the same way as professing Christians. For nearly two centuries the Jewish financiers had been encouraged to carry on their activities in England for the benefit of the Crown. Now, impoverished as they were, their utility could be overlooked. Accordingly, Henry III's policy of restricting Jewish activities, and the Church's of suppressing usury, were combined and carried to their logical conclusion, in an attempt to prevent the Jews from lending money at interest on whatever security, and to divert their energies into productive channels.

The conception was not altogether a new one. Forty years before, when some Jews had been expelled from Leicester by Simon de Montfort, a movement had been set on foot by the Countess of Winchester and other landowners to admit the refugees to their estates, where they would be encouraged to work with their hands. This proposal was submitted to Robert Grosseteste, afterwards bishop of Lincoln, whose approval it received; but it does not seem to have had any practical outcome.[2] More recently Thomas Aquinas had urged similar action upon the Duchess of Brabant. 'If rulers think they harm their souls by taking money from usurers', he wrote, '. . . they should see that the Jews are compelled to labour.'[3] The same idea had entered the mind of Louis IX of France, who in 1253 sent home

[1] Proceedings were instituted simultaneously against a London citizen suspected to be guilty of the same offence: see (Sir) B. L. Abrahams, *The Expulsion of the Jews from England in 1290* (Oxford, 1895), p. 31. (The present chapter is necessarily dependent to a large extent on this admirable, though not exhaustive, work.)

[2] Grosseteste, *Epistolae*, ed. Luard, § v (pp. 33 ff.). He was then Archdeacon of Leicester.

[3] *Opusculum ad Ducissam Brabantiae* (1261-2?), § xxi. Cf. H. Liebeschutz in *Journal of Jewish Studies*, xiii (1962), 70-76).

instructions from the Holy Land that all Jews should leave his dominions, except those who became traders or took up manual toil.[1] This project does not seem to have been carried into effect. It was therefore left for Edward I to attempt to apply, for the first time, a radical solution to the Jewish problem in accordance with the ideas of his day.

§ 11

The *Statutum de Judeismo* was issued at Westminster in the Common Council of the Realm in 1275.[2] By it Jews were absolutely forbidden, as Christians were, to lend money at interest. Any person of whatever faith entering in future into a usurious contract, whether as borrower or lender, would be liable to punishment, and such agreements would no longer be enforcible at law. Outstanding transactions were to be wound up as soon as possible and pledges in Jewish hands redeemed by the following Easter, while no interest might henceforth be charged on former loans. Stringent rules were laid down limiting the right of distraint on land, no recovery being permissible on account of interest, and only one-half of the debtor's property (which even so might not include his chief residence) for the principal. As a further precaution the alienation of real estate by Jews without special licence was forbidden.[3]

The prohibition of usury left them without any means of livelihood. The restrictions were therefore accompanied by concessions. For the first time in English history they were empowered to become merchants and artisans, and for this purpose (though for no other) to enter into free intercourse with Christians. They were, moreover, authorized (though this licence was to expire after fifteen years) to lease lands for tillage and farming for terms not exceeding one decade. Simultaneously, as though to impress the fact that these concessions did not imply

---

[1] Laurière, *Ordonnances des rois de France*, i. 75 ('De Reformandis Moribus'); M. Paris, *Chron. Maj.* v. 361–2.

[2] *Statutes of the Realm*, i. 220–1 (the date is given in *Flor. Hist.* iii. 45 and *Ann. Mon.* iv. 408).

[3] As regards the possession of land, the *Statutum de Judeismo* was slightly more liberal than the legislation of four years earlier, which prohibited it entirely except for personal occupation. Moreover, in Easter Term 1278, the Justices of the Jews ruled that, notwithstanding the terms of the Statute, debts contracted before it came into force should continue to bear interest (Elman in *Historia Judaica*, i. 96).

any improvement in general status, various intolerant restrictions were renewed. Jews were to be allowed to live only in towns under direct royal authority, and only where chirograph-chests (now superfluous) had formerly existed. The obligation to wear the badge of shame was extended to all persons, of either sex, from the age of seven upwards:[1] while those above twelve years of age were to pay annually at Eastertide a poll-tax of threepence.

Immediately after the promulgation of the Statute the representatives of the Jewish communities of the realm met together to consider its effects, and drew up a long petition imploring the king and Council to modify certain details. It was inequitable, they pleaded, that if a debtor died without heirs and his estate devolved upon the overlord, or if he had nothing to offer as security save his principal residence, the right of distraint should be restricted. Notwithstanding the new prohibition poor Jews ought to be allowed to dispose of their houses to their wealthy co-religionists, rather than be forced to tear them down for the sake of the building-material. As far as the licence to trade was concerned, it was meaningless. Jews could not travel about safely, as Christians could, nor was there any likelihood that they would be paid if they gave credit. Hence they would have to buy dearer and sell dearer than other men, and in such circumstances could not hope to make a living. The petition closed with a pathetic plea for mercy, that the supplicants might continue to live peaceably under Edward as they had done under his predecessors since the Conquest.[2]

This carefully reasoned appeal had no effect, except perhaps in some relative trivialities. (There is some evidence, for example, that outstanding transactions were not immediately wound up after all.) For it was not in its details, but rather in its spirit, that the *Statutum de Judeismo* was impracticable. On the surface it was a well-meaning and indeed conscientious attempt to emancipate the Jews economically. Yet it did not go far enough. Under medieval no less than under modern conditions, economic

---

[1] Seven years was earlier than was customary on the Continent, where the Badge generally had to be worn from the age of thirteen in the case of boys and twelve in that of girls. The Council of Oxford of 1222 explicitly extended the obligation to women.

[2] *Select Cases in Court of King's Bench, Edward I* (Selden Society, 1939), vol. iii, pp. xxxi, cxiv.

emancipation was impossible without social emancipation.
Men cannot transact business unless they meet as equals; merchants cannot make a living if there is a lack of understanding
with their customers; artisans need a friendly environment in
which to serve their apprenticeship, to practise their craft, and
to dispose of their productions. All this was expressly excluded
by the terms of the Statute, which affirmed and extended (instead of modifying) the former discrimination, and forbade the
Jews to be 'levant and couchant' amongst the general population. In the towns, buying and selling was confined to burgesses.
For Jews to be admitted to their number was already highly
exceptional;[1] but it was now expressly forbidden, on the ground
that they were the king's vassals. To enter the Gild Merchant
which controlled trade, or the Craft Gilds which controlled
industry, was similarly out of the question; for these bodies,
besides having a definite religious aspect, presupposed feelings
of social sympathy absent between Jew and Christian. Moreover, the Jews were deliberately and expressly excluded from
the protection given to merchants, native and foreign, by the
famous Statute of Acton Burnell in 1283.[2] In farming, these
precise difficulties did not apply. Nevertheless, rural solitude
had no attraction for men whose lives were under constant
menace, while any sense of security and permanence was made
quite impossible by the limitation of the experiment to a period
so short that it would barely have sufficed for the necessary
training. The restriction of residence to a few urban centres
constituted yet another obstacle, which should have been obvious enough: yet it was aggravated by periodical orders, beginning in 1277, for the arrest of those persons not living in the
handful of authorized Jewries[3] (perhaps in consequence of the
report of Hugh of Digneueton, who in that year was com-
missioned to investigate how far the new regulations were being
obeyed).[4] To change in short the Jew's manner of life while he
remained subject to the same insecurity, the same prejudices,
and the same differentiation as before was an impossible task.
    Moreover, notwithstanding his pious resolve to renounce the

---

[1] Cf., however, the case of Benedict of Winchester, below, pp. 114, 119.
[2] *Statutes of Realm*, i. 221.
[3] *E.J.* iii. 317, 319; C.R. 1284, p. 256 (28 June 1284).
[4] P.R. 1277, p. 240.

source of revenue so profitably exploited by his father, the king continued to impose extraordinary levies on his Jewish subjects as though their wealth were undiminished. Almost simultaneously with the enactment of the *Statutum de Judeismo*, on 24 November 1275, instructions were issued to seal the chirograph-chests, preliminary to the exaction of a tallage of £1,000 on the old basis. Ruined by the new legislation, the greater number of the Jews were unable to pay, though the amount was comparatively moderate. In the following year all those whose dues were outstanding were imprisoned once again, their chattels sold for the benefit of the Treasury, and their wives and children deported overseas.[1] Notwithstanding the difficulties on this occasion, in 1276 yet another tallage of 3,000 marks was imposed, other raids following at intervals. The Justices of the Jews were kept in being, rapaciously active; and the new poll-tax, rigorously exacted, was no negligible burden for the poor. For the Jews to obtain money to satisfy these demands by the economic activities to which they were now confined by law was impossible.

§ III

Edward's well-meaning experiment hence ended in failure. A number of the wealthier financiers were able to turn to wholesale trade in corn and wool—commodities on which they had previously been accustomed to make advances, and in which they had traded when forced to foreclose. In provincial centres this branch of activity proved particularly attractive, Jews of Bristol, Canterbury, Exeter, and Hereford engaging largely in the corn-trade, while at Lincoln, Norwich, and Oxford they were interested also in wool.[2] Licences to trade were issued also to a number of notable Londoners. It was relatively easy, too, for some of the former pledge-brokers to deal in trinkets and jewellery, as they had doubtless done previously when the occasion offered. But only a very few persons rented lands for the stipulated period, and even so probably it was for the sake of wood-cutting rather than agriculture.[3]

[1] P.R. 1275, p. 126; *E.J.* iii. 103-4.     [2] See Note IV (a), p. 274.
[3] Cf. *E.J.* iii. 128-9, 297-9. Cases are recorded at Hereford of indebtedness in terms also of geese, cheeses, and loads of hay (*Trs. J.H.S.E.* i. 148 ff.). The conclusion of the 49th provision of the Synod of Exeter of 1287 (Wilkins, *Concilia*, ii. 155; below, pp. 77, 96) is the sole indication that lands were leased for cultivation.

The poorer, however, were in many cases faced with starvation, finding their old source of livelihood cut off and the substitutes offered illusory. Some are said to have taken to highway robbery. Others, less adventurous, were driven to apostasy, the number of pensioners of the *Domus Conversorum* in London rising suddenly to nearly one hundred.[1] Large numbers saw no alternative but to carry on their old profession clandestinely, availing themselves of the devices invented by Christians usurers to evade canon law—the 'false chevisaunce', or making out agreements for larger sums than had actually been lent, or veiling the nature of the transaction by stating it in terms of commodities, or charging a 'courtesy' instead of interest. Many, on the other hand, forbidden to make any profitable use of their capital in a legal fashion, endeavoured to eke a living out of it illegally by 'clipping' the coinage: that is, filing the edges and putting it back into circulation while melting the clippings into bullion. It was an offence of which the Jews of northern Europe were not infrequently accused in the Middle Ages: for as the chief owners of money they were tempted to indulge disproportionately in this type of dishonest practice.[2] Nevertheless, though they were punished more savagely than others if clipped coins were found in their hands, they received only incidental mention in the Assize of Money and other regulations of the reign of John concerning the currency[3] and in 1238 offered the king £100 for an impartial inquiry into the abuse and the banishment of those guilty, a commission of Jewish magnates going on circuit with the Justices to take part in the investigation. Ten years later, an official inquiry placed no more responsibility on the Jews than on their Cahorsin competitors and the Flemish wool-traders, the other classes through whose hands large sums of money passed.[4] With the enactment of the *Statutum de Judeismo*,

---

[1] Adler, *J.M.E.*, p. 306.

[2] The offence is bitingly condemned in the twelfth-century ethical work, *Sepher Hassidim*, §§ 305–6, and is recorded as one of the causes for the expulsion from England by Rabbi Meir of Rothenburg in his *Responsa* (cf. *Trs. J.H.S.E.* xviii. 73–78). So also the chroniclers, Ibn Verga and Usque, in their accounts of the last tragedy; and, less sceptically, Isaac Abrabanel in his *Yeshuoth Meshiho*, p. 46—probably derived from Profiat Duran's lost 'Record of Persecutions' (*Zichron haShemadot*), which he cites in connexion with English affairs.

[3] P.R. 1205, pp. 47*b*, 54*b*.

[4] Cf. C.R. 1244, p. 245; 1246, p. 433; P.R. 1238, p. 228; Lib. R. 1243, p. 187; 1244, p. 242; *Rot. Fin.* 1246, i. 461; M. Paris, *Chron. Maj.* iv. 608 (but see ibid. v.

however, and the cutting off of what had formerly been their solitary channel of livelihood, conditions changed. Prosecutions became more frequent,[1] until at last the king took drastic steps and appointed a special judicial commission to look into the matter.

On 17 November 1278 the Jews throughout the country were arrested, and a house-to-house search was made in their quarters in each city. Those against whom any evidence could be found were sent for trial: the chroniclers reported exaggeratedly that 680 were imprisoned in the Tower of London. Their punishment was savage, a large number being hanged there next year, besides some in other cities: their property, of course, escheating to the king. Amongst the victims were some of the most noteworthy figures in English economic life, who can hardly have needed to resort to such paltry dishonesty—persons like Benedict fil' Licoricia, one of the most prominent Jews of Winchester, and the affluent woman financier Belaset of Lincoln, who herself had been engaged in business on a large scale.[2] A few more saved their lives by a timely realization of the verity of Christianity. The Christians implicated in the crime were treated more leniently, only three being condemned to death, though many others were heavily fined. That prejudice had entered into the proceedings was obvious even to contemporaries.[3] The initial imprisonments had provided ample opportunity for personal enemies to introduce evidence of guilt into their houses; and some Jews, who had the courage to sue for an investigation into the ownership of tools for coin-clipping discovered among their property, were duly acquitted.[4] Similar

---

15 and *Hist. Angl.* iii. 76); J. de Oxenedes, p. 253; Rigg, *P.E.J.*, pp. xxvi–xxvii. The outcome of the trial in 1230 of a number of Shropshire Jews for stealing cloth and clipping the coinage (C.R. 1230, p. 304) is not known.

[1] *E.J.* iii. 277, 290–1, 309, &c.; Hundred Rolls, ii. 82.

[2] For Benedict fil' Licoricia of Winchester (not to be confused with the honoured Benedict fil' Abraham) cf. *Trs. J.H.S.E.* x. 204. The house confiscated from Belaset of Lincoln is still standing in Steep Hill. As late as 1293 twenty men of this city were indicted for concealing the property of condemned Jews (*Rot Parl.* i. 51a). For the official inventory of the property confiscated (extant only for Bristol, Devizes, and Winchester) see *Misc. J.H.S.E.* ii. 56–71. It is an ironic consideration that Edward I was the first English sovereign known to have resorted officially to clipping the coinage. The chroniclers' account of the events of 1278 seems to be partly fictional: cf. Richardson, *J.A.K.*, pp. 217–20.

[3] 'Nescio si juste vel injuste' remarks a monastic chronicler in reporting the escape of the non-Jewish moneyers from punishment (*Ann. Mon.* iv. 278–9).

[4] P.R. 1278, p. 285; cf. Rigg, *P.E.J.*, and *E.J.*, 1279, *passim*.

petty persecutions and new accusations followed all over the country, keeping the Jews everywhere in a constant state of alarm. At length, on 7 May 1279 an order was issued sharply prohibiting proceedings of this type without the fullest substantiation.[1]

This drastic action must have put an end to large-scale offences against the coinage. This very fact is likely to have driven the poorest class of Jew into the less culpable crime of clandestine usury. It became increasingly obvious that the attempt to effect a sudden revolution in the economic life of the English Jews had ended in failure.

§ IV

Theological odium, during the past decades, had increased more and more. Here and there throughout the country (particularly in Lincoln and Norwich) the shrines of reputed boy-martyrs, who were said to have been put to death by the Jews, were receiving universal veneration. At Oxford, there was near Merton College a cross, erected at the expense of the local community in expiation of the act of one of their number who, in a sudden frenzy, had thrown down a crucifix at that spot when it was borne in solemn procession to the shrine of St. Frideswide on Ascension Day in 1268.[2] All the anti-Jewish enactments fulminated by successive popes during the last century had been obeyed in England more promptly and more implicitly than in any other country of Europe. Nowhere was the Jewish badge more rigorously enforced. The Statute of Pillory, of 1267, forbade Christians to purchase meat which the Jews found ritually unfit. In 1272 (as once before, by 1243) the principal London synagogue was confiscated, on the pretext that the chanting disturbed the service in the neighbouring chapel of the Friars Penitent, to whom it was now assigned.[3] Worship

---

[1] C.R. 1279, p. 529. Those responsible for the accusations were in some cases persons of notoriously bad character. It seems that after this episode the sale or export of bullion by Jews was prohibited; cf. P.R. 1283, pp. 56, 79.

[2] C.R. 1268, pp. 14–15, 553; 1269, pp. 22–23; there is now a full account in Roth, *Oxford*, pp. 151–4. The part played on this occasion by Edward, who posted off to his father at Woodstock with the news, should be noted. The inscription to be found on the Cross is given by Tovey, *Anglia Judaica*, p. 175. In 1276 there was a question of repairing it—naturally, at the expense of the Jews (*E.J.* iii. 204).

[3] This site, at the north-east corner of Old Jewry, is now occupied, not inappropriately, by the offices of the Commissioners of the National Debt.

was henceforth carried on in the private oratories which some
of the wealthier Jews maintained in their houses. However, ten
years later, John Peckham, Archbishop of Canterbury, ordered
the confiscation and dismantling of these also, with one exception. His instructions were carried out with an excess of zeal by
the Bishop of London, who would allow no reservations, and
was with difficulty persuaded by his ecclesiastical superior to
permit the reopening of a single Bethel, in a private house.[1] In
the provincial centres matters were no better; at Bristol, for
example, certain Jews were put under the ban by the Bishop in
1275 on a charge of having insulted the chaplain of St. Peter's
when he came to administer the Holy Eucharist to a sick person
in the Jewry;[2] while at Hereford Bishop Swinfield broadcast
excommunications on both sides when some of his flock attended
a Jewish wedding despite his prohibition.[3]

Meanwhile, the Holy See took advantage of the favourable
atmosphere to urge on its repressive policy, assured in most
other countries of only theoretical obedience. In November
1286, in a letter addressed to the Archbishops of Canterbury
and York, Pope Honorius reaffirmed the decisions of the Lateran
Councils. He pointed out the evil effects of free intercourse
between Jews and Christians in England (which he depicted in
exaggerated terms), the pernicious consequences of the study
of the Talmud, and the continual infringement of the canon
laws on the subject. As though this were the most pressing
business which confronted Christendom, he sternly called for
counter-measures, including sermons and spiritual penalties, to
end this improper state of affairs.[4] His communication was taken
into consideration at the Diocesan Synod of Exeter in the following year, which obediently reinforced all the ancient canonical
strictures against the Jews, with a severity rarely paralleled.[5]
The king too had taken a hand. In 1276 he was personally
responsible for reviving an allegation of ritual murder that had

[1] Martin, *Registrum Epistolarum J. Peckham*, i. 213, ii. 407, 410.
[2] Adler, *J.M.E.*, p. 226.
[3] Below, p. 120.
[4] *Cal. Papal Registers*, i. 491. The fact that this communication figures in the
Register of the Bishop of Hereford (Capes, *Registrum R. de Swinfield*, pp. 139–40)
makes it possible that it was prompted by the reports of the recent conviviality
between Jews and Christians in that city; but it was also directed to France.
[5] Wilkins, *Concilia*, ii. 155.

been hanging over the London community since the close of the previous reign, when the body of a child, bearing what were supposed to be tokens of crucifixion, was discovered in the Thames.[1] This was the prelude to a massive onslaught. The Justices in Eyre at the Tower of London in the following year were instructed to inquire not only concerning those who had purchased Jewish property and debts in contravention of the recent legislation, but also the martyrdom of Christian children at Jewish hands: and they were informed (though they did not take any action) that two recent cases were recorded in the roll of the Chamberlain and Sheriffs.[2] Shortly afterwards the appalling charge was renewed in Northampton, where the Jews were accused in 1279 of crucifying a Christian boy and some suffered accordingly.[3] That same year the wealthy Norwich magnate Abraham fil' Deulecresse was burned on a charge of blasphemy, and there seems to have been a somewhat similar episode at Nottingham.[4] In consequence, the Justices in Eyre were now instructed to have public proclamation made in all places in which Jews lived, warning them under pain of death not to offend Christianity, and threatening converts who returned to Judaism (a not unknown happening) with the same penalty.[5] At the same time, the wearing of the Jewish badge even by women, and the prohibition of the employment of Christian servants, were reaffirmed—as they were once again in 1281, with other restrictions of the same sort.[6] Obviously under the impact of the recent events, the Mayor of London significantly omitted the phrase 'between Jews and Christians' in proclaiming peace in the City, and not long afterwards the London authorities, going beyond the recent governmental regulations, forbade houses to be rented from Jews or let to them, except within the precincts of the Jewry.[7] On 9 June 1280 Edward

---

[1] C.R. 1276, pp. 271–4.

[2] M. Weinbaum, London unter Edward I und II (Stuttgart, 1933), ii. 134. It is significant that in this year the London Jewry purchased immunity from the jurisdiction of the Justices in Eyre for £50.

[3] Florence of Worcester, Chronicon, ii. 222, repeated exactly by B. de Coton and J. de Oxenedes. See Note IV (b), pp. 274–5.

[4] F. Blomefield, Norfolk, i. 617: Ch.R. 1279, p. 213: P.R. 1280, p. 377.

[5] C.R. 1279, pp. 565–6.

[6] C.R. 1281, p. 176.

[7] Weinbaum, as above, i. 84–85: R. R. Sharpe, A Calendar of Letter Books of the City of London, pp. 215–19.

attended in person a General Chapter of the Dominican Order
held at Oxford by which (in accordance with the provisions of
the Papal Bull *Vineam Sorec* of the previous year) conversionist
sermons were instituted in England. This innovation was reinforced shortly after by the full weight of royal authority, in a
decree ordering all Jews to attend the discourses that were to be
arranged for their benefit during the coming Lent.[1] To encourage conversions, moreover, Edward waived for a seven-year
period his legal claim on the property of those who left their
faith. From now on they might retain one-half of what they
previously owned, though amassed in sin, the remainder (with
certain other income from Jewry, including the proceeds of the
recently instituted poll-tax) being devoted to the upkeep of the
*Domus Conversorum* in London.[2]

Though now reduced to the lowest depth of misery and degradation, the Jews continued to be harassed administratively
as well. On 6 February 1283 a special commission was set up
under Hamo Hauteyn, one of the Justices of the Jews, to investigate the charges made against certain of them who were suspected of selling foreign merchants plate made of clippings or
of silvered tin.[3] But the administrator of justice was himself far
from impeccable, and three years later he was removed from
office, after an inquiry held by the Earl of Cornwall, for gross
peculation in the discharge of his functions.[4] On 2 May 1287
there was a sudden reversion to the harsh methods of past reigns,
all the leading Jews being arrested and imprisoned as a preliminary to exacting a fresh tallage—reported by the chroniclers
as 20,000 marks, though in the course of a year only some
£4,000 was actually collected.[5]

Meanwhile, the Jewish arch-presbyter had once more come

---

[1] See P.R. 1280, p. 356, the royal instructions of 2 January to the local authorities to compel the Jews to listen to the sermons of the Dominicans. On the
Continent it was only at the period of the Counter-Reformation that the system
of conversionist sermons (for the institution of which in 1279 see *Bullarium Romanum*,
iv. 45) was perfected and systematically enforced.

[2] Adler, *J.M.E.*, pp. 301–2. For a case of Forced Baptism in London in 1290,
when redress was refused by the king, see *Rotuli Parliamentorum*, i. 46a.

[3] P.R. 1281–92, pp. 56, 79, 98, 187, 291, &c.

[4] *Select Cases in Court of King's Bench, Edward I* (Selden Society, vol. i), pp. clv–
clix. Hauteyn's colleague, Sir Robert de Ludham, was also cashiered (Madox,
*History of Exchequer*, ed. 1711, p. 173: *Trs. J.H.S.E.* xiv. 156–8).

[5] See Note IV (c), p. 275.

into unpleasant notoriety, for the instrument of the royal exactions could not be over-scrupulous in his methods. Hagin, son of the learned Master Moses of London, whose election by the communities of the realm in succession to Elias le Eveske had received royal sanction in 1258, had a troubled term of office. After the London massacre in 1264 (when he had saved his life by fleeing to the Tower) he took refuge in Normandy. Some time after his return he was accused of having concealed the death of an infant child of Cok fil' Aaron, the most illustrious victim of the massacre.[1] To escape the consequences he again fled to the Continent. Not long after, hoping that the scandal had died down, he ventured to return, but was immediately thrown into prison again. Further accusations and imprisonments continued intermittently until his death in 1280. He was succeeded in the following year by Cok Hagin fil' Deulecresse of London. The latter had not long before been excommunicated by his co-religionists for refusing to bear his share of the tallage, and owed his rehabilitation and present position to the influence of the queen-mother, in whose favour he stood high.[2] It was in his house alone that public worship was permitted after the destruction of the London synagogues in 1283. His seven-year tenure of office was destined to be the most tragic of all.

§ v

This was the condition of affairs when, in the summer of 1289, Edward returned to England from a prolonged visit to his continental possessions. His attempt to solve what he regarded as the Jewish problem had manifestly ended in failure: he had only succeeded in adding illegality to its other complications. Three possibilities were left. One was to extend to the Jews that social emancipation the absence of which made their economic emancipation an impossibility. This, however, was a conception which could not have occurred to the mind either of Jew or of

---

[1] The object of the concealment was apparently to save the boy's brothers (one of whom was his own son-in-law) from the necessity of paying an inheritance-tax for the second time within a very few years: *P.E.J.*, p. 73 ff.

[2] Stokes, *Studies*, pp. 35–37. Hagin fil' Deulecresse appears to have belonged to the family of R. Moses of London, being a nephew of his predecessor in office. He is conjectured to be identical with the Hagin who translated certain astronomical works of Abraham ibn Ezra into French and the *Image du Monde* into Hebrew: see, however, below, p. 128.

Christian in the thirteenth century. The times were not ripe for
it; neither side probably would have accepted it; and the extreme attitude which had been taken up during the king's absence both by the pope and by the English Church finally placed
it beyond the bounds of feasibility. The second possibility was
a confession of failure—to return to the previous state of affairs
and to legitimize money-lending once more. This solution was
certainly taken into consideration. To the period just before the
king's departure probably belongs a draft of a law in Norman
French, setting forth the manner in which the Jews had flouted
the various restrictions on their activity. To avoid this in future,
they were to be authorized to lend money again henceforth,
under the strictest control and at a specified rate of interest.[1] It
does not appear that this measure, though formally drafted,
was ever put into execution. All that was done apparently was
to reopen the chirograph-chests in the various Jewish centres in
order to control the liquidation of former transactions, and to
register those in which they were now engaged, presumably
with the intention of checking the worst irregularities.[2]

Only one possible method of coping with the issue remained:
to sweep away the problem which it had been impossible to solve.

The banishment of the Jews was by no means a new conception. It had been employed all over Christian Europe as early
as the seventh century. On the royal demesne in France it had
been effected by Philip Augustus, a century before, in 1182, and
again decreed by St. Louis (though the order relating to it was
never apparently carried into execution) in 1249. In England
a similar idea is stated to have crossed the mind of Henry III,
while in 1281, according to one report, Parliament had endeavoured to persuade the king to drive the Jews out of the
country, offering a levy of one-fifth by way of inducement. On
this occasion the danger had been averted, it is said, by a higher
offer on the part of the victims.[3]

---

[1] See Note IV (d), p. 275.

[2] The chirograph-chests seem to have been functioning normally at the time
of the Expulsion (cf. B. L. Abrahams in *Trs. J.H.S.E.* ii. 85 ff.), and the unpublished rolls of the Exchequer of the Jews give the same picture. The bonds
in terms of money registered in 1290 as being from the 'New Chests', numbering
only 138 as against 508 in terms of commodities (Elman, loc. cit., pp. 96–98),
must nevertheless refer to ostensibly commercial transactions.

[3] M. Paris, *Hist. Angl.* iii. 103–4.

Locally, matters had gone further. As we have seen, there were many cities in England from which the Jews had been expelled in the previous reign. The precedent had been followed under Edward—a striking instance (1273) was Bridgnorth, where only a year before they had been specifically committed to the protection of the sheriff.[1] In 1275 there had been a whole-sale measure of the sort when the queen-mother obtained letters patent expelling them from her dower-towns, including Marl-borough, Gloucester, Worcester, and Cambridge.[2] More recently still, the king had ordered their removal from the royal borough of Windsor (1283).[3] Even during the period of consoli-dation that followed the Barons' Wars, when the Jews timidly attempted to extend their area of settlement, they were harshly expelled time after time from those places where no chirograph-chests were functioning.[4] The citizens of Newcastle-on-Tyne as early as 1234, and those of Derby in 1260–1, had gone so far as to purchase the 'liberty' of excluding Jews from residence within their boundaries in perpetuity, the latter city carefully specify-ing Jewesses as well; and in 1284 the charters of the newly created boroughs of North Wales followed this model. At pres-ent, communities existed in fewer than twenty cities in the king-dom, all on the royal demesne, as against at least twice that number where they had at one time been found. In many cases these expulsions had been effected at the request of the burgesses, or were in conformity with their known desires; for (religious considerations apart) the latter had little liking for this alien element, who were in the town but not of it. The increase in population in those few Jewries which were now tolerated, and the perpetual influx of needy refugees from the centres whence they had been expelled, must necessarily have increased local animosity; and such occurrences as the riot of 1274 at

---

[1] Almost simultaneously the Jews were excluded from Winchelsea (as they had been from Romsey seven years before; P.R. 1266, p. 613).

[2] P.R. 1275, p. 76: Eleanor's dower-towns included also Bath, where, however, there were few Jews. The Gloucester community was removed *en masse* to Bristol, but afterwards scattered: Adler, *J.M.E.*, pp. 225–6.

[3] Rymer, *Foedera*, i. 634 (13 October 1283). The statement (*Trs. J.H.S.E.* vii. 56) that before the Expulsion the majority of the Jews of Winchester had removed to Southampton is based on a misinterpretation of the document printed ibid. ii. 102—a list of Winchester Jews headed 'Southampton' because the sheriff of Southamptonshire (= Hampshire) was the responsible authority.

[4] C.R. 1269, p. 116, &c.; above, p. 72.

Southampton, when the sheriff came to distrain for a debt owing to a Jew, or at Bristol in 1275, when fire was set to the Jewry and many houses were sacked, were becoming increasingly common.[1]

Ill-feeling had been stimulated as well by the obvious insincerity of most of the recent neophytes, prompted by convenience rather than conviction, and the reported return of a few of them to Judaism. Officially, indeed, the expulsion of the Jews from England (like the greater tragedy in Spain two hundred years later) was partially justified, if not actuated, by this consideration.[2] It was not altogether a fictitious plea. In 1274, for example, a number of prominent London Jews were accused of having abducted a woman convert and coerced her to go overseas in order to revert to Judaism;[3] and as late as 1290 the Oxford Jews assaulted a convert who had the temerity to come among them to collect taxes.[4] Meanwhile the Gascon authorities complained to the chancellor of England that the Inquisitors in Languedoc had ordered them to dispatch to Toulouse for trial certain Jews from England who were accused of having relapsed after conversion.[5] About the same time a *cause célèbre* of a more startling nature, which evoked universal scandal, occurred in the capital. Robert of Reading, a Dominican friar, had been stimulated by his study of Hebrew literature to embrace Judaism, assuming the name of Haggai and marrying a Jewish wife.[6] It was this event, according to some chroniclers, which was responsible for the oppressive regulations included in the

---

[1] P.R. 1274, p. 107; Adler, *J.M.E.*, pp. 214, 226–7. (This riot was led by William Giffard, formerly sheriff of Norfolk and Suffolk, who was deeply involved with Jewish money-lenders.) There were other disorders at the same time at Farningham (where two Jews were killed), Guildford, Bedford, and Winchester (*E.J.* ii. 44, 94–95, 142, 196, 227, 231, 263), and later at York (C.R. 1279, p. 577).

[2] Cf. especially Archbishop Peckham's complaint to the king on 2 November 1281 (*Registrum Epistolarum*, ed. Martin, i. 239), and that of Pope Honorius in his communication to the English Church five years later (above, p. 77).

[3] *E.J.* ii. 209–10, iii. 18, 41, 111; Adler, *J.M.E.*, pp. 33–34—an interesting case from the point of view of social history.

[4] P.R. 1290, p. 397: Roth, *Oxford*, p. 162.

[5] L'Anglois, *Philippe le Hardi*, p. 221 (1280). But it is possible that the reference is to Gascon Jews.

[6] Florence of Worcester, ed. Thorpe, ii. 214–16, supported by the Hebrew sources in *Trs. J.H.S.E.* vi. 256 ff. This episode is often merged in that of the Oxford deacon who married a Jewess fifty years before (above, p. 41), and the two are identified in the memorial tablet at Oxford.

*Statutum de Judeismo* and for the even more serious consequences which were to follow.

From the purely selfish point of view there was no reason for Edward to refrain from carrying his intention into effect. The Jews were no longer of primary importance to the Exchequer. A century before, their average annual contribution to the royal income in ordinary taxation has been estimated at about £3,000 or approximately one-seventh of its total: now it was reduced to some £700, which represented little more than one-hundredth of the amount to which the revenue had by now increased. Economically, too, the function they performed was no longer essential. Not only was the country better developed than at the time of their settlement, when the native middle class had been almost non-existent; but in addition the Cahorsin and Italian usurers, working under the highest patronage but concealing their activities by ingenious subterfuges, made their presence superfluous. If the state desired to borrow money the sums which could be provided by these foreign *consortia*, specializing in government loans, made the resources of the Jews appear negligible. On the other hand, their operations with private individuals were more of a danger than a benefit to a king who was endeavouring to build up a strong central authority. The middle tenants and lesser baronage had formerly been the Jews' most profitable clients, and the ultimate result of these operations had frequently been (as we have seen) the reversion of the estates pledged with them to the Church or the tenants-in-chief, the increase in whose power was one of the problems that engaged Edward's attention throughout his reign. Now that the Jews were no longer important to the Exchequer, no reason of state prevented him from supplementing his attack upon the barons by ridding the country of their instruments. The pope and the Church were appealing for action. The king himself, from otherwise unsuspected religious motives, was naturally inclined to obey. His queen was indeed notoriously availing herself of the medium of Jewish financiers and their activities to acquire fresh estates.[1] His mother on the other hand had plainly indicated her prejudices on more than one occasion, and is even reported to have instigated the final step from the

---

[1] Peckham's *Registrum*, ed. Martin, ii. 619 (to the queen, 1283) and iii. 937 (to Master Geoffrey Aspal, 1286).

nunnery whither she had now retired. The experimental period of fifteen years during which the Jews had been empowered to lease farms by the *Statutum de Judeismo* expired in 1290, shortly after the king's return to England. Not many months later, giving up both the attempt at radical reform and the idea of restoring the former state of affairs, he set about applying to the Jewish problem the only solution which logically remained.

## § VI

The fatal step was taken on 18 July 1290 by an act of the king in his Council. It happened to be (as was long after remembered with awe) the fast of the ninth of Ab, anniversary of manifold disasters for the Jewish people, from the destruction of Jerusalem onwards.[1] On the same day writs were issued to the sheriffs of the various English counties, informing them that a decree had been issued ordering all Jews to leave England before the forthcoming feast of All Saints (1 November); any who remained in the country after the prescribed day were declared liable to the death penalty. The news was greeted by the general population with joy, and the Parliament which had assembled only three days before indicated its approval by prompt assent to the royal demand for a fifteenth of movables, and a tenth of the spiritual revenue, in taxation.[2]

[1] The date is preserved in Isaac Abrabanel's commentary on Jeremiah ii. 24, apparently quoting from Profiat Duran's lost *Record of the Persecutions of Israel*; the day corresponds with that of the writ to the sheriffs of 18 July, which must therefore have been issued simultaneously with the edict of expulsion, now lost.

[2] Richardson (*J.A.K.*, pp. 213–33) presents the events leading up to the expulsion of the Jews in a somewhat new light. He suggests that the reasons hitherto suggested for the change of policy—the growing impoverishment of the Jews, coupled with the undermining of their position through the competition of the Italian financiers —were relatively unimportant. The onslaught made on the Jews in 1278 on the pretext of clipping the coinage (which he shows to have been insincere, the number of the victims, however, being exaggerated) had resulted in large-scale escheats and confiscations, which suggested the possibility of an even more confiscatory attack. In 1288 Edward had entered into heavy financial commitments to ransom his cousin, Charles of Salerno, nominal king of Sicily. It was probably to meet the expenditure necessitated by this and other extravagances that the Jews were expelled from Gascony early in 1289, after thorough spoliation. The financial success of this led to its imitation in England in the following year. On 18 June 1290 instructions were issued to the sheriffs to seal the *archae* ten days later—a portent of what was to follow, the edict of expulsion being issued on 18 July.

The plea that the step was justified by the conduct of recent converts to Christianity was insincere, but there can be no doubt that the problem existed: in 1282 the Mayor and Sheriffs of London were ordered to arrest and imprison thirteen

The edict was executed with superficial fairness, and almost humanity, unlike subsequent proceedings of the sort on the Continent. Public proclamation was made in every county that no person should 'injure, harm, damage, or grieve' the Jews, in the time which was to elapse until their departure. Those who chose to pay for it were escorted to London. The Wardens of the Cinque Ports were instructed to see that the exiles were provided with safe and speedy passage across the sea and that the poor were enabled to travel at cheap rates.[1] Individual safe-conducts were issued to some of the more important.[2] They were allowed to take with them all cash and personal property in their possession at the time of the edict, together with such pledges deposited by Christians as were not redeemed before a fixed date. Their bonds and real estate, however, including their cemeteries and synagogues, escheated to the Crown. Nevertheless, a few individuals who enjoyed especial favour (such as Cok Hagin, the last arch-presbyter) were allowed to dispose of their houses and fees to any Christian who would buy them.[3]

On the morrow of St. Denis's Day (Tuesday, 10 October 1290)[4] the London Jews of the poorer sort started on their way to the coast 'under the custody of the Lord King', bearing their Scrolls of the Law.[5] Many of the richer had embarked at London, with all their property. At Queenborough, at the mouth of the Thames, anchor was cast at ebb-tide, and the ship grounded on a sandbank. The master then invited his passengers to disembark with him to stretch their legs. When the tide began to rise, he ran back to the side and climbed back on deck, recommending the unhappy Jews to call upon their prophet Moses, who had rescued their fathers at a similar juncture in the past. The

---

Jews—eleven of them women—who had 'returned to their vomit' (*The Jews in England. Exhibition of Records at the Public Record Office, 1957*, pp. 15–16). The Jews are said to have been arrested simultaneously on the prescribed day all over the country 'between the first and third hour' (W. of Guisborough [= Hemingburgh], ed. Rothwell, p. 226). Immediately afterwards inquiries were held by mixed juries concerning the extent of Jewish property: in Oxford this took place on 2 August (*Cartulary of St. John*, ed. Salter, ii. 152–4).          [1] P.R. 1290, p. 278.

    [2] e.g. Bonami of York (P.R.1290, pp. 379, 382) and Moses of Oxford (ibid., p. 381).
    [3] The beneficiaries seem to have been the chattels of notables: for example, besides Cok Hagin who 'belonged' to the Queen, Aaron fil' Vives (below, p. 97).
    [4] Not St. Denis's Day itself, as in Abrahams, *Expulsion*, p. 70: see the official entry from the King's Remembrancer Memoranda Roll in *Trs. J.H.S.E.* ix. 187, and Prynne, *Short Demurrer*, ii. 115.
    [5] 'Una cum libris suis' (Bart. de Coton, *Historia Anglicana*, R.S., p. 178).

whole party, without exception, was drowned, and the property left on board divided amongst the sailors. However, the news got about and after their return to England the culprits were tried and hanged. A tradition was long current that, however calm the weather, at the spot where the outrage took place the waters of the Thames are never still. But these were not the only victims.[1]

A considerable body of exiles, numbering 1,335 in all, and consisting largely of the poorer class, were transported to Wissant near Calais, at a charge of fourpence for each person.[2] It was the stormiest season of the year. Some of the vessels were lost with all aboard: others of the passengers were cast destitute upon the coast. Despite a papal protest, a number of the refugees were allowed by the French king to settle in Amiens, and others in Carcassonne. In the following year the 'Parlement de la Chandeleur' decreed that all those who had arrived from the English possessions should leave the country by the middle of the following Lent.[3] Thus these asylums were broken up.

The ultimate fate of the exiles is obscure. Notwithstanding this harsh enactment, it is probable that many of the fugitives from England, speaking as they did the language of the country, were able to remain in France undisturbed. In a roll of Paris Jewry, dating from four years after the Expulsion from England, several names appear with the addition of 'l'Englesche' or 'l'Englois', while isolated individuals are encountered at Vesoul and elsewhere.[4] A little group was settled in Savoy:[5] while the Clerli

---

[1] In 1294 certain sailors received a pardon at Portsmouth from their outlawry for their late murder of Jews on the high seas (*Gascon Rolls*, iii. 187, 188, 191). There seems to be a vague echo of the Queenborough episode in the Jewish chroniclers' account (e.g. S. Usque, *Consolaçam às Tribulaçoens de Israel*, iii. § xii) of the pavilion erected over the sea, into which those English Jews who adhered to their faith were enticed to be drowned: but see Note IV (*e*), p. 276 and p. 282.

[2] Abrahams, *Expulsion*, p. 71; Jacobs and Wolf, *Bibliotheca Anglo-Judaica*, p. xvii.

[3] Laurière, *Ordonnances des rois de France*, i. 317; *R.E.J.* iii. 221; Abrahams, loc. cit. Among the refugees later found in Paris was Bonami of York (cf. *Bibl.* A. 10. 28 and below, p. 88) who was authorized by Philip le Bel to settle where he pleased in France and to dispense with the Jewish badge in return for a tallage of 100 livres tournois yearly (Langlois in *Notices et extraits des manuscrits de la Bibliothèque Nationale*, xxxiv. 18).

[4] *R.E.J.* i. 66–69, xxxviii. 242, xliii. 298. Bonami of York is mentioned in the first of these lists, and Cok Hagin, the last arch-presbyter, possibly in the last.

[5] A document of 1329 published by M. Stern (*Urkundliche Beiträge über die Stellung der Päpste zu den Juden*, i (Kiel, 1893), p. 9), mentions among the Jews of Chambéry 'Eliottum anglicum', 'Manisseum anglicum' and 'Dominum Crescenterm dictum anglicum'.

family of Venice, long after, traced its descent legendarily to English exiles. The surname Ingles was found occasionally amongst the Jews of Spain, and Inglesi in the obscure island of Gozzo, near Malta.[1] Hebrew manuscripts written in England found their way to Germany, Italy, and Spain. The title-deeds of an English monastery were discovered in the lumber-room attached to the ancient synagogue at Cairo—obviously brought there by an English refugee.[2] Except for such random recollections, English Jewry of the Middle Ages became entirely assimilated in the greater body of their co-religionists overseas.[3]

## § VII

In England the traces left were inconsiderable. On the departure of the Jews, certain categories of their property, as we have seen, fell into the hands of the king. This comprised their synagogues and cemeteries, their houses, and their bonds—partly for the repayment of money, partly for the delivery of wool and corn. The annual income of the real estate, after all allowances had been made, came to about £130. The value of the debts, as shown in the register made by the officers of the Exchequer, was a little over £9,000. However, the king would only touch the original capital of this amount, piously waiving his right on any interest that might have accumulated.[4] Naturally there was a good deal of evasion, which affected even the highest circles. On his way home from the Papal Curia at Rome in 1292 John le Romeyn, archbishop of York, encountered in Paris his old acquaintance Bonami the Jew, and acquired from him his claim to a debt of £300 outstanding from the monastery of Bridlington, which he did his best to exact. The episode became known, and in the following year the Primate was impeached for his action.[5] In the event, the amounts due to the Crown were not fully collected. Payment was permitted to be deferred. Renewal of the renunciation of interest in 1315, and again in 1327, shows how long some of the debts remained outstanding. Finally, in response to a petition of the Commons in this year, Edward III

---

[1] Roth, *History of the Jews in Venice*, p. 168; F. Baer, *Die Juden im christlichen Spanier*, i. ii. 304; *Trs. J.H.S.E.* xii. 192, 199, 209.
[2] E. N. Adler, *Catalogue of Hebrew MSS.* (Cambridge, 1921), p. vi.
[3] See Note IV (*e*), pp. 275-6.
[4] Rigg, *P.E.J.*, p. xli.
[5] *Rotuli Parliamentorum*, i. 120a.

gave up all claim to the payment of amounts still owing to him.[1] Originally it had been intended to devote to pious uses the value of the houses which had escheated to the Crown. In fact a considerable proportion was given away to the king's favourites.[2] Till the sixteenth century at least, certain property was still designated in the conservative legal phraseology as being in the king's hands 'through the expulsion of the Jews'.

In the popular mind the impression left was slight. In the greater cities throughout the country, the old Jewries continued to be designated by their former names. In many places stone houses remained to recall the former owners' legendary skill as builders. In Lincoln an authentic synagogue has survived to the present day. Here and there newly granted borough charters, imitating those of an earlier date, automatically excluded the Jews, regardless of the fact that they were no longer tolerated in the country.[3] The cult of the hypothetical boy-martyrs continued till the period of the Reformation, commemorated in numerous ballads and still strong enough to poison the mind of the gentle Geoffrey Chaucer a century later. English cathedrals —Rochester, Winchester, probably others—displayed in the conventional fashion a symbolic statue of the blindfold and dejected Synagogue, in contrast to the triumphant Church.

Equally slight were the effects of the Expulsion upon the life of the country generally, though the momentary shortage of capital which ensued may have been responsible in part for the financial crisis of 1294. A further consequence deserves consideration. Impoverished though the Jews were, their potential importance to the Treasury even in the last years was not negli-

---

[1] Ibid. ii. 8a, 11b; *Statutes of Realm*, 255. Up to this time frequent payments 'for acquittance against the Jews' (i.e. debts formerly owing to the Jews) are registered in the Charters (cf. Ch.R. iii. 157 (1310) and 228 (1315)). The sums received by the Crown were not, however, inconsiderable, amounting in 1294 alone to £1,850. 13s. 4d. In 1293 it was decided that arrears of rent on property which had escheated to the Crown were to be paid to the landlords (*Rotuli Parliamentorum*, i. 98–99).

[2] Cf. the lists of grants in *Rot. Orig. in Scaccario*, pp. 73–76. Abrahams is not quite justified in stating (*Expulsion*, p. 73) that 'they were nearly all given away to the King's friends'. Thus, though the Canterbury synagogue was made over to Queen Eleanor's tailor, the rest of the real estate belonging to ten Jewish property owners devolved on the Prior and Convent of Christchurch: cf. *H.M.C.* ix, App. I for the proceedings of the jury of citizens which inquired into the escheated property.

[3] e.g. Overton (1292): so also in the confirmation of older charters, as that of Beaumaris as late as 1562.

gible. It was not without its importance in the development of the English constitution that this uncontrolled, and uncontrollable, source of royal revenue was finally removed. From this date the detailed regulation of finance by the representatives of the people became possible. It is thus not without its significance —though the importance of the fact should not be exaggerated —that the Model Parliament of Edward I assembled, and the English constitution received its shape, four years after the Expulsion of the Jews.[1]

For nearly four centuries England disappears almost entirely from the horizon of the Jewish world. References to her in Hebrew literature are sparse, and the accounts of English events subsequent to the period of the Third Crusade are garbled to a degree.[2] In the chronicles the name of the country remained a prototype of cruelty and oppression. The reputation was undeserved. Nevertheless, England had played an important and unenviable role in the martyrdom of the Jewish people. It was here that the Ritual Murder Accusation, which subsequently proved responsible for such widespread misery, first reared its head. At no other time in the blood-stained record of the Middle Ages were the English horrors of 1189-90 surpassed. And there was one other aspect, which Jewish writers fully appreciated. The final tragedy of 1290 was the first general expulsion of the Jews from any country in the medieval period. Local precedents only had been known before. But it was Edward I who set the example for the wholesale banishment of the Jews, which was followed with such deadly effect in France sixteen years after, by Philip le Bel, and two centuries later by Ferdinand and Isabel of Spain, in the culminating tragedy of medieval Jewish history.

[1] Mention should be made also of the conjecture that certain English legal practices—the writ *elegit*, certain details of the system of mortgage, and the separate examination of husband and wife in the procedure of final concords—owe their origin to the Jewish procedure familiarized through the Exchequer of the Jews (cf. F. A. Lincoln, *The Starra, their Effect on Early English Law and Administration*, Oxford, 1939). There is contemporary authority for the statement that the inclusion of the word 'defend' in property-transfers was intended in the first place to meet the case of the Jews: cf. *Year-Book of XXX Edward I*, ed. A. J. Horwood, p. 190.

[2] Cf. particularly Joseph haCohen's *Chronicles of France and Turkey* (English trans. by C. F. H. Bialloblotzky, London, 1835), where the account of fifteenth-century English history is barely recognizable. Contemporary references to the closing stages of the history of the Jews in England are little less inaccurate.

# V

# ANGLO-JEWRY IN THE MIDDLE AGES

§ 1

THE Jewish community that maintained a precarious existence in England from the close of the eleventh century to
the close of the thirteenth was essentially artificial in origin.
It was tolerated by the Norman and Plantagenet rulers for an
express purpose, and enjoyed virtually no rights except in connexion with these limited functions. It possessed in consequence
a remarkable homogeneity and compactness, and thus has a
significance for the historical student out of proportion to its
magnitude or its achievements. It may be considered in fact
the type of the 'feudal' Jewry of the Middle Ages, as regards
composition, activity, and organization. For this reason, its
structure deserves detailed examination.[1]

Of the Jewries in the principal countries of western Europe
in the Middle Ages, indeed, that of England was indubitably
the least important, both numerically and culturally. At the
time of the Expulsion of 1290 it was believed to comprise
approximately 16,000 souls, but this number is probably far
higher than the facts warrant.[2] This body was scattered
throughout the country, though most thickly in the eastern and
south-eastern counties. In the thirteenth century there were
twenty-seven centres in which *archae* for the registration of
Jewish debts were established—Bedford, Bristol, Canterbury,
Colchester, Devizes, Exeter, Hereford, Huntingdon, Ipswich,
Lincoln, London, Northampton, Norwich, Nottingham, Oxford, Stamford, Wilton, Winchester, and York; Berkhamsted,
Cambridge, Gloucester, Marlborough, Sudbury, Wallingford,
Warwick, and Worcester. At the time of the Expulsion of 1290
they were excluded from the eight places last mentioned, only
nineteen communities then existing.[3] Besides these towns there

---

[1] Some of the points elaborated in this chapter have already been referred to
cursorily above.          [2] See Note V (*a*), pp. 276–7.

[3] The usual enumeration has been corrected: there is no evidence that the Jews
had been excluded from Huntingdon and Devizes, while Ipswich is to be added to
the number of places with an *archa*.

were a few others where settlements had at one time been found, though not provided with an *archa*: these comprised Bury St. Edmunds, Leicester, Coventry, Derby, Winchelsea, Bridgnorth, Newcastle, Newport, Wycombe, Southampton, Newbury, and some others. In one or two more centres, such as Lynn, the community exterminated by the massacres of 1190 had never been re-established, though individuals may have managed to obtain a foothold. Before the decree of 1253 limiting residence to those towns where communities were then established, isolated households or groups were to be found also in rural centres throughout the country; subsequently, too, some managed to establish themselves in such places, from which they were periodically expelled.[1] The settlement was thickest in the south and east of England. No community existed north of Newcastle-on-Tyne or west of Exeter, though individuals were certainly to be found in Cornwall.[2] None are encountered in Scotland in pre-Expulsion times, but Jewish financiers did business from time to time with the Scottish sovereign, and they were settled in those parts of Wales under English influence (Chepstow and Caerleon, and perhaps elsewhere as well). In Ireland we know little of their condition or distribution, but their numbers justified the appointment in 1232 of Peter des Rivaulx to plenary authority over those resident there.[3]

It is by no means easy to gauge the relative density of the various communities. To the 'Northampton Donum' of 1194, that of London contributed rather more than one-quarter—a

---

[1] Expulsions from all places without a chirograph-chest took place in 1269, 1277, and 1284. Nevertheless, the inmates of the *Domus Conversorum* between 1280 and 1308 included former Jews from Merton, Bury, Arundel, Cricklade, Gillingham, and Kendal (Adler, *J.M.E.*, p. 306), while in 1272 they were resident at Guildford, Chichester, Lewes, Arundel, Seaford, Hatcham, Bottisham, and Holm, Cambridgeshire (Rigg, *P.E.J.*, pp. 68–70), and in 1273–5 at Bradesworth, Berham, Farningham, Hungerford, Royston, Sandwich, and Tickhill (*E.J.* ii, *passim*). Officially a Jew residing without royal licence in any place from which Jews were excluded was punished by confiscation of his property (Rigg, *P.E.J.*, p. 82). For Jews in Southwark cf. *Bibl.* A. 8. 22. The total number of settlements is about 200: below, pp. 277, 293.

[2] Cf. Jacobs, *J.A.E.*, pp. 186–8, quoting from the *Liber Rubeus*. The passage would indicate that the Jews were interested in tin-mining. (On the Continent—Italy and Spain—Jews were certainly engaged in mining at this period, so that the suggestion is not entirely fanciful.) Nevertheless, the *Jews' Tin* and *Jews' Houses* of more modern times are in all probability based on an erroneous folk-etymology. For the Jews in Cornwall see *Bibl.* A. 8. 137–40.

[3] *Bibl.* A.8. 152: B. Shillman, *History of Jews in Ireland* (Dublin, 1945).

proportion perhaps unduly high by reason of the concentration there of the greatest capitalists and propinquity to the seat of government. Even if we accept the highest estimates of the total Anglo-Jewish population, the community of the capital cannot have comprised more than 2,000 souls, as contrasted with the 2,000 households who impressed the imagination of the medieval Jewish historians:[1] but one-fifth that number is probably nearer the mark. The two communities next in size, those of Lincoln and Canterbury, were perhaps half as large. At the time of the Expulsion, the former included some sixty persons engaged in business transactions on their own account, in many cases, however, belonging to the same family.[2] The average small community is unlikely to have comprised more than fifty to a hundred souls all told.

## § 11

Medieval English Jewry derived in the main from northern France, like the Norman conquerors in whose wake they followed. Their usual port of embarkation (we are informed in Rabbinic sources) was Dieppe, whence, if the wind were good, the English coast might be reached in one day.[3] Relations were close also with the Rhineland. A minority came from farther afield—from Spain, from Italy, even from Russia.[4] The original element remained, however, predominant. Among themselves the English Jews spoke and even jested in Norman French.[5] They were generally called, too, by French equivalents to their Hebrew names. For the men we find Deuleben or Benedict (Berechiah, Baruch), Bonevie or Vives (Hayyim, generally

---

[1] e.g. Ibn Verga in the Hebrew chronicle *Shebet Jehudah*, § xviii. For the extent of the London Jewry see *Bibl.* A. 8. 13 and below, pp. 123–4.

[2] Cf. lists in *Trs. J.H.S.E.* ii. 76–105.

[3] Moses of Coucy, *Major Book of Precepts*, § xxv.

[4] See the name-lists in Jacobs, *J.A.E.*, pp. 345–71. The name *Lumbard*, found throughout this period, plainly indicates immigrants from Italy as a whole rather than from the northern provinces. (That it denotes 'money-lender', as has been maintained, would be in the case of Jews a distinction without a difference; but possibly—especially when used as a praenomen—it may signify 'Long-Beard'.) Jacobs, *J.A.E.*, p. 73, identifies Isaac of Russia, who was in Hampshire in 1181, with Rabbi Isaac of Chernigov, and suggests that he was 'possibly the first Russian in historic times who put foot on English soil'; but the dates do not tally.

[5] The passage from Giraldus Cambrensis cited below (p. 279) is incomprehensible except on the assumption that the medium of conversation was French.

rendered as Hagin),[1] Bonenfaund (Tob-Elem), Deulesault (Isaiah), Deulecresse or Cresse (Solomon, sometimes Gedaliah), Diai or Deu-ai (Eleazar), Deudone (Nathaniel), Bondi or Bundy (Yom-Tob), Amiot or Bonami (probably Benjamin). Isaac, in its Hebrew form, was shortened by the omission of the first syllable into Cok or Hak, which might be given the diminutive form Hakelin, while by a similar process Jacob became Copin and Samuel, Molkin. So, too, Benjamin was anglicized as Bateman, while Asher, with obvious allusion to Genesis xlix. 20, became Sweteman. Purely non-Jewish names, such as Thomas or Peter (corresponding to Perez), are occasionally found, the tendency increasing in the thirteenth century.[2]

For women a Hebrew equivalent was considered unnecessary, and we find picturesque appellations such as Belaset (Bellassez), Duzelina, Gentilia, Pucella, Precieuse, Licoricia, Regina, Chera, Pasturella, Glorietta, Mirabilia, Brunetta, Bona: with some Anglo-Saxon forms such as Swetecot, Gertelot, or Alfild.[3] Surnames, so far as they were in use, indicated place of origin (Lumbard, Peitevin, Angevin,[4] le Français, de Hibernia, &c.), occupation (le Mire, le Scriveneur or l'Escrivein, le Pointur),[5] or personal peculiarity (Rufus, le Gros, le Long, le Enveyse, le Fort, l'Aveugle). Only in a few cases like l'Eveske (Cohen),[6]

---

[1] Pronounced, however, *Hayin*, the *y* sound being generally rendered by *g*. That the name means 'life' was realized even at Court; hence Henry III's pun (C.R. 1266, p. 208): 'the King wishes to Master Hagin son of Moses, a better state of life'.

[2] Anglo-Jewish nomenclature is discussed by Stokes, *Studies*, pp. 63–71, and Loeb, *R.E.J.* xvi. 296–9 and xviii. 152. The curious surname 'Arrow' (ץ ח) suggested in Davis, *Shetaroth*, p. xv, is based on a misreading; see below, p. 118 n. Some of the name-equivalents in the text are subject to revision: Bonevie was probably used as equivalent to Benjamin, and Bundy sometimes to Benedict, while Deulecresse seems to have been simply a name of good augury. The much-discussed Manser clearly stands for Menahem: compare Davis, *Shetaroth*, p. 356, with the corresponding Latin in *Starrs*, ii. 115.

[3] List in Adler, *J.M.E.*, p. 21. Belaset corresponded to Rachel: cf. Gen. xxix. 17.

[4] These three are also found, surprisingly, as praenomens, Peitevin and Angevin of Canterbury being brothers. The name 'le Turk' indicates origin from Thouars in Poitou (Latin *Thuarcium*), and 'De Brug'' a resident of Bridgnorth, not of Bruges in Flanders. [5] Below, pp. 118, 278.

[6] The identity of *Eveske*, or *episcopus*, with the Hebrew *Cohen* is obvious, though Jacobs endeavoured to prove that it indicated Rabbinic functions. For a discussion of the point see Stokes, *Studies*, pp. 18–22. There is a curious reference (*King's Remembrancer Memoranda Roll, 1230–1* (P.R.S. 1933, p. 64) to Solomon fil' Benedict, 'episcopus de conventibus judaeorum'. But, as the dealings referred to in the document are with a prioress and nuns, this is presumably a notarial witticism. Richardson (*J.A.K.*, pp. 124–5) maintains that *episcopus*, *eveske*, implies public office.

Comitissa (*nessiah*: apparently deriving from the name of an ancestress), or Kokhab (= Star: perhaps applied to a family originating at Estella in Navarre) did they correspond to surnames in the modern sense. More distinctively English in form were the agnomens Russell (Ursel), Bullock, Barlibred, Hariprid, Furmentin, or Bigelin. But it was more usual for a Jew to be distinguished from others of the same name by indicating his city of residence, the name of his father, or, exceptionally (perhaps when the father died young, or was less prominent in business) that of his mother. Rabbis were generally referred to, even in secular records, as 'Master' (*Magister*).

Outwardly the English Jew of the Middle Ages resembled his contemporaries. In the thirteenth century the most usual external garment for men was a hooded cloak, though the typical pointed Jewish hat, the *pileum cornutum* (as prescribed by the Council of Vienna in 1267), was also worn. The hair, but not the beard, was allowed to grow long. Women wore the crown-shaped head-dress and wimple characteristic of the period.[1] The superficial resemblance to the general population must indeed have been considerable in order to justify the Jewish Badge, which was enforced in England earlier and more consistently than in any other country of Europe after its establishment by the Lateran Council of 1215. It was first put into vigour in 1218 by the earl marshal, who ordered that every Jew, at all times, in the city or outside it, walking or riding, should wear upon his outer garment a piece of white cloth or parchment whereby he might be distinguished from Christians. This sign was to take the form of the so-called *tabula*—the legendary shape of the Two Tables of Stone which bore the Ten Commandments—as symbolizing the Old Testament. The injunction was repeated in 1222 at the Council of Oxford, when it was enacted that all Jews of either sex should wear on the breast a badge two fingers wide and four long, of a different colour from the rest of the garment. In 1253 Henry III renewed the clause, ordering the

---

[1] Four caricature-portraits of English Jews of the medieval period are extant: one (1233) of Isaac of Norwich and two of his agents, of whom Mosse Mokke wears the *pileum cornutum* and Abigail is dressed as a woman of the period (see Adler, *J.M.E.*, frontispiece); one of Aaron of Colchester, whose son Isaac was involved in a forestry offence in 1277; a third in a roll of 1240; and now a fourth in my own collection. All are illustrated in my 'Portraits and Caricatures of Medieval English Jews' in *Jewish Monthly*, IV. i, reprinted in *Essays and Portraits*.

*tabula* to be borne in a prominent position. Edward I returned to the charge in his *Statutum de Judeismo* of 1275. In order to secure greater prominence, he stipulated the colour of the badge and increased the size. A piece of yellow taffeta, six fingers long and three broad, cut in the same shape as before, was henceforth to be worn over his heart by every Jew above the age of seven years (elsewhere the age-limit was much higher).[1] Two years later an inquiry was instituted into the manner in which this and other regulations were being obeyed. The result was seen in 1279 when orders were issued once more emphasizing the necessity for Jewish women as well as men to wear the Badge of Shame. The Synod of Exeter, in 1287, repeated the ecclesiastical injunction. There was plainly very little opportunity for forgetfulness; it was not one of the occasions when medieval legislation expressed only an ideal.

§ III

As elsewhere in Europe in the Middle Ages the Jews were reckoned *servi camerae regis*, or Serfs of the Royal Chamber. Nowhere, indeed, was this laid down more explicitly. Henry III's Mandate concerning the Jews of 1253, repeating the terms of an ordinance of 1233, started with the specific injunction that 'no Jew remain in England, unless he perform the service of the King: and immediately any Jew shall be born, male or female, he shall serve Us in some manner'. In the so-called 'Laws of Edward the Confessor' (which, though apocryphal, faithfully represent the point of view of the middle of the twelfth century), the constitutional theory of the period is succinctly summed up: 'All Jews, wherever in the realm they are, must be under the King's liege protection and guardianship, nor can any of them put himself under the protection of any powerful person without the King's licence, because the Jews themselves and all their chattels are the King's. If therefore anyone detain them or their money, the King may claim them, if he so desire and if he is able, as his own.'

---

[1] Cf., for the history of the Jewish Badge, Ulysse Robert, *Les Signes d'infamie au moyen âge* (Paris, 1891), and above, pp. 40, 42, 59, 71. It is shown in the stipulated English form in the caricature of Aaron of Colchester and other contemporary representations (including a corbel at Lincoln) illustrated in my article referred to above: cf. Richardson *J.A.K.*, pp. 178–80, for the exemptions before 1253.

Apart from this general authority, a power yet more absolute was exercised over the king's 'demesne Jews' resident in the royal boroughs or Crown lands.[1] This absolute proprietorship was sometimes demonstrated by the concession of wealthy individuals as a gift to Court favourites, with the sole right of exploitation. Thus, at the close of the reign of Henry III, his son Edmund was presented with Aaron fil' Vives, a conspicuous member of the London community. The latter was unusually fortunate in certain respects, for he received permission to establish himself in any city of the kingdom that he pleased, and was exempted by his new master from all extraordinary financial burdens in return for an annual tribute of a pair of gilt spurs. The profit expected to accrue through his activities must, on the other hand, have been very great, as a special chirograph-chest was to be maintained for him wherever he might be resident and an assessor was appointed to act in the Jewish Exchequer in his master's interest should any case concerning 'his' Jew come before it.[2] Magnates indeed regarded the presence of Jews on their demesne as highly desirable, would invite them to settle on payment of a purely nominal tribute (such as a pair of silver spoons), and would obtain from the Crown letters of protection to safeguard them.[3] Even the queen, the papal legate, or the Archbishop of Canterbury did not disdain to solicit special privileges for some favoured individual.[4]

As a natural consequence of this state of utter dependence, the Crown expected to profit—and to profit immoderately—at every stage of the life and activity of the Jew. A heavy payment —sometimes as much as 2,000 marks—was exacted from foreigners for permission to reside and carry on business in England. When a business transaction was registered at the *archa*, a fee was paid by both parties. The profits of justice, if a lawsuit resulted, belonged as a matter of course to the king. Moreover, before initiating judicial proceedings, the Jew had to pay twenty shillings—three times as much as a Christian did in similar circumstances; and if he procured a writ of recovery

[1] Cf. C.R. 1255, p. 396, &c. In granting Guy de Roquefort the castle of Colchester and the lands belonging to it Henry III expressly excluded 'the wood of Kingswood and the Jews of the town' (P.R. 1256, p. 482).

[2] Rigg, *P.E.J.*, pp. 62–63; P.R. 1270, p. 440; 1271, p. 515.

[3] Tovey, *Anglia Judaica*, p. 84; C.R. 1226, p. 123.

[4] P.R. 1268, p. 204; 1254, p. 318; 1281, p. 433.

(costing one bezant) one-tenth of the proceeds devolved on the Exchequer. No acquittance was valid unless properly enrolled, a fee being of course exacted.[1] During the last phase, moreover, each individual had to pay a poll-tax, ultimately devoted to the upkeep of the *Domus Conversorum* in London. The routine profits of Jewry, during the eight lean years after the Battle of Evesham, amounted on an average to upwards of £400.

This regular revenue was, however, only a detail of the total obtained. In certain circumstances a debtor would make a cash payment to the king so as to be absolved from the payment of the interest, or even principal, of his debt to a Jew; alternatively, on a plea of penury, he might obtain an order for an 'extent' or valuation of his means, which would be followed by instructions to his creditor to grant 'reasonable terms' (sometimes derisory) for repayment. Jews, on the other hand, sometimes paid heavy sums for an undertaking, not always observed, that no 'extents' affecting them would be made during a specified period.[2] For a variety of misdemeanours a Jew's entire property might be confiscated, though in exceptional circumstances sufficient would be left for his sustenance. Even when one became converted to Christianity everything he had previously possessed went to the Crown, as having been amassed in sin.[3] Although the Third Lateran Council had expressed its disapproval of this practice, it was only under Edward I that the right was waived, the convert being permitted henceforth to retain half while the rest was devoted to the *Domus Conversorum*. But there was an even more paradoxical practice: if a Jew, excommunicated by his co-religionists, failed to make his peace with them within forty days, the Crown confiscated all his worldly goods.

The normal occurrences of life were no less sedulously exploited; and though such payments were not the prerogative of any single section of the nation, the Jew was a far more regular

[1] Many of these payments were almost in the nature of a stamp-duty, and were not exacted from Jews only. But the scale in their case was frequently far higher, and as they engaged in a larger number of formal transactions than their neighbours the burden on them was infinitely greater.

[2] P.R. 1262, pp. 201, 205; 1265, p. 522; C.R. 1267, p. 423. It goes without saying that, if the creditor appealed against the findings, a fee was exacted (C.R. 1250, p. 423).

[3] There was a more sordid reason for this. The Jew was authorized to use his capital only for the king's benefit: when this became impossible, he was deprived of it.

source of profit than his neighbour. He would pay for permission to change his place of abode, or to live in some place where there was no settled community, or to enter into partnership, or to alter his name,[1] or to marry the person of his choice, or to be divorced, or to attend a wedding in London, or to employ a Christian nurse for his son, or to have the custody of children. The communities of the realm would find money for proceedings to be taken against some person whose conduct they considered compromising, or to be withheld from some person whom they thought innocent. Moreover, a levy would be made, from the generality or from individuals, on the occasion of the marriage of a member of the royal family, or when the king returned safe from a journey, or when the queen was in childbed. Sometimes the spoliation called for no excuse at all.[2]

From the reign of John the principal source of income from the Jews was by tallage, hitherto regarded as an extraordinary expedient resorted to only in emergency. So commonplace did this become that under Henry III, when a marriage was arranged between young people, it was thought necessary to make special provision to meet this probable contingency:[3] while a London financier, by a species of primitive insurance, paid heavily for a guarantee that he would not be tallaged at a higher rate than 100 marks annually for a specified period of years.[4] There was no limit to the violence that might be employed on the occasion of a levy, the imprisonment of all the Jews or the leading householders, sometimes accompanied by their wives and children, often serving as a preliminary.[5] At times of greater moderation, representatives of the communities of the realm might be summoned together at some central spot

[1] *E.J.* ii. 19; but why Abraham Motun desired to change his cognomen is not easy to understand.

[2] Cf. C.R. 1251, p. 544: 'The King wills that the gold cup he has purchased from Elias Episcopus Jew of London for 250 marks [cf. Lib.R. 1249, p. 264] should remain the King's by gift of the Jew, and the money shall be restored to him.'

[3] Thus, Yom-Tob, son of Rabbi Moses of Norwich, betrothing his daughter Zionah to Solomon, son of Eliab, in 1249 bound himself 'to acquit the amount of their tallage if it should be imposed upon them during that year' (Davis, *Shetaroth*, pp. 33–35).

[4] P.R. 1250, p. 71. The pitiless activities of the tax-gatherers are feelingly described in the 'Fox Fables' of Berechiah haNakdan (of Oxford? see below, p. 126) § ci—the fable of the Merchant, the Robbers, and the Knight.

[5] That the reality was not always as drastic as the theory on these occasions is suggested by the allegations against the Constable of the Tower, *E.J.* iii. 103.

to divide the burden among themselves. Alternatively, it would be apportioned by a special commission, consisting sometimes of as few as two, and sometimes of as many as twelve prominent Jews appointed by the Crown; they occasionally acted in conjunction with an elected or co-opted element, which, however, was always in a minority.[1] Sureties, up to forty in number (sometimes identical with the assessors), would be nominated on occasion and held responsible for the collection of the full amount. In each community there would be a small committee of 'tallagers' in which the three economic classes—wealthy, well-to-do, and poor—might have separate representation:[2] in accordance with Rabbinic law, however, members had to stand aside when the contribution of a close relative came up for consideration. Taxpayers had the right to appeal against their assessment, a mixed jury inquiring into their means.[3] On the other hand, a community which was not represented in the Assessment Commission might make a payment to the king to ensure that one of its members should be present to watch its interests when the time came.[4] Generally speaking, those with a capital of less than forty shillings did not have to contribute, though under John this amount was exacted even from the poorest. The levy was usually preceded by an inspection of the *archae*, by which it was possible to ascertain what outstanding credits every business man possessed. In case the full contributions were not paid, the recalcitrant were banished and their property confiscated, unless they had anticipated this by flight—a contingency which the authorities did everything to prevent. The Jews on their side enforced payment by means of excommunication, the only weapon at their command; but this was superfluous when they were in agreement with the authorities, and futile when they were not.[5]

---

[1] C.R. 1246, p. 395; 1247, p. 506; 1252, p. 138; P.R. 1237, p. 187; 1249, p. 46. To be a tallager was an unwelcome burden, exemption from which might be purchased: *E.J.* ii. 13.

[2] Cf. the detailed regulations of 1219 published by Stokes, *Studies*, pp. 250–1. The same system is once found for the selection of the general tallagers, four nominated members of the wealthier class having to co-opt two from each of the other sections to assist them 'so that the rich be not spared and the poor not too much grieved' (P.R. 1249, p. 46). This tripartite economic division was common in the medieval Jewish community, particularly in France and Spain.

[3] C.R. 1252, p. 178: cf. Davis, *Shetaroth*, p. 370. Deferred payment was sometimes permitted, on condition that in case of unpunctuality double the amount would be exacted (*E.J.* ii. 46).          [4] C.R. 1247, p. 504.

[5] There is a particularly detailed account of the mechanism for levying two

The royal prerogatives over the Jew included that of confiscating his property on his death (as on his conversion), on the ground that it had been acquired by sinful methods. This right —which applied to non-Jewish usurers as well—was carried into execution by Henry II in the classic case of Aaron of Lincoln, and was reaffirmed by Henry III a century after as regards real estate.[1] Yet it was seldom so drastic in reality as it was in theory; for it was obviously to the royal interest to leave the heirs sufficient to carry on business and amass taxable profit. Generally, on the death of a wealthy Jew, his estate was attached and liquidated by a mixed jury sitting in conjunction with representatives of the family. A third part would be retained by the Crown, while the rest would be allowed to devolve according to Jewish law of inheritance or the testamentary dispositions of the deceased.[2] It was presumably in order to forestall this right that gifts of houses were sometimes made *inter vivos*. Thus, for example, grandparents would transfer rights over their property to a grandson on the express condition that they could continue in occupation as long as they lived.[3] Often the king's portion of the assets of a deceased usurer was commuted by a fine or 'relief'. This was payable by instalments, the estate being released as soon as adequate security was furnished. The amounts thus exacted were huge. When Hamo of Hereford died in 1232 his family paid a total of 6,000 marks as a relief, this being a very great deal more than the maximum which could legally be exacted from the son of an earl.[4] Frequently, moreover, the Crown

small tallages of 500 and 1,000 marks respectively for Richard of Cornwall in P.R. 1255, pp. 439-40, 441-4; three Jews of each community were selected to assess the levy, and guarantors varying in number between two and four were designated in each place.

[1] Cf. C.R. 1249, p. 346: 'Of ancient custom prevailing in our realm we ought to succeed to the houses and land bought by Jews.'

[2] Cf. *Cal. Inq. Misc.* i. 163 for a detailed instance of an inquiry preceding such a settlement (estate of Copin of Oxford, 1252). The composition of the estate is interesting: bonds, £142. 14s. 4d.; working capital (gold), £66. 14s. 4d.; miscellaneous property and real estate, £25. 13s. Master Elias of London on his death in 1284 left credits to the value of £185; miscellaneous effects worth £266. 13s. 4d.; rents in London bringing in £19. 16s. 0d. a year; and a house worth £5 a year.

[3] Davis, op. cit., pp. 259-62.

[4] Adler, *J.M.E.*, p. 146. Hamo (for whom see *Trs. J.H.S.E.* iii. 191 ff.) figures in the tallage rolls as the richest Jew in Hereford, and was a partner of Aaron of York. The duty on the estate of Leo of York (1244) was 7,000 marks; of David of Oxford (1246) 5,000. The heirs of Isaac of Norwich paid in 1241 as *arrears* £4,878. 7s. 10d. (Adler, loc. cit., but cf. above, pp. 33, 35).

lawyers might make out a case for complete confiscation on the ground of some alleged misdemeanour. If the deceased left infant children the king assumed the right of wardship as a matter of course, granting release only on the payment of a substantial fine and taking similar toll in the event of marriage. In the case of Aaron of York, Henry III avariciously began the exaction of the death duties before his demise; but this was an unprecedented abuse.

§ IV

Apart from this continual financial exploitation, the Jews of England were submitted to a number of petty vexations. At one time they were prevented from burying their dead until all claims upon the property were settled. (This abuse was specifically prohibited by the traditional charter of liberties.) They were not permitted to sell to Christians meat found ritually unfit for Jewish use. Synagogues, or even private houses, might be seized and destroyed because they were in proximity to Christian churches.[1] As in many places on the Continent—particularly in southern Europe—they were compelled on occasion to act as torturers and executioners, and in this capacity they incurred great obloquy at the close of the reign of John.[2]

In certain respects, on the other hand, they enjoyed unmistakable privileges.[3] If they were the property of the king and whatever they possessed or amassed belonged to him, it followed that he was vitally interested in protecting them and giving them facilities to carry on their business. They were the only persons in the country expressly authorized to lend money at interest. They could sue in the royal courts for recovery, and distrain upon their security with the assistance of the royal officers. They were empowered to travel about the country without interference, though not allowed to emigrate unless they had special licence. Up to the middle of the thirteenth century they might settle where they pleased, with the exception of the few towns from which they had been excluded. They were exempt from paying any custom or toll or any due on wine,

---

[1] C.R. 1265, p. 146; above, pp. 43, 76–77.

[2] For John's use of the Jews as executioners, cf. Chronicle of Mailross, *sub anno* 1216. This abuse obtained also in the Byzantine Empire, Corfu, Sicily, Spain.

[3] The 'Rightlessness of medieval English Jewry' is over-emphasized by F. Schechter in his article *J.Q.R.*, N.S., iv. 121–51.

in just the same way as the king himself whose chattels they
were.[1] They followed the royal Court and did business in the
royal ante-chamber. Though their conversion was encouraged,
the employment of force for that purpose was forbidden; and
the children of converts were allowed (nominally at least) to
choose freely what religion they desired to follow.[2] To counter-
balance the reduction of debts due to Jews, the king might order
a commission of 'honest and trustworthy men' to inquire into
the means of a recalcitrant debtor, and see whether he was in
fact unwilling or unable to pay what he owed. They were consistently protected against violence or attack. The sheriffs and
other royal officers always intervened to shield them when
necessary, and the royal castles were generally open for them to
take refuge in times of emergency. When in 1267 certain Jews
paid the king a fine in order to remain at Bridgnorth, they
stipulated that they were to be allowed the use of the castle in
time of danger.[3] In Winchester Castle their habitual refuge went
by the name of the Jews' Tower.[4]

In their external relations the Jews were governed in accordance with a somewhat indeterminate body of privileges, regulations, precedents, and customary law, probably never codified,
known as the Assize of Jewry.[5] They could look, as of right, to
the king for justice, which, as Edward I wrote,[6] 'we are bound to

[1] Towards the end of the thirteenth century, however, special tolls were
authorized to be charged at the newly constructed bridges—1d. for every Jew on
horseback and ½d. for one on foot: cf. P.R. 1279, p. 331 (Huntingdon); 1284, p. 116
(Moneford). For a dead Jew, the charge was 8d., for a burial in London 1½d.

[2] C.R. 1236, p. 358. In some cases converts reverted to Judaism even after
taking the preliminary steps in an ecclesiastical career (Lib.R. 1247, p. 133; C.R.
1245, p. 298). Most surprising of all is that a suit for defamation of character was
entertained on the grounds of an untrue allegation of baptism (C.R. 1288, p. 500).
Innocent IV's prohibition of baptism by force (1246) was sent to England as to
other countries (M. Stern, *Beiträge über die Stellung der Päpste zu den Juden*, ii. 45–46)
and generally obeyed; though see above, p. 79.

[3] Gross in *Papers A.J.H.E.*, p. 192. At such places as Oxford (P.R. 1259, p. 60)
and Norwich (Lib.R. 1236, p. 240) the offices of Constable of the Castle and
Keeper of the Jews were explicitly combined.

[4] Lib.R. 1249, pp. 235–6. The Tower may have been used for their periodical
imprisonments.

[5] *E.J.* i. 43, &c.; C.R. 1267, pp. 404–5; P.R. 1267, p. 154, and many other
contemporary sources use this phrase, which may conceivably refer to a written
body of regulations now lost. Its terms have been hypothetically reconstructed by
Jacobs, *J.A.E.*, pp. 329–37. Cf. now also Richardson, *J.A.K.*, pp. 176–197.

[6] *Gascon Rolls*, ii. 789 (28 December 1284). But Walter Map excluded Jews and
Cistercians from his oath to do justice to all men.

administer to Jews as well as to Christians'. Jurisdiction in cases in which they were involved was reserved to the Crown—a profitable monopoly, indeed, but one that must necessarily have saved them from much unfair discrimination.[1] In the law-courts the Jew enjoyed certain prescriptive rights. If he summoned a Christian for the payment of a debt, he was allowed to produce in evidence the agreement drawn up between them. In commercial suits a jury composed of twelve Jewish business men was assembled to inquire into the facts. Instead of bringing eleven 'compurgators' to attest to his character, a Jewish suspect who found it difficult to muster this number might purge himself by his bare oath while holding a Scroll of the Hebrew Pentateuch—a solemnity regarded with the utmost awe. If, on the other hand, he stood his trial, he enjoyed (except during an interlude after the accession of Edward I) the privilege of having a mixed jury, on which Jews and Christians were represented in equal numbers.

In certain cases (such as sacrilege, blasphemy, illicit connexion with a Christian woman, or striking a clerk) the Church claimed jurisdiction. This was hotly disputed by the royal courts, in which the accused might acquit himself if he produced a Christian and a Jew to testify to his innocence, and the question became part of the larger issues between the ecclesiastical and secular tribunals. However, in 1258, at the Council of Merton, it was decided that those who refused to plead before the Bishop's Court in such cases should be placed under an interdict, the faithful being forbidden under pain of excommunication to traffic, contract, or converse with them.[2] A social and commercial boycott of this sort was a very serious matter even for Jews, and it is probable that the attempt to reduce them to obedience was successful. In Oxford there was a prolonged dispute, regarding the jurisdiction in cases between students and their Jewish creditors, between the Constable of the Castle and the Chancellor of the University, but it was ultimately settled in favour of the latter.[3]

---

[1] In London, disputes between Jews and Christians regarding pledges up to the value of 40s. were adjudicated by the Constable of the Tower, who had custody of those committed to prison (C.R.R. 1261, p. 385).

[2] Above, p. 54–55.

[3] Trs. J.H.S.E. xiii. 302–3; Rashdall, Universities of Europe, ed. 1936, iii. 85–86; P.R. 1260, p. 105; 1261, p. 360; 1286, p. 236; Cal. Geneal. 1261, p. 97. Cf. Cal.

§ v

The main occupation of the Jews of England down to the last years—the pretext for the toleration which they enjoyed and the sole official *raison d'être* of their existence—was the profession of money-lending, forbidden by canon law yet indispensable for the exigencies of daily life. In this the smooth-tongued infidels were ubiquitous. There was no limit on the nature of the pledges which they were prepared to accept, from wearing apparel to agricultural produce, from jewellery to loads of hay, from books to knightly armour. They would make advances to the king on the security of the ferm of the shire and to the housewife on the security of her household pots.[1] The only restrictions legally imposed were with regard to blood-stained[2] cloth (which might have been acquired as the outcome of violent robbery) and church vessels used in Divine worship. However (as has been seen), the latter restriction was so far neglected under Henry II that they actually made loans on the security of holy relics.[3] Priests and religious houses raised money by pledging their Gospels, Decretals, and theological works.[4] There is nevertheless no basis for the statement that Oxford students pawned so many of their books with the Jews that they could not go on with their studies.[5] The most lucrative transactions, however,

*Inq. Misc.* i. 93 (1261): 'The Chancellor takes no fines from either scholars or Jews, but only nourishes peace and quiet between them, and affords speedy justice to both sides'. See now, more fully, Roth, *Oxford*, pp. 126–150.

[1] See Note V (*b*), pp. 277–8.

[2] 'Pannus sanguinolentus' cannot very well mean scarlet cloth, as has been suggested: for there was no reason why Jews should not have had this in their hands, and their dealings in it were in fact legally recognized (cf. Rigg, *P.E.J.*, p. 111).

[3] This was forbidden also by Jewish authorities from the second half of the twelfth century, whether from religious scruples or from nervousness (L. Finkelstein, *Jewish Self-Government in the Middle Ages*, New York, 1924, pp. 178, 188–9): it was thus a double offence.

[4] Loans to religious houses were restricted after 1188 when the Cistercians (previously excellent clients: see above, p. 15) were forbidden to pay usury or to borrow money from Jews in any circumstances (D. Knowles, *The Monastic Order in England*, Cambridge, 1940, p. 656).

[5] Cf. Roth, *Oxford*, p. 135. Rigg, *P.E.J.*, pp. 103, 114 gives an inventory of books deposited with certain Oxford Jewesses and an estimate of their values—an intimate glimpse into academic life. No less than fifty-four Latin books, sold (with one in Hebrew) for 9s. all told, were among the effects of Salum of Chippenham in 1285 (*Misc. J.H.S.E.* ii. 62). For books pledged with Jews, cf. my *Intellectual Activities*, pp. 7–11, and *Trs. J.H.S.E.* viii. 78–97.

were on the security of land or rent-charges, many houses falling into Jewish hands by this means, especially in London. This continued until late in the reign of Henry III, when the new restrictions virtually confined the erstwhile Jewish financier to pawnbroking.[1] So closely did the details of the process of lending money on landed security resemble the later system of mortgage that it is not wholly unreasonable to trace its origin to these Jewish transactions.

There was a considerable co-operative element in this activity. Not only did the greater of the financiers maintain local agents everywhere, but also—in part for convenience, in part for security, in part because of the difficulty of providing large sums at short notice—they worked in close collaboration, sometimes amounting almost to partnership, with one another. There thus came into existence an elaborate system of inter-related loan offices, always prepared to furnish reciprocal assistance for any lucrative transaction. The recurrence on the records of certain names, time after time—e.g. in the thirteenth century, those of Aaron of York, David of Oxford, Moses of London, or Hamo of Hereford—suggests that the most important business was carried on in the name of a few leading personalities, the capital used by whom represented the united riches of the entire nexus at the head of which they stood. Every son and son-in-law would in due course enter into the family business, each thus having at his command what appeared to his simple clients to be unlimited resources.[2]

The rate of interest was high, though it tended to decrease after one or two preliminary operations had instilled mutual confidence.[3] Exceptionally it would reach 60 per cent. or even 87 per cent., though there would be special reasons for so high a rate.[4] More usually it varied between one penny and two-pence in the pound weekly, or $21\frac{2}{3}$ to $43\frac{1}{3}$ per cent. per annum. This last figure, recognized as a fair charge in the twelfth century, was fixed under Henry III as the maximum rate even for

---

[1] See Note V (c), p. 278.

[2] There is a detailed analysis of various Jewish economic transactions in medieval England in Caro, op. cit. i. 313–49.

[3] Thus, in the second Hebrew bond that has been preserved (Davis, *Shetaroth*, pp. 3–4) a debt of £160 to Emma de Beaufoi is charged with a yearly interest during her lifetime of ten marks, or only $4\frac{1}{8}$ per cent.

[4] It is found in one case (ibid., p. 47) between Jews.

Oxford students.[1] In consideration of the extreme uncertainty that always prevailed, and the crushingly heavy dues exacted by the Crown, this was not excessive, even by modern standards.[2] Moreover, even in the case of Jewish loans, interest nominally began to run (at least on some occasions) only after the lapse of five or six months, so as to avoid the appearance of usury.[3] Compound interest on the other hand was strictly forbidden. This fact obviously caused a greater rapacity or greater disingenuousness on the part of the creditor, for whom a fresh operation with enhanced capital was far more profitable than a protraction of the old one. Notwithstanding all these restrictions, a sum lent out at the legal rate would double itself in a couple of years. This fact explains what appeared to be the unlimited resources of the Jews and their prodigious power of recovery.

After a year and a day, the Jewish creditor had the right to realize the pledge deposited with him. Sometimes, accompanied by the royal officers, he would go to distrain upon the property which was now legally his own; an operation which invariably led to resentment and sometimes to blows. In the case of real estate, he took formal 'seisin', and received the fealty of the tenants.[4] Since, however, a Jew could not hold land in fee[5] he would either sell his acquisition after holding it for a year to establish his claim, or else administer it and recoup himself out of the income. In the first part of the reign of Henry III the former process led to considerable transference of property, to the detriment in some cases of the feudal prerogatives of the Crown. As has been seen, the right to make loans on the security of real estate was from this period progressively restricted.[6] Even

---

[1] C.R. 1248, pp. 114, 216. That this was the economic rate is shown by the fact (Davis, pp. 72–75) that it was charged by a Jew to his own brother-in-law. In southern Europe, where exploitation of the Jews was less severe and security was generally greater, the standard rate was far less—23 per cent. to 37 per cent. in Italy, 20 per cent. in Spain. I do not believe that there is any recorded instance of a medieval Jew charging anything like the 266⅔ per cent. exacted in the south of France by the Gianfigliazzi firm of Florence: cf., however, *E.J.* i. 34.

[2] The English Money-Lending Acts of today regard 48 per cent. as a not unconscionable rate of interest.

[3] Cf. the instance in Rigg, *P.E.J.*, p. xix. It should be borne in mind that the taking of interest even by Jews was against the letter of canon law, since it was regarded as a *probrum contra homines* as well as *contra Deum*.

[4] Cf. the case described in C.R.R. 1208, p. 169.

[5] Bracton's *Note Book*, ed. Maitland, iii. 342 (§ 1376): but cf. above, pp. 10–11, 66.

[6] Above, pp. 64 ff. A case of 1305 reported in Horwood, *Year Books of XXXII–*

before this it had become usual, in disposing of property, to bar
subsequent re-transfer to Jews (as to the Church) which might
result in the loss of feudal rights by the tenant-in-chief; and over
a long period the insertion of the clause *exceptis locis religiosis et
judeismo* was customary in all such contracts.[1]

As elsewhere in Europe, the financial operations of the Jews
were not looked upon with unmitigated odium, the methods of
their irregular Christian competitors being even more disliked.
Robert Grosseteste, the great bishop of Lincoln, scornfully compared the fixed rate of interest charged by Jewish money-lenders
with the crafty system of the Cahorsins, who would make out a
bond for half as much again as the amount of the loan, payable
at the end of the year, thus exacting 50 per cent. interest for
however short a period.[2] Another method practised by the latter
was to lend the amount free of interest for the first three months,
but to charge as much as 50 per cent. for every three months
afterwards. It is noteworthy that, in the petition of the barons
presented in 1258 at Oxford, complaint was made of the grinding activities of the Christian usurers only: with respect to the
Jews the solitary abuse mentioned was that the great magnates
to whom they sold their debts abused their position, by absorb-
ing the pledged property into their demesne farms. In the thirteenth century the notorious Chamberlain of the Exchequer,
Adam de Stratton, made a practice of buying up Jewish debts
as extensively as possible, leaving them in the names of the
former principals. The latter thus became mere collectors on
behalf of a Gentile, Stratton being in effect one of the most important money-lenders of his day. Great magnates also bought
up debts owing to Jews which they exacted themselves—for

---

*XXXIII Edward I* (R.S.), p. 354, vividly illustrates a transaction on landed security.
Simon the Jew was to be repaid for a loan by two annuities, of £100 and 100 marks
respectively, secured on the income of a certain manor. When the arrears amounted
to £600 he sued for repayment 'in the Jewry', and was granted the manor in
demesne. He then made it over to an ancestor of William de la Souche, against
whom a writ of Cosinage was brought in 1305 on the grounds that the transference
had been illegal.

[1] The practice goes back at least to the beginning of the thirteenth century:
cf. an instance of 1204 in Jacobs, *J.A.E.*, p. 221. A similar provision begins to
make its appearance in Burgage tenements from 1228.

[2] M. Paris, *Chron. Maj.* v. 404. There was of course the great difference that the
Cahorsins were ostensibly merchants or money-changers, whereas the Jews were
deprived of any such protective camouflage.

example, William of Valence, Henry III's half-brother, or even the notorious Jew-baiter Gilbert Claire, earl of Gloucester.[1]

The economic function performed by the Jews could not easily have been dispensed with. Thus at Oxford, it was only after 1240, when the St. Frideswide's Chest and similar funds were founded, that the needy student had any alternative but recourse to them when he required assistance; and it was some time before the new public institutions were able to replace them adequately. For two major occupations of the Middle Ages—building and warfare—the assistance of the Jew was indispensable. The great English capitalists of the twelfth century, such as Aaron of Lincoln, were responsible in part for a good deal of the ecclesiastical construction which characterized that period. A Jew advanced money to the adventurers who raided Ireland in 1169; and the Third Crusade, from which the Jews of England suffered so terribly, was rendered possible largely by their monetary assistance. In normal times they were resorted to by the baronage for ready money to defray their 'scutage', whereby they acquitted themselves of their obligations to the Crown without direct military service. Jewish activities thus assisted in a certain measure in building up a strong central authority on the ruins of the feudal system. The unending expenses of medieval litigation could sometimes be met only with the help of some accommodating Jew. Thus at each stage of the long process between 1159 and 1163 by which the young aristocrat Richard of Anesty recovered his family lands—obtaining the king's writ from across the sea, sending his clerks to Rome, pleading in the various courts, having his writ of appeal sealed, making payments to the Exchequer, and every other point of the interminable procedure—it was to some Jewish financier that he turned for help.[2] And it was to Jews, too, that the king regularly resorted for crude gold for his personal use, so that in the thirteenth century they filled a function almost equivalent to that of official bullion-brokers to the Crown.[3]

---

[1] See Note V (d), p. 278.

[2] See Hubert Hall, *Court Life under the Plantagenets*, pp. 36–37 and 204 (with plate facing); Palgrave, *Commonwealth*, II. xxiv–xxvii.

[3] C.R. 1250, p. 255; Lib.R. 1250, p. 272. Jews could not, however, purchase gold bullion without licence (Pp.R. 1189–90, p. 110). In C.R. 1266, p. 208 there is an instance of a comparatively advanced banking transaction carried out for the Crown by Hagin of London, who was instructed to make certain payments out of the money received by him on the king's behalf.

From the period of the reorganization under Richard I these activities were carefully regulated and controlled. In each of the major communities of the country a so-called *archa* or chirograph-chest was established. This was administered by four 'chirographers', of whom two were Jews and two Christians, assisted by two copyists and a Clerk of the Escheats. The chirographers were chosen by mixed juries summoned by the sheriffs, consisting of Jews and Christians in equal number, and on election were required to find sureties for their good conduct.[1] In their presence all contracts between Christians and Jews had to be drawn up and registered.[2] These were in the form of an indenture, the bond being written on a strip of parchment, together with a duplicate copy or memorandum to the same effect. The two sections would be divided by cutting in an irregular line through the word *Chirographum* written in bold characters across the entire width. The original was sealed and delivered to the creditor, the duplicate retained by the debtor or deposited in the *archa* constituting a safeguard against fraudulent alteration.[3] In the middle of the thirteenth century the practice was altered, the sealed part being retained by the chirographers and counterparts issued to both of the parties concerned. Each transaction was, moreover, recorded in three special rolls—one kept by the clerks, one by the Christian chirographers, and one by their Jewish associates (in this case, in Hebrew).[4] Later, yet a fourth was prepared, for consultation in case of need by the Clerk of the Escheats. The presence of a majority of the officials was necessary for any valid transaction.

On the repayment of the loan the Jew would make out an acquittance. This was called by the Hebrew term *Shetar*, which, under its Latin form *Starrum*, passed into general currency, and may possibly have given its title to the notorious Star Chamber

[1] C.R. 1265, p. 42. The appointment seems to have been regarded as a burdensome one: cf. (P.R. 1260, p. 129) a grant for life to a burgess of Bristol that he should not be made a King's Cofferer of the Jews against his will.

[2] For a day-to-day account of the activities of the Norwich chirographers in 1224–6 see 'The Norwich Day Book' (*Trs. J.H.S.E.* v. 243–75).

[3] It has been conjectured (F. A. Lincoln, *The Starra*, Oxford, 1939) that the conventional English system of duplication owed its origin to the practice of the Exchequer of the Jews, but in fact it goes back to the twelfth century.

[4] C.R. 1252, p. 164: cf. K. Scott, 'The Jewish *Arcae*', in *Cambridge Law Journal*, x. 446–55.

at Westminster.[1] These documents were generally written in Hebrew with a Latin transcript, sometimes in Latin alone—in one or two instances in Hebrew characters—occasionally in Norman French. They were signed by the creditor in Hebrew, and his seal was appended (English restrictions in this respect did not go quite as far as those in France, where after 1223 the use of official Jewish seals ended). A receipt of this nature entitled the debtor to the cancellation and delivery of the *pes*, or foot, of the original bond of indebtedness. However, from the middle of the thirteenth century at least, no acquittance was valid unless enrolled at the Exchequer of the Jews—a regulation which incidentally brought considerable profit to the Treasury. Sometimes the receipts would be given in the form of a wooden 'tally' with notches and cuts indicating the amount, which was split longitudinally so as to make a duplicate record. A large number of these, recording Jewish transactions of payments, are still preserved.[2]

As co-ordinating authority over the provincial *archae*, the Exchequer of the Jews (*Scaccarium Judaeorum*), established under Richard I, continued its activities in its official chamber on the west side of Westminster Hall.[3] Its functions were threefold. In the first place there was the financial side, as it supervised the collection of tallages and other income derived from Jewry.[4] Secondly, it was an administrative body, acting as the channel of communication between the Crown and the Jewish communities, all new members of which had to present themselves before it for enrolment. Finally, it was a judicial body, deciding in disputes involving Jews or those which arose, directly or indirectly, out of transactions between them and Gentiles.[5] It

---

[1] Its later stellar decoration may have derived from the name, not vice versa.

[2] *Bibl.* A.4. 11.

[3] C.R. 1235, p. 100. At times the Exchequer of the Jews followed the royal Court about the country; thus in 1277 it sat in Shrewsbury Abbey (*Select Cases before the King's Bench, Edward I* (Selden Society, 1938), II. lxxiii f.).

[4] See Note V (*e*), pp. 278–9

[5] Cf. C.R. 1257, p. 23: the Justices in Eyre are instructed that Jews are to plead and be sued only before the Justices of the Jews. In London, however, cases regarding real estate were assigned in 1250 to the Mayor's court, and later on were tried in Chancery; it was only after 1271 that they again returned to the cognizance of the Exchequer of the Jews (Rigg, *P.E.J.*, p. xxii). In 1276 the London Jewry purchased exemption from the jurisdiction of the Justices in Eyre by a payment of £50. It was permissible for Jews to be represented before the court by an attorney (*narrator*; cf. Rigg, *P.E.J.*, p. 54).

had cognizance ultimately in all cases in which property once in Jewish hands was concerned. Thus it played quite an important part in the judicial administration of the country, sometimes in matters in which Jews were not immediately implicated, a large part of its business dealing with land transferred to fresh ownership because of the activities of Jewish financiers.

At its head, as we have seen, were the Wardens or Justices of the Jews (*Custodes Judaeorum, Justitiarii ad custodiam Judaeorum assignati*, &c.) varying in number between two and five. Sometimes, though not always, there was nominally included among them the *Presbyter Judaeorum*, who attended their sessions as technical adviser in specifically Jewish matters and kept certain records.[1] If he were unable to be present, he had to appoint a deputy.[2] One of the Jewish chirographers of the London *archa* generally acted as clerk of the court, while there was also a Jewish escheater to supervise the liquidation of those estates which fell into the king's hands, and an assessor to collect the *aurum reginae*, of 10 per cent. on the renewal of leases and granting of charters, which was due to the queen.[3] The Justices of the Jews were, however, subordinated, on certain occasions to a higher official more directly amenable to control, to whom the king 'committed the superior care of his Jewry'.[4]

The careful system of recording all operations carried on by Jews, to which the Jewish Exchequer owed its origin, was of considerable importance. Through this it became possible for the wealth of the financiers to be assessed and taxed without any possibility of evasion. Moreover, henceforth the levies were not necessarily paid in cash. When it was desired to exact a new tallage, the *archae* could be impounded and bonds to the desired

---

[1] For the *Presbyter Judaeorum* see above, pp. 30–31. In 1249 the arch-presbyter Elias le Eveske and Aaron fil' Abraham, another prominent financier, were given equal rights at the Exchequer, both having the status of Justice of the Jews (C.R. 1249, p. 179). It does not seem to have been an unprofitable office: *E.J.* i. 71. Locally, the term presbyter denoted purely synagogal functions: Stokes, *Studies*, p. 22, and Richardson, *J.A.K.*, pp. 121–4.

[2] C.R. 1243, p. 51.

[3] C.R. 1252, p. 271. There were also various subordinate officials such as the sergeant: the Exchequer of the Jews claimed jurisdiction in all cases where they were concerned.

[4] Above, pp. 49, 60. That there was a branch of the Jewish Exchequer in Ireland, as usually stated, is not the case, though Peter des Rivaulx was appointed in 1232 to custody of the Irish Jews, who were instructed to be 'intendent and respondent' to him: see above, pp. 49, 92.

amount sent to the Exchequer in a closed pyx.[1] Ultimately the
Crown preferred to levy its dues in the form of well-secured
debts rather than promissory notes which might not be met
punctually. Again, it was by no means unusual for bonds of
indebtedness to change hands, by purchase or otherwise. They
served almost as bank-notes, and their existence considerably
increased the available currency.[2] It is not difficult to imagine
that a Jew of London, whose business took him to Exeter, would
purchase from one of his co-religionists a well-secured debt
registered in the local *archa*. The bond relating to this (suitably
endorsed) he would take with him to cash or to discount upon
his arrival. In this way the Jews stimulated the development of
the credit system of the country as a whole.

It is out of the question that the entirety of English Jewry can
have been engaged in the predominant occupation of money-
lending. The communal magnates were certainly financiers.
Dependent upon them, however, directly or indirectly, there
would necessarily be numerous subordinates—agents and clerks
to help in their business, synagogal officials to carry out divine
worship, scribes to draw up their business documents or to copy
out their literary and devotional compositions, attendants to
perform the household services forbidden by the Church to
Gentiles. No roll of the community of London, in the twelfth
century, contains more than forty names, but it can hardly be
doubted that this represents only a minority of the total number
of heads of family. Some of the great financiers—Jacob of
London or Benedict of York—seem to have maintained numerous household staffs. Aaron of Lincoln and his homonym, Aaron
of York, had their agents all over England.

Though the overwhelming majority of the documents at our
disposal deal with the financiers, a minority was engaged in
other professions. The records furnish the names of at least
eighteen physicians. We meet with one even at a small place
such as Lynn, where his practice must have been almost exclusively amongst the general population: while at Norwich, in
the thirteenth century, the profession was hereditary in one
family.[3] Master Elias (Elijah Menahem) of London, just before

[1] *E.J.* ii. 54.
[2] The Lincoln *archa* contained in 1240 bonds to the value of £1,000.
[3] A deed of 1266 published by Davis, *Shetaroth*, pp. 132–5, introduces us to the

the Expulsion, enjoyed such reputation that he was summoned by the Count of Hainault to go overseas to attend upon him.[1] An occasional Jewish goldsmith is encountered, including one in the service of King John.[2] If the admission of Benedict fil' Abraham to the merchant-gild at Winchester in 1268 was not an empty compliment, it is obvious that he must have engaged in trade.[3] At Norwich we encounter Diaia le Scalarius ('the ladder-maker'), and at Gloucester Abraham le Skirmiseur, or fencing-master.[4] The money-lenders, too, might be involved in commercial operations when the pledges in their hands—especially jewels and luxury articles—remained unredeemed. Some persons, up to 1271 at least, could have lived comfortably from their rent-rolls, though from the close of the reign of Henry III there was an increasing tendency to confiscate all real estate in a Jew's hands on his death.[5] Hebrew sources indicate that the Jews in England, as elsewhere, were engaged to some extent in peddling, particularly of cloth;[6] and they certainly imported wine on a large scale, and not only for their own use.[7] After the

*herbier* of Solomon the physician, son of Isaac the physician, in Saddlegate-street, Norwich. (Dr. Charles Singer informs me that this is the first private herb-garden of the Middle Ages of which he knows.) It is to be presumed that Jacob le Mire (*E.J.* iii. 29, &c.), Leo le Mire (*Misc. J.H.S.E.* ii. 63), and Salle le Mire (Davis, op. cit., p. 391) were also physicians. One chirurgeon, Sampson of London, is encountered (*E.J.* ii. 14). See details in my *Intellectual Activities*, pp. 65–69.

[1] *Bibl.* A.4. 47.

[2] Above, p. 32. (There were also several converts engaged in this calling: cf. Rigg, *P.E.J.*, p. 113, and Adler, *J.M.E.*, pp. 293, 296.) The fact that several persons engaged in other professions than money-lending are mentioned only once in the records makes it probable that others are not mentioned at all—an important factor in considering the composition of medieval English Jewry.

[3] Below, p. 119.

[4] *Trs. J.H.S.E.* v. 256–7: C.R. 1250, p. 329. A contemporary Jewish fencing-master in Germany is mentioned in the *Responsa* of Meir of Rothenburg (1215–93), ed. Berlin 1891, § 335. The teaching of fencing, as of dancing, was one of the characteristic professions of Italian Jews at the close of the Middle Ages. In Bristol, a family went by the name of *Furmager* (Adler, *J.M.E.*, p. 196). They may have been the accredited cheese-makers to the Jewish community, who would not eat cheese made by Gentiles without supervision. The mysterious 'Jewish Lawyers' who figure in Jacobs, *J.A.E.*, *passim*, should be 'law-worthy Jews' (*Judaei legales*), and 'le Scalarius' above is a misreading for 'le Fraunceys'. [5] See Note V (*f*), p. 279.

[6] *Trs. J.H.S. E.* xii. 112. This has an important bearing on the problem of the Jewish population in England in the Middle Ages: the official records at our disposal relate almost exclusively to the financiers. For the general question see now P. Elman's study, 'Jewish Trade in 13th-Century England' in *Historia Judaica*, i (New York, 1939), pp. 91–104.

[7] Above, pp. 102–3; C.R. 1243, p. 111; Adler, *J.M.E.*, p. 135. The importation of wine by Aaron of York was not apparently a unique case, as Jews were

*Statutum de Judeismo*, as has been seen, the Jews tended to engage especially in the corn and wool trades. A legend of some antiquity preserves the name even of a Jewish artist, Marlibrun of Billingsgate, who, like his contemporaries in Spain, did not scruple to paint holy images.[1] Several suggestively Biblical names, such as Isaac of York, figure on the coinage of the twelfth century as minters, in which calling a Canterbury convert was certainly engaged at this time.[2]

Jewesses played a significant part in economic life. Every roll of English Jewry mentions the names of women who contributed important sums to the Exchequer—not always the widows of dead financiers, but frequently wives or perhaps even spinsters in business on their own account. Belaset of Wallingford, and Licoricia, widow of David of Oxford, were among the most active English financiers of the thirteenth century. Even Margaret, daughter of Jurnet of Norwich and a wealthy heiress,[3] is found engaging in independent business transactions. Such activity was assisted by the conspicuously high judicial and social status of women in Jewish life, which compared very favourably with that of the ordinary Englishwoman of the period.

## § VI

While completely subject to the Crown in external matters, the Jewish communities of the kingdom enjoyed amongst themselves a considerable degree of autonomy. As elsewhere, they exercised the right of levying domestic taxation.[4] Their communal regulations, licensed by the Crown on the payment of the inevitable

occasionally enjoined to furnish various royal nominees with a supply (C.R. 1237, p. 409), or even allowed to reckon the value of wines taken for the king's use as part of their tallage dues (C.R. 1272, pp. 488, 493-4, 498-9). Nevertheless, an English Rabbi of the thirteenth century deplored the absence of wine in England (*Steinschneider Festschrift*, Leipzig, 1896, p. 207). See also below, p. 119, n. 1.

[1] R. Newcourt, *Repertorium ecclesiasticum parochiale Londinense* (London, 1708), i. 240, 765; *Bibl.* A.4. 24; *Trs. J.H.S.E.* xiv. 93-94.

[2] Jacobs, *J.A.E.*, pp. 259-60; Adler, *J.M.E.*, p. 65. (On the Continent Jews often acted as minters.)

[3] Her mother was not, however, a Christian, as long believed: see above, p. 10. The role of the Jewish woman in medieval England is described in Adler, *J.M.E.*, pp. 17-45.

[4] The organization and machinery of this are not made clear by the records at our disposal. We read, however, in a Hebrew deed (Davis, *Shetaroth*, p. 98) of a 'Synagogue Tax' levied on real estate.

fee, were enforced even by the civil power. Domestic disputes
were decided by their own authorities in accordance with Talmudic law—a right envied by the Church which was apparently
granted by Henry II, confirmed by John, and utilized when
convenient by the authorities. On one occasion, for example,
application was made to the *Capitula Judeorum* for a ruling
upon the vexed question whether it was permissible for one Jew
to take usury from another,[1] and on another, they were allowed
to decide that a person who did not intimate his religious allegiance immediately he was questioned could no longer be considered a Jew.[2] The Jewish courts were regularly resorted to for
decision in matrimonial cases, and institutions of Jewish civil
law (such as the right of a widow to a prior claim on her late
husband's chattels for the repayment of her dowry[3] or the
Rabbinic institution of usucaption or prescriptive right)[4] were
unquestioningly admitted by the authorities. However (by a
sort of counterpart of the law of *praemunire*, which forbade recourse to ecclesiastical tribunals abroad), steps were taken to
keep such jurisdiction within the realm and to prevent appeal
from the English Rabbis to authorities on the Continent.[5] This
judicial autonomy was qualified only in cases of the so-called
'pleas of the Crown' (homicide, assault, rape, housebreaking,
larceny, arson, treasure trove, and mayhem) which always had
to be tried before the royal justices. In many cases an exclusively
Jewish jury of twelve persons was sworn, it being presumed that
they would have a greater knowledge of the facts.

[1] Pp.R. 1193, p. 117. The decision is not recorded, but was presumably in the negative, unless the English Rabbis were in violent disagreement with their continental contemporaries. Nevertheless, it is obvious from Rigg, *P.E.J.*, pp. 65–66, and Davis, *Shetaroth*, pp. 47 ff., 63 ff., &c., that legal fictions (e.g. the nominal interposition of a Christian intermediary) were used in order to evade the legal prohibition.

[2] Rigg, *P.E.J.*, pp. 82, 95–96. Anglo-Jewish Rabbinical conventions and ordinances may be inferred from *Shetaroth*, p. 34.

[3] The unconverted wife of a converted Jew, Augustine of Canterbury, went so far as to assert (though unsuccessfully) her dower-right according to Jewish law over a house which he had made over to the abbey of St. Augustine's, and which had been subsequently purchased by another Jew (C.R. 1234, p. 555; cf. C.R. 1265, p. 66).

[4] C.R. 1252, p. 110. In the code of Mordecai ben Hillel (thirteenth century) there is an instance of the acceptance by a Jewish court as evidence of death of the testimony of a thief who, before execution, confessed to the murder some time previously of a Jew who was taking £10 from a certain Judith in Lincoln (cf. Davis, *Shetaroth*, pp. 298 ff.) to her brother in York.    [5] *Bibl.* A.4. 23.

All legal documents between Jew and Jew were drawn up in Hebrew, and according to the Rabbinic formulae. Their wills, made in accordance with the Talmudic prescriptions, were recognized as valid by the courts, while if a person died intestate, his property was divided among his heirs in accordance with Jewish practice.[1] The ultimate sanction for the enforcement of internal regulations was that of excommunication, which was recognized by and on occasion turned to the profit of the Crown. (As we have seen, a person who remained under the ban for more than forty days had his property confiscated to the exchequer.) More than once licence was given for putting under the ban those who failed to pay the amounts promised for the upkeep of the cemetery in London, with the proviso that any eventual profits should accrue to the king.[2] The Jews of every city claimed a voice in determining the composition of the community. Thus, in 1266, those of Canterbury bound themselves by oath not to allow any 'liar, improper person, or slanderer' from another town to come to live there, and stipulated what should be done in case some undesirable immigrant were provided with royal licence.[3]

The internal organization of English Jewry in the Middle Ages was very similar to that which prevailed elsewhere in Europe. Life centred about the synagogues (*scholae judaeorum*),[4] of which, down to the close of the thirteenth century, all the important communities had more than one. These were mostly small establishments, often maintained by wealthy magnates in their own houses.[5] Here, as places of general assembly,

---

[1] *Cal. Inq. P.M.* i. 242. The enforcement of Hebrew agreements by the civil authority was ensured by stipulating a forfeit to the king, &c., in case of non-fulfilment.

[2] Rymer, *Foedera*, i. 274; P.R. 1250, p. 72.

[3] Adler, *J.M.E.*, p. 83. The right of the Jewish community to control immigration by means of the Settlement Ban (*Herem haYishub*) was a regular institution of Rabbinic law, and it is clear that the issue on this occasion was the ratification of such an agreement by the civil power: cf. *Misc. J.H.S.E.* iii. 76–79. See also P.R. 1262, p. 205, for a case of the expulsion from Bedford of the rivals of a Jewish woman financier.

[4] It must be pointed out that the term *schola*, &c., applied to the synagogue has no essential educational significance, indicating nothing more than the meeting-place of a corporate body: cf. Blondheim, *Les Parlers judéo-romans et la Vetus Latina* (Paris, 1925), pp. 106–8. From Archbishop Peckham's letter, *Epistolae*, ii. 407 (in which he speaks of the synagogues *quas vocant scholas*) it would appear that the former London synagogues were decorated with mural paintings.

[5] See Note V (g), p. 279.

communal meetings would be held, excommunications fulminated, and announcements made. The synagogue formed also the
channel of communication with the civil authorities, necessary
proclamations being made in it, both in Latin and in Hebrew,[1]
on two or three Sabbaths in succession. Inquiries were made in
it, too, concerning outstanding debts. If a man were banished
he had to 'abjure the realm' there publicly, holding a Scroll of
the Law in his arms.

At the head of the community (*Universitas* or *Communitas
Judaeorum*) of each place stood its *baillivus*, corresponding to the
Hebrew *parnas* ('Pernaz' in the records). The *gabbai*, or Treasurer,
is also mentioned frequently. The salaried officials included
the *shohet* or ritual butcher, the *hazan* or reader ('Chanteur',
'Chapeleyn', 'Capellanus'), and presumably the sexton.[2] The
institution of the professional Rabbi had barely made its
appearance, though 'masters of the Jewish law' (well-known
business magnates in some cases, as well as scholars) were to be
found in most places.[3] The authority they exercised was princi-
pally moral, though none the less effective: yet they claimed the
power to inflict physical punishment on stubborn members of
their flock.[4] England had its representatives of the German
ascetico-mystical school of *Hasidim* (literally 'pious'), who, in
the twelfth and thirteenth centuries, are found in more than one
centre.[5] The average English Jew of the Middle Ages followed

[1] i.e. Judaeo-French?

[2] For these officials see Davis, *Shetaroth*, p. 129; *E.J.* i. 145; Stokes, *Studies*,
chapters v–viii. That *Capellanus = Hazan* is evident from a Northampton deed
(*Trs. J.H.S.E.* xv. 161) but Stokes considers that it may have become an hereditary surname in view of the fact that persons so described were commonly
engaged in financial transactions, and in one instance even in a forest offence.
The records also mention the *Sopher* or Scribe (Davis, p. 356: equivalent to the
*Scriveneur* or *Escrivein*) and also the *Pointur* (probably identical with the *Nakdan*
who punctuated codices after they had been written: see Note V (*k*), p. 280, and
the discussion in Adler, *J.M.E.*, p. 199); but these cannot very well have been
full-time employees. The offices are now discussed by Richardson, *J.A.K.*, pp.
285–92.

[3] A Canterbury Jew signs himself, however, 'Jehozadak son of Jehozadak,
Judge and Teacher' (Davis, *Shetaroth*, p. 338), and a Lincoln scholar 'Abraham
Hayim son of Joseph, Teacher' (Adler, *J.M.E.*, p. 45, correcting Davis, pp. 296,
302) apparently indicating Rabbis by profession.

[4] *J.Q.R.*, N.S., xix. 35. (This can hardly imply the pillory.)

[5] Cf. Simeon, murdered in Germany in 1146 (above, p. 10); Joseph of Bungay
(*Shetaroth*, p. 5); and Abraham, father of Aaron of London (Adler, *J.M.E.*, p. 269).
The term in the twelfth and thirteenth centuries clearly meant more than 'the
pious' in the conventional sense.

the hardly less strenuous path of normal observance, though there were occasional instances of laxity. The synagogue ritual was very similar to that followed in France, though not lacking independent features.[1]

Up to the reaction at the close of the twelfth century the Jews seem to have lived on tolerable terms with their neighbours. They discussed religious questions together in a friendly spirit. To the surprise of Jewish authorities they drank together (the specially prepared wine for their use being imported normally from France or Germany).[2] They rode together on journeys.[3] No objection was raised even to their presence in churches and monasteries, where they sent their chattels confidently for safe keeping.[4] They might enter into arrangements with their debtors even in the ante-chamber of the Archbishop of York.[5] Irregular sexual intercourse was by no means unknown. Converts to Judaism included clerics as well as laymen, some of whom apparently escaped untoward consequences.[6] Down to the very end the wheel did not turn full circle. It was possible for a Jew of Oxford to find twelve burghers to testify that he had been 'brought up amongst them from infancy, and bore himself ever leally in all manner of lealty'.[7] In Winchester Benedict fil' Abraham was admitted in 1268 into 'full membership of the liberty of the city, and citizenship, and gild rights in the Merchant Gild, with all the privileges in the said liberty'.[8] A Jewess

---

[1] It ts described, from a unique manuscript, by D. Kaufmann in *J.Q.R.* iv. 20 ff.

[2] Jacobs, *J.A.E.*, p. 269; C.R. 1280, p. 60 (importation from Gascony of seven tuns of 'good wine made according to the Jewish rite'). *Tosaphoth* on *Aboda Zara*, f. 61 (*Hisronoth haShas*, § 127, p. 39a, omitted in modern editions): 'The wine bought by Gentiles in Germany, which is exported to England under seal in order to be sold there to Jews, was permitted for consumption by Rabbi Jacob of Ramerupt towards the end of his days' [notwithstanding the fact that it was not under continual surveillance].

[3] See Note V (*h*), p. 279.

[4] Above, p. 23 &c.: C.R. 1205, p. 20b. On one occasion the king ordered the prior of Norwich to receive into his custody the tallies and charters of the local magnate, Isaac (C.R. 1223, p. 523); but compulsion was usually unnecessary.

[5] C.R. 1201, pp. 389–90.

[6] Above, pp. 41, 83.

[7] *E.J.* i. 88.

[8] P.R. 1268, p. 223. It is possible that this exceptional concession was due to Benedict's patron, the papal legate; for two years later the relations between Benedict and his neighbours were such that the king had to take the Winchester Jews into his protection (ibid., 1270, p. 417). Owing to a misunderstanding of the records, Benedict received posthumous promotion, at the hands of recent historians, to the dignity of mayor of Southampton. Cf. now Adler in *Misc. J.H.S.E.* iv. 1–8.

of the same city, in 1258, bequeathed a ring to the king, as though he were the most benevolent of monarchs.[1] Conversely, the royal charity extended even to a Jewish cripple.[2] In 1277 there was a famous case at Colchester, when Jews and Christians were arraigned together for the offence of chasing a deer through the town.[3] As late as 1286, when the gloomiest period in the history of English Jewry had dawned, a wealthy financier of Hereford invited his Christian friends to his daughter's wedding, which was celebrated with great pomp. Bishop Swinfield, aghast at such conviviality, prohibited attendance under pain of excommunication, but even this was an insufficient deterrent.[4] Down to the eve of the Expulsion, despite the attempt to enforce segregation, Jewish visitors to London would lodge with their attendants and horses at the houses of Christians.[5] During the unrest at the time of the Barons' Wars they were frequently able to take refuge in the houses of their neighbours, or deposit property with them. Sometimes, indeed, the latter would place it with their own in church, where it would be safe from molestation.[6] When order was restored, it was a friendly Gentile who was sent abroad to bring the infant son of the martyred Cok fil' Aaron back to England.[7] Generally speaking, crimes of violence against the Jews were punished like any others, though the system of frank-pledge (or mutual responsibility among members of a tithing) did not apply in the case of members of the Jewish community.[8]

Inevitably the English Jews shared the prejudices and

---

[1] C.R. 1258, p. 229. The bequest may not have been spontaneous; a legacy to the pope was mandatory, later on, for the Jews of Avignon.

[2] C.R. 1228, p. 65.

[3] J. Jacobs, *Jewish Ideals*, pp. 225–33; it was this episode which gave the scribe the opportunity to make his caricature of 'Aaron fil' Diaboli'.

[4] W. W. Capes, *Registrum R. de Swinfield*, pp. 120, 121; above, p. 77. The account of 'displays of silk and cloth of gold, horsemanship or an equestrian procession, sport and minstrelsy' seems exaggerated.

[5] Rigg, *P.E.J.*, pp. 58–59. A decree of Edward I (C.R. 1281, p. 176) as well as a Canterbury anecdote of the previous century (Jacobs, *J.A.E.*, p. 153) seem to point to the existence of inns (*hospicia*) kept by Jews, in which Christians were henceforth forbidden to lodge.

[6] Cf. (*E.J.* i. 133) the case of Aaron of Sittingbourne. Not only did the townspeople look after his property, but they consented to surrender him only when de Montfort's followers threatened to burn their houses.

[7] Cf. the extremely interesting details in Rigg, *P.E.J.*, pp. 73–76.

[8] 'Nec fuit in franco plegio, quia illud accidit in Judaismo' (*Munimenta Gildhallae, Liber Albus*, i. 99 (1237–8)).

superstitions of their environment. Eminent scholars, such as
Rabbi Elijah Menahem of London, dabbled in magical prescriptions for medical purposes, or to save houses from fire; and the
imprisonment of a demon in a signet-ring was an achievement
credited to one English Jew of the period. In cases of sickness
they might resort to the care of Christian women who specialized
in charms, though it was more common for Christians to consult
them regarding their future fate and actions.[1] They were quite
prepared to regard barnacle geese as a vegetable product,
though not with quite the same credulity as their neighbours,
who, in controversy with them, adduced the same mythical
creature as proof of the possibility of the Virgin Birth.[2]

The standard of conduct amongst English Jews was not
supernaturally perfect. The majority of the offences encountered amongst them were naturally connected with their business,[3] though there can be no doubt that at the close some were
driven to the sordid offence of coin-clipping. Crimes of violence
were not rare, the medieval English Jew not being by any means
a paragon of meekness, whether his own co-religionists or
Gentiles—even soldiers[4]—were involved. We find a few cases
of murder[5] and some trespasses against the Forest Laws.[6] Sexual
offences are not common, and the most circumstantial allegation
on record failed to result in a conviction.[7] Though the Assize of
Arms deprived them after 1181 of the possession of weapons,
some English Jews had no objection to settling their differences

[1] *J.Q.R.*, N.S., xix. 32; *Trs. J.H.S.E.* v. 156 (quoting Harley MS. 12 (24),
ff. 314–17); Jacobs, *J.A.E.*, p. 153; Wilkins, *Concilia*, i. 671 (Decree of Synod of
Worcester, 1240).

[2] Jacobs, *J.A.E.*, pp. 54, 92–93. For Jewish credulity on the subject see *Trs.
J.H.S.E.* xii. 110.

[3] Jews were, however, sometimes the victims rather than the perpetrators of
business offences: cf. *Gascon Rolls*, 1254, § 3863.

[4] P.R. 1182, p. 165; 1183, p. 142. Cf. P.R. 1278, pp. 287, 290, for a brawl
between Jewish and Christian women, and Rigg, *P.E.J.*, pp. 11–12, for a lively
account of an episode at Warwick in 1244, when a Jewess was stated to have
'eaten the mouth and ears' of another. There is a hardly credible story (C.R.
1248, p. 108) of a riot of the Oxford Jews against the house of Master John Maunsell, Henry III's minister.

[5] See Note V (i), pp. 279–80.

[6] Above, p. 120: cf. also P.R. 1201, p. 93; 1268, p. 78.

[7] Rigg, *P.E.J.*, p. 104.
Details of an extraordinary episode are given in *E.J.* iii. 311–12—the case of
Sampson fil' Sam', who assumed the habit of a Minorite Friar and parodied
Christianity. The punishment was even more picturesque than the crime.

by the ordeal of battle, like true sons of their age.[1] That they were
not lacking in military proficiency is apparent from the fact that
a French Jew named Hanuchin was given special licence to live
in England because of the good service he had done during the
wars in Normandy under King John.[2] They seem to have been
found particularly suitable as cross-bowmen and sergeants-at-
arms, who needed special technical training and did not form
part of the feudal levy; and several converts from Judaism are
found serving in these capacities.[3]

As was customary at the period betrothals were arranged
between children too young to undertake the responsibilities of
marriage, the ceremony being deferred as long as four years
after the preliminaries.[4] After the wedding the young couple
would live in the house of the bride's father for a year or more,
the latter undertaking to provide them with food and clothing,
to discharge any tallage which might be imposed during that
period, and even to engage a teacher with whom his son-in-
law might continue to study.[5] If a girl were left an orphan
her brothers would bind themselves by deed to find her a
'becoming and pleasant spouse' and to give her an adequate
dowry, as well as to make proper provision for their mother.[6]
The marriage settlement made by the bridegroom would normally amount to as much as £100 'according to the custom of
the Isle'—a striking commentary upon the general prosperity of
the community.[7]

The Jews were pioneers in the art of domestic architecture.
Their high standard of comfort, their foreign connexions and

---

[1] C.R.R. 1194, p. 79.                                   [2] P.R. 1204, p. 47.

[3] Adler, *J.M.E.*, pp. 294–7, and idem in *J.C.*, 5 Aug. 1898. It is not perhaps
a coincidence that the maintenance of cross-bowmen was regarded as a special
obligation of the Jewish community: cf. Adler, *J.M.E.*, p. 141; *Trs. J.H.S.E.* xiii.
308, and other cases. For the alleged manufacture of Greek fire by the London
Jews see above, p. 61. The name Miles, occasionally found among medieval
English Jewry, does not indicate 'the Knight', as has been stated, but is clearly a
variant normally of the Hebrew *Meir*. Cf. however 'Benedictus miles' and 'Benedict
le Chivaler', apparently identical.

[4] Davis, *Shetaroth*, p. 299.

[5] Ibid., pp. 33–35.                                     [6] Ibid., pp. 43–46.

[7] Ibid., p. 302. It is possible that, as in northern France (cf. Tosaphoth, *Ketuboth*
54*b*; *J.Q.R.* N.S., xxx (1940), pp. 221 ff.), this was a nominal figure; yet, although
the daughters of other families received only ten marks (Davis, op. cit., pp. 43–46)
or £40 (C.R. 1237, p. 464), we have a case (P.R. 1250, p. 81; C.R. 1251, p. 420)
of the official allocation of a dowry of as much as £200.

experience, and above all their need of security, all combined
to bring this about. They were apparently among the first to
introduce the use of stone houses for ordinary occupation into
England, and in the capital their residences were sufficiently
desirable to be taken over by some of the wealthiest among the
nobility. Throughout the country the Jews long remained
associated in popular lore with certain ancient dwelling-houses,
for no apparent reason other than their solidity of construction.
The authentic examples at Lincoln are the oldest private residences in this country still in occupation.[1]

Generally, the infidels lived by themselves in a special street,
even before the canon of the Third Lateran Council which made
it obligatory. This was universally known as the Jewry (from the
Old French *juierie*), a term which continues to the present time
as a street-name in several of the older English cities. This was
not a Ghetto in the technical sense, nor were the Jews confined
to it by law. In York, indeed, they were specifically allowed to
go where they pleased, even so late as 1278;[2] and the great
magnates had their residences in the heart of the city—in
Micklegate, Feltergayle, and elsewhere—as well as in the main
Jewish quarter in Coney Street. Lincoln Jewry had its centre in
one of the principal roads leading up to the Minster, where the
architectural relics to which reference has been made may still
be seen. In London the original Jewry extended from Cheapside
across Lothbury to what is now Coleman Street, and into the
adjacent Ironmonger Lane, where the first synagogue was situated. At a later period they seem to have been crowded out of
this area, the 'Old Jewry' (as it is still termed) being superseded
even before the Expulsion of 1290. The Church made a point of
establishing centres of activity amongst the infidel (the Hospital
of St. Thomas of Acre, or Acon, on the site of the birthplace
of Thomas Becket, and two ordinary places of worship, were

---

[1] Colour is given to the legends associating such houses with Jews by such
references as 'two stone houses, late of Moses of Cambridge' (Ch.R. 1227, p. 55;
cf. ibid., 1228, p. 76). The 'stone house' of Master Elias in the London Jewry had
an extensive *solarium* attached (P.R. 1286, p. 224). Less authentic than the Lincoln
examples are 'Moses Hall' at Bury St. Edmunds, and 'Music' (Moses?) Hall at
Norwich, &c. There was formerly a 'Jew's House' at Southampton (J. S. Davies,
*History of Southampton*, 1883, p. 456). For an account of the Lincoln houses see
M. Wood in *Archaeological Review*, xcii (1935), pp. 194 ff.

[2] Adler, *J.M.E.*, p. 132; but his reference, C.R. 1279, p. 577, hardly bears his
interpretation—they were permitted to traffic, not live, where they wished.

introduced in the course of the twelfth century alone). In addition, the barons who desired lodgings near the tilting-ground in the Cheap seem to have been especially attracted by the mansions of the wealthy Jews. In the year of Magna Carta, no fewer than three earls were occupying houses formerly in the possession of members of the community. As a result, the centre moved a little westwards, up Cat Street and Lad Lane (now Gresham Street, where the church of St. Lawrence Jewry bears witness to their numbers) and down the side turnings about the Cheap, especially Milk Street and Wood Street. In the turbulent times which followed, a few Jews seem to have taken refuge in the salutary neighbourhood of the Tower, where Jewry Street (formerly known as 'Poor Jewry') off Aldgate, is believed to preserve the memory.[1]

## § VII

The standard of education was characteristically high. We do not meet a single illiterate Jew in the considerable mass of documents of the period which have survived.[2] Even an isolated householder, living in a country village, would have a tutor for the instruction of his children.[3] In a famous Lincoln case of 1271 the most important item in the bride's dowry was a beautiful Massoretic Bible.[4] English liturgical codices were known in France,[5] and the beauty of the manuscripts looted at York excited the admiration of the Jews of Cologne, whither they were brought for sale.[6] A few Anglo-Jewish manuscripts of this

[1] The medieval English Jewry was not, of course, provided with gates and gate-keepers, like the later continental Ghetto; the illustration in *Encyclopaedia Judaica*, vi. 654, confusingly depicts the old archway leading into Duke's Place, Aldgate (the heart of the eighteenth-century colony) as the entrance to the former Ghetto. The 'Jewry Wall' at Leicester is now proved to have been part of the Roman basilica. For 'Poor Jewry', London, see *J.C.*, 4 Apr. and 20 Aug. 1902.

[2] Compare nevertheless *E.J.* i. 17 for an indication that not all English Jews were literate.

[3] Cf. Pp.R. 1191–2, pp. 32, 173 (Isaac *magister puerorum* of Birdfield, Essex). In connexion with the Jewish preoccupation with scholarship, it may be pointed out that there was little else with which the unfortunate usurer could occupy his extensive leisure.

[4] Davis, *Shetaroth*, pp. 298–302; Adler, *J.M.E.*, p. 43.

[5] L. Zunz, *Die Ritus des synagogalen Gottesdienstes* (Berlin, 1859), pp. 62–63.

[6] Above, p. 25. An interesting revenue entry of 1192 records a payment of 100s. from Josce Crispin and the two daughters of Morell 'for their share of the books of the said Morell' (Jacobs, *J.A.E.*, pp. 53, 145, 408, endeavours to identify

period have survived to the present day.[1] Josephus was also
familiar to English Jews.[2] The religious practices current in 'the
isle of the sea' (as it was generally called)[3] were quoted with
approval by the continental authorities, though it was regarded
as a matter of surprise that they did not scruple to drink wine
prepared by Gentiles and in their company, or even to make use
of signet-rings which contained the likeness of the human figure
(the practice, as we know from actual example, of Aaron of
York). Though as a rule the Jews were unable to write in Latin
characters, whether French, English, or Latin were in question,
they could generally decipher (and, exceptionally, even forge)[4]
those languages. All contracts between themselves, and their
own set of the rolls recording their transactions, were drawn
up in Hebrew, in which tongue they usually endorsed Latin
deeds when necessary. Master Elias of London, however, corresponded freely in French.[5] Women were not overlooked in
the educational system. Nevertheless, it was found necessary to
translate the domestic service on Passover Eve into the vernacular, for their benefit and that of the children.[6]

From the literary standpoint, the status of English Jewry was
not remarkable. In this respect too they were on the whole an
offshoot of the communities of northern France, upon which
their literature continued to be dependent. Many of their foremost intellectual figures came from abroad, such as the first
Anglo-Jewish scholar known to us by name, Rabbi Joseph or
'Rubi Gotsce', who played a leading role in the London

the scholar here in question with the eminent Sir Morell of Falaise). When David
of Oxford died in 1244 it was expressly stated that if any book 'against the law
of the Christians or of the Jews' were found in his library, it should be condemned.
The Pope had recently issued a Bull ordering the Talmud and kindred works to
be burned as blasphemous: cf. Roth, *Oxford*, p. 123.

[1] e.g. the work treated of by D. Kaufmann (*Bibl.* A.10. 220), a liturgical frag-
ment described by M. Abrahams (*Bibl.* A.11. 11) and perhaps the Bury Psalter
in the Bodleian Library, Oxford. For a study of the books recorded in the possession of English Jews in the Middle Ages see Stokes in *Trs. J.H.S.E.* viii. 78 ff.;
some further titles in Adler, *J.M.E.*, pp. 222–3, and my *Int. Act.*, pp. 7–11.

[2] See Note V (*j*), p. 280.

[3] The phrase is a biblical one (Isaiah xi. 11, &c.). Occasionally the term used
was *Kezeh haArez* (for which see Deuteronomy xxviii. 64)—a literal translation of
what was supposed to be the meaning of *Angle-Terre* ('The Corner of the Earth').

[4] See above, p. 41 n.

[5] *Revue des Etudes Juives*, xviii. 256–61: *Trs. J.H.S.E.* xv. 54–55.

[6] *Trs. J.H.S.E.* iii. 38; see, however, *R.E.J.* xvii. 156.

community in the time of Henry I. Thereafter several business men mentioned in the English records are distinguished by the title of 'Magister', indicating prominence in Rabbinic (or possibly medical) studies. Under Henry II various foreign scholars visited England. Foremost among them was the famous Abraham ibn Ezra, that restless, versatile Spaniard who wrote on almost every subject which could interest the medieval mind, and had at least a glimmer of the principles of Higher Criticism. He was in London (whither, indeed, he is said to have returned to die) in 1158, writing there his *Jesod Morah* ('Foundation of Reverence') and probably his *Iggereth haShabbath* ('Sabbath Epistle'), under the patronage of Joseph de Moreil.[1] Jacob of Orleans, a distinguished *Tosaphist*,[2] perished in the London massacre of 1189; Yom-Tob of Joigny, a liturgical poet whose hymns are even now recited in the synagogue, was the central figure in the tragic events which took place at York in the following year; Berechiah haNakdan, author of the famous Fox Fables, and translator into Hebrew of the *Quaestiones Naturales* of Abelard of Bath, may perhaps be identical with Benedict le Pointur of Oxford.[3]

The following generation witnessed a greater degree of indigenous activity, stimulated no doubt by this influx of scholars.[4] Jacob ben Judah, the *hazan* or reader in the synagogue of London, composed a code of religious law known as *Etz Hayyim* ('The Tree of Life'), which incidentally comprises the text of the Jewish liturgy in use in pre-Expulsion England, and one or two original hymns.[5] Yomtob ben Moses of Bristol, and later Oxford,

---

[1] *Bibl.* A.11. 41–42, 46. M. D. Davis, in *J.C.* 27. viii. 1894, attempts to identify Joseph de Moreil (for whose association with England see a passage quoted in Neubauer's *Catalogue of Hebrew MSS. in the Bodleian Library*, i. 436) with 'Rubi Gotsce'. This seems correct: see my *Intellectual Activities*, pp. 19–20.

[2] The name given to the school of Jewish scholars which had its seat in northern France and wrote additions ('*tosaphoth*') to Rashi's Talmudic commentaries.

[3] See Note V (*k*), p. 280, and my *Oxford*, pp. 117–18.

[4] Something of the background of the literary activity of this generation is revealed by the title *Nadib*, or 'The Generous', appended in the Hebrew records to the names of some of the wealthy financiers of the thirteenth century—e.g. Isaac of Norwich and his son Samuel, Aaron of York, and Jacob fil' Moses (from whom Walter de Merton purchased the property which constituted the nucleus of his college at Oxford): the term implies 'patron' or 'mæcenas'.

[5] Now being edited by I. Brodie (pt. I, Jerusalem, 1962). Among the scholars reverently cited in the work is Isaac ben Perez of Northampton—untraceable unfortunately elsewhere or in the secular records.

was the author of a work, perhaps juristic, entitled *Sepher haTenaim* ('The Book of Conditions') now lost.[1] Moses haNakdan, his son, familiar in the English records as Magister Moses of London, wrote a standard treatise on Hebrew punctuation and grammar.[2] Among his pupils was Moses ben Isaac haNessiah, whose *Sepher haShoham* or Onyx Book, described as first in time and probably in value of the grammatical works produced in northern Europe at this period, vividly illustrates the range of knowledge of the medieval English Jewry.[3] Rabbi Meir of Angleterre composed a handbook of the laws incumbent upon a mourner, and is possibly identical with that Meir ben Elijah of Norwich who wrote some involved liturgical and didactic poems.[4] Most distinguished of all, perhaps, was Rabbi Elijah Menahem (Elias) of London, son of Magister Moses mentioned above, who besides being an affluent business man and enjoying a considerable reputation as a physician, composed among other works a notable commentary on the *Mishnah* (the second-century code which lies at the basis of the Talmud) much used by subsequent scholars.[5]

The names and opinions of a few other scholars, who left no independent writings, are also remembered. Menahem, the reader of the London synagogue, was highly considered in his day. One or two English Jews, such as Elijah of York, a victim of the massacre of 1190, are mentioned with deference in the *Tosaphoth* and other literary records of the time. Berechiah (Benedict) of Nicole or Lincoln, a further son of R. Moses of London, is now beginning to emerge as a figure of some importance, as is the case also with his fellow-townsman Joseph of Nicole. R. Benjamin of Canterbury, or rather Cambridge,

---

[1] See the discussion in my *Jews of Oxford*, pp. 113-15.

[2] Often published: *Bibl.* A.11. 85-86.

[3] New ed. by B. Klar with English introduction by C. Roth, pt. I (London, 1947).

[4] See the works and articles listed in *Bibl.* A.11, especially §§ 18, 38, 63 ff., 81-85, with B.15. 1: also Renan, *Les Rabbins français au commencement du quatorzième siècle* (Paris, 1877), pp. 484-7; W. Bacher in *R.E.J.* xii. 73-79; and M. Waxman, *History of Jewish Literature*, ii (New York, 1933), pp. 7-8. Moses ben Isaac, who must have been one of the most learned men in England in his day, had some acquaintance with Arabic, and even cites a Russian root communicated to him by Isaac of Chernigov (above, p. 93 n). Meir of Norwich signs himself החזה and was presumably the reader in the local synagogue.

[5] There is a detailed monograph on Elijah of London in *Trs. J.H.S.E.* xv. 29-62, and his Hebrew writings have been published, ed. M. J. L. Sacks, Jerusalem, 1956.

grammarian and exegete, is probably to be identified with the
Magister Benjamin who flourished in the latter city in the reigns
of Richard I and John. Rabbis Aaron of Canterbury, Vives of
York, and Joseph of Bristol were also authorities of note in their
day.[1] Elhanan (Isaac) ben Iakkar, of London, was the author
of two distinct commentaries on the mystical classic, *The Book
of Creation*, and some similar works, showing considerable influence from Christian sources.[2] The conjectured connexion with
England of Joseph Behor-Shor of Orleans, Sir Leon of Paris and
other Tosaphists; of Elhanan ben Isaac, the liturgical poet and
author of *Sod haIbbur* ('Secret of Lunar Intercalation'); of Hagin,
who translated the *Image du Monde* and other works of Abraham
ibn Ezra into French; and of a number of other celebrities
claimed by patriotic Anglo-Jewish scholars,[3] is open to considerable doubt.

In spite of the comparative paucity of names in this list, it is
possible to see that the intellectual horizon of English Jewry was
by no means restricted. They cultivated poetry, biblical exegesis,
belles-lettres, and, above all, grammar, in which their contributions were of solid importance. But—true to the tradition of
Franco-German Jewry, to which the English communities owed
their origin, and with which they continued so closely associated
—their interests were, above all, devoted to the study and formu-
lation of religious law and practice. Pope Honorius, in his
mandate to the archbishops of Canterbury and York in 1286,
complained of the influence in England of the book commonly
called 'Thalamud', which the Jews of the realm put forth as
being of greater authority than the law of Moses.[4] Correspondence was carried on with, and inquiries addressed to, all
the greatest rabbinical authorities of the age, from Jacob ben
Meir of Ramerupt ('Rabbenu Tam') to Meir of Rothenburg.
Through the former, the recent persecutions on the Continent

[1] I have dealt with this subject in detail in a separate monograph, *The Intellectual Activities of Medieval English Jewry* published by the British Academy in 1949. The Eleazar and Jekutiel of London and Elijah of Warwick mentioned by some writers are illusory. For new material on Rabbis Benedict and Joseph of Lincoln and Benjamin of Cambridge, &c., see *Journal of Jewish Studies*, i. 67–81 and iii. 56–61.

[2] G. Vajda, 'Dequelques infiltrations chrétiennes dans l'œuvre d'un auteur anglo-juif du xiiie siècle', in *Archives d'histoire doctrinale et littéraire du moyan-âge*, xxviii (1961), 15–34.

[3] See Note V (*l*), pp. 280–1.

[4] *Cal. Papal Registers*, i. 491, &c. (above, p. 77).

soon became known to the inhabitants of the 'Isle of the Sea',
who mourned them whole-heartedly,[1] while on the other hand
English massacres were commemorated in the Franco-German
martyrologies and dirges.[2]

In non-Jewish circles, knowledge of Hebrew was somewhat
greater than was once imagined. The impetus came through
clerks trained at the abbey of St. Victor in Paris, some of whom
were in personal contact with Jewish scholars. In particular,
Andrew abbot of Wigmore and Herbert of Bosham, Thomas
Becket's biographer, studied Hebrew fairly intensively and drew
heavily on the commentaries of the north French exegete Rashi
in their works of Biblical interpretation.[3] In the thirteenth century his work was carried on by the new Franciscan order,
sponsored by Robert Grosseteste and reinforced by the enthusiasm of Roger Bacon, who composed a notable Hebrew grammar.[4] Yet interest in Jewish lore was mainly prompted by
controversial and conversionist motives. As early as the reign of
William Rufus, Gilbert Crispin, abbot of Westminster, set down
the tenor of a religious discussion that had taken place in London between him and a certain Jew educated in the famous
rabbinical school of Mainz.[5] A less capable controversialist
imitated this some thirty or forty years later in the *Altercatio
judaei cum christiano de fide christiana*, addressed to Alexander,
bishop of Lincoln.[6] Towards the close of the thirteenth century
Bartholomew, bishop of Exeter, addressed his *Dialogus contra
Judeos* to Baldwin, later archbishop of Canterbury, who in turn
included a polemical sermon on Jewish blindness in his *Liber de
commendatione fidei*:[7] while Peter of Blois, while archdeacon of

---

[1] Neubauer and Stern, *Hebräische Berichte über . . . der Kreuzzüge*, p. 68.

[2] *Trs. J.H.S.E.* i. 8–14; S. Salfeld, *Das Martyrologium des Nürnberger Memorbuches* (Berlin, 1898), pp. 153, 235, 278. The 'martyrs of England' were long included
in the traditional German martyrologies.

[3] See for a general summary R. Loewe in *Trs. J.H.S.E.* xvii. 225–49 and in
*Three Centuries*, ed. V. D. Lipman, pp. 125–48, wtth the detailed studies listed in
*Bibl.* and in *Nov. Bibl.* A.11. Attributions of direct knowledge to Hebrew to Bede,
Alcuin, &c. cannot be substantiated: they derive their material from older writers.
Matthew Paris (*Chron. Maj.* iv. 553) mentions one Robert of Arundel who trans-
lated several works from Hebrew into Latin.

[4] *Bibl.* A.11. 19.                                     [5] Above, pp. 5–6.

[6] *Maxima Bibliotheca Patrum*, vol. xx: cf. A. Lukyn Williams, *Adversus Judaeos*
(Cambridge, 1935), pp. 381–3. B. Blumenkranz considers this a student's exercise,
the dedication being fictitious.

[7] A. Morey, *Bartholomew of Exeter* (1937), p. 164.

London, wrote his *Contra perfidiam judaeorum* specifically for use against argumentative Jews.[1] Robert of Cricklade, prior of St. Frideswide in Oxford, endeavoured to convince the Jews of their error on the authority of the suspected Christological passages of Josephus. A greater sense of actuality was ostensibly shown by Peter of Cornwall, prior of Holy Trinity in London, who in 1208 set down the arguments he had used to secure the conversion of a Jew named Simon, subsequently canon of the priory:[2] William of Arundel, archdeacon of Huntingdon, was so optimistic as to try to get a conversionist pamphlet, which he completed in 1240, translated into Hebrew. Duns Scotus, though imbued with the ideas of the Hebrew Avicebron (Ibn Gabirol), did not waste his time on controversy, but advocated forcible baptism for the Jewish children, and the exercise of threats to persuade their fathers to follow the example.[3] Few English writers of the medieval period show indeed much sympathy with the Jews, though the historian Thomas de Wykes, commenting on the London Massacre of 1263, says:

And though the Jews were not of our religion, it seemed base and impious to kill them, when we ought to love them because they are men and have been created in the image of God: 'because the remnant shall return, even the remnant of Jacob, unto the Almighty God'.[4]

The foregoing gives some idea of the nature and the composi-

[1] *P.L.* ccvii. 825–70. The 'John, Bishop of Worcester' to whom the treatise is addressed is presumably John of Coutances (1196–8) rather than John of Pagham (1151–8). The author implies that the Jews, owing to their greater familiarity with the Bible, enjoyed a distinct advantage in their discussions with the Bishop. It is not perhaps without its significance that the Jews had favoured Archbishop Baldwin's opponents in Canterbury, and that Peter of Blois was heavily in their debt (Adler, *J.M.E.*, pp. 51, 60).

[2] R. W. Hunt in *Essays Presented to F. M. Powicke* (1948), pp. 143 ff.: Roth, *Oxford*, p. 121. B. Smalley, *The Study of the Bible in the Middle Ages*, 2nd ed., pp. 338 ff., has shown that Grosseteste's *De cessatione legalium* was not as so frequently stated a conversionist tract aimed at the Jews. It may be observed that on the other side R. Tomtob of Joigny, the outstanding victim of the York massacre, was a venturesome polemist: see *Revue des Études Juives*, iii. 4–5, as was also Benjamin (of Canterbury?): ibid., xlix. 48.

[3] In order that the old prophecies should not be falsified he suggested that a handful of Jews should be dispatched to a distant island and maintained there until the second coming of Christ.

[4] Wykes, *Chronicon*, p. 221. Ralph de Diceto (*Ymagines Historiarum*, ii. 76) condemned the massacre at Bury St. Edmunds in somewhat similar terms, and Matthew Paris's references are sometimes not unkindly.

tion of the Anglo-Jewish community in the Middle Ages. It presents, indeed, few points of differentiation from the greater Jewish agglomerations of the Continent. Its importance consists rather in its *typical* character. It is rigidly self-contained, within the boundaries of the Norman Conquest on the one hand and the Expulsion of 1290 on the other, with just sufficient qualification at either extremity to remind us that in Jewish, as in all history, it is impossible to generalize too sweepingly. The community was immersed in, and indeed given its economic justification by, the profession characteristic of the Jews of the medieval world, more exclusively than was the case in any other country of western Europe; but at the same time, there were enough exceptions to prove that wider interests were not excluded. Its components were all of recent origin in the country; there was thus no ancient settlement, as was the case elsewhere, to continue association with the soil. The royal control was peculiarly close and comprehensive. The strength of the central government was such as to ensure uniformity of treatment and thus to facilitate generalization. Moreover, thanks to the magnificent preservation of the English records, we are particularly well informed on the subject.[1]

Every characteristic facet of medieval Jewish history, moreover, finds its reflection in England during the two centuries in which the Jews were settled in the country—encouragement degenerating into persecution, which finally culminated in expulsion, of which England provided the first general example. Even in their intellectual activities, the Jews of the country were eclectic, immersing themselves—without important consequences, and with a strong bias in certain specific directions —in all current branches of Hebrew literature and thought. It is because of this typical character that medieval Anglo-Jewish history has its individual quality and interest.

[1] A newly published case (C.R.R. 1230–2, n. 1027) throws a novel and vivid light on some aspects of medieval Anglo-Jewish life and organization. We are introduced to buying and selling in the London Jewry, an allegation of assault on two Flemish merchants with intent to rob, a Christian *serviens de Judaismo*, and the excommunication by Josceus Presbyter (? Josce fil' Isaac the Archpresbyter, exercising Rabbinic functions) of any Jew who withheld information bearing on the affair.

# VI

# THE MIDDLE PERIOD

## 1290–1609

### § 1

THE exclusion of the Jews from any land, however rigidly it may be prescribed by law, is unlikely to be absolute. England, in the period following the fatal year 1290, provides the classic exemplification of this general rule.[1] Across the Channel and the North Sea the victims of persecution sometimes cast longing eyes at this potential haven of refuge, forgetting all they had suffered there before. At the close of 1309 Magister Elias—from his title a physician or Rabbi—was given a safe-conduct by Edward II to come to England to treat 'on certain matters relating to Us'. He was presumably that medical practitioner who arrived with five companions in the course of the following summer. Though he may have come in a professional capacity, it was thought that his object was to obtain permission for his co-religionists to re-establish themselves in England.[2] He does not appear to have met with any success. There is, however, a persistent report in both Jewish and non-Jewish sources of a second expulsion under Edward III (the year is given in a Hebrew chronicle, circumstantially, as 1358);[3] and it is not altogether impossible that a few surreptitious settlers may have been ejected about that time.

Throughout this period, notwithstanding the edict of expulsion, Jews trickled into the country. In 1318 a knight hospitaller captured by the infidel brought back with him from the Holy Land a Jew named Isaac to whom he had been made over,

---

[1] For a complete bibliography illustrating this chapter see *Bibl.* A.5. 1–29 and *Nov. Bibl.* A.5. 1–12 with *Trs. J.H.S.E.* xix. 1–12.

[2] See Note VI (*a*), p. 282.

[3] Joseph haCohen, *Emek haBakha*, p. 54. For allusions which would corroborate this cf. Thorold Rogers *apud* Neubauer, in *Notes* (*Collectanea*, ii. 314) (Jews in Oxford throughout Middle Ages): *Collectanea Franciscana*, ii. 150 (Jews expelled under Edward III).

who remained until ransom had been paid.[1] In 1376 the Commons complained that the Lombard (i.e. Italian) usurers harboured Jews and Saracens in their midst; and, though religious toleration was not conspicuous in the Italian mercantile centres at this period, there may have been some justification for the statement.[2] Solomon Levi (later more famous as Pablo de Santa Maria, bishop of Burgos and member of the Council of Regency of Castile) was in London possibly as a hostage in 1389, though it is not quite certain whether before or after his conversion.[3] In 1410 the ailing Henry IV summoned from Italy Elias Sabot (Elijah Be'er ben Sabbetai, of Bologna, subsequently physician to Popes Martin V and Eugenius IV), who was empowered to practise medicine in any part of the realm; and he brought with him ten followers, sufficient to form the quorum requisite for Jewish public worship. In the previous year, Richard Whittington, mayor of London, had obtained permission to invite to London to attend upon his wife another Jewish physician, Master Samson de Mirabeau. In 1421 an Italian Jewish apothecary named Job was found in the country with his son, and both were compelled to accept baptism.[4]

Meanwhile, the *Domus Conversorum* founded by Henry III had never been quite empty. At the time of the Expulsion it contained nearly one hundred persons, men and women.[5] After

[1] P.R. 1318, p. 254. The safe-conduct was prolonged for one year on 11 January 1319.

[2] *Rotuli Parliamentarum*, ii. 332a. It has frequently been suggested that the Spanish and Italian merchants who traded in England at this time comprised many Jews: but, notwithstanding a careful inspection of the available material, I have been unable to trace a single name in corroboration of this hypothesis. Thus in A. Beardwood's *Alien Merchants in England, 1350–1377*, the only possible names which occur are those of Benedict Zacharie (a Lombard), David Jacobi of Lucca, and Solomon de Alman, goldsmith of Norwich. None of these is sufficiently distinctive to justify any further deduction.

[3] A letter from him, bemoaning the cheerless state of London during the Purim festival, is extant (*Bibl.* A.5. 4; cf. also L. Landau, *Das apologetische Schreiben des Josua Lorki*, Antwerp, 1906). But it is not out of the question that the document is a satire upon the ex-Rabbi [cf. now *Nov. Bibl.* A.5. 2].

[4] Cf. *Bibl.* A.5. 25, 26. There is no evidence, other than the biblical first name, for believing that David Nigarellis of Lucca, who attended on Henry IV in 1412, was likewise a Jew. The 'Jeweis' of Abingdon, who gave a performance before the eight-year-old Henry IV in 1427 (Rymer, *Foedera*, x. 387), were clearly not Jews but *joueurs*, or players.

[5] A comprehensive account of the *Domus Conversorum* in the Middle Period is given by M. Adler in *J.M.E.*, pp. 306–79, superseding that in *Trs. J.H.S.E.*, vol. iv; cf. also *The Jews in England* (Public Record Office Catalogue, 1957), pp. 9–14.

these original collegiates died out the utility of the institution did not end, as might have been imagined. Down to its decline at the beginning of the seventeenth century, there were always a few inmates to justify its existence—poor Jews who had drifted to England from overseas and embraced Christianity; foreign converts attracted by the endowments; rascals who immigrated expressly to enjoy these advantages. The persons in question (who, in certain instances, had been living in the country for some while before their conversion)[1] came from many parts of the Jewish world: France, Flanders, Italy, Sicily, Germany, Spain, Portugal, even Morocco. Besides these, there were a few apostates who did not avail themselves of the benefits of the *Domus*—as for example the enterprising charlatan who professed to be able to detect thieves by magic, and was consulted professionally in 1390 by the Council of the Duke of York.[2]

One or two of the sordid parade subsequently attained a certain distinction. Thus under Edward II, Alexander le Convers, parson of Leatherhead (probably a survivor of the Expulsion of 1290), became successively agent for securing money and ships for the royal service, collector of Peter's Pence in Ireland, and Envoy to Flanders.[3] Still greater was the prominence achieved a century and a half later by a certain Portuguese Jewish soldier of fortune named Edward Brandão (he subsequently anglicized his name to Brandon or Brampton) who entered the *Domus Conversorum* in 1468. The fact that on his baptism Edward IV had acted as his godfather provided him with an introduction to Court, and in the stormy days of the Wars of the Roses he had ample opportunity of advancement. From 1472 onwards he received a succession of naval and military commands. After ten years he was appointed governor of the island of Guernsey, and in 1483 was raised to the knighthood. His devotion to the Yorkist cause proved disastrous to him when Henry VII triumphed at Bosworth Field, and he returned to his native Portugal. With him he took to wait

---

[1] In the fourteenth century the inmates included persons from Eton, Woodstock, Stratford, Leicester, and Dartmouth (Adler, *J.M.E.*, pp. 323–6).

[2] H. T. Riley, *Memorials of London* (London, 1868), pp. 518–19. He was subsequently pilloried and banished: R. R. Sharpe, *Letter-Books of London, H*, p. 351.

[3] M. Adler, 'Edward II and his converted Jews', in *J.C.* 5 Aug. 1898. But *convers* often signifies 'lay-brother'.

upon his wife an ambitious Flemish youth named Perkin War-
beck, who received from him a great deal of casual information
regarding life at the Court of Edward IV, which proved invaluable when he made his preposterous bid for the English
throne a little later on.[1]

### § II

A new and peculiarly tragic chapter in Jewish history began
in the year of the discovery of America. In 1492 Ferdinand and
Isabel expelled the Jews from Spain—a measure which was
speedily imitated in Portugal and Navarre. This drastic step
ended the immemorial connexion of the Jews with south-
western Europe. The whole distribution of the Hebrew people
was changed, the centre of gravity moving from West to East—
from the Iberian Peninsula to the Turkish Empire.

There were now left in Spain and Portugal only the Marranos—those crypto-Jews who, under an outward guise of
Catholicism, remained faithful at heart to the religion of their
fathers. It was in order to cope with these that the Inquisition
had been established, and their resistance to its persecutions
constitutes one of the most remarkable pages of history. They
were to be found in all walks of life—from playwrights to pastry-
cooks, from pedlars to physicians, from soldiers to monks.
Some of the most eminent persons in the Peninsula, who occupied positions of dignity and trust in the army, the administration, even the Church, were of Jewish descent; and the country
was periodically thrown into a turmoil by the news that one of
them had been haled off to the Inquisitional dungeons, from
which he might emerge only to be burned at the stake.[2]

For a long period, these New Christians (as they were termed)
were forbidden to leave their native land, lest they should shake
off the shackles of the religion so recently imposed upon them
by force. Such a prohibition could not be maintained in perpetuity, and before long Marrano fugitives were to be found in
all parts of Europe, joining or establishing open Jewish communities in Turkey, Italy, and ultimately Holland, Germany,

---

[1] *Bibl.* A.5. 24: *Nov. Bibl.* A.5. 8–9: *Essays and Portraits*, pp. 68–85. Brampton
subsequently revisited England, and a son of his was knighted at Winchester in
1500.

[2] See my *History of the Marranos* (Philadelphia, 1932), from which I have copied
some phrases.

and France as well. For stragglers to reach England was inevitable. The result was that the orientation of this country in Jewish life underwent a radical change. Whereas in the Middle Ages it had looked toward the Franco-German or *Ashkenazi*[1] group, the Spanish tragedy and its aftermath brought it for a period of some two centuries into the sphere of the Spanish and Portuguese, or *Sephardi*, nucleus.

There is evidence that in 1492 some of the exiles came to London with bills of exchange on local Spanish merchants. Apparently a few Marranos similarly sought refuge here, much to the indignation of the Spanish rulers. This 'infesting scourge' (as it was pedantically described, though the numbers in question must have been very small) continued till 1498, when, at the time of the negotiations for a marriage between the Prince of Wales and Catharine of Aragon the Catholic sovereigns formally protested against it. Laying his hand on his breast King Henry solemnly assured the Spanish envoys that he would prosecute without mercy any Jewish renegade or fugitive from the Inquisition who could be discovered in his dominions.[2] There is no indication that anything drastic was done; but in such circumstances there was plainly little chance of permanent establishment.

But, to an extent far greater than the Spaniards, it was the Portuguese New Christians (victims or descendants of victims of the comprehensive Forced Conversion of 1497, which put an end to the Jewish community in that country) who figured in the Iberian mercantile colonies abroad: for they played a role of disproportionate importance in Portuguese commerce. In 1512 the great Marrano mercantile and financial house of Mendes, which controlled the coveted pepper monopoly and at one time all but rivalled the Fuggers in the extent and importance of their transactions, established its Antwerp branch. Its operations, carried on largely through New Christian agents, speedily

[1] The biblical *Sepharad* (for which see Obadiah, verse 20) was consistently applied by the Jews of the Middle Ages of Spain. Similarly Germany was called *Ashkenaz* (Genesis x. 3). The terms *Sephardim* and *Ashkenazim* are today applied a little loosely to the two main historic categories of the Jewish people, according as they are descended from the Spanish-Mediterranean-Levantine, or the Franco-German-Polish, group. They are distinguished from one another by certain differences of background, of liturgy, and of Hebrew pronunciation.

[2] Text in Wolf, *Diplomatic History of the Jewish Question* (London, 1919), p. 126, where, however, the inferences drawn are more than the document justifies.

spread across the North Sea. Ultimately it became entrusted with the loan transactions of the English treasury; and when in 1532 proceedings were taken on a charge of Judaizing against Diogo Mendes, the head of the Antwerp establishment, Henry VIII personally intervened on his behalf. In 1536, on the death of Diogo's elder brother Francisco, his widow Beatrice (later, when she had openly reverted to the faith of her fathers, known as Gracia Mendes, the most adored Jewish woman of the age) went to join her brother-in-law at Antwerp, and on her way paid a short visit to England. With her came her whole family, including her nephew and future son-in-law the young João Micas, who was to bring his kaleidoscopic career to its climax as the Jew Joseph Nasi, duke of Naxos and the Cyclades, all-powerful adviser at the Sublime Porte.

The Marrano community which they found in London comprised at least thirty-seven householders.[1] Organized religious life was not absent. Services were regularly held at the house of one Alves Lopes, to whom newly arrived fugitives would come for assistance and advice. Christopher Fernandes, one of Diogo Mendes's local agents, would send to intercept the Portuguese spice-ships touching at Southampton and Plymouth, and warn Marranos on board if danger awaited them in Flanders. Antonio de la Roña, a kinsman of the Mendes family, who was described as 'master of Jewish theology', was probably the spiritual leader of the group: it was his practice to help refugees to realize their property, providing them with bills of exchange on Antwerp. The settlement was rich in medical practitioners. The most eminent was Dionysius Rodriguez, formerly physician to the Court of Portugal and a medical author of some reputation, who had fled to London for safety and was later on to be burned in effigy by the Lisbon Inquisition. With him had come his three sons, of whom one, Manuel Brudo, was likewise an accepted medical authority and had a distinguished clientèle in Court circles.[2] Better known than either (though as writer,

---

[1] The history of the Marrano community in Tudor England was unknown until 1928–9, when Lucien Wolf began to publish the results of his remarkable researches into the records of the Portuguese Inquisition (*Bibl.* A.5. 24a, 27, 28). Previously the only information available was that in Sidney Lee's 'Elizabethan England and the Jews' (*Bibl.* A.5. 19) which may still be consulted with profit: see also *Bibl.* A.5. 22 and Wolf's earlier paper on the Middle Period of Anglo-Jewish History, *Bibl.* A.5. 29, with the general survey in *Trs. J.H.S.E.* xix. 1–12.

[2] See Note VI (*b*), pp. 282–3.

not as physician) was that versatile personality variously called
Isaiah Cohen, Diego Pires, and Pyrrho Lusitano, later of
Ragusa, who became famous as one of the foremost Latin poets
of the sixteenth century.[1]

In 1540 news arrived in London that proceedings had been
opened at Milan against the Marrano refugees. Antonio de la
Roña was summoned to Antwerp to attend the meeting which
discussed relief measures; and he subscribed one hundred ducats
—partly in English crown pieces—to the emergency fund. But
the crisis had more serious repercussions than could be realized
at the moment. One Gaspar Lopes, a cousin of Diogo Mendes
and formerly his London agent, who was among those arrested
by the Milan commissioners, turned informer. In consequence
of his depositions, amplified by the details elicited in the course
of the subsequent proceedings in Flanders, the secret of the
little London community was laid bare. The Spanish authorities
presumably communicated the outcome of their inquiries to
the English government, and about Christmas, 1541, orders
were given for the arrest of 'certain persons suspected to be Jews'
and the sequestration of their property. The proceedings were
lengthy, for a special messenger was sent to Lisbon to make
investigations and a commission of inquiry appointed meanwhile. At the same time, the prisoners enlisted the interest of the
King of Portugal and the Queen Regent of the Netherlands,
who repeatedly wrote letters blandly testifying that they were
good Christians. At the beginning of March accordingly three
high officers of state waited on the Imperial envoy and informed
him that, as a token of friendship, the King had ordered those
accused to be released; on the 9th, the Commissioners presented the Privy Council a report exonerating them. The episode
was nevertheless a portent of danger, and it seems that before
long the little community dispersed.[2]

It was not long before the infiltration was resumed, for the

---

[1] Possibly to be identified with the 'Master Diego' on whose behalf the Netherlands government intervened in 1542 (Wolf, *Essays*, p. 77); but the poet was then
very young. The Marrano colony in London at this time included also two of
Michel de Montaigne's uncles, Martin and Francesco Lopes (T. Malvezin, *Michel
de Montaigne*, Bordeaux, 1875, pp. 108–9): the former's family subsequently played
an important role in the Calvinist Consistory at Antwerp.

[2] *Acts of Privy Council*, vii. 304, 325; viii. 76, 94; *Letters and Papers, Henry VIII*,
xvii. 36, 76; xviii. 34, 146; *Spanish State Papers*, vi. 270. Lucien Wolf's account
(*Essays*, p. 83), which I previously followed, is misleading.

total exclusion of such furtive refugees was impossible. By the close of the reign of Edward VI we find a diminutive Marrano community not only in London but also in Bristol: for this city maintained a considerable trade with the Peninsula, in which Spanish Jews had been interested for centuries past.[1] Among the residents here was Antonio Brandão, a young surgeon from Santarem (nephew of Amatus Lusitanus, the most illustrious medical annalist of his age, who mentions him more than once in his writings),[2] and a physician named Henrique Nuñes. The latter and his wife were the leaders of the group. Services were held regularly at their house: they periodically received the dates of the festivals from London: they were in touch with the latest Jewish literature, reading avidly Usque's famous martyrology, *Consolaçam às Tribulaçoens de Israel*, recently published at Ferrara. Of the community of London at this stage we have less detailed information; but the names of eight householders belonging to it are recorded.

The Marranos of this period were presumably regarded as Protestant refugees—the obvious guise to assume if they wished to escape interference and even secure sympathy. Hence, with the reaction against the Reformation under Mary, when native Protestants were burned and the Spanish alliance threw the shadow of the Inquisition over England, no safe course remained for them but to leave the country. Henrique Nuñes retired with his family to France, and probably other members of the two communities followed his example. Though even now a slender residuum remained, the colony was once more scattered to the four winds.

§ III

In that remarkable period of expansion which opened with the accession of Queen Elizabeth, the foreign mercantile settlement in London ('the dinning-room of Christendom' as Middleton called it) increased prodigiously. At the beginning of the reign there were less than 3,000 aliens in the city; at its close there were some 10,000. Among them was inevitably, as before,

---

[1] The Pamplona archives show that the Jews of Navarre were trading in green cloth 'from Vristol', in considerable quantities, between 1400 and 1433 (Jacobs, *Sources of Spanish Jewish History*, London, 1894, pp. 118–19).

[2] *Centuria V*, iv, vi, xvi. Cf. M. Lemos, *Amato Lusitano*, Oporto, 1907, pp. 9, 10, 40, 74, 124.

a considerable sprinkling of Spanish and Portuguese New Christians, again encouraged by the possibilities of tolerance heralded by the overthrow of Roman Catholicism. The intensification of commercial intercourse with southern Europe gave these refugees fresh opportunities, and during the war with Spain they were used by London merchants as a cloak for trade with the Peninsula. Thus the Marrano community again expanded, its hundred or more members including a few persons of outstanding ability and some prominence in public life. At their head was Hector Nuñez (generally known as 'Doctor Hectour'), one of the handful of persons who had remained throughout Mary's reign, an important figure in the city. Though a qualified and practising physician, he also engaged in foreign trade on a large scale. His widespread business and personal connexions abroad were found extremely useful by the government. He enjoyed the confidence both of Burleigh and of Walsingham, and on one occasion left his dinner-table to bring the latter the first news of the arrival of the Great Armada at Lisbon.[1]

The most prominent of the Marrano merchants after him was Jorge Añes (anglicized as Ames), whose family had been settled in London at least since 1521. One of his sons, Francis, became a soldier of fortune, and was employed by Sir Francis Drake for intelligence work in the Azores; subsequently he held a command in the English garrison at Youghal, in Ireland, of which he was thrice the Mayor, and earned the commendation of the Earl of Ormonde for his gallant defence of the town against the rebels.[2] Dunstan Ames, his brother, was purveyor to the queen, and traded extensively with Spain. The latter's daughter brought them into touch with Court circles, for she was the wife of the well-known Dr. Roderigo Lopez. This was another Portuguese New Christian who, after qualifying in medicine in his native country, settled in London. Here he was a member of the College of Physicians (before which he delivered the annual Anatomical Lecture in 1569), and was the first house-physician appointed at St. Bartholomew's

[1] See Note VI (c), p. 283.
[2] Nuñez's brother-in-law, Bernaldo Luis, also did extensive espionage work for Burleigh in Spain, where he was arrested in 1588 (Trs. J.H.S.E., xi. 5-6, 36; L. de Alberti and A. B. W. Chapman, *English Merchants and the Spanish Inquisition in the Canaries*, London, 1912, pp. 77-78).

hospital. Later he became medical attendant to the all-powerful
Earl of Leicester, and then in 1586 to the queen herself, who
recommended him warmly in correspondence. He was connected by marriage, as it happened, with Alvaro Mendez (alias
Solomon Abenaish), the ex-Marrano Duke of Mytilene, who
had succeeded to much of Joseph Nasi's influence at the Sublime Porte, and, as one of the architects of the Anglo-Turkish
*entente* against Spain, was in continuous correspondence with
the English Court where, though known as a Jew, he seems to
have been highly esteemed. Lopez threw himself into the
political game with unnecessary zest. Taking advantage of his
close relations after Leicester's death with his stepson, the Earl
of Essex, he began to intrigue industriously to secure English
intervention on behalf of Dom Antonio, prior of Crato, the
Pretender to the Portuguese throne. The latter (whose financial
agent in London was Dunstan Ames) was himself, as it happened, of Jewish blood, being the son of a member of the old
royal house through an irregular union with the beautiful New
Christian, Violante Gomez; and the Marranos had high hopes
that his triumph would secure them some measure of relief.
In 1592 he was brought over to England by Essex and the war
party, and Lopez was constantly with him in the capacity of
secretary and interpreter.

The degree of religious observance in the furtive London
community is obscure, but its members were Jewish in more
respects than by mere descent. It is on record that they collected funds for the maintenance of the secret synagogue at
Antwerp, forwarding them through the medium of Dr. Lopez.
In 1592, when an envoy of Alvaro Mendez named Solomon
Cormano was in London on diplomatic business, religious
services were held at his house in full traditional style; and the
crypto-Jews of the capital gratefully took the opportunity to
attend. Though their marriages and funerals were performed
of necessity in accordance with Protestant rites, there is evidence
that baptism was neglected. So far as possible, too, they were
laid to their last rest side by side in Stepney Churchyard, some
way from their actual area of residence. During a lawsuit
brought in 1596 against one of the Marrano merchants who had
been trading with the Peninsula in partnership with an Englishman, the Jewish ceremonies observed at his home in Duke's

Place, London, were alluded to in Court without any sense of incongruity, and (what was more remarkable) without any untoward results.[1]

In the year 1593 (according to an ancient legend, which need not be discredited in all its details) the community was reinforced for a short space of time by a party of visitors of particular religious zeal. A brother and sister, Manuel Lopez Pereira and Maria Nuñez (whose parents had suffered from the persecutions of the Inquisition) set sail from Portugal with a small body of Marranos, in the hope of finding a place of refuge in the freer lands to the north. The vessel was captured on the journey by an English ship, and brought to port. The queen herself expressed a desire to see the fair prisoner, was captivated by her charm, took her in the royal coach when she drove about London, and gave orders for the vessel and all its passengers to be set at liberty. In spite of this token of royal favour, the visitors, 'leaving all the pomp of England for the sake of Judaism' (as the old chronicle puts it), pursued their way to Amsterdam. Here, after other vicissitudes, they managed to establish an open Jewish community, which, constantly recruited by fresh Inquisitional fugitives, became known before long as one of the most important in western Europe, and was subsequently to play an important part in the formal readmission of the Jews to England.[2]

Occasionally professing Jews also found their way into the country. The most remarkable instance was that of a certain Joachim Ganz, or Gaunse, one of the 'mineral men' brought from Germany by the Company of the Mines Royal. From 1581 he was working in England, where he introduced improved methods into the copper-mines at Keswick in Cumberland and at Neath in Wales. He remained undisturbed for a number of years. However, in September 1598 he was arrested at Bristol for certain incautious words let fall during a discussion with a local clergyman. On being brought before the Mayor and Aldermen, he openly declared himself a Jew, born at Prague in Bohemia, adding that he had never been baptized and 'did not beleeve any Article of our Christian faithe for that he was

[1] C. J. Sisson, 'A Colony of Jews in Shakespeare's London' in *Essays by Members of the English Association*, xxii. 38–51.
[2] See Note VI (*d*), p. 283.

not broughte uppe therein'. The local authorities, scandalized, sent him up to London for trial before the Privy Council. Though further information is lacking, it is to be presumed that he was expelled from the country.[1]

### § IV

Towards the close of the century, the Marrano community in England began to decline. The reason was in part political. After the failure of Drake's expedition against Portugal in 1589, Lopez and his associates had quarrelled with the prior of Crato, an incompetent figure-head at the best, and began to favour an agreement with Spain. Naturally, this embroiled him with Essex and the war party, who resented the fact that his position gave him easier access to the queen than they themselves had. The Spanish Court seized the opportunity to enter into secret negotiations with him, offering a heavy bribe if he would make away with the Pretender. Whether he actually intended to do this cannot be ascertained, but (whatever the reason—he himself explained it on perfectly plausible grounds) he did not reject the overtures outright. The relations which he thus began with the national enemy provided his opponents with a weapon. In October 1593 he was arrested and accused of plotting to poison Elizabeth herself, at the instigation of the king of Spain. Sir Robert Cecil championed him: the queen was plainly unconvinced: but to no effect. His trial, hopelessly partisan, dragged on for months before a special commission, which included some of the highest officers of the state. In the end he was found guilty, and executed at Tyburn on 7 June 1594.[2] There can be little doubt that, though his aims and methods were not above suspicion, he was innocent of this particular

---

[1] *Bibl.* A.5. 3. Another indication of Jewish life in England at this time is provided by the fact that Nathaniel (Judah) Menda, baptized with great pomp in 1577 (on which occasion the sermon was preached by John Foxe: *Bibl.* B.6. 1), had been resident in London as a Jew for six years. John Florio's father, Michelangelo Florio, preacher to the Italian Church in London and biographer of Lady Jane Grey, was also of Jewish birth, but converted before he came to England. The Ipswich records for 1572 include a memorandum of the payment of sixpence 'for whippinge of a Jewishe man'—three times the rate for whipping a Welshman (*H.M.C.* ix, App. 249b). There is much on Gaunse in M. B. Donald, *Elizabethan Copper* (London, 1955).

[2] *Bibl.* A.5. 9, 15, 18; A.10, 32; *Trs. J.H.S.E.* vi. 32–55, xvi. 163–84. Bird's *Memoirs*, i. 149–58; *H.M.C. Hatfield*, iv. 512–13; S.P.D., 1593–4 *passim*. The queen's incredulity is reflected in her generous treatment of Lopez's widow.

charge. A miniature anti-Semitic storm was nevertheless aroused in England. During the period between the sentence and its execution the most popular play on the London stage was Marlowe's *Jew of Malta*, the extravagances of which seemed to anticipate the character as well as the fate of Dr. Lopez. Meanwhile Shakespeare was at work on his *Merchant of Venice*, in which the character of Shylock clearly reflected in its cruder facets the popular abhorrence of the new Judas and his machinations.

The atmosphere which thus developed can have been by no means encouraging for the dead man's associates and kinsmen. The heyday of the Marrano community in England was now ended. The decline of trade relations with Spain discouraged the settlement of further New Christians, who now found a powerful counter-attraction in the newly established community at Amsterdam.[1] The two most prominent of the London group were by now dead—Hector Nuñez in 1591 (his profession of faith in his will had been noteworthy for the absence of any Christian colouring, notwithstanding strong monotheistic allusions) and Dunstan Ames in 1594. Of the latter's family some remained in the country, where they became utterly assimilated with the general population. Others made their way to the Levant, where in after-years English travellers were surprised to encounter, openly professing Judaism, persons born in Crutched Friars in London.[2]

Finally, in 1609, six years after James I's accession to the throne, an unfortunate quarrel took place amongst the members of the little colony. One party avenged itself by denouncing its opponents as Judaizers, and the authorities were compelled to instruct the Earl of Suffolk, as Lord Chamberlain, to take the necessary steps. As the result of his inquiries all Portuguese merchants living in London who were suspected of Judaizing were expelled from the country.[3] It was necessary to wait half a century before the Marrano settlement again became numerous and was officially authorized.

---

[1] Hugh Broughton was informed by an Amsterdam Jew in 1608 that many of his co-religionists in that place had been in England (*Our Lordes Famile*, Amsterdam, 1608).

[2] Cf. Coryat's account in *Purchas his Pilgrimes*, II. x. 1824–5.

[3] See Note VI (*e*), pp. 283–4, and E. R. Samuel, 'Portuguese Jews in Jacobean London', in *Trs. J.H.S.E.* xviii. 171–230. Nevertheless, the Amsterdam 'santa companhia de dotar orphas' (1615) specifically admitted English members.

§ v

Meanwhile, under the stimulus of the Reformation, England had witnessed a revival—or rather a birth—of Hebrew studies. These were represented after the thirteenth century only by nominal lectureships at the universities, established in obedience to the Bull of Pope Clement V of 1312, which insisted on the necessity of including Hebrew in the curriculum. One reason for the fresh orientation is to be found in Henry VIII's matrimonial difficulties, which had a theological as well as a political aspect. For his desire to annul his long-standing marriage there was biblical authority in Leviticus xviii. 16, in which an alliance between a man and his brother's wife is categorically forbidden. On the other hand, in Deuteronomy xxv. 5, such a union is expressly prescribed if the brother had died childless, in order that his name should be perpetuated. The problem of interpretation was highly perplexing. In consequence the importance of Hebrew tradition for the correct comprehension of Holy Writ was suddenly realized. Since Jews were now excluded from both England and Spain, it was to the Jewish quarters of Italy, and especially to that of Venice, that both sides turned for guidance. Richard Croke, who had been sent to collect opinions on behalf of Henry from eminent canon lawyers, applied for assistance to the famous Venetian humanist, Fra Francesco Giorgi. The latter had no difficulty in finding Hebrew scholars who were willing to support the English thesis—notably one Marco Raphael, a recent apostate from Judaism, and inventor of a new invisible ink for use in the secret diplomacy of the Serenissima, who showed himself more than eager to oblige. Hardly a day passed, reported Croke from Venice at the beginning of 1530, when he did not confer upon the matter with some monk or some Jew, and the names of six of the latter, conforming or converted, are mentioned in his dispatches.

Henry insisted on having the rabbinical opinions submitted to him for personal consideration. Despite an attempt of the Spanish ambassador to waylay them, Raphael and Giorgi reached London safely at the beginning of 1531: and there the former drew up a report to the complete satisfaction of his patron. He was, however, borne down by weight of learning and of numbers. Almost all of the Italian Rabbis were ranged against him. Worst of all, at this very period a levirate marriage took place in Bologna between a Jew and his brother's widow. This completely discredited all arguments on the other side, and the breach between England and Rome was brought nearer. Nevertheless, the episode had a real importance in Jewish history; for it was this which, combined with the contemporary Reuchlin–Pfefferkorn controversy in Germany, began to re-habilitate Hebrew literature from the discredit which it had suffered in Europe since the rise of Christianity.[1]

So vivid did interest in Hebrew become in England with the stirring of the Reformation that the Act of Uniformity (1549) authorized its use in private devotions, while the medals struck in 1545 to commemorate Henry VIII's recognition as head of the Church, and two years later on the occasion of his son's accession to the throne, both bore lengthy inscriptions in what was optimistically considered to be the language of the Old Testament.[2] Hebrew printing in England goes back a couple of decades earlier still, the first examples being included in Wakefield's *Oratio de utilitate trium linguarum*, published by Wynkyn de Worde in 1524. A few productions of the Hebrew presses recently established in Venice and elsewhere were to be found in some of the greater religious houses before their dissolution.[3] In 1549, just before his death, Paul Fagius, the famous German Protestant divine and humanist, was appointed to the chair of Hebrew at Cambridge—the first more or less competent scholar to occupy such a position in England.[4]

Obviously, for the serious investigation of so remote a tongue the assistance of some person with first-hand acquaintance was indispensable. Accordingly, from this period a few Jews by birth (generally converted) began to haunt the purlieus of the universities. The earliest was John Immanuel Tremellius, a native of Ferrara, who had been converted to the Roman Catholic faith by Cardinal Pole, but afterwards went over to

---

[1] For the Royal 'Divorce' in its Jewish associations, see D. Kaufmann, 'Une Consultation de Jacob Rafael Peglione de Modène sur le divorce de Henri VIII' in *Revue des Études Juives*, xxx. 309 ff.; and 'Jacob Mantino', ibid. xxvii. 30 ff. (especially 47 ff.). Raphael remained attached to the English Court, accompanying Henry to France in 1532. He was not (as often stated) a nephew of Giorgi, whose family had no Jewish associations.

[2] *Trs. J.H.S.E.* v. 113–14.

[3] Some specimens are preserved in the libraries of Oxford and Cambridge colleges. [4] Stokes, *Studies*, pp. 207 ff.

Protestantism. Owing to the wars of religion in Germany he sought refuge in 1547 in England, where he enjoyed the hospitality of Archbishop Cranmer at Lambeth. After Fagius's death, he succeeded to his position at Cambridge, and was appointed simultaneously to a non-residential canonry at Carlisle. On Mary's accession and the beginning of the Catholic reaction, he fled to the Continent, where he ultimately became professor of Hebrew at Heidelberg, and published a number of works; but he paid another visit to England in 1565.[1]

Less distinguished was Philip Ferdinand, subsequently professor of Hebrew at Leyden. Born in Poland in 1555, he embraced Christianity, made his way to England, and studied at Oxford. Here he proved his capacity by giving tuition in Hebrew in several colleges, after which he transferred himself to the sister university. A little book of his on the precepts of the Mosaic law, published here in 1597, was the first serious contribution to Jewish scholarship to see the light in this country.[2] At the beginning of the seventeenth century professing Jews began to make their appearance, beginning with a 'Rabbi Jacob' who was teaching about this period at Cambridge. He is perhaps identical with the Oxford scholar Jacob Barnett, whose Hebrew learning attracted much attention, and who in 1609 became secretary to the distinguished Protestant humanist, Isaac Casaubon. After long discussions he was persuaded to submit to baptism, but, when the day for the ceremony arrived, was nowhere to be found. It is not remarkable that not long after there is a record of the banishment of 'Jacobus Bernatus' from England.[3]

The record of these scattered Hebraists is not peculiarly distinguished or inspiring. Nevertheless, the role they played was

[1] *Bibl.* A.10. 271-2: for Hebrew studies in England generally, cf. the material listed ibid. A.11, and most recently E. J. Rosenthal, 'Rashi and the English Bible', in *Bulletin of the John Rylands Library*, vol. xxiv (1940), and S. Levy, 'English Students of Maimonides' in *Jewish Annual*, 1940-1, pp. 72-87; and now R. Loewe in *Three Centuries*, ed. V. D. Lipman, pp. 137 ff.        [2] *Bibl.* B.11. 2.

[3] Roth, 'Jews in Oxford after 1290' in *Oxoniensia*, xv. 63-80. In the subsequent period we find a few additional names to add to the foregoing list. Early in 1626 Queen Henrietta Maria asked the University of Oxford to favour her servant, Antonio Maria de Verona. A little later Alessandro Amidei, a Florentine convert, taught Hebrew at Oxford, and contributed to a miscellany published there in 1658: subsequently he became professor of Hebrew in Edinburgh. Mention is deserved also by Paul Jacob, a converted Jew, who petitioned King James for an allowance in 1623, on the ingenious plea that, since the sceptre had departed from Judah, the petitioner was the English monarch's child and subject.

not without importance. In the first place, they familiarized
the Englishman, for the first time for three centuries, with the
existence and the appearance of the authentic Jew (albeit in
most cases converted). Moreover, limited though their knowledge sometimes was, they did a great deal to promote and
diffuse Hebrew studies in England. Their disciples outdid them
in earnestness and in importance. By the reign of James I
there was in the English Church a small but competent nucleus
of native-born Hebrew scholars of real ability. The result was
seen in that great achievement, the 'Authorized' version of the
Bible, published in 1611. Executed direct from the original
tongues[1] by a competent band of scholars, it was as faithful as
the age and the circumstances would permit. Though no Jews
participated, the spirit of the ancient Hebrew commentators
was immanent, and their works were always at hand for consultation. The result was a magnificent rendering, which almost rivals the grandeur of the original, and has been the most
potent influence in moulding the English language from that
day onwards. Though the Jews were still jealously excluded
from England, there was no country in which the Hebraic
spirit was so deeply rooted or so universally spread.[2]

[1] In this respect the Authorized Version was a great advance on that of Cover-
dale, who knew no Hebrew. His precursor, William Tyndale, was, on the other
hand, a fair scholar. Whittingham, who took a leading part in producing the
Geneva or 'Breeches' Bible (1560), was similarly familiar with Hebrew, as also
were a few of the translators who participated in the 'Bishops'' Bible (1568).
The earliest English Hebraist of any eminence was Hugh Broughton (1549–1612),
some of whose works are listed in *Bibl.* B.14. 4–10: while the first Hebrew grammar
for English use was John Udall's *Key to the Hebrew Tongue* (Utrecht, 1593), composed
while he was in prison for his share in the Marprelate Tracts: cf. also D. Daiches,
*The King James Version* (Chicago, 1941), and I. Baroway in *Jewish Social Studies*,
xviii. 3–24.
   Much material on the relations of English travellers with Jews abroad in the
Elizabethan period (see Note VI (f) pp. 284–5) is assembled in A. Cohen, *An
Anglo-Jewish Scrap Book*, 1600–1840, London, 1943. For the relations with the
English Court of the poet Salomon Usque, of Constantinople, see H. G. Rosedale,
*Queen Elizabeth and the Levant Company* (London, 1904) and my article 'Salusque
Lusitano', *J.Q.R.* n.s. xxxiv (1943), pp. 65–85. The statement once made that
Alvaro Mendes was knighted by Queen Elizabeth is inaccurate: he was a Knight
of the Spanish Order of Santiago. Comprehensive guidance on the literature about
Jews and crypto-Jews in Elizabethan England is now given in S. A. Tannenbaum's
*Shakspere's The Merchant of Venice* (*A Concise Bibliography*), New York, 1941. For
the very important relations with Jewish merchants in Morocco, see T. S. Willan,
*Studies in Elizabethan Foreign Trade* (Manchester, 1955).

# VII

## READMISSION

### 1609–64

#### § 1

THE religious developments of the seventeenth century brought to its climax an unmistakable philo-semitic tendency in certain English circles. Puritanism represented above all a return to the Bible, and this automatically fostered a more favourable frame of mind towards the people of the Old Testament. With this was intermingled the hope that the Jews, so long deaf to popish or episcopal blandishments, would be unable to withstand a pure form of Christianity, once they had the opportunity of becoming acquainted with it at close quarters.

There were not lacking those who carried their new-found biblical enthusiasm to, or beyond, its logical conclusion. Certain extremists regarded the 'old' dispensation as binding, and even reverted to its practices of circumcision and the observance of the seventh-day Sabbath. In 1600 the Bishop of Exeter complained of the prevalence of 'Jewism' in his diocese,[1] and such views were comparatively common in London and the Eastern counties. Numerous persons were prosecuted here for holding what were termed 'Judaistic' opinions, based on the literal interpretation of the Old Testament.[2] As late as 1612, two so-called Arians died at the stake (the last persons to suffer capital punishment in England purely for their religion) for teaching views regarding the nature of God which approximated to those of Judaism. The followers of the Puritan extremist, John Traske, went so far on the path of literalism that they were imprisoned in 1618–20 on a charge of Judaizing. In this case, the accusation was so far from being exaggerated that a few of them settled in Amsterdam and formally joined the Synagogue.[3]

[1] *H.M.C., Hatfield*, x. 450.  
[2] See Note VII (*a*), p. 285.  
[3] See Note VII (*b*), p. 285.

In certain cases the tendency took a bizarre form. Some of the so-called saints and others (such as Everard the Leveller, or Robert Rich the Quaker philanthropist) styled themselves Jews, while a few 'ranters' actually claimed that they were designated to lead the Jewish people, providentially converted and renewed, back to the Promised Land.[1] A distinguished lawyer, Sir Henry Finch, suffered imprisonment for his remarkable treatise, *The World's great Restauration, or Calling of the Jews* (London, 1621), in which he invited the ancient people of God to reassert their claim on the Promised Land and Christian monarchs to pay homage to them.

Apart from this philo-semitic tendency, there was an incipient movement in favour of religious toleration as such. As separatist sects multiplied, the adherents of those which could never hope for a majority began to clamour that the principle of rigid uniformity should be modified. Generally speaking, it was not disputed that allegiance to the universally accepted principles of Christianity was a necessary prerequisite. Among the Baptists, however, more generous views prevailed, and it was urged that religious tolerance should be extended to all, without any restriction whatsoever. A number of writers belonging to this sect thus found themselves logically compelled to plea for a toleration that should extend even to Jews, and inferentially for the readmission of the Jews to the country.[2] As early as 1614 a member of the body, Leonard Busher, published for presentation to James I a memorable tract entitled *Religions Peace, or, a Plea for Liberty of Conscience* (reprinted in 1646). In this, the earliest English publication in which religious liberty in its fullest sense was advocated, the point was made for the first time that, by the exclusion of the Jews, their

---

[1] Thus in 1650 Joshua Garment proclaimed a half-demented farmer named John Robins as King of Israel, declaring that before the coming Michaelmas he would divide the sea like Moses and bring the Jews of the world back to Palestine. At much the same time Thomas Tany, a London silversmith, discovered that he was a Jew of the tribe of Reuben, and announced the imminent rebuilding of the Temple at Jerusalem, with himself (most unorthodoxly) as High Priest (R. Matthews, *English Messiahs*, London, 1936; *Bibl.* B.6. 10, B.16. 4, B.17. 2).

[2] For a detailed analysis of these publications and of the gradual change in English sentiment see W. K. Jordan, *Development of Religious Toleration in England* (4 vols., London, 1932–40). The authorities for the history of the resettlement of the Jews in England are listed in *Bibl.* A.6. 1–37, and the contemporary publications relating to it in B.1. 5–29. For Finch see now *Trs. J.H.S.E.* xvi. 101–20.

conversion was impeded; and the author went so far as to
suggest not only that they should be readmitted, but that they
should be allowed to engage in religious disputations (which
could only end in their defeat) without hindrance. The lead
was followed in the next year by another Baptist, John Murton,
in an anonymously produced work, *Objections answered by way of
dialogue, wherein is proved . . . that no man ought to be persecuted for
his religion* (1615). This tract, the popularity of which is shown
by its frequent republication (1620, 1630, 1662), insisted on the
validity of private judgement in matters of religion, with the
corollary that Jews should be converted by argument only, and
no longer submitted to persecution. John Wemyss, writing in
1636 (*A Treatise of the Foure Degenerate Sonnes*), argued that the
Jews should be permitted to live and maintain their synagogues
in a Christian commonwealth, so long as they behaved modestly
and refrained from disseminating their religion. In his striking
monograph, *The Bloudy Tenent of Persecution for cause of conscience
discussed in a conference between Truth and Peace* (1644), Roger
Williams similarly voiced the plea that the Jews could be good
citizens even though they were unbelievers, and must be given
the opportunity to demonstrate it. The tract was publicly
burned by the Common Hangman in August—just after its
author had sailed for America with his charter for Rhode
Island, conceived on the same tolerant principles. Nevertheless,
the tide of sympathy continued to rise.[1] The Civil War was
giving it a strong impetus, some persons being convinced that
the country's tribulations were in punishment for its maltreatment of the Jews in the past.[2] The Baptists found themselves
reinforced by persons such as Hugh Peters, one of the most
influential of the Puritan ministers, in his pamphlet, *A Word for*

---

[1] Another champion of religious toleration, on different grounds, was Sir Thomas
Browne, who in his *Religio Medici* (published only in 1642, but circulated in manuscript some years earlier) stalwartly maintained that persecution served to confirm
the Turks and Jews in their erroneous opinions. The influence of scholarly intercourse at this period should not be under-estimated. It was not easy, for example,
for James Primrose, the eminent physician, to maintain an anti-Jewish attitude after
he had published a commendatory letter from Abraham Zacuto of Amsterdam as
preface to his *Popular Errors*. For Wemyss's proposals see *J.Q.R.* n.s. xxxix. 379–95.

[2] This point of view was expounded most elaborately by Edward Nicholas,
for whom see below, p. 153. But it was widely held: cf. Roger Williams, *Hireling
Ministry none of Christs*, 1652: 'for whose hard measure the nations and England
hath yet a score to pay'.

*the Army, and Two Words to the Kingdom* (1647), in which he set
down as one of the remedies for the evils which were afflicting
the country that 'strangers, even Jews, be admitted to trade and
live with us'.

This development was not due only to the fact that sym-
pathetically inclined sectaries were now in the ascendant, but
also to its corollary—the collapse of the national church, the
only body which hitherto had sufficient strength to persecute
those who held minority views in the matter of religion. Henceforth, no single element was physically capable of carrying on
the tradition, though the Presbyterians displayed a strong in-
clination to do so. An ordinance passed in 1648, during the period
of their greatest political influence, declared the denial of the
Trinity, of the divinity of Jesus, or of the inspiration of Scripture,
punishable by death; but it was never acted upon, perhaps
because the abolition of the Court of High Commission seven
years before had left no tribunal competent to deal with such
cases.[1] Moreover, attention was now diverted from the Jews
not only by numerous bizarre Independent bodies, but also by
such minorities as the Roman Catholics, who, besides being
unpopular were, at this stage, politically dangerous. It was
hence not so much that the Jews became more acceptable, as
that the inacceptability which was once theirs alone was now
shared with many others. Thus, after the parliamentary triumph,
the sympathy which had previously been academic became
active, and, in the experiments for a constitutional settlement—
which at the same time had to be a religious settlement—the
position of the Jews assumed a symbolic prominence.

It was in the winter of 1648–9 that the question first came up
in a practical form.[2] Immediately after 'Pride's Purge' had

---

[1] There was a significant episode in 1649 when, notwithstanding the remon-
strations of the Assembly of Divines, the secular courts ordered the discharge of a
follower of Traske, Anne Cyrtyn, though 'a professed Jew and causing three children to be circumcided', on the grounds that the offence was 'merely ecclesiasticall'
(J. C. Jeaffreson, *Middlesex Sessions Rolls*, ii. 186–7).

[2] The following account of the premature attempt to secure the recall of the
Jews to England in 1648 is completely new: it is based on a collation of the data
assembled in my *Life of Menasseh ben Israel* (Philadelphia, 1934), pp. 197–200;
Jordan, op. cit., ii. 119–31; and A. S. P. Woodhouse (ed.), *Puritanism and Liberty*
(Army Debates from the Clarke MSS., 1647–9), London, 1938. It is comical to
note how, in the course of the debates which failed to extend toleration to the
Jews of the seventeenth century, the precedent of those of biblical times is con-
stantly and reverently cited.

swept away the Presbyterian dominance in Parliament, the Council of Officers began to discuss a new constitution based upon what was known as the Agreement of the People. This had been drawn up by a committee representing the army and different sects included in the Republican party, under the inspiration of such advanced theorists as John Lilburne, and stipulated that there should be a wide measure of liberty for all men to preach and advance their opinions in a peaceable manner. Clearly, considerable latitude was possible in the practical application of this. The Council of Mechanics, meeting at Whitehall, boldly passed a resolution in favour of universal tolerance for all religions 'not excepting Turkes, nor Papists, nor Jewes'.[1] This policy was endorsed by the Council of War when it met on Christmas Day[2] and it was apparently suggested that a clause to this effect should be embodied in the new constitution. The Council of Officers was no less favourable but preferred a different approach to the question, petitioning Parliament on its own account to consider the repeal of the banishment of the Jews (it was in these terms that the whole discussion was conceived) 'in regard it was not held fit for mention in the Agreement'. At about the same time, a petition was presented through Lord Fairfax, the Commander-in-Chief, from two Baptists from Amsterdam, Joanna Cartwright and her son Ebenezer, requesting the readmission of the Jews 'to trade and dwell in this land, as they now do in the Netherlands'.[3] It was agreed that this should be taken into consideration immediately the present urgent public affairs were dispatched— not a very imminent contingency in the month of the king's execution. Meanwhile there was in the press a more elaborate plea, *An Apology for the honourable nation of the Jews, and all the sons of Israel*, by Edward Nicholas, who spoke of the tribulations that the country had suffered in punishment for her past maltreatment of the people of God, and averred that it was only by making amends that she could hope to enjoy the Divine blessing again as she had done in former times.

The general opinion in the responsible body remained

---

[1] *Mercurius Pragmaticus*, 19–26 December 1648.

[2] *History of the Independency*, ii. 50.

[3] *Bibl.* B.1. 6 (facsimile reprint, San Francisco, 1941). On the whole question, see my article 'The Attempt to recall the Jews to England, 1648', in *Jewish Monthly*, i. 12 (1948) pp. 11–17.

lukewarm, its members being unable to envisage the possibility of toleration outside the bounds of Christianity. It was in vain that William Erbury, the chaplain of Skippon's Regiment, demonstrated that this attitude made a favourable reply to the Cartwright petition impossible ('To what purpose', he asked, 'will you give that liberty to the Jews and others to come in, unless you grant them the exercise of their religion?'), and that Captain Butler inveighed against the principle of attempting to define religious truth. On 20 January, the modified *Agreement of the People* was laid before Parliament, reserving religious freedom for such only as should 'profess faith in God by Jesus Christ'. The ideal of universal toleration thus received what was to prove a final set-back, and with it the Gentile movement for the recall of the Jews to England on finely conceived idealistic grounds.[1]

## § 11

The question now entered a new phase. Though the disinterested champions of religious liberty did not give up hope, the movement was overshadowed henceforth by another, narrower in scope, in which mysticism and material considerations were oddly interwoven, and Jews and Christians were equally involved. The Puritan theologians found a kindred spirit beyond the North Sea in the famous Rabbi Menasseh ben Israel, alias Manuel Dias Soeiro. He had been born in Madeira in 1604 of crypto-Jewish parentage, but had been brought early in life to Amsterdam. Here he made a name while still a very young man as one of the most productive, if by no means most profound, theological writers of his age. Gentiles as well as Jews thronged to hear him preach, and when Henrietta Maria, queen of England, visited the Amsterdam synagogue in 1643, it was he who gave the address. Savants and statesmen, both at home and abroad (including many in England) were in the habit of consulting him on matters of Jewish scholarship. He had thus become a representative figure in Gentile eyes, and considered himself qualified to speak to those in authority on behalf of his people as a whole. In common with the other members of the group to which he belonged, he considered the salient fact in contemporary Jewish life to be the tragedy of the

[1] See Note VII (c), pp. 285–6.

Marranos of Spain and Portugal, persecuted with unrelenting
severity by the Inquisition. To this was added in 1648 the trail
of massacre which followed the Cossack rising against the Poles.
The whole of central Europe was filled with penniless fugitives,
fleeing from the scene of slaughter.[1] It was the culminating
disaster in contemporary Jewish history, and the opening of a
land of refuge became desperately important.

A curious episode set Menasseh ben Israel's mind at this
juncture on England. A Marrano traveller named Antonio de
Montezinos, recently returned from America, claimed that
about 1641 he had discovered near Quito, in Ecuador, certain
natives belonging to the lost Hebrew tribes of Reuben and of
Levi, who practised various Jewish ceremonies. On his return
to Holland he embodied his account in an affidavit executed
under oath before the authorities of the Amsterdam community
—including Menasseh himself, who was immediately bom-
barded with inquiries on the subject by his English correspondents. These communications forced on him the more remote
implications of the report. The prophet Daniel had intimated
(xii. 7) that the final Redemption would begin only when the
scattering of the Jewish people was complete. On the other
hand the Book of Deuteronomy plainly stated (xxviii. 64) that
the dispersion was to be universal 'from one end of the earth
even unto the other'. Hebrews had now been found in America:
they were missing only in Great Britain. Moreover, the classical name for England, in medieval Jewish literature, was 'the
end of the earth'—an over-literal translation of the French
Angleterre. It followed that if they were introduced into the
British Isles, the prophesied Dispersion would be completed,
and the messianic Deliverance would begin. Under the impetus
of this idea, Menasseh produced in 1650 a treatise in Latin, in
which he dealt with the recent discoveries and their implications. This he entitled *The Hope of Israel* ('Spes Israelis').[2]

The book proved an instantaneous success. Before the year
was out, it had been published in English, dedicated to Parliament, whose 'favour and good-will' were respectfully solicited
for the scattered Jewish nation: the translation running through

[1] The late Lucien Wolf stated in conversation that a boat-load arrived in England; but it has been impossible to find confirmation of this.
[2] See Note VII (d), p. 286.

three editions in as many years. It occasioned a spate of publications. John Sadler, the town clerk of London; Hamon l'Estrange, a versatile theologian and historian; the Sabbatarian pastor Henry Jessey, an accomplished Hebrew and rabbinic scholar and former correspondent of Menasseh's, were among the many who rushed into print. But the most memorable contribution to the discussion was written by Sir Edward Spenser, knight of the shire of Middlesex, who, as a member of the body to which the work had been directed in the first instance, took it upon himself to compose a formal answer. It was entitled: *An Epistle to the learned Menasseh ben Israel, in answer to his, dedicated to the Parliament* (London, 1650); and, following the cue given by Menasseh himself in his Dedication, it discussed seriously the conditions, of somewhat ludicrous severity, upon which the settlement of the Jews in England might be allowed. The question thus entered into the sphere of more or less practical politics.

Early in 1651 an English mission headed by Chief Justice Oliver St. John, one of the outstanding Republican stalwarts, arrived at The Hague to negotiate an alliance between England and the United Provinces. During a trip to Amsterdam its secretary, John Thurloe, seized the opportunity to become acquainted with the famous Rabbi, whom he apparently advised to make formal application to the English government for the object he had at heart. It was on 10 October—the morrow of the passage of the Navigation Act—that the Council of State took into consideration the communication which resulted, appointing an influential committee (of which the Lord General, Oliver Cromwell, was a member) to answer it. It presumably reported that direct conversations should be opened up in order to discuss terms. Before Menasseh could set out for London, war broke out between England and Holland; but though he allowed himself to be persuaded by his friends to turn back ('for certain political reasons', as he afterwards recorded) he did not give up hope. Immediately the news of the assembly of Barebone's Parliament reached the Low Countries he addressed this new body in the same sense as he had its predecessor. A petition to a similar effect was simultaneously submitted at Westminster by one Samuel Herring; and a formal motion 'that the Jews might be admitted to trade as well as in Holland' was discussed by the House. Nothing practical, indeed, was done: though the three 'Generals of the Fleet' became interested in the project, and were reported to have presented to the government a petition endorsing it.

As, owing to the war and subsequent sickness, Menasseh was still unable to follow up his advantage in person, his place was now taken by a Marrano merchant named Manuel Martinez Dormido,[1] ruined by the recent Portuguese reconquest of Brazil, who was accompanied by the other's son, Samuel Soeiro. Immediately on arrival, he submitted (3 November 1654) two petitions to Oliver Cromwell, who, since the last days of 1653, had been ruling England as Lord Protector, with more absolute power than any recent monarch had possessed. One recounted his personal history, and requested that diplomatic representations should be made to assist him in recovering his fortune. The other, after a vivid description of the tyrannies of the Inquisition calculated to make Protestant blood run cold, went on to recount the sufferings of the Marranos, their constant flight to northern Europe, and their potential value to national finance and commerce. On the strength of this Dormido pleaded that the government should readmit the Jews to England, 'graunting them libertie to come with their families and estates, to bee dwellers here with the same eaquallnese and conveniences which your inland subjects doe enjoy', with himself as their Consul.

Cromwell was a realist. Though his Puritan background naturally stimulated his interest in the people of the Old Testament, he had little sympathy for the mystical tendencies that had hitherto coloured the movement for their readmission to England, and consistently opposed both the millenarians and the literalists who based religious observance on the Mosaic code. Though in advance of his age in his spirit of tolerance he confined it theoretically to Christians and in practice only to Protestants (though for political reasons not Episcopalians). It was preposterous, he maintained, that toleration should be 'stretched so far as to countenance those who deny the divinity of our Saviour, or to bolster up any blasphemous opinions contrary to the fundamental verities of religion'. Religion did not, however, weigh with him in this matter so much as

---

[1] Not Menasseh's brother-in-law, as generally stated.

practical considerations. A primary factor in the foreign policy of the Commonwealth was the protection and encouragement of English commerce. This was the cause of the war with Holland, and it played its part in that with Spain. But negative steps to protect trade were not sufficient. It was patent that Jewish merchants had been very largely responsible for the recent growth and prosperity of Leghorn, of Hamburg, and especially Amsterdam. Were they persuaded to settle in London, they might do as much there as well. Fugitives from Spain and Portugal would transfer their capital thither, instead of to the Low Countries, and perhaps some of the Amsterdam colony might be persuaded to follow them. With them they would bring, not only their wealth and their ability, but also their world-wide commercial connexions, which must inevitably enrich their country of residence. In the West Indian trade also Jewish influence was strong, and their introduction might prove no less useful than naval and military action in making English commerce supreme in the Spanish Main. The whole question of the readmission of the Jews was, from one point of view, simply an episode in the Anglo-Dutch and Anglo-Spanish rivalry. It is impossible to fathom the entire complex of reasons that drove Cromwell himself in this direction, but the intensity of his personal interest in the question of the readmission of the Jews is certain.[1]

## § III

The ordinary Englishman realized only imperfectly what the Protector knew very well, that infiltration had already begun on a small scale. The recovery in English commerce under the Commonwealth had resulted in the formation in London once more of a settlement of Spanish and Portuguese merchants, many of whom were New Christians—especially so after 1630, when the recrudescence of persecution in Portugal drove hundreds of that category into exile. Moreover, the formation of

---

[1] Recent writers (e.g. M. P. Ashley, *The Commercial and Financial Policy of the Cromwellian Protectorate*, Oxford, 1934), tend to minimize Cromwell's economic, and especially his commercial, interests. His friendly attitude towards the Jews has to be reinterpreted in view of this; but the importance of the economic factor is shown by the interest taken in the question by the Dutch government: Roth, *Menasseh ben Israel*, p. 237, and in *Three Centuries*, ed. V. D. Lipman, p. 6.

open communities in the other great commercial centres of northern Europe made it natural for agents, correspondents, or rivals to settle beyond the North Sea. An impetus was given to the process in 1632, when, in consequence of internal dissensions, the crypto-Jewish congregation which had sprung up at Rouen was denounced to the authorities and temporarily broken up.[1] One of its principal members had been Antonio Ferdinando Carvajal, a native of Fundão in Portugal, but long resident in the Canary Islands. He, with perhaps one or two others, had settled in London. Notwithstanding at least one prosecution for recusancy owing to his failure to attend church,[2] it did not take him long to establish his position in his new home. Before many years had passed, he was among the most prominent merchants in the City. He possessed his own ships, trading with the East and West Indies, as well as the Levant, in a large variety of commodities. He imported gunpowder and munitions on an extensive scale, brought large quantities of bullion from abroad, and during the Civil War was grain contractor for Parliament. When in 1650 informal hostilities began with Spain his goods were expressly exempted from seizure by the Council of State, and he was given facilities for continuing his commercial operations.[3]

After Carvajal the most interesting character in the Marrano colony was Simão de Caceres, a fiery merchant formerly settled in Hamburg, who supplied Cromwell with valuable information and was anxious to be avenged on the Spaniards for their cruelty towards his co-religionists: a little later he laid before the government a plan for an expedition against Chile, in which a Jewish contingent was to take part, and another for the fortification of Jamaica. Other members of the group came from Amsterdam, whence, according to the Venetian envoy, a number of Jews had been brought over in 1643, at the outset of the Civil War, when there was difficulty in exporting goods from England, to smooth the process of trade. Thereafter more than one Dutch Jewish house maintained its representative in

---

[1] See my article, 'Les Marranes à Rouen', in *R.E.J.* lxxxviii. 133–55.

[2] J. C. Jeaffreson, *Middlesex County Records*, ii. 147 (1640).

[3] *Bibl.* A.6. 35. See *High Court of Admiralty Examinations*, ed. D. O. Shelton and R. Holworthy, 1932, § 435, and E. Sainsbury, *Court Minutes of East India Company*, 10 March 1640, for further illustrations of his commercial activities (shipping goods to Madeira and importing musk into England).

London.[1] The Marrano group lived for the most part as titular Catholics, attending Mass in the chapel of the French or Spanish ambassador. It was pretty notorious, however, that their sympathies with any form of Christianity were lukewarm, and in view of recent developments it was less necessary for them to conceal the fact than had formerly been the case. 'Touching Judaism', James Howell wrote in 1653 to a friend in Amsterdam, 'some corners of our city smell as rank of it as doth yours there.'[2]

With all this Cromwell was quite familiar. He knew that a large proportion—perhaps a majority—of the Spanish and Portuguese merchants in the City were in sympathy with Judaism. Yet Judaism was no more obnoxious to him than Papistry. Besides, he was finding the reports from abroad provided by some of the group—thanks to their widespread connexions—invaluable in certain of his political projects.[3] He was accordingly predisposed to give a benevolent hearing to Dormido's petitions. They were immediately referred to the Council, which appointed a small committee to consider the matter. A month later it reported, but unfavourably; and in the Protector's absence the Council decided that 'there was no cause to make any order'.

Cromwell's attitude towards this decision may be deduced from the fact that, early in the next year, he went out of his way to write to the King of Portugal, requesting compensation for the losses which Dormido had suffered in Brazil. Seeing that the latter was a foreigner and a Jew (he was even referred to as such in the letter), and had been resident in the country for no more than a few months, it was an extraordinary proceeding, and showed plainly in which direction the Protector's personal sympathies lay. It would appear that at the same time he

[1] S.P.V. 1642–3, p. 252. For the trade of the Dutch Jews with England, see too H. I. Bloom, *The Economic Activities of the Jews of Amsterdam in the 17th and 18th Centuries* (Williamsport, 1937), pp. 106–7. From A. M. Vaz Dias, *Spinoza Mercator* (The Hague, 1932), p. 54, it appears that Spinoza's family had as their London agent at this time Francisco Lopes d'Azevedo, alias Abraham Farrar.

[2] That Jews were not unknown outside London, too, appears from an entry of 1634–5 in the Borough Act Book of Plymouth, indicating that a 'Hebrew High German' had been 'maintained at the charity of the town' at a cost of £2. 18s. (Worth, *Plymouth Records* (1893), p. 158). Some interest is attached too to the impostor who appeared at Hexham in 1653, claiming to be a converted Italian Jew—an episode which occasioned the publication of several pamphlets (*Bibl.* B.1. 13–15).

[3] Wolf, *Cromwell's Jewish Intelligencers* (reprinted, with emendations, in his posthumous *Essays in Jewish History*).

intimated to Dormido that he was completely in favour of his project, but considered it desirable for Menasseh to come over and treat of the matter in person.

Samuel Soeiro returned to Amsterdam to lay the matter before his father. The latter, though not yet fully recovered from his illness, was now no longer to be kept back. In the middle of September (just before the Jewish New Year festival, which was celebrated in London in due form on this occasion, for the first time probably for 365 years), Menasseh arrived. With him he brought, ready for distribution, a little English pamphlet which he had prepared some time before, *To His Highnesse the Lord Protector of the Common-wealth of England, Scotland, and Ireland. The Humble Addresses of Menasseh ben Israel, a Divine, and Doctor of Physick, in behalfe of the Jewish Nation*, in which he eloquently pleaded that the newly constituted English government would 'with a gracious eye have regard unto us, and our Petition, and grant unto us . . . free exercise of our Religion, that we may have our Synagogues, and keep our own publick worship, as our brethren doe in Italy, Germany, Poland, and many other places'. This was presented at Whitehall together with a personal petition requesting that all laws against the Jews should be repealed; that the principal public officers should take an oath to defend them; that synagogues and cemeteries should be permitted in all parts of the English dominions; that they should have unrestricted rights of trade; and that they should be allowed internal jurisdiction, subject to appeal to the civil judges. On the other hand, a special official was to be appointed to maintain control over immigration, and those who were admitted were to swear allegiance to the government and to be kept under strict surveillance.

On 12 November 1655 Cromwell brought this petition with him to a meeting of the Council of State, resolved to secure its acceptance with the minimum of delay, and a motion was tabled to the effect that 'the Jewes deservinge it may be admitted into this nation to trade and trafficke and dwel amongst us as providence shall give occasion'. To the majority the question appeared too complicated to be decided there and then. Accordingly a sub-committee was appointed to take the matter into consideration. This body, not over-enthusiastic, recommended that outside opinion should be consulted.

The course of the negotiations was watched with the utmost interest both at home and abroad, and the printing-presses were kept busy pouring out a flood of literature on the subject. The balance of opinion was hardly cordial. It was alleged that the Jews had made an offer of half a million pounds for St. Paul's Cathedral in London, which they proposed to convert into a synagogue, and that the bargain would have been carried through had not Parliament insisted on the increase of the purchase price to £800,000. A messenger, ostensibly sent to purchase the Cambridge University Library, was rumoured to have stopped on the way at Huntingdon, Cromwell's birthplace, to inquire into his genealogy, so as to confirm the report that he was the promised Messiah. A Russian Jewish apostate named Eliezer bar Jesse or Paul Isaiah, who had served in Rupert's horse, and who experimented in all gradations of Christianity from Catholic to Anabaptist, was encouraged to write a succession of pamphlets (1652–5) indicating the incorrigible hatred of the Jews for Jesus, and the extreme unlikelihood of their conversion.

Above all, William Prynne, who had lost his ears for his virulence against the queen twenty years before, was prompted by what he saw and heard in the streets of London to compose what was to be one of the most effective pamphlets of the period, a monument of learning as well as of acerbity: *A Short Demurrer to the Jewes Long discontinued Remitter into England*.[1]

It was in this atmosphere that a representative conference, comprising some of the finest brains in the political, legal, theological, and business life of the country, met in the Council Chamber in Whitehall on Tuesday, 4 December 1655. The opening meeting was presided over by the Lord Protector himself, who, with characteristic clarity and common sense, narrowed down the questions before the Conference to two: first, whether it was lawful to admit the Jews, and secondly, if it were lawful, on what terms it was 'meet' to receive them. The first point was purely technical. The two juristic experts in attendance, Sir John Glynne, Chief Justice of the Upper Bench, and William Steele, Chief Baron of the Exchequer, pronounced

---

[1] The second part of this work, published a little later, is still fundamental for the study of Anglo-Jewish history, and served as the basis for Tovey's more systematic, and more accessible, *Anglia Judaica* of 1738.

that, contrary to the general impression, there was no law which forbade the return of the Jews to England (for the Expulsion of 1290 had been an act of royal prerogative, and applied only to the persons immediately concerned). The issue before the Conference thus resolved itself into a discussion of the second point, to which the remaining sessions (7, 12, 14, 18 December) were devoted. As the debates continued, a stubborn body of reactionary opinion manifested itself. The theologians professed to regard the public exercise of the Jewish religion in a Christian country as nothing less than blasphemous, and to dread the possibilities of proselytization, while seeing little prospect of compensatory victories for the Gospel. With unbelievable credulity, some went so far as to envisage a revival of Moloch-worship in England. Only a small minority supported the political representatives in their plea for unconditional readmission.

On the occasion of the fifth meeting (Friday, 18 December) the doors of the Council Chamber were thrown open, and the debates were listened to by a none-too-orderly mob, keyed up to a considerable pitch of excitement by Prynne's recently published *Demurrer*, which was now in every hand. The argument centred around the commercial and economic aspects of the problem. In this the narrow outlook of individuals carried more weight than the larger interests of the country. Merchant after merchant added his voice to the tide of protest, hinting darkly that the admission of the Jews would enrich foreigners at the expense of the natives, and cause the decline of English trade. Sir Christopher Pack, a former lord mayor, eloquently voiced the apprehensions of the City of London, his speech being one of the most effective delivered during the whole course of the discussions. Even those who favoured readmission agreed that it could be permitted only under stringent conditions, inspired by a hasty re-reading of the medieval codes: Jews were not to be admitted to any judicial function, to be allowed to speak or act to the dishonour of Christianity, to profane the Christian Sabbath, to employ Christian servants, to hold public office, to print anti-Christian literature, to convert Christians to Judaism, or finally, to discourage persons who attempted to propagate the Gospel amongst them.

The night was far advanced when, rising from his chair of

state, Cromwell intervened in the discussion. ('I never heard a man speak so well', one who was present subsequently recorded.) It was clear, he said, that no help was to be expected from the Conference, and that he and the Council would have to take their own course. He hoped that he would do nothing foolishly or rashly, and now asked only that those present would give him the benefit of their prayers, that he might be directed to act for the glory of God and the good of the nation. With these words he stepped down abruptly from the dais, and the Conference was brought to an end.

§ IV

The anticipated sequel failed to materialize. Christmas passed. The days lengthened into weeks and the weeks into months; but still the Lord Protector did not announce his decision. Public opinion was too strong: the Council, if consulted, was unhelpful. Accordingly he determined simply to maintain the state of affairs that he had found, permitting such Jews as were established in London to observe their ancestral rites undisturbed as they had hitherto done.[1]

Matters were at this stage when the little group of London Marranos was alarmed by a new development in foreign affairs. In the autumn of 1655 war had broken out between England and Spain. Early in the following March the Council of State issued a proclamation declaring all Spanish moneys, merchandise, and shipping to be lawful prize. The possible repercussions on the nascent community were obvious. Its members had been born, almost without exception, in Spain, or else in Portugal when that country had been under the Spanish yoke. They had indeed fled, for the most part, from the rigours of the Inquisition, and had no thought of returning. Nevertheless, they were Spanish subjects in the eyes of the law. One of the most affluent among them after Carvajal (recently endenizened and therefore safe from molestation) was Antonio Rodrigues

---

[1] Owing to a slight misinterpretation of the report of the Tuscan envoy, coupled with a confusion between the 'Old' and 'New' styles of reckoning, it was maintained by Lucien Wolf that Cromwell privately gave a favourable reply to the petition of the Jews between 14 and 28 January 1655-6; and in consequence an annual celebration of 'Resettlement Day' took place in the early years of the present century on 4 February. As I showed in my paper, 'New Light on the Resettlement', in *Trs. J.H.S.E.*, vol. xi, this hypothesis is completely untenable.

Robles, a wealthy merchant of Duke's Place. A jealous com-
patriot, incited by a scrivener named Francis Knevett, denounced him to the authorities; and orders were immediately
issued for the seizure and sequestration of all his property,
including two ships lying in the Thames.

The entire group was thrown into consternation. If Robles's
property was confiscated, few could consider themselves safe.
It was agreed even by those who had previously been satisfied
with their anomalous status that the best course was to throw
themselves upon Cromwell's mercy, declaring themselves openly
as Jews, and requesting his protection. On 24 March—only
ten days after the first steps had been taken against Robles—
a petition was presented to him requesting written permission
to meet for private devotion according to Jewish rites in their
houses without fear of molestation, as they had hitherto done,
and to have a burial-place for their dead. Cromwell immediately referred the request to the Council for decision. Even at
this, his third attempt, he could not have his way—it is an
interesting sidelight on his imagined omnipotence. Only after
three months, apparently, did the Council take the question on
which the Lord Protector had set his heart into serious consideration at last. Nevertheless, the lead given by his associates indicated to Robles what was the wisest course to follow. On the
same day that they presented their petition he submitted a
request for the restitution of his property on the grounds that
he was not a Spaniard, but a Portuguese 'of the Hebrew nation'.
On 15 April he followed this up by a fresh memorandum in
which he recounted his life-story—how he was a Jew, born in
Portugal; how his family had been driven from place to place
by reason of the Inquisition; how his father had lost his life, his
mother been maimed, and many of his kindred burned alive, in
consequence of its persecutions; how he himself had come after
many vicissitudes to England, hoping to find peace and security
at last. The whole document was admirably calculated to
arouse the sympathy of the pope-hating, Inquisition-fearing
Englishman of the period. In the following week affidavits
confirming his statement that he was 'of the Hebrew nation and
religion' were sent in by a number of his Marrano associates,
who thus ranged themselves at his side. In the subsequent investigations it transpired that there were in London over twenty

such families, some of whom had resided there for a considerable time.

Consideration of the case did not take long. The Council of State sent the papers to the Admiralty Commissioners, requesting a prompt decision. The latter, after summoning the witnesses, reported that they were unable to give any definite opinion on the question of nationality. The affair thus had to be decided from the other angle—that of religion. On 16 May the Council of State ordered all the warrants to be discharged, and reinstated Robles in the possession of his property. As a Spanish Catholic his position had been open to question. As a refugee Jew he was safe.

Meanwhile, the Council of State had delayed taking action for as long as possible on the petition of 24 March. There is evidence that it was at last considered favourably on 25 June —possibly under pressure from the Lord Protector, to whom it was returned on the following day, and who presumably communicated the welcome decision to Menasseh ben Israel and his associates. But this fact has only been established very recently, as for some reason the pages of the Council Book comprising the deliberations for that day were subsequently torn out—perhaps by an enemy of the Jews trying to remove the evidence. Possibly indeed the Council's assent was hedged about by restrictions, and it certainly did not amount to the formal Recall of the Jews originally desired. Menasseh, bitterly disappointed in his grandiose expectations, and seeing no prospect for his own future, seems to have become estranged from his co-religionists. They, however, felt themselves sufficiently secure to rent a house in December in Cree Church Lane for use as a synagogue,[1] and a couple of months later a cemetery was acquired. The Jews had not been recalled to England, but their presence there was henceforth considered legitimate.[2]

[1] According to the parish accounts, the workmen engaged in adapting the house for its new use were 'warned' before the Court of Aldermen, but nothing came of it.

[2] The process is described at length in the light of the latest investigations in my paper, 'The Resettlement of the Jews in England in 1656', in *Three Centuries*, ed. V. D. Lipman, pp. 1–25, reprinted in my *Essays and Portraits*. The legality of the residence of Jews in the country was emphasized by the fact that before the year was out a son of Manuel Martinez Dormido was admitted a licensed broker without taking the prescribed Christological oath. About the same time, the prevailing philosemitic tendencies were strikingly illustrated by the collection made by Henry Jessey and John Dury for the relief of the distressed Jews of Jerusalem,

## § V

The debate on the Jewish question had spluttered on mean-while in a running fire of pamphlets, for and against, culminating in 1656 in James Harrington's plea in his *Oceana* for settling distressed Jews in Ireland, and in Menasseh ben Israel's noble *Vindiciae Judaeorum* refuting the superstitious allegations which had been brought up in the course of the polemic. This was the latter's last production before he returned to Holland to die, broken-hearted at the apparent ruin of his hopes. For such exiguous toleration as had been won, wholly dependent upon the benevolence of one man, was very far from that ample, formal recall for which the Amsterdam dreamer had worked, and Jews throughout Europe hoped.

By reason of this informality, the Lord Protector's death in September 1658 was a serious menace to the position of the little community. Hardly was the breath out of his body when London merchants recommenced their intrigues, and a certain Richard Baker presented to Richard Cromwell in their name *The Merchants' Humble Petition and Remonstrance*, in which he solicited the expulsion of the Jews and the confiscation of their property. Meanwhile, Thomas Violet, 'the great Trappaner of England', who eked out his living alternately as an informer and an exporter of contraband bullion, was ferreting around the City, and discovering all that he could about the mysterious foreign colony which centred in Cree Church Lane. In December 1659 (six months after Richard Cromwell's withdrawal into private life) he made an application before the courts for the law to be set in motion against the intruders, only to be told that, in the present delicate state of political affairs, considera-tion had better be postponed.[1]

Not long afterwards, the exiled Charles Stuart heard the church bells frenziedly pealing as he landed at Dover. Soon the reaction was complete. It was only to be expected, in such circumstances, that the readmission of the Jews by 'the late

---

some £300 being transmitted to Rabbi Nathan Spira in Amsterdam (who, how-ever, did not come to England for the purpose, as formerly stated).

[1] The best account of what follows may be found in H. S. Q. Henriques, *The Jews and English Law* (London, 1906), or in the chapters from this work previously pub-lished under the title, *The Return of the Jews to England* (London, 1903). Henriques, however, with his rigid legal mind, was unable to appreciate the fact that the pres-ence of Jews in England was recognized some years before it was legally authorized.

execrable Usurper' would have been reversed, with so much of his other work. His connivance at the Resettlement had been a characteristic and unpopular item in his policy. Moreover, many of the persons who had taken a prominent share in the movement and in the Whitehall Conference—Peters, Rowe, Lisle, and others—were among the Regicides, a fact which cannot have escaped notice. In the reaction against Puritanism as a religious system the sympathy for the Jews which it engendered not only lost its appeal, but might well have been changed to a deeper hatred. It would therefore have been natural had the precarious advantages, won so painfully during the course of the past three or four years, shared the fate of the remaining policy of the Commonwealth.

Popular opinion certainly expected this. The Lord Mayor and the Corporation of the City of London lost no time before presenting a petition complaining in exaggerated terms of the great increase of Jews in England, their interference with the trade of the citizens, and their treasonable correspondence with their co-religionists in other states, and beseeching the king 'to cause the former laws made against the Jews to be put into execution, and to recommend to your two Houses of Parliament to enact such new ones for the expulsion of all professed Jews out of your Majesty's dominions, and to bar the door after them with such provisions and penalties, as in your Majesty's wisdom shall be found most agreeable to the safety of religion, the honour of your Majesty, and the good and welfare of your subjects'. Thomas Violet (who had meanwhile attempted without success to discredit the community by passing a packet of counterfeit foreign coins upon its newly appointed minister) could not remain inactive in such circumstances, and renewed his application in the courts, by which he was advised to lay the matter before the Privy Council. He did so, in a petition of extreme virulence, in which he asserted that it was felony for any Jew to be found in England, and suggested that those who had broken the law should be arrested at prayer on Saturday morning, have their property confiscated, and be kept in prison until they were ransomed by their wealthy brethren abroad. Petitions to a similar effect were presented at the same time by some other zealots, such as Sir William Courtney.[1]

---

[1] See also Wolf in *J.C.*, 22 Nov. 1889 and *Essays*, pp. 119 ff.

The little London community, which had already begun to take precautions ('since the King's coming in', wrote an interested contemporary, 'they are very close, nor do admit any to see them but very privately'), was thrown into panic and hastily prepared a counter-petition. But meanwhile other influences had been at work. Charles II was essentially tolerant in a manner in which Cromwell was not, simply because religion was to him a matter of minor consequence. On conscientious ground, he had no objection whatsoever to the presence of Jews in his dominions. He realized, too, that he might find them useful in the future, as he had in the past, when he had received advances from the King of Portugal through the medium of Jeronimo Nuñes da Costa, his agent in the Low Countries. The readmission of the Jews to England had been present in his mind even at that period. During the course of the discussions in England, he had attempted to raise a loan from the Jews of Amsterdam, assuring them that if they were amenable 'they shall find that when God shall restore us to the possession of our rights and to that power which of right doth belonge to us we shall extend that protection to them which they can reasonably expecte and abate that rigour of the Lawes which is against them in our several dominions'. The results were not as satisfactory as he had hoped. Yet the pronouncement indicated the direction of his personal sympathies, and gave the Jews a prospect of success whatever party was victorious.[1]

Nothing but a strong expression of opinion on the part of the sovereign can explain the action of the Privy Council when the petitions of the City and merchants and counter-petition of the Jews were read before it on 7 December. No order was made, but instead the rival documents were referred to Parliament—not for adjudication, but so that measures might be taken into consideration for safeguarding those concerned, the desirability of whose presence in the country was assumed to be beyond discussion. On 17 December Denzil Holles, the spokesman of the Council, presented the documents before the Commons, 'as specially recommended to them for their advice

[1] The strength of the royalist element among the Jews, and the extent of their understanding with Charles, previously overstated, are correctly assessed in *Trs. J.H.S.E.* xiv. 39–79.

therein, touching protection for the Jews'. The House determined to consider the matter at an early opportunity. A week later, before anything was done, the Convention Parliament was dissolved, and it does not appear that the City of London even received a reply to its address. But the Crown's attitude was clearly defined; on the question of tolerating the Jews Charles II had taken up much the same position as Oliver Cromwell.[1]

Other alarms were in store. On 26 February 1663 the House of Commons voted 'that a Committee be appointed to prepare and bring in laws to prevent encroachments in trade by the Jews or French or any other foreigners'. Thanks again perhaps to the royal protection, nothing resulted. In the following year (1 July 1664) the Conventicle Act came into force, prohibiting assemblies for prayer except in accordance with the liturgy of the Church of England. Though this was aimed only against Christian nonconformists, it put an obvious weapon into the hands of mischief-makers, of which they were not slow to take advantage. Immediately afterwards a certain Mr. Rycaut interviewed the heads of the congregation and informed them that by continuing to hold services in their synagogue they had made themselves liable to all manner of penalties and forfeitures. Almost simultaneously (in all probability by collusive arrangement) the Earl of Berkshire intervened, saying that he had been verbally instructed by the king to protect them; he would not do so, however, unless they came to an arrangement with him, in default of which he would himself commence proceedings and confiscate their property.[2] The Jews, instead of falling into the trap, addressed the king himself, asking to be allowed to remain in the realm under the same protection as the rest of his subjects. The petition was referred to the Privy Council and elicited a written assurance that no instructions had been given for disturbing them and that

---

[1] These events are referred to in the synagogue accounts for 1661: 'The congregational funds owe me £80, which I paid in advance . . . for the action which the traders brought against us in order to drive us from the realm' (L. D. Barnett, *El Libro de los Acuerdos*, Oxford, 1931, p. 58).

[2] The Rycaut involved in this attempt is probably Paul Rycaut, who was later to be secretary to the English Embassy in Constantinople and to write a classical account of the Turkish Empire and its Jews (he had been present at the last session of the Whitehall Conference). The Earl of Berkshire was a son of that Earl of Suffolk who had been responsible for the expulsion of the Marranos from England in 1609.

they might 'promise themselves the effects of the same favour as formerly they have had, soe long as they demeane themselves peaceably & quietly with due obedience to his Ma^ties Lawes & without scandall to his Governement' (22 August 1664).[1] Thus, the residence of the Jews in England was authorized, for the first time, in writing.

In this manner there was obtained easily—almost casually— from Charles Stuart that formal instrument which Menasseh ben Israel had despairingly endeavoured to procure from the all-powerful Lord Protector.[2] It was paradoxical; but it is not, after all, surprising. The only legislation of the Commonwealth which was maintained after the Restoration was the Navigation Act, intended to foster English trade. Cromwell's Jewish policy was actuated in part by the same motives; and if only for this reason, it would not have been wise or statesmanlike to reverse it. This indeed was not decisive. Stuart promises were short-lived, and, at a period of general reaction such as burst upon England in 1660, it was not normally to be expected that considerations of equity, gratitude, or advantage would be preponderant. That the resettlement of the Jews escaped the same fate as the Commonwealth and everything associated with it was, in fact, because of what Menasseh ben Israel had considered his failure. Nothing had been formally effected. There was nothing, therefore, to reverse; and the Cromwellian settlement was allowed to remain simply because it was so casual, and so elusive, as to defy attack.

Even had this not been the case, the success of the negotiations of 1655 would have left the Jews in England, a few years later, in a much worse position than that which they actually achieved. Menasseh's proposals had been considered extravagant by contemporary opinion. Nevertheless, they were based upon the principle of differentiation, and were removed only in

---

[1] Facsimile in *Bevis Marks Records*, ed. L. D. Barnett (Oxford, 1940), vol. i, plate III. It is significant that neither in the petition nor the reply is there any mention of a Jewish community, a synagogue, or religious observances, reference being made only to 'Jewes tradeing in & about yo^r Ma^ties City of London'. It was only in 1673 that the religious status of the Jews in England was legally secured (below, pp. 181–2).

[2] According to the regulations (*Ascamot*) of the Spanish and Portuguese synagogue in London (London, 1784), § xxix, a recommendation against intermarriage (to which tradition adds proselytization) was made by Charles II as a condition of his toleration. It is possible that this statement is well founded.

degree from the repressive system that obtained in the less enlightened parts of the Continent. With the slightest modification in public sentiment, the Ghetto might have been introduced in all its German or Italian severity. But the characteristic feature of the subsequent period of Anglo-Jewish history was the utter absence of this spirit. (What disabilities there were—and these were relatively trivial at their worst—were shared with a large body of nonconformists, Protestant as well as Catholic, among the general population.) That this was so was due entirely to the unobtrusive and informal manner in which the Resettlement was effected. The fruits of failure proved more generous in the end than those of success could possibly have been.[1]

[1] Recent research on the events leading up to the Resettlement of the Jews in England is listed in *Nov. Bibl.* A.6 (pp. 38–40), and some other fresh sources are indicated in my new article referred to above, p. 166 n. Among the notable pleas for toleration in the reign of James I was that of Thomas Helwys, who maintained in his *Short Declaration of the Mystery of Iniquity* of 1612 (for which he was committed to Newgate) 'Man's religion is betwixt God and themselves. . . . Let them be heretics, Turks, Jews or whatever, it appertains not to the earthly power to punish them.' In 1614/15 the Spanish ambassador vainly attempted to have Samuel Palache, the Sultan of Morocco's representative in Amsterdam, condemned in the English courts for piracy in connexion with his privateering activities, and he spent some time in England in consequence, living as a Jew. It was alleged later on that there were a number of baptized Jews among the medical quacks in London (N. Briggs, *The Vanity of the Craft of Physic*, 1647). There were also various teachers of Hebrew, baptized and unbaptized (cf. preface to John Davis's *Hebrew Grammar*, 1656: 'Idle vagabonds . . . and false *Hebrew* deluders') some of whose names are recoverable: among them Jacob ben Samuel, who claimed to have been Menasseh ben Israel's 'clerk' and to have accompanied him when he visited the Speaker and Master of the Rolls (MS. in Chichester Diocesan Archives). No copy is unfortunately traceable of the satirical 'Act for admitting the Jews to England, with a short provision for banishing the Cavaliers', referred to in *Centuriae libri theologici, &c.*, London, 1653. A newly discovered Hebrew letter describes Charles II as jovially telling the leaders of the community at the time of the blackmailing attempt of 1664, 'laughing and spitting', to come to him when they were in trouble.

# VIII

# THE JEWRY OF THE RESTORATION

## 1664–1702

### § 1

NOTWITHSTANDING the absence of a formal legislative instrument inviting the Jews back to England, as visionaries on both sides had anticipated during the long negotiations, the newest congregation of the Marrano diaspora slowly expanded. Fresh immigrants periodically arrived from abroad—fugitive Marranos from the Peninsula and the Canary Islands, or enterprising merchants from Amsterdam, Hamburg, Leghorn, and the south of France. In 1660 some thirty-five heads of families belonging to the community may be enumerated. Within three years fifty-seven fresh names are added to the roll.[1] By 1663 the community felt itself sufficiently secure to draw up its first body of *Ascamot* or regulations[2]—modelled on those of the Congregation of Amsterdam, as the latter in turn had been on those of the Ponentine synagogue of Venice—and to bring over from Amsterdam as its first Rabbi the learned Jacob Sasportas, at one time Moroccan envoy in Spain.[3] As its distinctive name the new community adopted the title 'The Gates of Heaven', reflecting faithfully the function which it performed for more than one generation of fugitive Marranos, who obtained here their first experience of the religion of their sires. Outside London there was as yet barely any trace of Jewish settlement in England, but as early as 1660 there was a diminutive

---

[1] Wolf in *Trs. J.H.S.E.* v. 19; but the rate of increase seems extraordinarily rapid. The original synagogue accommodated about 85 men and 25 women: it was enlarged in 1674–5 to provide room for 172 men and 84 women. A nominal roll of the community made by a visitor in 1680–4 (*B.M. Records*, i. 16–20) enumerates 414 souls. In C. Dodsworth's 'Proceedings against the Exportation of Silver' (*Bibl.* B.1. 35) the number of Jewish families in 1690 is given as 70 to 80.

[2] Published *in extenso* in English translation in *El Libro de los Acuerdos* (ed. L. D. Barnett, Oxford, 1931); see below, pp. 188–9.

[3] The tradition that Sasportas had accompanied Menasseh ben Israel to London is incorrect; see *Trs. J.H.S.E.* xi. 119.

colony in Dublin. Its principal member was Manuel Lopes Pereira, alias Jaques Vanderpeere, whose family had played an important part in crypto-Jewish life in Rouen, London, and elsewhere.[1] The Dublin community was not, however, to attain any importance for another generation.

By now the synagogue in Cree Church Lane was one of the sights of London. A certain John Greenhalgh was taken there one Saturday morning in the spring of 1662 by 'a learned Jew with a mighty bush beard' and gave a minute description of all he saw in a letter to a friend.[2] There were in the synagogue on this occasion, he said, about one hundred 'right' Jews and one proselyte: all gentlemen, and most of them richly clad. Samuel Pepys, who had already indulged his curiosity on one occasion before the Restoration, repeated the experiment on the after-noon of 14 October 1663. It happened to be the feast of the Rejoicing of the Law, when the Jew traditionally allowed him-self some licence even in synagogue. The Diarist, however, was not aware of this fact and could not repress his disdain when evening came and he set down his impressions of the day. In the end, this constant stream of Gentile visitors (especially women) became a nuisance, and the governing body ordered that 'to avoid the scandal and hindrance that it causes in this Holy Congregation . . . on the occasions when English ladies come to see the ceremonies of our religion, it is forbidden and ordained that from this day henceforth no members of this Holy Congregation may bring them to it, nor rise nor move from his place to receive them'.[3]

In 1665, when the Great Plague devastated London, the Jewish community suffered heavily, though not perhaps in the same proportion as their neighbours. Six identifiable burials took place in the newly opened cemetery in Mile End, and between them is space for fifteen other interments of which, in that awful time, no record was made. Jacob Sasportas, the newly appointed Rabbi, fled overseas to avoid the contagion.[4] In the following year the Great Fire of London spared the synagogue area, and the Jews were not molested when violence

---

[1] Wolf, *Jews in the Canary Islands* (London, 1926), pp. xxxiii–xxxvii, 184, 194, 197; *Trs. J.H.S.E.* xi. 143 ff., 162 f.

[2] Ellis's *Original Letters Illustrative of English History*, second series, IV. ccix (anno-tated reprint in *Trs. J.H.S.E.* x. 49 ff.).          [3] *Libro*, p. 15 (summer, 1664).

[4] *Misc. J.H.S.E.* iii. 7–14; but cf. *Trs.* xix. 180.

was offered to Roman Catholics and foreigners in general, who were accused of having attempted to destroy the city. This period of tribulation called attention to one important hiatus in the congregational organization, and just after the outbreak of the Plague, in the spring of 1665, there was founded an Association for Visiting the Sick—the earliest of the network of voluntary organizations which were in time to cluster about the synagogue and fulfil every social requirement of the community.[1]

These portents prepared the way for a fever of a different sort. The Messianic craze which swept Jewry in 1666, when Sabbatai Zevi made his comet-like appearance in the Levant and sent a wave of hysteria sweeping throughout the world, did not leave England untouched. Reports were current to the effect that a barque with silken sails and cordage, manned by a crew speaking only Hebrew, had been sighted off Scotland.[2] Benjamin Levy, an employee of the congregation, received regular reports through Raphael Supino of Leghorn (an enthusiast who had followed Menasseh ben Israel to England, but on the failure of the Whitehall Conference had returned to his native place). Spanish and Portuguese merchants of New Christian extraction living in London were waited upon by devout compatriots, who begged them to declare themselves Jews in order to have the opportunity to participate in the joys of the Messianic era. João d'Ilhão, of Amsterdam (who not long before had led a colonizing venture in Curaçao), presented a petition requesting a pass for a Dutch ship which was to transfer him and some fifty Jewish families who desired to go to Palestine. God, he concluded, had at length begun to gather in His scattered people, having raised up a prophet for them, and they would pray for His Majesty when they arrived in Jerusalem. Henry Oldenburg, secretary of the Royal Society, was so impressed by all he heard that he wrote to Spinoza asking his opinion on the recent events. The enthusiasm penetrated

[1] Ibid., pp. 10–11.

[2] *Bibl.* B.18. 12. Several other contemporary tracts (ibid. B.18. 13–19 and Addenda, B.18. IIa) illustrate the intensity of interest in the episode. The English connexion with the Sabbatacan movement is not only superficial, as the pseudo-Messiah's father had been dragoman to English merchants at Smyrna, and it is conjectured that through their means the young man heard and was influenced by the millenarian ideas of the Fifth Monarchy Men.

even among business men on the Exchange, one of whom wagered large sums, at long odds, that his hero would be recognized within two years by all the princes of the East. Almost the only prominent Jewish leader in the whole of Europe to preserve his sanity was Jacob Sasportas, who, from his refuge in Hamburg, poured scorn on the pretender's Messianic claims, and in the end succeeded in restoring a sense of proportion to the Jewish world.[1]

## § II

Meanwhile the Jews were beginning to play a part of increasing significance in England. Charles II was liberal in issuing patents of endenization,[2] several score of them being distributed to members of the community in the twenty-five years of his reign. He was on affable terms with Augustin Coronel Chacon, 'the little Jue', who had perhaps been useful to him during his exile. On the Restoration the latter became consular and financial agent for the King of Portugal in London, and it was he who first suggested to Monk the match between Charles and Catherine of Braganza. In reward for his services he was raised to the knighthood, though he prepared himself for the dignity by seceding from the synagogue.[3]

In Catherine's train, when she arrived from Portugal, there was a distinguished group of Marranos. The most important was Duarte da Silva, an opulent New Christian merchant of Lisbon, whose operations extended to many parts of the New World and the Old, and whose arrest by the Inquisition in 1647 had caused a slump in the Portuguese exchange abroad.[4] He had ultimately been released and was now delegated to accompany the Infanta to England to administer her dowry. This

[1] See Note VIII (a), p. 286.

[2] i.e. naturalization, in a slightly modified form: see below, p. 213.

[3] Burnet, *History of My Own Times*, ed. Airey, i. 290. For Coronel's career, see *Trs. J.H.S.E.* v. 17–18; S.P.D. 1665–6, p. 118; and *H.M.C., Heathcote*, pp. 34, 46–47.

[4] A. Baião, *Episodios dramaticos da Inquisição Portuguesa*, ii (Rio de Janeiro, n.d.), pp. 266 ff. (The account in *Trs. J.H.S.E.* v. 18–19 is mainly inaccurate.) Cf. also Pepys's *Diary*, 19 June 1667 (the name is given incorrectly as Silon), and Clarendon's *Life* (Oxford, 1827), ii. 164, 192. Another important New Christian later in the entourage of Catherine of Braganza was her body-physician, Fernando Mendes; the statement that he was accompanied by a brother named Andrea, the queen's chamberlain, is based on a misunderstanding: cf. Wolf in *Trs. J.H.S.E.* v. 20–22. Alvaro da Costa was, however, her *moço da camera*.

was to have totalled 2,000,000 Portuguese crowns, or about £350,000, one-half to be paid on the princess's arrival and the remainder a year later. In fact she brought with her only a derisory amount, largely in jewels and sugar, the balance being in bills of exchange on Da Silva and Coronel. The king, who had already raised large sums from the London goldsmiths on the security of his expectations, pressed for payment. Coronel was able to meet the demands made only by borrowing from Alderman Backwell, the London banker, thus being driven ultimately into bankruptcy. Da Silva proved less malleable, and in October 1662, to the queen's indignation, was thrown into the Tower for six months to heighten his sense of responsibility.[1]

Though Da Silva did not join Judaism officially on his arrival in England, he came into the open as a declared opponent of the intolerant religious policy of Portugal, and from this time London became a principal centre of intrigue against the Inquisition. He professed his readiness to provide his native country with enormous subsidies of money and munitions, including ships of war, in return for some diminution in the power of the Holy Office. It was even rumoured that he requested permission to establish an open synagogue in Lisbon. His attempts were seconded by a more devoted London Jew, Fernando Mendes da Costa, who set on foot independent negotiations through the medium of his brother at Rome in the hope of curbing the worst excesses of the Tribunal. In the result, all this came to nothing, though it paved the way for the activities of Father Antonio Vieira and the suspension of the Portuguese Inquisition from 1674 to 1681.[2]

Another Jew who touched the main stream of English history at this period was an adventurer named Francisco de Faria, who, born in Brazil, subsequently lived in Antwerp as an artist, in Holland as an officer in the army, and in England as

[1] D. K. Clark, 'Edward Backwell as Royal Agent' in *Economic History Review*, xi (1938), pp. 51–52. Da Silva had been asked to assist in handling the Dunkirk purchase money also; W. D. Macray, *Privy Council Notes* (London, 1896), § 74.

[2] J. L. D'Azevedo, *Historia dos Christãos Novos Portugueses* (Lisbon, 1921), p. 282; Roth, *History of the Marranos*, pp. 340–1; *Trs. J.H.S.E.* v. 31–32. Da Silva subsequently removed to Antwerp, where he died—still nominally a Catholic—in 1677. His son Francis, who had been associated with him in London, did distinguished military service in the Low Countries, and was raised to the dignity of Marquis of Montfort. The second marquis returned publicly to Judaism, and the family retained its English connexions until late in the eighteenth century.

interpreter to the Portuguese Embassy. In 1680, at the time of the frenzy over the 'Popish Plot', he came forward with some startling disclosures, accusing the Portuguese Ambassador of having attempted to bribe him to murder the Earl of Shaftesbury and others. In return for these revelations, made with considerable éclat before the Privy Council, he received a government allowance, but, when the popular excitement died down, tactfully disappeared from view.[1]

The community comprised many another character who was equally colourful and more creditable. Almost all its members had known the vicissitudes of Marrano existence in Spain or Portugal; hardly one but had some close relative who had been immolated in the flames of the *quemadero*; and when the news of a fresh *auto-da-fè* reached London, special services would be held in the synagogue and special prayers recited in memory of the victims. From time to time the Inquisition at Lisbon or the Canary Islands would receive from some shocked Catholic a detailed account of their lives in their place of refuge. The Francias (according to a deposition made by a friar at Las Palmas) 'had left Malaga and come to live in London for fear of the Holy Office which intended to punish them because of their religion, they being Jews professing the creed and following rites and ceremonies of the Jewish Church, whereas in London they can live freely in their religion without fear of the censure or punishments of the said Tribunal, and this he frequently heard from the English in the Bourse'.[2] A Lisbon denunciation of 1659 introduces us to Manuel da Costa de Brito (perhaps a relation of Abraham Israel de Brito, one of the signatories to the petition of March 1656), who lived in London and was intriguing to bring his family to join him there: 'and the wife of the said Manuel da Costa said that the God of Israel would bring her children to her, to give them to Judaism and the holy covenant, and she gave thanks to the God of Israel to find herself in a land of liberty, where she might invoke His holy name.' Another person figuring in this denunciation was

---

[1] *Bibl.* A.10. 76, B.3. 5–6. Military interests were exemplified also in the convert Paul Gomes, who after serving in Tangier for two years petitioned for appointment as lieutenant in one of the royal ships (S.P.D. 1665–7, p. 148). Faria (with the apostate Hebraist, Lewis Compeigne de Veil) was employed by the secret service: J. Y. Akerman, *Secret Services of Charles II and James II* (C.S. 1851).

[2] Wolf, *Jews in the Canary Islands*, p. 212.

Abraham Peregrino, 'said to be French and a Capuchin friar, who became a Jew'.[1] Not that these former New Christians, freshly introduced to Judaism, were the only proselytes in the community. Notwithstanding the nervousness which prevailed on this score and the outright prohibition in the communal by-laws, it was impossible to check the ardour of some Puritan enthusiasts who followed their devotion to the Old Testament to its inexorable conclusion. A handful of English converts was therefore to be numbered among the congregation almost from its foundation.[2] Some Marranos, on the other hand, found diffi-culty in attuning themselves to the Jewish tradition from which they had been so long divorced. A few remained only semi-attached for years, causing no slight perplexity to the official community, who determined that if any person died in such circumstances he should be denied burial in the congregational cemetery.[3] The Canary Inquisition was once informed of a cer-tain member of the Francia family in London who 'being in synagogue dressed in the vestments of his church, said: "Gentle-men, all this is suited either to very great fools or very wise men", saying which he took off his vestment, threw down his book and went out'.[4]

§ III

Meanwhile the legal position of the Jews in England was being elucidated in a series of judicial decisions. In 1667 the Court of the King's Bench pronounced that Jews might give evidence in a court of law and be sworn on the Old Testament in accordance

[1] *Bibl.* A.7. 5. This Abraham Peregrino (= Proselyte) is apparently iden-tical with the contemporary controversialist and firebrand, Abraham Guer (= Proselyte) of Cordova, alias Lorenzo Escudero (Roth, *Marranos*, p. 329). Another Catholic priest who lived in London as a Jew was Don Joseph Carreras, who was at one period in the service of the Spanish Ambassador (Wolf, op. cit., pp. 178, 205–7).

[2] e.g. the proselyte whom Thomas Greenhalgh saw at prayer in the Synagogue in 1662: the pious Deborah Israel, who left all her property to the congregation on her death in 1669 (*Libro*, pp. 28–29): or Moses Israel, who is recorded with his brood of seven children in the nominal roll of 1680–4. Though capital punishment for heresy disappeared only with the abolition of the writ *De Heretico Comburendo* in 1677, it had already fallen into desuetude. Legally, on the other hand, apostasy from Christianity remained a penal offence in England.

[3] *Libro*, p. 23; *Trs. J.H.S.E.* v. 22. In the roll of 1680–4 specific mention is made of several persons who had not yet formally embraced Judaism.

[4] Wolf, op. cit., p. 205.

with their own practices (the degrading special formula, which had obtained before the Expulsion and was still applied in almost every part of Europe, was overlooked and henceforth never came into force). In 1677 the venue of a case was altered so as to save a Jewish witness from the necessity of appearing on a Saturday. In 1684 there was a more momentous decision, when Judge Jeffreys refused to entertain the plea that, as the Jews were 'perpetual enemies' in law, the religion of a Jewish plaintiff made it impossible for him to bring an action for the recovery of a debt. Meanwhile, in 1672, an endenized Jewish burgher of New York, on appeal to the king in Council, had established his right to protection notwithstanding his faith and foreign birth.[1]

Not that the period was without its alarms. In February 1670, when the anti-popery craze was at its height, a select committee of the House of Commons was appointed to investigate the causes of the growth of Papistry, with instructions also 'to enquire touching the number of the Jews and their synagogues, and upon what terms they are permitted to have their residence here'. The pressure of public business was too great to permit much time to be spared for this, and the committee's report dealt only with the question of Roman Catholicism.[2] But these complications obviously caused some alarm in Jewish circles, and the accounts record 'various expenses in solicitors and goings and comings to the Parliament and bottles of wine that were presented and £6. 7s. 6d. for a paper of the Court of the Aldremans'.[3] A little later the second Conventicle Act was passed, prohibiting assemblies for prayer, except in accordance with the liturgy of the Church of England. The measure was directed, however, only against native Dissenters, and, as aliens, the Jews were undisturbed.

A more serious threat followed. In the spring of 1672 Charles II issued his Declaration of Indulgence, by which the right of public worship was conferred on Papists and Dissenters. The Jews, whose position had been guaranteed by the royal promise of nine years previous, were not directly affected by this. However, the withdrawal of the measure in the following March, as

---

[1] Henriques, *The Jews and English Law*, pp. 183–90; *Pub. A.J.H.S.* v. 52–55. The Jewish oath obtained, however, in the West Indies.

[2] Henriques, op. cit., pp. 148–9.        [3] *Libro*, pp. 53–55.

the result of the widespread agitation which it caused, gave an opening to their enemies. At the Quarter Sessions at the Guildhall during the next winter the leaders of the Jewish community were indicted of a riot, on the grounds that they had met together for the exercise of their religion. A true bill was found against them by the Grand Jury. In consternation they petitioned the king, who, on 11 February 1673/4, issued an Order in Council to the effect that 'Mr. Atturney Generall doe stop all proceedings at Law against The Petitioners'.[1]

A disturbance of a different sort followed seven years later, when, learning that a young Dutch Jewess had run away to London with one of her father's employees and become baptized, some friends of the family instituted legal proceedings with a view to having her arrested and returned to her home. A great commotion was caused when the news was generally known. The Bishop of St. Asaph called for steps to vindicate the honour of the Christian religion and the English nation, and the Lord Mayor, thoroughly aroused by this 'affront to the religion and nation of the land', ordered an abstract of the laws on the statute book directed against the Jews to be prepared.[2] These all pointed in one direction: the constitution of the Jews as a juridical entity, accompanied by the medieval prohibition to be 'levant and couchant' among the general population, which had developed in contemporary Germany, Italy, and southern France into the Ghetto system. It cannot be a coincidence that immediately afterwards the Bishop of London and Sir Peter Pett, the eminent lawyer, drew up a memorial suggesting that the Jews in England should be segregated on pre-Expulsion lines, under the control of their own Justiciar (the first was to be Pett himself), who was to be responsible for the collection of taxes and to supervise their relations with the Crown. The Lord Privy Seal, Lord Anglesey, was interested in the project, and discussed it in a couple of audiences with the king. The latter, in turn, easy-going as ever, submitted the

[1] Henriques, op. cit., p. 149. In the following year, the congregational accounts mention the outlay for the Duchess of Buckingham in the house of Isaac Alvarez Nuñez, the fashionable jeweller and a pillar of the community (*Libro*, p. 90). The object of these negotiations was possibly to have the Jews included in the terms of the duke's Bill of Indulgence for Protestant Dissenters, which he introduced not long after; but nothing resulted.

[2] *Bibl.* B.6. 39; S.P.D. 1680, p. 120.

proposals to the Privy Council, which (probably acting under instructions) dropped them completely. No scheme of the sort was ever seriously considered in future.[1]

In February 1684/5 Charles II, to whose good-natured indifference the Anglo-Jewish community owed so much, breathed his last, and James II ascended the throne, determined to secure the position of Roman Catholicism in England. The moment was considered propitious to attempt further proceedings against the Jews. A publicist named Hayne prepared the ground with a pamphlet in which he gave an abstract of the various statutes concerning aliens in England, with observations proving that the Jews broke them all.[2] It was above all their exemption from alien duties (granted in the normal course of events in their patents of endenization) that caused resentment, as it put them in a position to compete with native-born merchants on equal terms. The late king had been petitioned in vain to abolish the obnoxious privilege; but an ingenious customs officer named Pennington now suggested that by his death the endenizations which he had granted became void, and that the Jewish merchants (all of whom had been born abroad) were henceforth liable to pay aliens' customs. The Corporation of London joined in the pursuit, maintaining in a petition to the Crown that in any case the exemptions violated the ancient privileges of the City.[3] Though the agitation proved unsuccessful it encouraged a further attack on confessedly religious grounds. One day, in the autumn of 1685, the community was thrown into consternation by the arrest of nearly half of its members, thirty-seven in all, as they were following their occasions on the Royal Exchange. A certain Thomas Beaumont, in conjunction with his brother Carleton, an attorney, had applied for a writ against them and another eleven, who escaped arrest, under an anti-Catholic law of Queen Elizabeth, which inflicted a penalty of £20 a month for non-attendance at church. Once

---

[1] *Trs. J.H.S.E.* iv. 184 ff., 192–3. Menasseh ben Israel had of course envisaged something in the nature of a Ghetto system when he laid his proposals before Cromwell, and Dormido, in anticipation of it, had offered himself as consul for his co-religionists (ibid. iii. 90). On one occasion during the restoration period a suggestion was made (probably not seriously) that the Jews should be segregated in the Scilly Isles. There is an improbable story, too, in Spence's *Anecdotes* that under Queen Anne the Jews offered Godolphin £500,000 for the town of Brentford, where they wished to set up a super-Ghetto.

[2] *Bibl.* B.1. 31.                         [3] Wolf, *Essays*, p. 125.

more the Wardens of the congregation threw themselves on the mercy of the Crown, petitioning His Majesty to permit them to 'abide here free in y<sup>e</sup> Exercise of their Religion as heretofore'. A douceur of some £300 secured the favour of the Earl of Peter-borough, who sponsored the application at court.[1] As a result James followed his brother's example, issuing an Order in Council by which the Attorney-General was instructed to stop all proceedings: 'His Majesty's Intention being that they should not be troubled upon this account, but quietly enjoy the free exercise of their Religion, whilst they behave themselves duti-fully and obediently to his Government' (13 November 1685).[2]

In the sequel the Jews were nearly involved in the consti-tutional struggle between the king and his subjects. The very next day the House of Commons protested against the exercise of the royal prerogative to dispense Roman Catholic officers from the operation of the Test Act—the first episode in the drama which was to end in James's loss of his crown. The result was the prorogation of Parliament, on 20 November, and it was never summoned again during the reign. In the following spring, when a collusive action was brought against Sir Edward Hales, a Roman Catholic who had received a military com-mission, a packed bench decided that it was part of the king's prerogative to dispense with the penal laws as he saw fit and necessary. Meanwhile the two Beaumonts had been emboldened by the general feeling in the country to continue their proceed-ings, despite the Attorney-General's intervention. Once more appeal was made to the sovereign, and on 4 December Sir Edward Herbert, the Lord Chief Justice (who was later to give judgement in the Hales Case), was instructed to send for Carle-ton Beaumont and examine him.[3] The matter was far too trivial to serve to thresh out so vital an issue, for men were interested in the Roman Catholics, and were not particularly interested in the Jews. The confirmation by the courts, not long after, of the legality of the Dispensing Power automatically disposed of

---

[1] Records of Spanish and Portuguese Synagogue, London.

[2] Henriques, op. cit., pp. 2–3, 49–51, 153–4: Calendar S.P.D., Feb.–Dec. 1685, n. 1856.

[3] Order of Council of 4 December 1685, in muniments of the Spanish and Portuguese Synagogue, London (facsimile in *B.M. Records*, i, plate VI). For the Beau-monts and their Jewish obsession, see W. S. Samuel in *Jewish Monthly*, ii. (1948), 360–5.

the lesser question; and, though the problem of Roman Catholic privileges remained an issue of primary importance in the history of England, the right to practise Judaism was never again seriously questioned.

§ IV

A new chapter in the history of the community opened with the coming of William of Orange in 1688. The expedition which led to the Glorious Revolution, inspired as it was by Englishmen and executed by Dutchmen, was to a large extent financed by Jews. Francisco Lopez Suasso, of The Hague, subsequently raised to the dignity of Baron d'Avernas le Gras, advanced the prince the enormous sum of two million crowns, free of interest, for his adventure. (It is said that he refused a receipt, on the plea that if the enterprise were successful, he would certainly be repaid, whereas if it were not, he would no less certainly lose.) The commissariat of the campaign was supervised by Francisco de Cordova, acting on behalf of Isaac Pereira, who provided bread and forage for the troops.[1] Small wonder that special prayers for the success of the expedition were offered up in the Dutch synagogues, and that the Marrano poets of Amsterdam (who continued the literary tradition of Madrid and Lisbon on the banks of the Amstel) hymned the enterprise in stately Spanish periods.[2]

For the next fourteen years England and Holland had their government controlled by the same ruler and pursued the same policy. Relations between London and Amsterdam became closer than ever before, and the community of the former city was swollen by immigrants from the latter, the metropolis of the Marrano diaspora. A number of families who were to play an outstanding role in subsequent Anglo-Jewish history trace their origin to this period. The synagogue established in Cree Church Lane in 1657, which had been drastically remodelled and enlarged in 1674, soon became inadequate. In 1699,

[1] Bibl. A.7. 88. For Pereira see also S.P.D. 1703, p. 686, Cal. Treasury Papers 1696, p. 318, &c. It is stated that William conceded the territory of Labrador to Joseph de la Penha of Rotterdam, who saved him from drowning about this time: L. M. Friedman, Early American Jews, pp. 146–51; Hebräische Bibliographie, o.s., iii. 117.

[2] Cf. M. Kayserling, Biblioteca española-portugueza-judaica (Strassburg, 1890), pp. 57, 87, 95.

accordingly, the congregation acquired a site in Plough Yard, Bevis Marks, upon which a new synagogue—the first specifically constructed for the purpose in England since the thirteenth century—was dedicated in the autumn of 1701. One of the beams in the roof, according to legend, was presented by the sovereign himself.[1] Moreover, on the day of the opening, the builder— a Quaker—returned all the profit he had earned from the erection of a fane to the universal God.[2]

Developments in London were paralleled on a smaller scale in Ireland. The Duke of Schomberg, in the campaigns before and after the Battle of the Boyne, depended to a large extent on the firm of Machado and Pereira, who had supervised the commissariat in the various Dutch campaigns since 1675.[3] The wealthy members of the London community were browbeaten by the authorities into making a loan to assist this venture, and a number of them settled in Dublin in consequence.[4] Thus the Irish synagogue, the existence of which for the past thirty years had been shadowy, knew a brief period of florescence. Its principal member was David Machado (de Sequeira), a writer of some distinction. We catch a glimpse of him in London, in 1707–8, engaged in a plan for bringing relief to his persecuted brethren in Portugal by diffusing there Father Antonio Vieira's recent attacks on the Inquisition. He even prepared a letter to send to the king of Portugal with the work, but changed his mind on realizing that it might prejudice the position of the Marranos instead of assisting them.[5] Closely connected with the Dublin community was a diminutive settlement at Cork, which had an evanescent existence shortly after.[6] However, when peace was restored, the Dublin community lost its importance and, though it continued to function under the auspices

[1] According to tradition, by Queen Anne (though she had not yet come to the throne), who had visited the synagogue in 1681, and whose husband, later Lord High Admiral, could have provided the mast from a man-of-war which is reported to have been used.

[2] Bibl. A.8. 58–72.

[3] The head of the firm was Moses Alvarez Machado, whose assistance in the campaigns in the Netherlands was so important that William wrote to him: 'Vous avez sauvé l'état.'

[4] S.P.D. 1689–90, p. 453; Trs. J.H.S.E. xi. 165–6. See also below, p. 194.

[5] Ibid., pp. 166–7; Roth, History of the Marranos, pp. 397–8.

[6] B. Shillman, A Short History of the Jews in Ireland (Dublin, 1945), pp. 138–42: A. M. Hyamson, The Sephardim of England (London, 1951), p. 146.

of the London synagogue, it never regained the promise which it had shown at the time of the Campaign of the Boyne.

In external matters there were occasional disturbances under the new sovereign: yet now they were disturbances which affected the Jews only incidentally, and not as Jews. That which attracted most attention was connected with the perennial problem of alien duties. On William's accession Pennington had renewed his contention that the exemptions granted in the patents of endenization issued under Charles II were now void, and he entered actions against twenty merchants, all of whom were Jews, for arrears amounting to £58,000. In this he had the encouragement of the king himself, who over-hastily declared that he would not abate a threepenny-bit of what was legally due to him. The Privy Council acted with greater deliberation, and on being petitioned by the other side ordered proceedings to be stopped. The English merchants supporting Pennington refused to acquiesce, spreading rumours that this result had been obtained by bribery, that the Treasury stood to lose £10,000 yearly besides the arrears, and that English trade and English traders were seriously imperilled by this decision in favour of the interlopers: and they enlisted the support of the Commissioners of Customs, who viewed the matter only from the point of view of revenue. Ultimately, on 14 October 1690, the Privy Council issued instructions for the duties payable by aliens on exported commodities to be levied, notwithstanding previous decisions to the contrary. No mention, however, was made of the arrears; and in the following December the increased duties were abolished by Parliament, making the victory an empty one.[1]

It has already been pointed out that, though this attempt mainly affected the Jews, who were the most prominent foreign-born element among the mercantile community, their association was in fact only incidental. This was not the case in connexion with another episode in the financial history of the reign, the outcome of which was of decisive importance in establishing the legal status of the English Jew. In past history the Jews throughout Europe had always been subjected to special taxation, of disproportionate severity, collected by their own authorities, who paid the proceeds over to the government.

[1] *Trs. J.H.S.E.* ix. 58–66; Tovey, *Anglia Judaica*, pp. 287–95.

This was still the case in the Ghettos of Italy and the Juden-
gassen of Germany and the teeming Jewries of Poland and even
the enlightened communities of Amsterdam, Hamburg, and
Leghorn.[1] The practice was essentially discriminative and
thereby prepared the ground for the establishment of an inferior
Jewish status in law: yet Menasseh ben Israel had assumed it as
a matter of course when he laid his proposals before Cromwell.
After the Restoration a Jew of Prague, named Jacob Aszik, had
attempted to secure the concession of farming the special taxes
which, he considered, could profitably be imposed upon his
co-religionists in London; yet, although he offered £3,000 a
year for the privilege, nothing was done.[2]

The financial exigencies of the country after the Revolution,
and the wars which followed in its train, brought the idea forward once more. In the autumn of 1689, in accordance with the
recommendations of a special committee which had recently
been set up, the House of Commons passed a resolution ordering
a bill to be introduced to levy £100,000 from the Jews, apart
from their ordinary contributions to taxation and their quota
of £10 each, rich or poor, to the newly instituted poll-tax, for
which all Jews were assessed as merchant strangers. In consternation the community prepared a petition indicating the manner in which English commerce benefited from their presence
and their inability to support any new burden. The Commons
refused to entertain any petition against a financial measure,
and the bill was introduced and read a first time on 30 December. The Jews, however, continued to fight strenuously against
the innovation, and in the end the unfairness or impracticability
of the proposals was realized, and the measure was dropped.
The idea of differential treatment in the matter of taxation
lingered on a little longer, for in the Act of the same session which
fixed the poll-tax for the next year, Jewish merchants were
placed in a separate category and assessed at £20 each—twice
as high as the rate payable by other merchant strangers. This
discrimination disappeared in 1691, when the new Poll Tax Act
failed to make any special provision for the Jews—a precedent
which was thereafter faithfully observed.[3]

[1] It applied, too, in the English possessions in the West Indies.
[2] Wolf, *Menasseh ben Israel's Mission*, p. lxxxiii (special financial treatment would
follow judicial autonomy); *Trs. J.H.S.E.* iv. 184; *H.M.C.* xi, App. vii. 38 (c. 1673?).
[3] Ibid., ix. 38–66. It is possible that the abolition of the special tax was a partial

Finally, when in 1698 a Bill was introduced into Parliament 'for the more effective suppressing of Blasphemy and Prophaneness', it was so phrased that its provisions did not apply to persons of Jewish birth. Objection was raised to this, and in the House of Lords the measure was amended in such a way as to make persons professing Judaism liable to the extremely severe penalties it imposed. By 140 votes to 78, the Commons refused to accept the amendment, and the Bill passed in its original form. Thus the practice of Judaism at last received parliamentary sanction in addition to royal protection.[1]

§ V

The community set up in 1657 was now in its heyday, its supremacy undisputed as yet by any rival body. Its administration lay in accordance with the *Ascamot* of 1663-4 in the hands of an executive body called the *Mahamad*, consisting of the two *Parnassim* or wardens together with the *Gabbay* or treasurer. There was little limit to the range of their activities. They appointed officials, issued ordinances, interfered with totalitarian absolutism in the private lives and extra-synagogal activities of members, acted as a court of arbitration to prevent quarrels between Jews from being aired publicly, suppressed commercial practice and speculations which created public prejudice,[2] imposed stringent monetary and social penalties on the recalcitrant, and at times went so far as to appoint their own successors. Their power was in fact all but absolute, and it was sometimes exercised with more vigour than tact.

The congregational organization was much like that of any other throughout the Jewish world. It was governed by its own constitution as laid down in the *Ascamot*, periodically enlarged

compensation for the unofficial forced loan raised from the Jews at this time (see below, pp. 193, 285). The Jews were indeed taxed *qua* dissenting aliens (above, p. 187).

[1] Henriques, pp. 13-18, 167; Luttrell, *Brief Relation of State Affairs*, 22 March 1697/8. The opposition was encouraged by the same Samuel Hayne who had led the agitation of 1685 and now published a 'manifesto of near one hundred and fifty knights . . . merchants and citizens of London, against the Jews now in England' (*Bibl.* B.1. 39), in the hope of influencing opinion. The practice of Judaism had already received incidental recognition in an act of 1695 'for granting to His Majesty certaine rates and duties upon Marriages'.

[2] e.g. speculating on the price of currency (1695), exporting bullion, except for the Peninsula and West India trade (1689, 1696) or raising insurance policies on political contingencies (1691): cf. *B.M. Records*, i. 21-23.

or renewed. From the very beginning (as seen in the code of 1663) meticulous provisions were enacted to govern communal life. It was prohibited under heavy penalties to establish any rival congregation. The order of Divine service was minutely prescribed in all its details. It was forbidden to make any disturbance in the synagogue, whether by over-vocal piety or by offering physical violence in the sacred precincts. The goodwill of the outside world was courted by prohibiting proselytization or religious disputations. A rigid censorship was established on literature published by members of the community, in order to preserve its faith unsullied (obviously the victims of the Inquisition had learned something from its methods). No member might print any lampoon or defamatory libel against any co-religionist, nor prosecute him in the courts of law for brokerage or similar dues, nor suborn his landlord or his maidservant. Romance was thwarted by a prohibition against participation in a secret marriage ceremony, while intriguers were warned against interfering with political affairs under the pretext of being spokesman of 'the Nation'. All this code was enforced by means of the lavish employment of excommunication—an effective remedy when social life was so painfully restricted: no ritually killed meat was supplied to the recalcitrant, nor would his sons be circumcised, nor if he died would he be buried in consecrated ground.[1]

Special attention was, of course, paid to education. It was the duty of the Rabbi or *Haham* (literally 'sage'), besides acting as Reader when required, 'to declare the *Dinim* (Jewish laws) on all days continuously and to preach on all Sabbaths and Holydays, and to give lessons to the students of the Talmud'. He was assisted in his labours by at least one assistant teacher, or *Ruby*. In addition the congregation had its own physician, and it was considered a desirable qualification for the Beadle to be at the same time a Cupper. The communal budget was derived in the main from a tax upon brokerage and commercial operations, ultimately consolidated as the *Finta*, or income-tax.

This was of course supplemented by voluntary offerings. Every Thursday the Beadle went round the congregation, from

[1] *Libro*, pp. 1–29, and *B.M. Records*, vol. i, *passim*: so also for the details given below.

house to house, to collect their oblations, which were distributed to the needy on the Friday.

The members piously preserved the culture of the countries in which they or their fathers had been born. Thus the synagogue of London, like those of Amsterdam, Hamburg, or Leghorn, became a little oasis of Iberian tradition implanted in a foreign soil. Spanish and Portuguese were the official languages. In those tongue sermons were preached, laws were drawn up, literature was composed, and correspondence conducted over half the civilized world. Most of the important families were international, members being settled in each of the greatest mercantile centres of Europe—no small advantage in trade.

Though the community was composed in the main of solid merchants and brokers it had to support a large number of indigent poor. One-quarter of the total number were on the border-line of poverty, and a very large proportion of the annual income was utilized in charitable work. So great did the burden become that in May 1669 the congregation lodged a complaint at the Mansion House against the swarm of mendicants by which it was beset and, on receiving a sympathetic hearing, made an order for all indigent strangers to quit the country within five days, in default of which they would be excluded from the Synagogue and its benefits: this was followed a week later by a fresh regulation refusing admission to the congregation henceforth to 'any person, of whatever quality, unless he should bring an order, arrangement or business for a lawful livelihood'. This was only momentarily effective, for within a few years, after a momentary decrease, as much as one-third of the total communal income had to be devoted to charitable purposes. In 1677 the attention of the City authorities was again called to the presence in London of a large number of destitute aliens who pretended to be Jews, and it was enacted by the Court of Aldermen that 'no Jews without good estate be admitted to reside or lodge in London or the liberties thereof'.[1]

In contrast to conditions in most other parts of the world, the Jews of England knew only minor annoyances. Anti-semitic sentiment was not indeed dead. Sir Josiah Child, the despotic chairman of the East India Company, might indeed champion the cause of the Jews in his economic pamphlets, and even

[1] *Libro*, pp. xx, 28, 116; *B.M. Records*, i. 29; Wolf, *Essays*, p. 123.

plead for their naturalization with a view to improving the country's commerce. John Locke could even argue in favour of the removal of all religious disabilities in his *Letter Concerning Toleration* of 1689. Men might laugh when the Danish *exalté*, Holger Paulli, called upon King William to baptize all Jews in his dominion in preparation for the coming redemption under his personal aegis.[1] But the mass of the people, though not violently antagonistic, was by no means benevolently disposed, and accusations of varying credibility were brought up from time to time—occasionally with unpleasant results. It was periodically alleged for instance that the Jews, working in conjunction with their co-religionists in North Africa, were responsible for the deplorable condition of the Englishmen en- slaved in Algiers, and for the difficulties in arranging for their ransom on reasonable terms; and wild threats were made that they would be expelled unless conditions improved.[2] Another recurrent complaint, voiced in 1690 by a committee of the House of Commons, was in connexion with the unlicensed ex- port of bullion—a suspicion which the Synagogue tried to sup- press by confirming the prohibition under religious sanction.[3] The City of London, hardly reconciled to their presence, was always on the look-out for breaches of privilege, petty illegalities, and undesirable immigration, and from time to time attempted drastic steps.[4] It was found necessary to mollify the authorities by occasional donations, and the communal accounts contain entries relative to pipes of wine presented on occasion to the Lord Mayor, with supplementary gifts for his son and even his sword-bearer.[5] Before long it became customary for the con- gregation to present each successive Chief Magistrate year by year with a silver salver embossed with the congregational arms, in anticipatory gratitude for his favour and protection.[6] Parish

---

[1] *Bibl.* B.1. 30, 34, 37; H. J. Schoeps, *Philosemitismus im Barock* (Tübingen, 1952), pp. 53–67.

[2] *Bibl.* B.1. 33 (1687); S.P.D. 1681, p. 458; *The Case of the Jews Stated* (1689: cf. *Trs. J.H.S.E.* ix. 46).

[3] Ibid.—a private attempt to begin proceedings against various Jews on a charge of exporting silver: Macaulay, *History of England*, ed. Firth, v. 2750; *B.M. Records*, i. 22. For later instances of the charge see *H.M.C. Portland*, iv. 693 (1711); *H.M.C.* x, App. iv. 34 (1730).

[4] For instances see above, pp. 181, 182.                    [5] *Libro*, p. 92.

[6] Roth, *Essays and Portraits*, pp. 108–12; *B.M. Records*, i. 11–12. The practice continued for about one hundred years, from 1677 to 1780, though after 1731 a

funds were frequently supplemented by the process of electing Jews to the office of Churchwarden: unwilling to serve in this capacity, they had to pay heavy fines in order to escape the unwelcome honour.[1] Occasionally the Jews were compelled to support apostates from their faith; for proselytization was carried on by enthusiastic churchmen with optimistic zeal. In 1702, in consequence of a *cause célèbre*, an act was passed compelling Jewish parents to make adequate provision for any of their children who should embrace the Protestant religion.[2]

## § VI

Meanwhile the Jews were consolidating their economic position. By the close of the seventeenth century they had established themselves securely in English commercial life. Jealously prevented from opening retail shops in the City—a privilege confined to freemen, which they were not allowed to become[3]—they were driven into wholesale commerce. They carried on a considerable trade with foreign parts, particularly with the other great centres of the Marrano diaspora, in the New World and the Old—even with Spain and Portugal, though, for obvious reasons, assumed names were adopted for this purpose.[4] They exported considerable quantities of English woollens, importing in return bullion and staple foreign commodities. Others, newly arrived from Italy, imported Turkish goods via Leghorn, to the resentment of the Levant Company, which claimed the monopoly of the Constantinople trade.[5] Commercial intercourse

purse of guineas frequently took the place of the dish. Similar presentations were made by the elders of the French and Dutch churches. They had a counterpart in Barbados in what was termed a 'Jew Pie' presented to each incoming governor, the crust covering a pile of gold coins, minor officials having 'tarts' and 'tartlets'.

[1] *Trs. J.H.S.E.* x. 48, 84–85. The records of the City parishes are replete with instances; but from the middle of the eighteenth century Jews not infrequently elected to serve. (From *The Case of the Jews Stated*, it appears that this was sometimes the case even in the seventeenth century, but as late as 1789 Lord Stowell considered it improper.)

[2] *Bibl.* B.3. 3; Henriques, *Jews and the English Law*, pp. 167–9.

[3] There were occasional exceptions to this: Rowland Gideon, the father of Samon Gideon (below, pp. 206–8, 215), was admitted a freeman, as well as a liveryman, in 1697.      [4] For specimens cf. *Misc. J.H.S.E.* 1. xxiv and *Trs. J.H.S.E.* xi. 167.

[5] *Journal of Commissioners for Trade and Plantations,* 1704–9, *passim*; below, p. 206. In 1695 a diplomatic incident was occasioned at Smyrna over a Jewish merchant from Leghorn who had been taken by the Levant Company into English protection. (Letter of W. Pagett of 31 May 1695: Mocatta Library.)

with Venice, the parent-congregation of the Marrano diaspora, was on a considerable scale, the export to that city and its dependencies of salt fish from England, and the import of Zante currants, being to a large extent in Jewish hands.[1] The first few Jewish settlers brought to England some £1,500,000 in specie, and their assured turnover was estimated at one-twelfth of the total commerce of the United Kingdom. Within thirty years of the Restoration they claimed that they had paid about £200,000 in customs dues alone.[2] In 1677 twenty members of the community were assessed at £20 each as their share in the communal imposts for the half year, representing transactions to the extent of some £32,000 per annum in each case.[3] In the spring of 1690 thirty Jewish merchants contributed (not quite spontaneously) a total of £45,000 to the loan advanced on the security of the twelve-penny aid, Isaac Pereira, the contractor, providing no less than £36,000 of this.[4] Diego Rodrigues Marques started on his career in England with £15,000 capital, and at the time of his death had gold and silver to the value of more than 1,000,000 milreis on the way from Portugal.[5] When in 1672 a ship called the *Falcon* was captured by the Dutch, it was estimated that £60,000 of the cargo belonged to London Jews.[6] The acquisition of Bombay in 1661 as part of Catherine of Braganza's dowry had brought with it a nucleus of Portuguese Marranos, who were reinforced from London before long; and there was a small community, with its own Rabbi, established also at Fort St. George (Madras) before 1688. It was largely

---

[1] S.P.V. 1672, p. 11, &c. Cf. letter from Venice of C. Broughton to Sir J. Astley, M.P. for Great Yarmouth, in Bodleian Library: 'I humbly conceive that if a Law was made that no Jewes should export Fish or import Currants directly or indirectly under a severer penalty to be Inflicted upon them & those who Couller this trade for them, it must do very well. . . . At least, the Italians, Dutch, and Germans, nor Jewes, will not eat the bread out of his Maj^tles subjects' mouths who live here and at Zante. . . .'

[2] See Note VIII (*b*), p. 286.

[3] Picciotto, *Sketches*, p. 50. Solomon de Medina (below, pp. 287–8), paid in 1678 an impost on a turnover of £80,000 (including brokerages). An interesting discussion of the position of the Jews in English economic life at this time is to be found in the *Athenian Gazette*, vol. vi (1692), no. 24: 'Whether it be for the advantage of England that the Jews be permitted to live and trade here.'

[4] See Note VIII (*c*), p. 287.

[5] Wolf, *Essays*, pp. 112–13. Cf. for further illustrations of affluence the letter of his associate, Paiva, in Roth, *Anglo-Jewish Letters*, pp. 78–81.

[6] S.P.V. 1672, pp. 68, 271.

due to the activities of this group that the market for diamonds, which had formerly been situated at Goa, was removed to the English factories.[1] Joseph Cohen d'Azevedo was among the directors of the interloping Scottish East India Company which was set up and suppressed in the reign of William III.[2] Trade with the West Indies, where Jews had been established in the various English possessions since the Protectorate, was also a vital Jewish interest.[3] The Glorious Revolution had (as we have seen) sent to England a handful of Jewish army contractors —a characteristic occupation of the higher economic strata of continental Jewry, demanding as it did not only capital but also trustworthy agencies and powers of organization—and this, too, became for a time an important calling among English Jews.[4] Two members of the Francia family were among the earliest contractors for the lighting of the London streets.[5]

Several pillars of the community were sworn brokers on the Royal Exchange, to which one of the pioneers had been admitted as far back as 1657; indeed, a not inconsiderable proportion of the congregational income was derived from a tax upon their operations. Towards the close of the century, however, their position was gravely threatened. From time to time attention had been called to the unauthorized operators who cut brokerage rates and tended to be less punctual in meeting their obligations; in 1680, for example, the Court of Aldermen requested the Lord Mayor Elect 'to consider and direct the prosecution of some speedy and effectual course for the suppressing of all brokers acting on the Royall Exchange without Admission, and Especially Jewes'.[6] At length, in 1697, parliamentary authority was obtained for carrying out a thoroughgoing reform. According to the arrangement first envisaged Jews would have been completely excluded. They were not disposed to accept this fate quietly, and fought hard to regain their footing. In the end the Corporation agreed to admit twelve of them among a total of 124 to the privilege of the

[1] *The Case of the Jews Stated* (1689); Miguel de Barrios, *Historia Real de la Gran Bretaña* (Amsterdam, 1688), p. 56. James de Paiva, founder of the Madras community, first suggested the establishment of the European militia in India, which comprised from the outset a number of Jews.
[2] Luttrell, *Brief Relation of State Affairs*, iv. 8.    [3] See Note VIII (*d*), p. 287.
[4] See Note VIII (*e*), pp. 287–8.    [5] *Notes and Queries*, clxxxi (1941), 7.
[6] Guildhall Repertories, lxxxv, fol. 245.

Exchange. This figure, though it marked a numerical reduction, was proportionately far higher than the actual numbers of the Jewish population warranted. It equalled the strength of all other alien brokers together; and, while the number of the Christian brokers was reduced by one-half, the Jews suffered a decline to the extent of only one-third, being moreover the only category who could be admitted without being Freemen of the City. It is not without reason that this arrangement has been termed the first step in Anglo-Jewish emancipation.[1]

The position of the Jew in the commercial life of the City and of the country was thus officially recognized.[2] The next century

---

[1] *Bibl.* A.7. 82, A.8. 1. The Jews on the Exchange congregated in the south-east corner, under the colonnade, between the Portuguese merchants and the Spanish and just behind the French. This corner was long known as 'Jews' Walk' and figures under that name in the old maps (e.g. in the *London Guide* of 1755).

The brokers (agents for the sale and purchase of commodities) who practised on the Royal Exchange are confused by E. Halévy (*History of the English People in the Nineteenth Century*, i. 315) with stockbrokers, the number of Jews among whom he wrongly asserts to have been limited in 1774 (?) to twelve. Though there was no formal limitation on the number of Jewish stock-jobbers, they had like others to receive a licence from the Court of Aldermen, which was extremely expensive. There was a test-case in 1764, when Joseph Ferdinando Silva was fined £450, after a lawsuit in the King's Bench, for practising without a licence (W. Maitland, *London*, ed. Entick 1775, additions p. 56). On the other hand, stock-jobbers were already familiar: cf. the prologue to Granville's *Jew of Venice* of 1701: 'Today we punish a stock-jobbing Jew.'

[2] From the beginnings of their resettlement, indeed, the Jews had entered into social life with little obstacle. As early as 1667 a piece of doggerel invited to the newly established coffee-houses 'you that delight in wit and mirth/and long to learn such news/as come from all parts of the earth/Dutch, Danes, and Turks, and Jews'. Before long, Jews were succumbing to the questionable delights of the Restoration theatre, to the distress of the Rabbi (Y. da Sylva, *Discursos* (Amsterdam, 1688), p. 93), Dryden averring that 'Like Jews, I saw 'em scatter'd through the Pit' (Epilogue to 'An Evening's Love', 1671). In 1679 the East India Company's sale was postponed so as to avoid the feast of Tabernacles (Benjamin Harris's *Domestic Intelligence*, 26 Sept. 1679). A sternly worded communal regulation of 1688, prohibiting participation in any political question or voting in any political contest, seems to suggest an active interest in public affairs, unless this was intended to prevent ostentatious partisanship at the time of the Revolution. When the interests of the community were threatened, they could take vigorous action: thus when a Bill of 1695–6 excluded aliens from trade with the Colonies, 'those of the Hebrew Nation residing in England' successfully protested, on the ground that refugees from the Inquisition could not be considered aliens in the normal sense *Journals of the House of Commons*, xi. 440). On the other hand, although special taxation was not explicitly imposed on the Jews after the Restoration, it was notorious that they were envisaged when in 1668 a special rate was fixed for the poll-tax on aliens who would not take the sacrament according to the liturgy of the Church of England: cf. *Journals of the House of Commons*, ix. 71 (30 Mar. 1668) and *Diary of John Milward*, ed. Robbins, p. 239: 'Voted . . . that aliens in all capacities shall pay

and a half were to show the position thus painfully acquired consolidated: the extension of this toleration from commercial to social life and finally to political rights, and the evolution of the Anglo-Jewish community as a free and undifferentiated body.

double, and the Jews more.' For the subject-matter of this chapter see now also E. R. Samuel in *Three Centuries*, ed. V. D. Lipman, pp. 27–44.

# IX

# THE JEWS UNDER ANNE AND THE FIRST
# HANOVERIANS

## 1702–60

### § I

By this time the composition of the London community had
begun to change. By the side of the original Spanish and
Portuguese colony there had grown up a settlement of
Jews of less compromising if less picturesque antecedents—the
so-called *Ashkenazim*[1] of the German-Polish group. The persecutions of the Middle Ages, in which that country had excelled,
had nevertheless not entirely effaced the Jewish communities of
Germany, which could trace their origin back to the days of
the Roman occupation of the Rhineland. After the Cossack
Rebellion of 1648–9 their numbers were recruited by refugees
from the terrible massacres in Poland, where during the past
couple of centuries the world's largest Jewish nucleus had come
into being. Those of this group were clearly distinguishable
from their *Sephardi*[1] brethren, particularly from those of Marrano
antecedents. Their pronunciation of Hebrew was different, as
well as their synagogal usages, their melodies, their cantillation,
and details of their rite of prayer. They were hyper-orthodox
in point of practice, cultivated Rabbinic scholarship with a
passionate intensity, knew little of secular lore, and spoke
among themselves the Judaeo-German dialect. Though one
in essentials, to the superficial observer the two elements were
obviously distinct.

Nevertheless, Ashkenazi Jews, forced by necessity, had been
quick to take advantage of the opportunities secured by their
co-religionists from Spain and Portugal in the various centres
of Marrano immigration of northern Europe; and it was a
logical impossibility to continue to exclude them once the others

[1] For an explanation of this term see above, p. 136, n. 1.

were admitted, whatever intolerance they may have encountered before. In the second half of the seventeenth century, accordingly, there was a considerable and increasing Ashkenazi settlement in Hamburg and in Amsterdam. Hence it extended, on the heels of the original immigrants, to London. Of the persons who became converted to Christianity in this country, from the Commonwealth period onwards, a good proportion were of German and Polish origin;[1] and in the records of the official community under the last Stuarts increasing numbers of distinctive names begin to appear, whether as recipients of relief, craftsmen, menials, or contributors. Of those in the last category, the majority belonged to affluent families of Hamburg or Amsterdam—above all, dealers in precious stones—ambitious members of which were naturally attracted to a new field of enterprise.[2] The most noteworthy was a certain Benjamin Levy, who arrived in London from Hamburg about 1670, and soon made a position for himself in almost every branch of overseas commercial enterprise. He was one of the twelve original 'Jew Brokers' and a Proprietor of the Western Division of the Province of New Jersey; and he was said to have been responsible for procuring the renewal of the Charter of the East India Company in 1698, with the result that his name was the second on its lists.[3]

As a matter of course he and his associates worshipped at the existing synagogue, notwithstanding the fact that the ritual was a little strange to them. But the official community was somewhat aloof in its attitude toward the *tudescos* (as it termed them), especially after the influx that may be presumed to have taken place from Amsterdam after the Glorious Revolution. In the following year the new arrivals banded themselves together to conduct divine worship in accordance with their own usages, and seven years later, through Benjamin Levy's

[1] Cf. the conversionist accounts (largely autobiographical) in *Bibl.* B.6. 38–48, &c.

[2] The continental background of the new settlement in England is vividly illustrated in the Memoirs of Glückel von Hameln and of Jacob Emden, both of whom give intimate details of Hamburg families, members of which—mainly gemdealers—settled in London, and in some instances an account of their business transactions. Thus the Norden family made its fortune by securing the agency for the sale of the newly discovered Brazilian diamonds, not yet placed openly upon the market.

[3] *Bibl.* A.10. 131 and scattered materials *penes me.*

generosity, they acquired their own cemetery. The community was henceforth self-contained and independent.[1] The traditions followed in the new synagogue (situated in Duke's Place, long the heart of London's Jewish quarter, in the immediate neighbourhood of the older place of worship) were those of the German-Polish group of Hamburg, from which city a majority of the original members hailed.[2]

The new community was recruited from abroad with great rapidity, the influx being yet further stimulated when the accession of George I brought England and Germany into a closer relationship. Composed as it was of persons of widely different status, occupations, and antecedents, it lacked the homogeneity and harmonious spirit of the older body. Its growth accordingly was expressed in a series of secessions, each of which resulted in the formation of a fresh congregation.[3] *Mutatis mutandis*, the new community was organized in much the same fashion as the old, though lacking a good deal of its external polish and its close discipline. There was the same communal hierarchy, though the power of the governing body was less absolute, the same system of raising revenue, though to a greater extent on a voluntary basis, the same network of congregational charities and institutions. By the side of the synagogue numerous voluntary associations came into being—mutual help societies, burial societies, societies for visiting the sick, for educating the young, for the relief of imprisoned debtors. The most characteristic were those for study, whose members would assemble after their day's work was done to pore over the Talmud or to hear ethical discourses. They would frequently remain behind to recite the evening service together: with the result that some of these bodies

[1] A visitor to London in January 1690 mentions that the London Jews had three synagogues 'but cannot contain them all' (Norman C. Brett-James, *The Growth of Stuart London* (London, 1935), p. 510). By 1695 there were in the East London parishes 853 Jews, one-quarter being Ashkenazi: cf. *Misc. J.H.S.E.* vi. 73–141.

[2] For the history of the earliest Ashkenazi synagogue in London see *Bibl.* A.8. 48–50, 74, and the present writer's *The Great Synagogue, London, 1690–1940* (London, 1950).

[3] The first took place as early as 1706, when in consequence of an internal dispute there was established the 'Hambro' Synagogue, so called because of the place of origin of its original members. (A previous attempt at secession, two years earlier, had been suppressed by the City authorities on the petition of the two existing congregations.) After the formation of the new community the original body, which was to play a particularly important part in Anglo-Jewish life, became known as the 'Great Synagogue'.

developed into subordinate Bethels, one or two of which still exist.[1] Just as the Spanish and Portuguese community endeavoured to perpetuate the atmosphere of Madrid or Lisbon amid the London fogs, so their Ashkenazi co-religionists transplanted with them from overseas something of the spirit of a central European ghetto. The language which they used for the communal business, for their studies, for their sermons, for domestic intercourse, was Yiddish, or Judaeo-German, written in Hebrew characters, and with a very strong admixture of the sacred tongue in its vocabulary. Medieval superstitions were rife. Weddings and betrothals were conducted in full continental style, with feasting and music and dancing spread over several days. (There was a notorious instance in 1720 when one of the City Halls was taken for the occasion, a guard of grenadiers accompanied the bridal procession, and the Prince of Wales came to gratify his curiosity.)[2] All necessary proclamations were made in synagogue by the Beadle, who also auctioned (for purposes of revenue) the various synagogal honours. As was the case with the older body, each congregation had its physician, who took his seat among the Wardens and assisted in their deliberations when the occasion demanded.

Socially and economically the new settlers generally belonged to a distinctly lower stratum than their precursors, who indeed refused to intermarry with them, to the amusement of the outside world.[3] At the head of the community there were indeed a few brokers, jewellers, and wholesale merchants of much the same type. They constituted, in this case, however, only a small proportion of the whole. Below them was an entire proletariat, composed to a large extent of the most recent arrivals, whose occupations extended from acting as servitors and footmen to their wealthy co-religionists to petty handicraft and retail trade.

The provenance of the immigrants was varied. The majority were from the old-established Jewish communities of Germany —not only great centres such as Frankfort and Hamburg, but also the smaller in the central and southern parts of the country, in Bavaria or Franconia, with a handful, imperfectly Gallicized,

[1] *Misc. J.H.S.E.* iii. 1 ff. From the middle of the century Friendly Societies on the English model began to make their appearance: ibid. ii. 90–98.

[2] *H.M.C., Portland*, v. 602; *Weekly Journal* of 27 Aug. 1720. The couple were not *Ashkenazi*, but members of the Coronel family.

[3] *Monthly Review*, 1763, p. 570.

from Alsace. Amsterdam and the other Dutch cities continued to provide their quota. A certain proportion were from farther east—Silesia, Moravia, Bohemia, and Poland; though as yet this great reservoir of Jewish life contributed in only a comparatively small degree to direct immigration.[1]

The nomenclature of the new-comers was as characteristic as their appearance. Whereas the Sephardi Jews had established surnames previous to their arrival in England (generally the Gothic patronymics assumed by their baptized ancestors), this was the case with their Ashkenazi co-religionists in only a minority of cases. In the synagogue a man would be called $x$, son of $y$. This generally formed the basis of the name by which he was known in the outside world: hence the appellations Abrahams, Isaacs, and Jacobs, which, with their biblical counterparts, now became the rule in the London Ghetto, fortified by a few places of origin and trades.[2]

## § 11

The influx from central and eastern Europe was paralleled on a much smaller scale by immigration from the Mediterranean world, by which the Sephardi community was reinforced. Throughout the first half of the eighteenth century it continued to be recruited by Marranos, fleeing from the rigours of the Inquisitions of Spain and Portugal; and more than one important Anglo-Jewish family owes its origin to this period.[3] In such circumstances it was inevitable that the Holy Office and its activities should remain a constant preoccupation of the older-established section of English Jewry. On the eve of the Day of Atonement prayers were offered in the synagogue on behalf of 'our brethren, who are imprisoned in the dungeons of the Inquisition'. Anglo-Jewish littérateurs introduced references to its activities in their writings,[4] and the bitter feelings which it engendered had local repercussions.[5] For many years London

---

[1] The records of the London and provincial synagogues frequently indicate the place of origin of the members, and make this generalization possible: see below, and *Trs. J.H.S.E.* xiii. 166–7, 182–3.

[2] See Note IX (a), p. 288.          [3] See Note IX (b), pp. 288–9.

[4] Cf. above all the verse translation of the Psalms, *Espejo Fiel de Vidas*, by Daniel Israel Lopez Laguna, published in London in 1720 with commendatory poems by local littérateurs—some in English.

[5] Thus when the distinguished ex-Marrano physician (not Rabbi, as in the

continued to be the headquarters of the campaign against it. David Nieto, formerly of Venice, *Haham* or Rabbi of the Spanish and Portuguese community from 1701 to 1728, and the most distinguished scholar to occupy that office, published in 1709 a telling refutation of the sermon delivered by the Archbishop of Crangranor at an *auto-da-fè* in Lisbon in 1705. This he followed up by *Recondite Notices of the Inquisitions of Spain and Portugal*, in Spanish and Portuguese, which he edited in 1722.[1] All this contributed towards the discrediting of the Holy Office. As the middle of the century approached its activity gradually diminished, and the tide of emigration that it forced automatically dwindled.

Though several members of the Spanish and Portuguese community enjoyed from the beginning a high degree of economic well-being, the problem of the poor was acute, even in this relatively wealthy section. Under George II an attempt was made to cope with it in accordance with the ideas of the day, by the systematic (though, as it finally turned out, fruitless) encouragement of emigration. When in 1732 Colonel Oglethorpe obtained his charter for establishing a settlement in Georgia, as a refuge for paupers and persecuted dissenters and a barrier for the British colonies against Spanish aggression, a few pillars of the Synagogue were among the agents appointed to solicit public subscriptions in aid of the scheme. Instead of handing over to the Commission the sum they collected from their co-religionists, they attempted to utilize it for financing the emigration of destitute Jews. This, however logical, was in excess of their powers, and they were compelled to surrender their commissions. Nevertheless, their activity resulted in the dispatch to the new colony in 1733 of two small batches of Jewish emigrants, belonging to both sections of the London community. Collaboration with the general scheme having proved impossible, in 1734 the

*Dictionary of National Biography*) Jacob de Castro Sarmento was proposed as a Fellow of the Royal Society, it was thought necessary to circulate a broadside exonerating him from the charge of having betrayed certain persons in Portugal to the Holy Office (*Bibl.* B.5. 8).

[1] Roth, *History of the Marranos*, pp. 347-8; *Bibl.* B.4. 7-9. Lea, *Inquisition in Spain*, iii. 285, associates the *Noticias* only with Antonio Vieira, the famous Portuguese Jesuit. But that Nieto had a hand at least in the publication is proved by the fact that this title figures, with those of the various works from his pen, in the background of a contemporary portrait painted by the Jewish artist D. Estevens, engraved by McArdell (see also above, p. 177).

Synagogue set up a special committee to apply for lands for an exclusively Jewish settlement in the new colony. The application was not granted, but three years later a tract was offered for the purpose in Carolina, though under conditions which proved inacceptable.[1]

In spite of this initial lack of success the committee continued in existence and in 1745 received an extension of powers and of income. Three years later negotiations were opened to establish a settlement in South Carolina, for which purpose the philanthropic but volatile John Hamilton, a London financier, petitioned the Council for Plantation Affairs for a grant of 200,000 acres. This scheme, too, fell through, though some individual families were sufficiently interested to emigrate to that colony not long after.[2] Meanwhile, in 1749, after the Peace of Aix-la-Chapelle, when the colonization of Nova Scotia was taken seriously in hand, an attempt was made to persuade poor Jews to settle there by the promise of a charitable allowance for three years from the congregation. In conjunction with the plan a Charitable Society was formed in the same year to apprentice boys to useful handicrafts, and to assist them in leaving the country. The prospect was in every sense a cold one, and there was no positive result.[3] There was nevertheless a steady trickle of emigration from both England and the Continent to the American colonies, and by the close of the reign of George II there were, besides the older settlements in the West Indies, half a dozen Jewish communities, largely of Spanish and Portuguese origin though no longer exclusively so in composition, reaching from Georgia to Rhode Island, and enjoying, in the untrammelled atmosphere of a new country, a rather ampler measure of tolerance than was the case nearer home.

§ III

Yet from the moment of the Resettlement there was probably no country in Europe in which the Jews received better treatment than England. Even in Holland they were excluded from certain towns and provinces, and in Turkey they received only

[1] Hyamson, *Sephardim*, pp. 99, 156–8: *Pub. A.J.H.S.* i. 5 ff., x. 65 ff.: lii. 169 ff.
[2] Hyamson, *Sephardim*, pp. 158–9: A. V. Goodman, *American Overture* (Philadelphia, 1947), pp. 168–83: B. Elzas, *Jews of S. Carolina* (Philadelphia, 1905), pp. 30–32.
[3] Picciotto, *Sketches*, p. 153.

the restricted rights of unbelievers. In Germany and Italy the Ghetto system still prevailed; from Spain, Portugal, and much of France, there was complete and even barbarous exclusion; Polish Jewry was terrorized and almost rightless; Danish Jewry was insignificant. In England, on the other hand, the Jews were under the protection of the law, could settle anywhere they pleased, and enjoyed virtual social equality. Not infrequently, indeed, some zealot published a conversionist pamphlet in which their beliefs were reviled, or a fanatical antiquarian advocated the enforcement of the restrictive legislation which existed on the statute-book. But that was all. Only on one or two isolated occasions was there any mob violence—never, however, receiving governmental sanction or connivance, or resulting in loss of life.

In 1732, indeed, a certain Osborne published a paper recounting in lurid detail how the Portuguese Jews in London had murdered a woman lately arrived from abroad and her new-born child, on the ground that the father had been a Christian. Similar conduct, according to the author, was frequent on the part of the culprits (it was indeed a sort of ritual murder accusation in a new setting). In consequence of these allegations some sections of the London populace were thoroughly aroused, and several Jews living near Broad Street, recently arrived from Portugal, were attacked by the mob. A case was brought with typical English coolness before the Court of the King's Bench, which found that the publication was an inflammatory libel upon the Jewish community as such, and ordered it to be withdrawn from circulation.[1] This was the sum total of the more violent manifestations of anti-Semitism in England in the century after the Resettlement.[2]

Administrative and even judicial annoyance, on the other hand, was by no means infrequent. Thus, for example, when a London Jew left a sum for the purpose of maintaining an institution

---

[1] Henriques, op. cit., pp. 9–10. Bad feeling continued nevertheless for some time: B.M. Records, i. 35.

[2] The alleged attempt against some members of the community in 1747-8 (Rubens, *Anglo-Jewish Portraits*, pp. 119–20) was hardly serious. On 4 June 1763, however, the discovery of a Jew picking pockets on Tower Hill led to an attack by a mob of half-drunken sailors on Duke's Place, where houses were sacked. In 1771 the Chelsea Murders (below, p. 235) caused an ugly outburst of feeling.

for Talmudical study, the court declared his legacy invalid as being devoted to a 'superstitious' purpose, and ordered that the amount should be diverted to what it considered the nearest legal object—viz., the instruction of the children at the Foundling Hospital in the rudiments of Christianity. Later, a legacy even for the support of a synagogue was declared invalid.[1] In 1720 an attempt was made (though ineffectually) to drive the Jew Brokers out of business, a petition being presented to the Lord Mayor and Aldermen in which it was attempted to show that their admission, not being authorized by the Act of 1697, was illegal.[2] Though this attempt was without result the fee payable for the transference of a broker's medal, originally quite moderate, was forced to a ridiculously high level; ultimately it rose to as much as £1,500, this constituting one of the most lucrative perquisites of the Lord Mayor's office.[3]

The most burdensome disability of all was the prohibition to acquire the Freedom of the City of London, where almost the totality of the Anglo-Jewish community resided, with the consequent impediments in all branches of economic life. One or two individuals managed to avoid the restrictions. But in 1737 the Corporation had an inquiry made into the 'scandal' caused by the granting of the Freedom to Jews, and ordered legislative action to be taken to prevent recurrence. Two years after, the religious test was upheld in the courts of law, and towards the close of the century (1785), with a cynical recognition of the questionable sincerity of conversions, the same bar was extended to baptized Jews.[4]

This disability was supplemented by exclusion from various mercantile organizations. When in 1727 Anthony da Costa was successful in an action against the Russia Company, which had barred him from membership on the score of his religion, the

---

[1] Henriques, op. cit., pp. 19–24. (Cases of *Da Costa* v. *De Paz*, 1744, and *Isaac* v. *Gompertz*, 1783–6. But the latter seems to have been an isolated case, as the London synagogues were in fact beneficiaries under many eighteenth-century wills.)

[2] R. Seymour, *Survey of London*, iii. 408. On the other hand an unsuccessful attempt was made in 1730 to have the number of Jew Brokers increased (*B.M. Records*, i. 35).

[3] Apsley Pellatt, *Brief Memoir of the Jews* (London, 1829), p. 201.

[4] *B.M. Records*, i. 36–37; Court of Aldermen Repertories, February 1737, 2 March 1737; Henriques, op. cit., p. 199; Wolf, *Essays*, p. 128; Picciotto, *Sketches*, p. 336.

Directors obtained from Parliament a modification of their charter which secured the right of refusal.[1] In the Russia trade,
indeed, Jewish interest was inconsiderable. But the same restriction applied to other branches in which the reverse was the case,
such as the trade with the Ottoman Empire. When in 1744 a
scheme was proposed in Parliament for the reorganization of
the Levant Company, which would have made the admission
of Jews possible, so great an outcry was raised that the Bill was
rejected: for critics professed to believe that if English Jews were
permitted to come into direct contact with their co-religionists
in Turkey, who were universally used as brokers and factors,
they would between them organize a monopoly of the trade and
squeeze out the Christian merchants. The reorganization scheme
was ultimately carried through in 1753, but a clause was inserted
forbidding Jewish members of the company to employ Jews as
factors in the Levant.[2]

Yet these disabilities were relatively inconsiderable, and on
the whole English Jewry, sure of their position under the House
of Hanover, and a little uncertain as to what continental con-
ceptions the Stuarts might have imbibed, had every reason to
support the existing order. (It was true that a London Jew of
Bordeaux origin named Francis Francia had been tried at the
Old Bailey in 1716–17 as an adherent of the Old Pretender, but
he was acquitted, and it is probable that this 'Jewish Jacobite'
was a government agent.)[3] Hence, at the time of the Young
Pretender's bid for London in 1745, the Jewish merchants and
brokers rallied whole-heartedly to the side of the government.
Samson Gideon [Abudiente], oracle of 'Change Alley, was one of
the few in the City who kept his head: helping the government

---

[1] *Bibl.* B.3. 9. The statement often made that Anthony da Costa (and Samson
Gideon after him) was a Director of the Bank of England is incorrect, as his name
does not figure in the official records. But the report goes back to the beginning of
the nineteenth century, and he may have been an unofficial adviser. The first
(and up to the present the only) Jewish Director of the Bank was Alfred de Rothschild, 1868–89. For Jews in its early days see *Trs. J.H.S.E.* xix. 53–63.

[2] A. C. Wood, *History of the Levant Company* (Oxford, 1935), pp. 155–6, 215;
*London Magazine,* 1745, pp. 521–30.

[3] *Bibl.* B.3. 5–6; *Trs. J.H.S.E.* xi. 190–205. A few years later a would-be
Jacobite agent entered into negotiations with some wealthy Jews in London and
The Hague with the object of bringing about a fall in English stocks and inciden-
tally making a profit for the shadow court of St. Germaine (A. and H. Taylor,
*Stuart Papers* (London, 1939), pp. 76–77), and Walpole is said to have threatened
condign punishment (*H.M.C., Portland,* vii. 416–18).

both with his shrewd advice and his vast credit, and taking a prominent share in raising the loan of £1,700,000 for the pressing needs of the moment. He and another Jew were among the dozen merchants who, when public confidence was at its lowest ebb, promoted the association to purchase Bank of England notes at par, if they were offered for sale; and the rest of the Jewish merchants, encouraged by the Synagogue, subscribed to a man to the Association Oath Rolls which thereafter were opened at the Guildhall and elsewhere. Others ostentatiously imported bullion from abroad and took it to the Bank. A quarter of the money raised on the security of the land-tax came from them, and two among their number placed at the disposal of the government several fully equipped vessels which were lying in the Thames. The lower classes enlisted in the civic militia; a service of intercession was held in the synagogues; and, when the emergency was over, a Jew was chosen—rare privilege—as a member of the delegation which went to present the City's humble congratulations to His Majesty.[1]

## § IV

By now there was to be found in England the nucleus of an acclimatized, English-speaking community. The most prominent among them were still of course the financiers and merchants, some of whom had begun to intermingle on friendly terms with English society; men like the charitable Joseph Salvador or Benjamin Mendes da Costa, both as well known for their liberality outside as inside the Jewish community; Solomon da Costa Athias, who presented to the British Museum in 1759 a collection of Hebrew books originally brought together for Charles II; or, in the sister-community, Moses Hart, for many years its lay-leader, and his kinsmen of the Franks family.[2] The most prominent of all was Samson Gideon [Abudiente], mentioned just above, who was consulted by successive Prime Ministers and Chancellors of the Exchequer, advised on the

---

[1] *Considerations on the Bill to permit persons professing the Jewish religion to be naturalized* (London, 1753), pp. 41–42; J. Francis, *Chronicles and Characters of the Stock Exchange*, pp. 88 ff.; *B.M. Records*, i. 38–39, 43. In the following year Jews figured among the body of merchants who advanced the government £2,000,000 at a day's notice to meet the exigencies of the war.

[2] Picciotto, *Sketches*, pp. 93–96, 155–6, 162–3, &c.; *Bibl.* A.10. 50a (Addenda).

consolidation of the National Debt in 1749, raised several
government loans during the War of the Austrian Succession
and the Seven Years War, and set the example of offering boun-
ties to recruits in the critical year 1757.[1]

These business magnates were said to be worth between them
some £5,000,000 sterling, of which £2,000,000 were invested in
government stock (one-tenth of it in the name of a single individual). However, only twenty families among them, it was
stated, could be reckoned really opulent. Then followed some
forty well-to-do brokers and stock-jobbers (including the twelve
authorized Jew Brokers), and a number of export merchants:
the development of the new textile industries in silk and cotton,
and of trade to the West Indies, owed a good deal to their enterprise and their widespread overseas connexions.[2] In the purlieu
of the circle of the brokers and stock-jobbers hovered financial
dabblers such as Jacob Henriques, the dealer in lottery-tickets
who claimed that his father had projected the Bank of England,
whose fantastic suggestions for restoring the national finances by
means of a guinea lottery were actually adopted in the Budget
of 1757;[3] or Philip Heilbuth, who in 1720 originated the idea
of a maritime insurance corporation, which ultimately led to the
establishment of what was afterwards Lloyd's.[4] A respected
figure in government circles, though only an occasional visitor
to England, was the eminent economist Isaac de Pinto of
Amsterdam (author of the *Traité de la Circulation et du Crédit*, one
of the great documents in the history of political economy): his
services in effecting a favourable arrangement regarding India
in the Treaty of Paris were so considerable that he was lavishly
rewarded by the East India Company.[5]

[1] *Bibl.* A.10. 84–85; *Pub. A.J.H.S.* xxxv. 27–37; *Annual Register*, 1758; autobiographical sketch in *B.M. Records*, i. 42–44. That Gideon advised Walpole in
the financial measures to be taken at the time of the bursting of the South Sea
Bubble in 1720, though stated on almost contemporary authority, is improbable,
as he was not born until 1699, and does not mention it himself.

[2] J. Tucker, *Second Letter concerning Naturalizations* (1753), p. 21; G. B. Hertz,
*British Imperialism in the 18th Century* (London, 1908), p. 89; Picciotto, *Sketches*, p. 93.
Of seventy-six insurance-brokers for whom William Braund underwrote at this
period twelve were Jews (all *Sephardim*): see the list in L. S. Sutherland, *A London
Merchant, 1695–1774* (Oxford, 1933), pp. 141–8.

[3] *British Magazine*, March 1761; *Bibl.* B.20. 15; H. Walpole, *Reign of George II*,
ii. 301–2.

[4] R. Strauss, *Lloyd's* (London, 1937), pp. 57–58.

[5] *Bibl.* A.10. 231; *English Historical Review*, lxii. 189.

Apart from the men of affairs there was a sprinkling of writers and scholars, especially physicians: men like the former Marrano Jacob de Castro Sarmento, a prolific medical writer, one of the earliest English advocates of variolation, or his namesake Jacob de Castro. The wayward Emmanuel Mendes da Costa, at one time clerk and librarian to the Royal Society, was perhaps the most eminent English natural historian of his day, member of many learned societies, and in correspondence with savants all the world over. His younger contemporary, Israel Lyons of Cambridge, mathematician and botanist, accompanied Lord Mulgrave's arctic expedition of 1773 as principal astronomer, and made his name known to the learned world in more than one book. In the sphere of belles-lettres, the lead was set by Moses Mendes (a grandson of that Dr. Fernando Mendes who had come to England in the train of Catherine of Braganza) who, secure in the fortune amassed as stock-jobber, and reinforced by baptism and marriage out of the Jewish faith, turned to literature and wrote several dramatic pieces, which were set to music by Boyce and Burney, and in some cases enjoyed long runs on the stage. Contemporaneously, his kinsman, Solomon Mendes, was a popular figure in the coterie of Richard Savage and James Thomson, while Abraham Prado of Twickenham, the commissariat contractor, was intimate with Horace Walpole and his circle.[1] Moses Mendes collaborated on occasion with a bad but prolific poet, Ralph Schomberg (assimilated son of the physician to the Great Synagogue), one of whose brothers entered the Royal Navy, supervised the landing of the troops at the capture of Quebec in 1759, was knighted, and was father of Admiral Sir Alexander Schomberg, the eminent naval writer.[2]

In other aspects of cultural life, too, English Jews were beginning to play some part. From the beginning of the eighteenth century their names figure in the lists of subscribers to new works.[3] During Mozart's first visit to England as an infant

---

[1] *Bibl.* A.10, *passim*, and *Dictionary of National Biography, sub vocibus*; *Anglo-Jewish Letters*, pp. 105–14, 122–3, 132–3, &c.; Walpole, *Letters*, ed. Toynbee, ix. 44–45, xii. 306, xiii. 353; Cobbett, *Memorials of Twickenham*, pp. 184, 338–9. One of Moses Mendes's sons (who adopted their mother's name) was father of Sir Francis Bond Head, who as lieutenant-governor suppressed the rising of 1837–8 in Upper Canada.

[2] *Dictionary of National Biography*, s.v. Schomberg.

[3] e.g. *Life and Acts of Edmund Grindal* (1720); Anson's *Voyage round the World* (1748).

prodigy several Jews showed their appreciation of him. With the court they patronized Handel almost as sedulously as the nobility boycotted him, and their support assisted in turning his *Judas Maccabaeus* from a failure to a success.[1] On the stage and the concert platform they were represented from the day of Hannah Norsa, who in 1732 made the fortunes of the newly opened Theatre Royal in Covent Garden by her astonishing performance as Polly Peachum in the *Beggar's Opera*, and of Giacomo Basevi Cervetto, who first acclimatized the violoncello in England, where he arrived from Verona in 1739. Another Italian Jew, Solomon Rieti, enlivened London life by laying out in 1742 the famous pleasure-gardens at Ranelagh.[2]

Persons of this type acquired easily and rapidly at least the appearance of anglicization. Quite soon after the accession of the Hanoverian dynasty it was remarked that beards were worn only by the Rabbis and persons newly arrived from abroad. The portraits which have survived from the beginning of the eighteenth century show little to differentiate the Jew from his neighbour. So long as it was in fashion he affected the irksome dignity of a periwig, which Rabbinical regulations expressly permitted him to comb out on the Sabbath. The younger generation habitually went about with swords; but on the day of rest, when they were enjoined to attach a wooden blade to the hilt, the majority preferred to do without. They were familiar figures, too, at the theatre, evoking thus the censure of some over-scrupulous moralists. Wagers (for instance, on the day of the arrival of the Dutch mail) were sufficiently common to require stringent supervision, and clandestine marriages reflected the atmosphere of the English playwrights rather than that of the Talmud. A breach of promise case which attracted much attention in 1734 disclosed an environment almost indistinguishable from that of a family in the same position in non-Jewish life.[3]

The English Jew soon yielded to the charms of the English countryside. Very soon after the Resettlement it became the

---

[1] Lecky, *History of England*, ii. 176.

[2] A. Dobson, *Eighteenth-Century Vignettes*, ii. 270.

[3] 'Gamaliel ben Pedahzur' (= Abraham Mears), *Religion, Ceremonies and Prayers of the Jews* (London, 1738), pp. 61–62; *Trs. J.H.S.E.* xiii. 329; *Misc. J.H.S.E.* ii. 7; Picciotto, *Sketches*, pp. 77–78; *Bibl.* B.3. 11, A.10. 274. Cf. also the runaway match illustrated in *Anglo-Jewish Letters*, pp. 170–6, and *Bibl.* B.5. 11.

practice of the wealthier to acquire residences in semi-rural retirement in the immediate neighbourhood of London. Defoe, in his *Tour of the Whole Island of Great Britain* (1727), was impressed by the fact that 'Jews have particularly fixt upon Highgate and Hampstead for their country houses'. Others spread westward along the Thames valley, about Isleworth and Richmond. So friendly were their relations with their neighbours that they attended the meetings of the Vestry, and even the local clergyman had no objection to entertaining a coach-load of Jews for a game at cards.[1] Jewish visitors to England, from the beginning of the eighteenth century, noted to their amazement how, already in the early spring, many of the communal magnates betook themselves to their rural residences and were thus unapproachable. That they were not without political interests, in a tentative fashion, is demonstrated by a resolution of the governing body of the senior community condemning interference in Parliamentary or local elections.[2]

It was not long before the reputation of English Jewry and the report of the favourable position which it enjoyed became known overseas, in an exaggerated form; and appeals for assistance, pecuniary and political, were constant from as far afield as Persia in the one direction or Rhode Island in the other. Jews established under British rule at Minorca or Jamaica requested intercession on their behalf with the governmental authorities when they were maltreated. The scholars of the Holy Land applied for support as a matter of course, sending special emissaries to London for the purpose. Mediterranean Jewry secured co-operation in the pious duty of redeeming the captives sold into slavery by the Barbary corsairs or knights of Malta. (Indeed, for these charitable objects special functionaries were appointed each year by the London Synagogue.) When, for economic reasons, the Swedish government made an attempt to encourage the settlement of wealthy Jews, the invitation was communicated officially to the Spanish and Portuguese community in London, which tactfully indicated that the continued kindness of the British king and Parliament did not permit them to leave the country. The Jews of Venice, now in sore straits, sent a delegation to raise a loan, for the repayment

---

[1] *London Evening Post*, 10 July 1753.
[2] See p. 189 above.

of which (never in fact completed) the Serenissima afterwards made special provision.[1]

But the most striking instance of all was in 1744–5, when the Empress Maria Theresa banished the Jews from Bohemia in revenge for offences said to have been committed by their co-religionists in Alsace. The community of Prague was one of the oldest and most numerous in Europe, and appealed to fellow Jews throughout the world, asking them to use what influence they could to obtain a reprieve. The leading members of the Great Synagogue in London, Moses Hart and Aaron Franks, immediately petitioned the king, who received them in audience and showed every sympathy, shaking his head and repeating, with tears in his eyes, 'It is not right that the innocent should suffer with the guilty.' Moses Hart, advanced in years though he was, was reported to have gone abroad to help, together with three members of Parliament; and Sir Thomas Robinson, the British Ambassador in Vienna, was instructed to associate himself with the Dutch envoy in making representations to the Austrian government. He was warmly sympathetic, and shocked by the empress's display of bigotry and prejudice. Thanks in part to his efforts, the refugees were allowed in the end to return to their homes. This was probably the first instance in modern history of diplomatic intervention by a European Power on behalf of an alien minority on purely humanitarian grounds.[2]

## § v

We have seen that, notwithstanding their generally favourable condition, there were various disabilities which weighed heavily upon the Jews. Just after the middle of the century an attempt was made to remove one which was found irksome by the upper classes. It resulted in complete failure, but attracted nevertheless a degree of attention out of all proportion to the real importance of the question at issue, with results which narrowly escaped being disastrous.

In the matter of naturalization, which secured to aliens the privileges of natural-born Englishmen (e.g. owning land and

[1] Picciotto, *Sketches*, pp. 164–8: *Bibl.* A.9. 134–5, B.1. 129.
[2] *Bibl.* A.7. 44; S. H. Lieben in *Jahrbuch der Gesellschaft für Geschichte der Juden in der tschechoslovakischen Republik*, iv (1932), pp. 353–479.

ships, and trading with the plantations), Jews were at a considerable disadvantage. It could indeed be procured in a qualified sense ('endenization') by letters patent, which, however, had no retrospective action, and did not permit the inheritance of land. This was legalized only when the process was effected in full form by Act of Parliament; but this method was not open to Jews since, long before the Readmission, at the height of the anti-Catholic agitation, it had been made obligatory for those who became British subjects by this means to have received the Sacrament within the past month according to the rites of the Church of England, as well as to take the Protestant oaths of Supremacy and Allegiance. Accordingly, Jews born abroad could avail themselves only of the costly method and more limited privileges of endenization, which from the time of Charles II they had done in large numbers—generally, owing to the great expense involved, in groups. A more liberal attitude had been advocated from time to time by some tolerant publicists such as Sir Josiah Child in his *Discourse about Trade* (1690) and John Toland, who, when the question of the naturalization of foreign Protestants began to engage the public attention, issued anonymously his far-reaching *Reasons for naturalizing the Jews in Great Britain and Ireland, on the same footing with all other nations* (1714)—one of the earliest pleas for a liberal attitude towards the Jews. But the voice of a Deist agitator was not likely to carry much weight at that period, and the work achieved nothing except to elicit a peculiarly scurrilous retort.[1]

For some time past it had been usual for the difficulties in the way of naturalization to be modified in favour of categories of persons who might prove of particular benefit to the state. Thus a statute of Charles II entitled aliens who had been engaged for three years in dressing hemp or flax, making tapestries, &c., to be naturalized after three years, and a statute of George II of 1740 conferred similar advantages on persons who had served for two years in the Royal Navy or on a merchant ship in time of war. In the same year, in an Act for naturalizing foreign Protestants and others settled in the American colonies (13 George II, cap. 7), the Sacramental test was dispensed with in the case of Jews who had lived there for seven years, who

---

[1] *Bibl.* B.i. 44–46. His plea was not, however, for the removal of political disabilities, dealing explicitly only with the naturalization of those born abroad.

were, moreover, relieved of the obligation to repeat the words 'Upon the true faith of a Christian' in the Oath of Abjuration.[1] Within the next fourteen years nearly two hundred West Indian Jews (the majority of whom lived in Jamaica) availed themselves of the opportunity offered by this measure. When in 1745 a similar Bill for naturalizing foreign Protestants in England was under consideration by Parliament, the Jews made representations to the government in the hopes of being included; but the time was inopportune, and in fact before long the measure was itself dropped.[2] This seems to have convinced them that it was better to make a preliminary experiment on a smaller scale. In 1743, accordingly, a Bill 'for naturalizing persons professing the Jewish religion in Ireland' (where the diminutive settlement had become yet smaller in recent years) was introduced to the House of Commons in Dublin, but was thrown out by the Upper House by two votes. Late in the following year it passed the Commons unanimously, and was presented to the Lord Lieutenant for transmission to England. However, through the influence of the Primate of Ireland, it was dropped quietly in council and never received royal assent.[3]

The magnates of the Spanish and Portuguese community in London anxiously watched these attempts, and after the second failure a 'Committee of Diligence' was appointed to see if anything could be done to forward the matter. There seems to have been an ulterior motive for this eagerness. In spite of a favourable opinion expressed by the Attorney-General in 1718, a certain element of doubt prevailed as to whether the acquisition by Jews of country residences and estates, and even city freeholds, was legally valid. An Act of 1722, which added to Roman Catholic disabilities by enforcing the Oath of Abjuration on all

[1] *Pub. A.J.H.S.* i. 93–98.

[2] *Considerations on the Bill* (1753), p. 23. The general attitude at the time is illustrated by a satirical suggestion of 1748 that the scope of the naturalization should be extended to 'all wandering Gypsies, Tartars, Persians, Chinese, Indians [and] particularly the Jews' (*Bibl.* B.1. 57).

[3] A letter of the Primate to Lord George Sackville of 18 January 1747–8 in *H.M.C.* iv, App. i. 299 (MSS. of Earl de la Warr), explains this curious (and hitherto unexplained) tergiversation. For the Irish Naturalization Bill see Picciotto, *Sketches*, pp. 114–15, *B.M. Records*, i. 39; and *Trs. J.H.S.E.* v. 236–8. For the whole question see now B. Shillman, *A Short History of the Jews in Ireland* (Dublin, 1945), pp. 50 ff. The fact that the Jews were expressly excepted from the provisions of the Irish Naturalization Act of 1783 shows to what an extent prejudice continued.

landowners, was followed the next year by a further measure (10 George I, cap. 4) exempting Jews from the necessity of including in it the words 'on the true faith of a Christian'; and at the same period several eminent authorities expressed their opinion that there was nothing in English law to prevent a natural-born Jew from owning real estate.[1] But the obvious self-consciousness on this point of the leaders of the Jewish community and their champions reflects the uncertainty that still prevailed. When Samson Gideon wished to acquire his country estate he considered it safest to validate his position by a special Act of Parliament, and there seems to have been a widespread desire that the problem should be finally cleared up, enabling English Jews, both native-born and otherwise, to acquire as well as to inherit estates and freeholds on the same terms as other Englishmen.[2]

This point was not stressed; titularly the intention was only to facilitate naturalization. The wealthy and popular Joseph Salvador (alias Joseph Jessurun Rodrigues) entered into touch with the government on behalf of his co-religionists of the Spanish and Portuguese community[3] (the *Ashkenazim*, poorer for the most part, were not vitally interested). Philip Carteret Webb, secretary of bankrupts in the Court of Chancery, was engaged to advise and supervise. The Newcastle government on its side showed itself warmly sympathetic. It was true, of course, that to English xenophobia the idea of naturalization on a large scale was known to be distasteful, even where elements less unpopular than the Jews were concerned. Three times since the beginning of the century measures had been brought forward for the naturalization of foreign Protestants; but the jealousy of the Church and the City had been aroused, and they had been dropped or repealed—in one instance after

---

[1] *The Question whether a Jew, &c.* (London, 1753; *Bibl.* B.1. 114), pp. 43–46; Henriques, op. cit., pp. 171, 241. The measure of 1723 is the first in which Jews are referred to as English subjects. The popular feeling at the time seems to be reflected in a letter of William Stratford, canon of Christ Church, to Edward Harley (19 March 1723/4): 'We hear that by the help of Lunn, the Jews have carried it against Jesus Christ' (*H.M.C., Portland*, vii. 377).

[2] An element of doubt had apparently been added by the publication of Tovey in 1738 in his *Anglia Judaica* of Henry III's previously unknown statute of 1271 prohibiting Jews from holding freeholds: above, p. 66.

[3] Cf. his memorandum of 14 January 1753 from the Newcastle Papers, in *Anglo-Jewish Letters*, pp. 128–30.

three years of legal validity. But notwithstanding these pre-cedents the proposals were pushed on.

The Bill drawn up provided simply that Jews who had been resident in Great Britain or Ireland for three years might be naturalized on application to Parliament without taking the Sacrament. The proposals were mild and unprovocative in the extreme—as Joseph Salvador had pointed out from the begin-ning, the expense of an Act of Parliament would prevent the poorer classes from being touched by them one way or the other. Only the rich were affected, being put in a position of equality with the dependants whom they had sent out to the West Indies; and, like all naturalized persons, they would still be unable to become members of the Privy Council or either House of Parliament, to obtain grants of crown lands, or to hold any office of profit under the Crown. But there was an incidental clause, ostensibly discriminatory, which prohibited Jews (whether native-born or foreign) from purchasing or in-heriting advowsons or presenting to any ecclesiastical benefice. The right of presentation went, of course, with estates: and this reservation implicitly confirmed the right of the Jews to hold land.[1]

The Bill was introduced into the House of Lords on 3 April 1753 by Lord Halifax, the 'Father of the Colonies', then Presi-dent of the Board of Trade. It was read three times in rapid suc-cession, and passed without a division. On 17 April it was read for the first time in the House of Commons, where at the beginning it appeared to have the prospect of a similar easy passage. At the second reading however, on 7 May, opposition began to develop, led by a former Lord Mayor, Sir John Barnard, one of the members for the City of London who opposed all naturalization measures. The House was asked what crime the people of the kingdom had committed that they should be deprived of their birthright not only as Englishmen but also as Christians. It was asserted that the Bill gave the lie to all the prophecies of the New Testament. One member even suggested that, instead of proceeding with the Bill, the

[1] The significance of the Naturalization Bill is generally misunderstood, many writers imagining that it conferred the rights of British subjects on the Jews of the country as a whole, and relieved them of religious disabilities. In fact, in its main clauses it only affected foreign Jews, whose naturalization it facilitated, touching the native-born (already British subjects) only incidentally and in a minor degree.

House should appoint a secret committee to inquire by what right the Jews were tolerated in the country at all. Nevertheless, the second reading passed by 95 votes to 16.

During the following fortnight the furore increased, both in the House and outside it. The Tory and Whig oppositions joined hands, attacking the measure with competitive virulence. Petitions against the Bill poured in, from conscience-stricken stock-jobbers and patriotic merchants who had to meet Jewish competition. The Lord Mayor of London, Sir Crisp Gascoigne, presided over protest meetings of Aldermen and Liverymen, and exhorted the citizens to resist this dangerous concession; while the Common Council denounced the measure as 'tending greatly to the dishonour of the Christian religion'. When the Bill was brought up for its third reading on 22 May, Lord Egmont moved the adjournment. Had the Opposition exerted all their strength it is probable that they would have carried the division; but, it was later said, their strategists imagined that the question would prove a more effective weapon in the country if the Bill were allowed to pass. The minority increased in numbers, in a sparse House, from 16 to 55, while the government supporters remained virtually stationary at 96. The Bill accordingly received the royal assent and passed into law.

Thereafter the struggle was transferred, over a period of nearly six months, from Westminster to the streets. An agitation against the 'Jew Bill' sprang up throughout the country— in part artificially sponsored by the opposition, in part a spontaneous expression of xenophobia—which has few parallels in English history. The walls were plastered with the slogan, incongruously combining two different antipathies: 'No Jews, no Wooden Shoes' (the last being considered the characteristic footwear of religious refugees from France). It was freely alleged that Jewish gold and ministerial treachery (the possibility of altruistic action was derided) had combined to corrupt Parliament. The member for Exeter was constrained to distribute papers to prove that he observed his Sabbath with other Englishmen, and therefore could not be seriously suspected of clandestine adherence to Judaism. The spiritual peers who had supported the Bill were roundly accused of delivering the Keys of the Church to those who had murdered their Saviour, and were hooted when they appeared in public: while the Bishop of Norwich was actually insulted by the rabble in more than one part of his diocese when he went to confirm. Grand juries, pocket boroughs, and city merchants competed with one another in the extravagance of the petitions which they presented imploring that the measure should be reversed; and the Corporation of Reading pathetically enjoined its members to protect the British Constitution and the protestant faith from Jewish machinations. Every constituency resounded with anti-Jewish and anti-government slogans, ranging from 'Christianity and Old England for Ever' in the capital to 'No Jews: Christianity and the Constitution' at Newton in Lancashire. Aspirant candidates for the forthcoming general election were considered only in relation to their conduct when the Bill had been before Parliament, a dark complexion becoming an insuperable objection. Ladies' trinkets were made in the shape of crosses; hogs' puddings and pork-banquets unexpectedly became patriotic fare; and 'no mass-house, no conventicle, no synagogue: High Church for ever' was the toast with which the convivialities closed. Prominent Jews, such as Salvador, were booed when they were seen in the theatre, and forced to withdraw. The Archbishop of Canterbury, kindly disposed towards them as he was, feared a general massacre.[1] Above all, the printing-presses were kept busy turning out pamphlets, squibs, ballads, and caricatures; and men like Jonas Hanway, the traveller and philanthropist, and William Romaine, the fashionable London preacher, reinforced the inevitable 'Christian', 'Britannia', and 'Timothy Tell-Truth' in denouncing the advance on the path of toleration.

The opposition indulged in ludicrous exaggeration. All the old anti-Jewish libels were revived, including the hackneyed fable of Ritual Murder. The Spanish laws against heretics were cited with approval, and it was suggested that the inhabitants of those countries where the Inquisition yet flourished would resent any amelioration in the treatment of those whom they burned so conscientiously at home, with disastrous results to the English export trade. It was alleged that the administration

---

[1] H. Maty's *New Review*, i (1782), p. 241. 'The world will not hear it [truth], and the proof is very evident from this abominable spirit that rages against the Jews. I expect in a little time they will be massacred. . . . We are now treating the Jews just as the Mohammedans treat the Christians.'

had received a bribe of half a million pounds sterling as an inducement to bring in the iniquitous measure. One pamphleteer, anticipating a mania of two centuries later, urged that passages glorifying the Hebrews (such as 'O pray for the peace of Jerusalem') should be omitted from the Psalms. Another paladin of orthodoxy suggested that the Bill might be allowed to stand, with a simple amendment to the effect that baptism should be a prerequisite of naturalization. Other opponents professed to believe that there would be an enormous influx of foreign Jews, who before long would divide England among their tribes as their ancestors had the land of Canaan, purchase all the estates, influence elections, enter Parliament, and aspire to evert the highest offices. The constitution of Church and State would be endangered, they said; Judaism would spread; and the country at large would invite the divine retribution which is the penalty of national apostasy. A satirist pictured—not without humour—the probable condition of England a hundred years later, when St. Paul's would be a synagogue, persons with grotesquely biblical names (such as Sir Nadab Issachar and the Right Honourable the Earl of Balaam) fill the highest offices of state, trade be ruined by the introduction of a second Sabbath-day in every week, the importation of pork become a penal offence, and a Bill for naturalizing Christians be rejected with contumely by the Sanhedrin. Scurrilous caricatures were sold in the streets, elaborating such titles as 'The Circumcised Gentiles, or a Journey to Jerusalem': 'The Jews' Triumph, and England's fears set forth', 'The Jews shaving Parliament, or the Knowing Ones taken in'. And the ballad writers found a superb opportunity:

> But, Lord, how surpris'd when they heard of the News
> That we were to be Servants to Circumcis'd Jews,
> To be Negroes and Slaves instead of *True Blues*,
> > Which nobody can deny.

The opposition was not, of course, allowed to have the wordy battle all its own way. Several pamphleteers entered the lists on behalf of the Jews—above all Josiah Tucker, later dean of Gloucester, the eminent economist and divine, whose work to some extent anticipated Adam Smith's. Some at least of the clergy showed themselves tolerant, and mounted the pulpit in defence of the unpopular measure. Of the newspapers, the *General Evening Post* and the *Public Advertiser* opened their columns to the voice of reason, in contrast to the scurrilities with which the *London Magazine, Westminster Journal,* and especially *London Evening Post* particularly distinguished themselves. The champions of the Bill accentuated the economic importance of the Jews and the benefits which they would necessarily bring to any country in which they could be induced to settle. They referred to their patriotic action at the time of general panic when the Young Pretender was marching on London eight years before, and their whole-hearted support of the Hanoverian dynasty both then and at other times. They quoted figures indicating the magnitude of their fortunes, the scale of their charities, the manner in which they had promoted English exports and the benefits which they had brought to the American plantations. They insisted on their invariable practice of supporting their own poor, who even in the event of an increase in number would be no burden upon the country. They inferred, not entirely without reason, that the opposition to so salutary a reform was due to the envy of a coterie of London merchants, who wished to monopolize foreign trade, to the manifest disadvantage of the country at large. One or two, who approached the question from an entirely different angle, went on to suggest that the naturalization was a necessary prelude to the general conversion of the Jews, and even urged the government, with arguments curiously anticipatory of later Zionism, to link it up with their restoration to Palestine. And a country gentleman, in his *Reflexions upon Naturalization*, developed Bacon's argument, that in order to achieve greatness an empire must show itself willing to absorb other stocks. But these tolerant voices were overwhelmed by the number and insistency of those which were raised on the other side. To champion the Bill, moreover, was not without its dangers, as Dr. Tucker found when he was attacked in the streets of Bristol by an angry crowd which, disappointed at seeing him escape, comforted themselves by burning him in effigy.[1]

[1] Upwards of sixty pamphlets on the Jew Bill are listed in *Bibl.* B.1. 60-124, and thirty satirical prints in *Trs. J.H.S.E.* vi. 216-33. The mass of propaganda was swollen by a spate of publications regarding two recent *causes célèbres*—one

So universal an agitation, on the eve of a general election, could not be overlooked. The Duke of Newcastle, whose agents kept him closely informed of the state of public opinion in the constituencies, feared that the results might be really serious; and the government determined very reluctantly to bow to the storm which it had aroused. On the opening day of the new session (15 November), the duke brought forward a fresh Bill in the House of Lords to repeal the unpopular measure, in a speech described by a contemporary as being 'rather worse than usual'. He maintained that the original proposals were wise and beneficial, but that the government had no choice but to yield to the clamour raised by secret enemies of the dynasty and of the Protestant Establishment. The Bishops of Oxford and St. Asaph supported him, admitting shamefacedly the necessity to bow to 'weak and misguided consciences'. Only Lord Temple raised his voice in violent protest against this surrender, under the influence of the public news-sheets, to 'an unchristian high church spirit'. Originally it was intended that the repealing measure should cover only that part of the original which facilitated naturalization, leaving unaffected the new statutory prohibition of presenting to advowsons. But this would have implied that this right was possessed under common law, and in consequence the repealing Bill was revised in committee so as to make this provision share the fate of the other clauses. It was read in the Lords for the third time on 22 November, Temple alone exercising his peer's right of recording his dissent.

In the Commons, the question had been brought up by the opposition without waiting for government action, Sir James Dashwood moving the consideration of repeal immediately the Reply to the Royal Address had been approved. His motion was supported from the government benches by Lord Parker; but on 23 November the new Bill reached the Lower House. A fierce debate followed, the discussion centring about the preamble, which suggested that the repeal was due to factious endeavours to arouse discontent in the country. Sir Roger Newdigate proposed a less objectionable alternative; but after a debate in which William Pitt condemned the persecuting

---

(*Bibl.* B.3. 15–21) occasioned by the adventures in Paris of a nephew of Samson Gideon with Edward Wortley Montagu, the other (*Bibl.* B.3. 22–26) by the difficulties of a foreign Jewish pedlar.

spirit, and Admiral Vernon praised the zeal of the country curates who had saved the country from being betrayed by the bishops, the amendment was defeated by 113 votes to 13. The repealing Bill was then passed unanimously through the House, receiving the royal assent on 20 December 1753.

Flushed by this success the opposition determined to carry its advantage further, in a frankly anti-Semitic spirit. Immediately the Bill had passed through the Commons, an attempt was made to effect also the repeal of the Act of 1740, which facilitated the naturalization of Jews in the plantations. But by this time popular interest had waned, and Parliament showed its determination not to embark on a programme of persecution by rejecting the proposals, in a House nearly twice as numerous as had divided on any previous occasion during the controversy, by 208 votes to 88.[1]

The altercation was over, and with it one of the strangest episodes of English history of the eighteenth century, which, like the Sacheverell Case or the Gordon Riots, showed how near the surface the old religious excitements still surged. For nearly three-quarters of a century the difficulties in the way of naturalization of foreign-born Jews remained, and those who wished to become British subjects had to choose the clumsy method of endenization. But save for this it is curious how little enduring was the outcome. One of the most remarkable, most universal, and most famous of all popular agitations of the day died down

---

[1] On the Jew Bill controversy see now A. Peskin in *Historia Judaica*, xix. 3–32. In Oxfordshire, notwithstanding an unprecedented expenditure and vast publicity, the government candidates were defeated in the subsequent election, in one of the most memorable electoral encounters of the eighteenth century: cf. R. J. Robson, *The Oxfordshire Election of 1754* (Oxford, 1949), vi. 86–99: 'Two Oxfordshire Gentlemen and the Repeal of the Jew Bill'. *Jackson's Oxford Journal* had derived a good deal of the satirical material used at the time from 'that augean stable of filth and calumny', the *London Evening Post*, in common with other provincial news-sheets. It has been suggested that 'No Jews, no Wooden Shoes' (referred to on p. 217) was not an anti-Huguenot slogan but Cockney rhyming-slang. See also Note IX (c–d), p. 289, and, most recently, Thomas W. Perry, *Public Opinon, Propaganda and Politics in Eighteenth Century England: a Study of the Jew Bill of 1753* (Harvard University Press, 1962).

Some curious details on journalistic activity at the time of the Jew Bill are given by G. A. Cranfield, *The Development of the English Newspaper* (Oxford 1962), pp. 137–40, 146–7. The government did everything in its power to stifle press criticism of its policy: a Nottingham man was prosecuted for selling the anti-Ministerial *Leicester Journal*, while the *London Evening Post* was for a time excluded from the mails.

as suddenly and as completely as it had begun. It had left
behind it no rancour; indeed, one of the strangest features about
the entire episode is that, notwithstanding the manner in which
feeling was excited, there was hardly any physical violence—
a fact which demonstrates its artificial nature. And, though the
results may have dashed the hopes of some of the upper class for
any substantial relief from the disabilities from which they
suffered (it was seventy years before the Jews again received
specific mention in any Act of Parliament), the lasting effects
were insignificant.

# X

# THE REIGN OF GEORGE III

## 1760–1815

### § 1

THE beginning of the long reign of George III, in which Anglo-Jewry was to witness the dawn though not the ful-filment of a new era, was marked by an innovation which ultimately was to prove exceptionally important. The recent political pre-occupations had not found the community entirely unprepared. For some while past (perhaps in imitation of the Deputies appointed to protect the civil rights of the Protestant Dissenters, who first met in 1737) the Spanish and Portuguese community had nominated from time to time its *deputados* to watch over political developments that might affect them, and to approach the government on its behalf should it be thought necessary. One such election was made, as we have seen, when the Irish Naturalization Bill was under discussion.[1] Similarly, on the accession of George III, in 1760, a standing committee was appointed to express homage and devotion to the new sovereign and thereafter to deal with any urgent political matters that might arise. Its immediate functions were satisfactorily per-formed. But a couple of weeks later, the sister-communities following the Ashkenazi rite presented a formal protest against their neglect on so important an occasion and nominated their own 'German Secret Committee for Public Affairs' to act for them in a similar capacity. It was preposterous for two such bodies to carry on independent activities; and towards the end of the year a motion was passed by the *Deputados* to the effect that, when any public affair should offer that might interest the two 'Nations', they would 'communicate to the Committee of

[1] Above, p. 214; *B.M. Records*, i. 39–40. It appears that negotiations with the authorities had previously been conducted by a person of experience in public affairs and with the necessary linguistic qualifications, corresponding to the *Shtadlan* in eastern European communities, who was known as the 'Solicitor' for the Jews: see below, p. 287.

the Dutch Jews' Synagogues' what they thought proper to be done. Thereafter joint meetings sporadically took place. This was the beginning of the London Committee of Deputies of British Jews (more commonly known today as the Board of Deputies) whose functions, though formal and intermittent until the end of the reign, were to attain considerable importance, and even statutory recognition, in the course of the nineteenth century.[1]

When the Deputies performed their first function at the close of 1760 they acted in the name of a community estimated to number between 6,000 and 8,000, the overwhelming majority of whom lived in London: their number having increased twelvefold since the Glorious Revolution seventy years before.[2] A quarter perhaps of the total, comprising, however, a majority of the more anglicized as well as of the well-to-do, belonged to the Spanish and Portuguese element: the Ashkenazim, though more numerous, were on the whole less assimilated, and (with some brilliant exceptions) belonged to a lower social stratum. But, on every section, the alembic of English tolerance was working with remarkable speed and with an efficacy which, from the sectarian point of view, was only too complete. Not only was this the case with the native-born upper class, in whom the process was more notorious, but with their more modest associates as well. An immigrant from Silesia, who at the outset of his career corresponded with his parents in Judaeo-German and was anxious for the welfare of the religious institutions of his birth-place, could develop within twenty years into a staid British merchant, with his sons married to English girls—one a sea-captain and another in the colonial service, and destined to be buried in Bath Abbey.[3] So, too (as we have seen), the sons of a London synagogue functionary, all born in Germany, could

---

[1] *B.M. Records*, i. 45–46; C. H. L. Emanuel, *A Century and a Half of Jewish History* (London, 1910), pp. 1–5.

[2] J. H(anway), *Review of the Proposed Naturalization* (1753), p. 142; *Considerations on the Bill*, p. 17. In 1738, according to Tovey (*Anglia Judaica*, p. 302), Anglo-Jewry was estimated to number 6,000, while in 1684 (above, p. 173 n.) it had comprised 414 souls.

[3] *Anglo-Jewish Letters*, pp. 150–5, 189–91. Probably the most remarkable instance of the entry of Jewish blood into the English aristocracy at this time was through a reputed daughter of Sir Edward Walpole by Maria Norsa, sister of the actress, who married the second Earl Waldegrave, and, after his death, the Duke of Gloucester, George III's brother; but the facts are not quite certain.

lose touch with their co-religionists and enter English life as playwrights, authors, physicians, and even naval officers.[1] This process was partially compensated by a modest though unmistakable trickle of proselytization, strenuously combated by the nervous communal leaders, which was to culminate most embarrassingly, notwithstanding their opposition, in the preposterous episode of the conversion to Judaism of the erstwhile Protestant champion, Lord George Gordon, in 1787.[2]

The change in sentiment was assisted by the spread of Freemasonry (in the English Lodges of which Jews held high office as early as 1723) which inculcated a generous degree of tolerance.[3] The mystical aberrations of the movement were strongly attracted to Jewish exponents of the occult, with results which were not without their importance in social history. Thus the notorious practical cabbalist and 'master of the Divine Name', 'Dr.' Samuel de Falk, was waited on by English and French nobles, from the Duc d'Orléans downwards, at his house in Wellclose Square.[4] Greater heights still were reached by the globe-trotting adventurer Simon von Geldern, great uncle of Heinrich Heine, who was one day found by Prince George of Darmstadt playing piquet with Their Majesties in St. James's Palace.[5]

The process of assimilation was illustrated by the growing use of English in the communal life, for purposes for which Spanish or Judaeo-German had previously been considered indispensable. In 1735 it was at last included in the curriculum of the public school of the Sephardi community. From the close of the reign of George II sermons and special orders of service frequently appeared in English translation, though the originals

---

[1] Above, p. 209.

[2] *Anglo-Jewish Letters*, pp. 125–8; *Bibl.* A.10. 97–102. In a seven-year period at the close of the reign sixty proselytes were converted to Judaism in London under the auspices of a single person—mainly women who married Jews (ibid. A.8. 2). The Jews were not directly affected by the Gordon Riots, though it was said that for safety many of them inscribed their doors with the prophylactic 'This house is True Protestant', and one was executed for taking part in the disorders.

[3] The coat of arms of the English freemasons was said to have been designed by Rabbi Judah Leão (called Templo) who exhibited a model of the Temple of Solomon at Court in 1675. The tolerance of English freemasonry in the eighteenth century contrasted with that of, for example, the Grand Orient Lodge in Berlin, which excluded the Jews.

[4] *Bibl.* A.10. 72–75. See *Essays*, 139–64, for his relations with Theodore of Corsica.

[5] F. Heymann, *Der Chevalier von Geldern* (Amsterdam, 1938), p. 343.

were in Hebrew or one of the other of the semi-sacred tongues. Purblind authorities long opposed the publication of the prayer-book in English, but in 1770 this inhibition was raised.[1] From the last decade of the century the minutes of various communal organizations also began to be kept in the vernacular.

§ 11

Notwithstanding the rapidity of this process of acclimatization, the foreign character of the community was maintained by the continuous influx from abroad. A spirit of restlessness was pervading the Jewish world. Discomforts in Germany, wars in central Europe, expulsion in Bohemia, massacres in Poland, petty persecutions elsewhere, combined with the glamour of a new field of opportunity to foster migration. Continental Jewries heard of the golden opportunities which England provided, and their scions went forth in an unending stream to try their fortune on the other side of the North Sea. And, once a settler had established himself, his younger brothers or other connexions would come to join him.

London was still the principal magnet, as the constant increase of its synagogal accommodation during the second half of the eighteenth century eloquently demonstrated.[2] Owing to the restrictions imposed here on Jews the new-comers tended to establish themselves outside the City boundaries—in the East End near the original settlement, and to a smaller extent in the West beyond Temple Bar. The well-to-do engaged like their precursors in wholesale commerce, brokerage, stock-jobbing, and trade in precious stones.[3] Then came a middle class of shopkeepers, silversmiths, and watchmakers. Lower down in the social scale were the artisans—pencil-makers, tailors, hatters, embroiderers, glass-engravers, diamond-polishers, necklace-makers, and so on.[4] But above all, the new arrivals turned their

[1] Cf. the lists in *Bibl.* B.8. 10 ff., B.9. 2 ff., B.10. 19 ff. The earliest English translation of the Jewish liturgy (excluding the malevolent production of the apostate 'Gamaliel ben Pedhazur', in 1738) was produced in 1761-6 in New York—according to report, owing to the objections raised by the authorities in England. On the other hand, a Spanish version appeared in London as late as 1771 (*Bibl.* B.8. 7a, 14).

[2] See Note X (a), p. 290.

[3] Comparatively few exercised in England the money-lending to which they had been forced by continental legislation, though they attracted disproportionate notice.　　　　　　　　　　　　　　　[4] See Note X (b), p. 290.

attention to two branches of activity which had been forced
upon them by the restrictions against trade and manufacture
which prevailed everywhere on the Continent, and which,
moreover, required neither training nor capital—trading in old
clothes, and peddling.

It was an economic function of some importance that they
filled. In the days before cheap tailoring (introduced by Jews
in the nineteenth century) it was out of the question for the
labourer to purchase a new suit of clothes at intervals; he had
to content himself with the cast-off garments of the wealthier
classes. Every street, lane, or alley in or near the Metropolis was
patrolled by some itinerant Jewish hawker, long-bearded and
speaking a barbarously mutilated English, prepared to purchase second-hand wear, battered hats, hare and rabbit skins,
old glass, broken metal, and almost every other conceivable
article of household or personal use discarded by tidy house-
wives.[1] It was the mainstay of a very large proportion of the
community—according to one careful authority, at the end of
the century there were 1,500 Jewish old-clothes men in London alone. Rag Fair and Rosemary Lane, near the Tower of
London, became the most populous, though far from the most
salubrious, part of London's Ghetto. Hither, the cast-off clothing of the upper classes, purchased after much haggling in the
areas of Westminster and St. James's, was brought to be recon-
ditioned by the dark-eyed daughters of Judah, who were famous
as needle-women. Then it would set out on its travels again, to
return at intervals, until the odyssey was ended as dirty rag to
be pulped into paper.[2]

Hardly less distinctive than the old-clothes men were the pedlars, who needed no shops and therefore could trade, even in
London, without interference. They were encouraged moreover
by the synagogal magnates, who, with practical benevolence,
did whatever was possible to place their indigent co-religionists,
newly arrived from abroad, in a position to support themselves,
and advanced them sufficient capital to begin their operations.
The orange men who paraded the London streets, the trinket
sellers who tempted the servant girls with home-made necklaces
and finery, the hawkers who inveigled schoolboys with pencils

---

[1] The autobiography of one of these Jewish street-traders is extant (*Bibl.* A.10.
223).                                           [2] See Note X (c), pp. 290-1.

and toys, were generally Jews. (Long after, it was from a Jewish lad in Piccadilly that Castlereagh bought the cheap knife with which he committed suicide.)

§ III

Before long the hawkers found competition in London too great, and began to push farther afield. Already in the first half of the eighteenth century the Jew pedlar was a familiar figure in the countryside. He filled an important gap in the mechanism of distribution, bringing the amenities of life within the reach of the isolated rural population, to whom they had hitherto been rarely accessible. We see him in innumerable sketches, ceramics, caricatures, engravings, and groups. He is foremost of the motley company shown jostling one another at the door of a wayside inn, in Rowlandson's expressive caricature, *Unloading a wagon*. Suspended from his back is his pack, ready to be swung round should a potential client appear. One can imagine its contents—buckles, cutlery, watches, lace, tobacco, sealing-wax, toys, and spectacles, with a selection of trinkets and jewellery to dazzle the eyes of the rustic beauties. With the inn as his head-quarters he will commence his circumambulation of the country-side, peddling his wares from door to door in the villages, push-ing his way to the remotest cottage and farmhouse, and making himself understood in the universal language of bargaining not-withstanding his ignorance of all but the vaguest rudiments of the English language. The calling was not without its dangers: the lonely Jew, with his burden of valuables, partly converted into money, was sometimes an irresistible temptation to foot-pads, and the baiting of these lonely strangers was a favourite rural sport. But there were few alternative vocations, and the number of those thus engaged rapidly grew. It was thus that rural England became reacquainted with the Jew.[1]

In those days of slow communication it was necessary for the pedlars to have some centre from which they could operate. Hence agglomerations, which gradually developed into

[1] There is a remarkable account of the activities of these Jewish pedlars in Israel Solomon, 'Records of my Family' (*Bibl.* A.10. 266; cf. *Pub. A.J.H.S.* xxv. 62–67, and Wolf, *Essays*, pp. 136–7). For instances of the murder of Jewish pedlars in the countryside, cf. *Gentleman's Magazine*, 1754, p. 44, 1760, p. 43: less violent maltreatment is illustrated in some contemporary engravings.

established communities, grew up[1] throughout the country, at the
more important provincial centres, market-towns, and especially
seaports, where the sailors constituted a regular and open-
handed clientele. The largest and oldest, probably, outside
London was that of Portsmouth, established in 1747 under the
auspices of a prosperous seal-cutter and engraver. In the same
year the community at King's Lynn received a rudimentary
organization. In Bristol a congregation was in existence in 1754.
The earliest synagogue at Plymouth (where Jews are mentioned
as far back as 1740) dates to about two years earlier. The congregational burial-ground was purchased at Canterbury in
1760, and the synagogue built in 1763. By the year of Waterloo
communities existed, not only at the places just named, but also at
Liverpool (1750), Exeter (1757), Falmouth (1740), Manchester
(1780), Birmingham (1730), Chatham (1750), Sunderland
(1768), Ipswich (1792), Bedford (1803), as well as Norwich,
Sheerness, Swansea, Gloucester, Bath, Coventry, Brighton, Pen-
zance, Dover, Hull, Yarmouth, and perhaps some other places.[2]
In addition individuals or families were to be found in almost
every town of any importance, at least in the south of the
country.[3] The more wealthy traders in the seaport towns became ship's agents; for the captain of every vessel in the Service
had to choose some person to act in this capacity for a period of
three years, and some twenty-five per cent. appointed Jews. The
official lists of navy agents at the time of the Napoleonic wars are
thus almost a directory of the Jewish communities of the period.[4]
Typical probably was the structure of the Jewish settlement in
Plymouth, the largest of the groups which, profiting from the
naval activity, grew up in the West of England seaports in the
mid-eighteenth century. Here, when a return was required at

---

[1] *The Case of the Jews* (1689) and Tovey (*Anglia Judaica*, 1738, p. 302) specifically
state that there was no Jewish settlement outside the capital as yet.

[2] See now the details in Roth, *Rise of Provincial Jewry*, London, 1950.

[3] e.g. Epsom (1718), Winchester (1763), Oxford* (1733), Cowes (1778),
Southampton* (1786), Arundel (1786), Nottingham* (1763), Chichester (*c.* 1763),
Cambridge* (1743), Edinburgh* (1691), Boston* (1799), Frome (1750), Poole
(1762), Lincoln (1766), Margate* (1766), Rochford (1791), Cardiff* (1797),
Sandwich (1794), Walton-on-Thames (1797), Chelmsford (1799), Leeds* (1772),
Jersey* (1765). (A majority of these details are from unexplored documentary
sources: at those places marked with an asterisk communities were established
subsequently.) The Dublin community was dissolved in 1791 and resuscitated in
1822.

[4] Cf. the excerpts in *Trs. J.H.S.E.* xiii. 183-7.

the time of the Napoleonic wars, the community included fifty-seven male aliens, mostly of German origin (only six having been born in Poland, five in Bohemia, and four in Holland). Most had arrived via Harwich: a few via Dover, Gravesend, and London; and many had lived in London or other places in the southern counties before settling in Plymouth. Twelve of them were silversmiths, including assistants; nine were chapmen and petty traders; eight old-clothes men; the remainder were opticians, cap-makers, umbrella-makers, pencutters, &c.[1] At the close of the Napoleonic wars this community included about thirty licensed navy agents.

The Jews of the organized provincial centres affiliated themselves at the outset with one of the London conventicles—generally the Great Synagogue—where probably they attended service on the more solemn occasions of the Jewish year if they were unable to make provision nearer home. Even after the local congregations had been organized (often on the model of the parent-body), this sentimental allegiance continued. Above all, the provincial communities, in which scholarship was at a premium, looked for guidance to the London Rabbinate. Hence the Rabbi of the Great Synagogue was venerated by Jews throughout England as their spiritual head, or rather intellectual guide. This was the case already at the close of the long period of office (c. 1704–56) of Rabbi Aaron Hart, brother of Moses Hart, during whose incumbency the congregation had grown from an inconsiderable handful to an influential body. But under Rabbi David Tevele Schiff (1765–92) the hegemony of the Great Synagogue and its Rabbinate was threatened, a considerable part of the Portsmouth community desiring to affiliate themselves to the Hambro' Synagogue in London and its Rabbi. There was a long and bitter dispute, which ultimately resulted not only in the acceptance of Schiff's supremacy but in its confirmation on terms carefully formulated and accepted by both sides. From this time onwards the spiritual head of the Great Synagogue was recognized as the principal, or 'Chief', Rabbi (or, to use the eighteenth-century term, 'High Priest') of

[1] Rumney in *J.C. Supplement*, January 1936; *A Picture of Plymouth*, 1812; Plymouth minute books in the Jewish Museum, London. Much the same picture is presented by the records of the Portsmouth congregation, all the members of which whose place of origin is indicated c. 1766 came from Germany (*Trs. J.H.S.E.*, xiii. 182–3). Rumney is in error in citing a 1740 edition of *A Picture of Plymouth*.

the Jews not only throughout England, but ultimately throughout the Empire.[1]

## § IV

While the 'German' community was being recruited constantly from abroad, and establishing offshoots throughout the country, the older body was in a different position. The gradual relaxation of the vigilance of the Inquisition, coupled with the decreasing enterprise of its victims, resulted in a progressive dwindling of immigration. After the Lisbon Earthquake of 1755 there was, indeed, a final stirring of consciousness on the part of the Portuguese Marranos, moved profoundly by that terrible cataclysm; and a number found their way to London. Not long after, with the reforms of Pombal, the Inquisition of Portugal lost its power, while that of Spain became less active for want of human material. Hence the tide of immigration gradually ceased. However, as late as 1795, many members of the Spanish and Portuguese congregation, in their Aliens Certificates, gave flight from the Inquisition as the reason for their coming to England; and one added the tragic detail that his mother had been burned by the Holy Office.[2]

The suspension of Marrano immigration was partially compensated from other quarters. The Synagogue was constantly reinforced from the mother-community of Amsterdam, with which most of its members had intimate family relations, as well as by Jewish 'Caribees' of similar origin who had made their fortune in the West Indies. But other elements, too, had by now come into evidence. One of the leading communities of the Marrano diaspora was that of Leghorn, which had been raised from a fishing-village to one of the most important seaports of the Mediterranean by the activity of the New Christians invited thither by the Grand Duke Ferdinando in 1593. This city was the headquarters of the coral trade, largely in Jewish hands. The principal outlet for this commodity was India, to which country it was exported via London and Amsterdam by Jewish gem-merchants, in return for precious stones. In connexion with this trade the Venetian trading- and banking-houses of Treves established a branch in London at the beginning of the eighteenth century, and a stream of Jewish

[1] *Trs. J.H.S.E.* xiii. 168–75.    [2] Wolf, *Essays*, p. 373.

immigrants came at their heels. In 1769, out of sixteen London houses engaged in the coral industry who petitioned the Directors of the East India Company, eight were Jewish. Prominent among them was the firm of Franco, ancestors of Lords Ludlow and Roborough, and Benjamin d'Israeli, grandfather of the prophet of British conservatism.[1]

Another staple import from Italy was the straw bonnet, associated with the name of Leghorn, which became popular in England owing to the patronage of the beautiful Misses Gunning. This industry was responsible for another small wave of immigration, which enriched English life with families of the calibre of the Montefiores. By the middle of the eighteenth century hardly a single important Italian Jewish community lacked its representative in London. Here they attached themselves (no matter what synagogal rite they had followed at home) to the once exclusive Spanish and Portuguese congregation. In 1787 a fierce outbreak of persecution at Rome (where a couple of children were seized for baptism without the slightest pretext) made that community think of emigration *en masse* to England. With pathetic optimism they wrote to London asking for advice. It is hardly surprising that the reply was discouraging; but, while such maltreatment persisted, emigration necessarily continued.[2]

At the close of the century there was an influx of different origin. When Gibraltar was ceded to Great Britain by the Treaty of Utrecht in 1714, the regard of its former owners for the orthodoxy of their erstwhile subjects was expressed in a clause by which Jews and Moors were forbidden to set foot on the Rock. Nevertheless, in 1729 a treaty was signed with the Emperor of Morocco (who was represented on this occasion by a Jew, Moses ben Attar) empowering his subjects of whatever religion to visit the fortress for business purposes for a period not exceeding thirty days. This limitation was soon neglected, and by 1749 a regular community was in existence.[3] By 1776

---

[1] *Misc. J.H.S.E.* i, pp. xxvi–xl; Wolf, *Essays*, pp. 154 ff.

[2] *J.Q.R.*, N.S., xvi, 105–16.

[3] *Bibl.* A.9. 136: the date of the foundation of the community is from manuscript material *penes me*. Jews had been resident in Gibraltar even before 1729, performing good service at the time of the siege of 1727. A close parallel to the establishment of the Jews under British aegis at Gibraltar was their settlement in Minorca during the interlude of British rule; *Bibl.* A.9. 134.

the Jews constituted one-third of Gibraltar's civil population of 3,000, and almost controlled its trade. In the course of the siege of 1779–83, when they served and suffered with the other inhabitants, every attempt was made to reduce the number of useless mouths. In June 1781 there arrived in England a number of destitute families from Gibraltar, who brought with them their Chief Rabbi and the scrolls of the law, rescued at great risk from the two synagogues of the beleaguered fortress. On the restoration of peace many of these immigrants preferred to remain.[1] In subsequent years a number of polyglot Jewish envoys—Jacob Benider (1772), Joseph Sumbal (1794), Masahod Macnin (1813), and Meir Cohen Macnin (1827)—came to the Court of St. James's on missions from the Sultan of Morocco, bringing with them others of their relatives or dependants.[2] Thus the community was revitalized with fresh blood—that of *berberiscos*, who a century before would have been rejected from full membership.

§ v

At the height of the period of expansion of which an account has been given in preceding pages, and to a certain extent because of it, a serious menace to the well-being of the community arose from within, in the allied problems of extreme poverty and delinquency. This did not affect the older Spanish and Portuguese community to any considerable degree, by reason of its better organization, its longer settlement in the country, its greater wealth, and the smaller proportion of its indigent. Among the Ashkenazim, on the other hand, the problem was extremely serious, owing to the constant influx of poor foreigners who had great difficulty in becoming self-dependent owing to the galling restrictions with which they were hampered. The principal reason for the scale of immigration from the Continent (apart from persecution abroad) was that it was so fatally simple and inexpensive. There was a regular service of mail-packets from Brill and Helvoetsluys in Holland. Three classes of passes were available to those who wished to cross to

[1] Picciotto, *Sketches*, pp. 190–2.
[2] *Anglo-Jewish Letters*, pp. 184–5; Wolf, *Essays*, pp. 243, 246, 400–1; *Misc. J.H.S.E.* ii. 84–90.

England by this means—whole (13s.), half (6s.), and gratis; and almost anyone who presented himself to the agent at the port of embarkation and pleaded poverty automatically received a free pass. Arrived in England, the ever-bountiful Synagogue could be relied upon to save him at least from starvation, a pittance of one shilling weekly being granted in all by the three London Ashkenazi congregations. Hence there was a constant influx to England of poor Jews, sometimes of low moral character, who were not only a serious burden to the community, but whose conduct was an actual menace to it.[1]

In 1768 a new wave of massacre began in eastern Europe, when lawless bands of rebels rose in the Ukraine and perpetrated horrors which had no parallel for generations. A fresh wave of penniless fugitives was driven across the Continent, and immigration into England assumed what was considered to be disturbing proportions. Within a period of thirty years it was estimated that the Jewish community increased threefold in numbers. Alarmed at the influx, the authorities of the Great Synagogue in London (which bore half the financial burden involved) resolved to refuse relief to foreign Jews who had left their country without good cause.[2] This restriction tended to aggravate difficulties, adding the menace of criminality to that of destitution. Public attention was drawn to the problem by a series of crimes, culminating in 1771 in a particularly brutal murder perpetrated at Chelsea by a band of Jewish malefactors with more than one infamy to their score. There was an ugly outburst of popular feeling. Jews were saluted in the streets with the cry 'Go to Chelsea'; and instances of physical violence were so common that the commiseration even of persons accustomed to continental standards of maltreatment was aroused.[3] The community found it necessary to dissociate itself from the malefactors in as public a fashion as possible, excommunicating them in the synagogue, withholding the last comforts at Tyburn, and refusing the bodies burial in consecrated ground.

The Wardens of the Great Synagogue (who, five years earlier, had offered their services to the authorities in the hope of checking

---

[1] J. Rumney in *J.C. Supplement*, December 1935; *Trs. J.H.S.E.* xiii. 332–3.

[2] Wolf, *Essays*, pp. 192–3 (the resolution does not belong to 1753, as stated in Booth, *Life and Labour of London* (1902), iii. 174).

[3] E. N. Adler, *London*, pp. 153–7; C. Pelham, *Chronicles of Crime* (1887), i. 227–9; *Trs. J.H.S.E.* xiii. 331.

Jewish delinquency) now took vigorous steps in consultation with Sir John Fielding, the blind Metropolitan magistrate who had tried the case. They insisted that the responsibility for the existence in London of large numbers of poor Jews without any means of livelihood did not rest with them, but with the disturbed state of Poland, and above all, the facilities afforded by the government itself for immigration from the Continent. In consequence of their representations the Secretary of State issued instructions to the Postmaster-General that in future no Jews were to be permitted to come to England on His Majesty's packet-boats except such as had paid their passages in full, and were furnished with passports from one of the ambassadors or ministers abroad. At the same time raids were made on Jewish pedlars throughout the country, and the Lord Mayor publicly offered free passes to any poor Jews who wished to leave England and return to their native lands.[1] By this means something was done to check the influx of undesirable elements, and the tide of criminality, if not turned back, was at least stemmed.

The problem of the Jewish poor was brought forward again in 1795, when the London magistrate and sociologist Patrick Colquhoun published his famous work on the Police of the Metropolis, which was to be the basis of Sir Robert Peel's reorganization of the Police Force thirty-four years later. The account which he presented of the lower classes of the London Jews and their general tendencies was a depressing one, and he insisted on the urgency for constructive action to save them from their degradation and criminal propensities. His observations attracted much attention. In particular Dr. Joshua van Oven, physician to the Great Synagogue, entered into correspondence with the author and suggested a scheme for the amelioration of the condition of the Jewish poor by setting up a systematic method of outdoor relief, supplemented by a grandiose House of Industry. The finances to support this (it was in this that the kernel of the proposals lay) were to be provided

---

[1] Cf. the authorities cited in the previous three notes; *Anglo-Jewish Letters*, pp. 155–7; H.O. Papers, 1770–2, p. 357; R. Leslie-Melville, *Life of Sir J. Fielding*, pp. 259 ff. In 1774 the Postmaster-General again gave orders that, while 'the industrious poor of all nations' could be transported to England gratis, Jews are not to be admitted on board the packets unless they paid full passage money (Advertisement of 10 October 1774). [See Note X (*d*), p. 291.]

out of a Jewish Poor Fund, established by Act of Parliament, and with two main sources of income: first, a compulsory levy on the synagogues and all Jewish householders, and secondly, an appropriation of the poor rate paid by Jewish parishioners but never utilized for the benefit of their co-religionists, who were so sedulously kept from being a burden on the public purse. The policy was approved by Colquhoun and taken up by some leading personalities in politics as well as in synagogal affairs. Opposition quickly developed from the parishes affected by the scheme, and the provision that part of the rates of Jewish districts was to go to the new Board was accordingly omitted. The revised plan was embodied in a Bill authorizing special taxation of the Jews for these purposes, which received the approval of the Chancellor of the Exchequer. At this stage objections were raised by the Spanish and Portuguese Synagogue, which argued that its members would contribute a disproportionate amount of the money but enjoy only an exiguous share of the benefits, and determined to petition Parliament against the scheme. An attenuated measure on the same lines, dealing with the 'German' Jewish communities only, was then prepared, and a petition in support of it was presented by George Tierney in the Commons on 25 February 1802. But meanwhile the proposals had come under fire within the community, pamphleteers pointing out that the scheme would act as a magnet to the poor of eastern Europe, who would stream over in such numbers as to make it bankrupt from the very outset, and that it was useless to teach the English Jews handicrafts unless they could be ensured that prejudices and snobbery would be modified so as to permit them to obtain employment once they were trained. In consequence the grandiose plan was reduced to the establishment in London, with money collected for this object some time previous, from benevolent Christians as well as Jews, of an Asylum and School for the poor of the Ashkenazi community—clearly a mild expedient which would only touch the surface of the question. That no success crowned this attempt, one hundred and fifty years after the Resettlement, to make English Jewry a separate fiscal entity was not altogether a misfortune; and it was remarkable how, within a generation, with growing liberality on both sides and the widening of opportunity, the specific problem which had attracted so much attention

in the decade before Trafalgar quietly and spontaneously disappeared.[1]

§ VI

A decisive factor in this change was the practical cessation of
immigration from the Continent during the Wars of the French
Revolution. From now on English Jewry was of necessity more
or less self-contained, and those of its members who had succeeded in acclimatizing themselves in the country were no longer
retarded or embarrassed by the constant influx of penniless co-
religionists from abroad. The burst of xenophobia at the outset
of the struggle, indeed, involved the Jews also, who were inevitably suspected of Jacobin sympathies; and at Ipswich the
magistrates had to intervene to save them from assault.[2] The
Aliens Act of 1793, which placed foreigners settled in England
under strict control, resulted in sporadic raids on Jewish pedlars
and petty traders throughout the country, and the deportation
of a number of them. Thereafter there were recurrent alarms.
When the French occupied Venice it was reported by the
British representative there that the Jews of the city were in
treasonable correspondence with their co-religionists in London.
Such suggestions were not taken seriously: indeed, the Synagogues were entrusted with the registration of Jews born abroad,
while the Seditious Meetings Bill of 1795 was modified so as not
to penalize them.[3]

The reaction of the Jews at the time of crisis was much the
same as that of any other class of Englishmen, though they were
debarred from holding commissions. As early as the middle of
the eighteenth century some had served before the mast in the
Royal Navy. In 1778 it was suggested that application should be
made for relief from the provisions of the Act for impressing men
for the king's service, but the proposal was considered unwise,
and in consequence a number of Jewish sailors fought under

---

[1] The contemporary publications regarding this scheme are listed in *Bibl.* B.1.
141–6, van Oven's letter to Colquhoun being reprinted in *Anglo-Jewish Letters*,
pp. 210–19. See also Wolf, *Essays*, pp. 195–8, and Rumney in *J.C. Supplement*,
January 1936.

[2] Clarke, *History of Ipswich*, 1830, pp. 319–20. In Birmingham, during the religious riots of 22 March 1813, the mob attacked the synagogue after wrecking
the Methodist chapel.

[3] *Misc. J.H.S.E.* iii. 97–98; Picciotto, *Sketches*, p. 243; Emanuel, *A Century and
a Half*, p. 9.

Nelson. In the army, too, they were to be found, though in smaller numbers.[1] On the renewal of the war with France, hundreds of Jews enlisted in the volunteer corps, the Chief Rabbi having 'expressed his highest concurrence to their taking the oaths of fidelity and allegiance to their king and country'; and at the great review in Hyde Park on 26 October 1803 the king was impressed at the prevalence of zoophoric names (such as Hart, Bear, and Lyon) in a regiment recruited in the east of London. At Dover, Plymouth, Bristol, Exeter, Liverpool, and Gosport Jews were enrolled; though at Portsmouth the mayor at first refused to accept their services.[2]

The exigencies of war gave an opening for outstanding service in a sphere with which Jewish ability is more usually associated —that of finance. This time it was the younger element in the community which was to the fore. The crisis in the affairs of the Dutch East India Company in the third quarter of the century had proved all but disastrous to many magnates of the Spanish and Portuguese group, whose families had long been in the practice of investing their money in it, and now found their capital reduced by some 90 per cent. For the first time the finances of the community were in disorder; and at the period of national crisis the opportunity was seized by new men. The vast requirements of the British Treasury gave ample outlets to the talents of two brothers, Benjamin and Abraham Goldsmid, members of a Dutch Jewish family long established in England.[3] After having been in business in London as bill-brokers for some years, the brothers began in 1792 to bid for government business, impinging on what had previously been regarded as the prerogative of a group of old-established banking firms, who had formed a ring to keep down prices. After one or two successful issues they took their place among the principal loan contractors in the City of London, handling a majority of the government issues. Their acumen, if immensely profitable to themselves, was greatly to the public advantage. The placing of loans

[1] See Note X (e), p. 291. Trs. J.H.S.E. xv. 1–28.

[2] Picciotto, Sketches, p. 276; H.O. Papers, 50: 43, 4 May 1798 (Public Record Office).

[3] The records of the Great Synagogue show the founder of the family occupying administrative office in 1742, nearly a quarter of a century before the date generally given for his arrival in England. It follows that Abraham and Benjamin Goldsmid were English born.

ceased to be a source of patronage: the unfair manipulations at the expense of the taxpayer ceased: the public henceforth had the best market-terms for their money; and the average rate of issue rose by at least three per cent., the Treasury benefiting by the difference.[1] The Goldsmids were thus the first Jews since the Middle Ages whose share in English financial history—at a period when finance was the life-blood of national existence—was of real significance. In the realm of charity they also played a distinguished part, both inside and outside the Jewish community. Benjamin committed suicide during a fit of insanity in 1808, and his brother on the failure of the government loan of 1810. By this time, however, Nathan Meyer Rothschild had begun his fabulous career in England, with foreign connexions so widespread and so faithful that he had an advantage over all his competitors, and sources of information so reliable that news of first importance often reached his ears before it came to the knowledge of the government. During the closing stages of the Napoleonic wars he was used for the transmission of subsidies abroad, and a masterpiece of organization made it possible for him to forward via Paris the bullion required for the payment of Wellington's forces in the Peninsula. Jewish capitalists had occasionally been useful to the government; now, for the first and probably the only time, they proved themselves irreplaceable. It was Rothschild (who had been attempting to keep up prices on the Exchange by extensive buying, in the face of an incredulous and falling market) who brought the news of Waterloo to the anxious Prime Minister. With the restoration of peace, a new era began.

[1] For fuller details see now P. H. Emden, 'The Brothers Goldsmid and the Financing of the Napoleonic Wars', in *Trs. J.H.S.E.* xiv. 225–46; and S. R. Cope, 'The Goldsmids and the Development of the London money-market', *Economica*, N.S., ix. 180–206. The Goldsmid brothers also attempted to straighten out the Prince Regent's embarrassed finances, with the incidental result of ruining one of the most respected Jewish banking-houses in Amsterdam.

# XI

# EMANCIPATION

## 1815–58

### §1

THE restoration of peace in Europe in 1815 found in England a Jewish community of some 20,000 to 30,000 souls, of whom not less than two-thirds lived in London.[1] Outside the capital there were communities—in no case exceeding one thousand souls, and in several not exceeding one hundred—in about twenty-five provincial centres of which Portsmouth, Plymouth, Birmingham, and Liverpool were the most important. The long sequence of disturbances abroad had thrown the community to an increasing extent on its own resources. In all sections there was by now a considerable native-born element, fully anglicized; among those of Spanish and Portuguese extraction, indeed, they were predominant. With Francis Cohen (Palgrave), Isaac d'Israeli, John Adolphus, and Lewis Goldsmith—all more highly considered in that day than in ours—they had begun to play a respectable part in English letters, while David Ricardo (baptized in early manhood) had founded a new school of political economy, and Benjamin Gompertz was among the outstanding contemporary mathematicians.[2] The requirements of the community were by now served by an increasing supply of literature in the vernacular. English sermons, though not yet the rule, were no longer unknown to the

---

[1] Colquhoun's estimate in 1795 was 15,000–20,000 in London (of whom 3,000 belonged to the Spanish and Portuguese element) and 5,000–6,000 in the seaports. Goldsmid in his *Remarks on the Civil Disabilities of British Jews*, 1830, pp. 69 ff. made an estimate of 18,000 Jews in London and 9,000 in the rest of the country, J. E. Blunt (*Establishment and Residence of the Jews in England*, p. 75), substituting 20,000 and 17,000 respectively. Apsley Pellatt (*Brief Memoir of the Jews*, 1829) suggests 25,000 all told.

[2] Jewish contributions to general English literature before 1837 are listed in *Bibl.* B.20. It is to be noted that the most important works of Moses Mendelssohn, which prepared the ground for Jewish Emancipation on the Continent, were translated at an early date into English (*Bibl.* B.20. 54, &c.).

Synagogue.[1] Though Hebrew scholarship was at a low ebb (the only noteworthy figure of English birth was Jacob Hart, who, under the name Eliakim ben Abraham, published a series of scientific brochures of high interest), the community had produced at last in men like David Levi, the erudite hat-maker of Whitechapel, scholars who were qualified to answer Christian polemists on their own level and in their own language. Whereas a century before the Jews had been an alien element, there was among them now at least a nucleus who were unmistakably Englishmen, though of distinctive origin and religious persuasion.

Economically, too, English Jewry had changed during the course of the quarter-century of war. The old-clothes men and pedlars had in many cases managed to establish themselves in more respectable walks of life as exporters, manufacturers, tailors, jewellers, or shopkeepers; and though the former callings were still largely followed by Jews, the age when the ascriptions were synonymous had passed. Moreover, the long period of intense activity which resulted from the naval operations had brought prosperity to the communities of the seaports: while the Industrial Revolution and the development of the Midlands and the north had established flourishing settlements in such new seats of activity as Birmingham and Manchester, where precedent carried less weight than in the ancient centres of British tradition. Whereas at the outset of the reign of George III the Jewish community had been restricted to a very few wealthy merchants and brokers in London, with dependants in lowly occupations distributed over a wider area, after Waterloo a large proportion were indistinguishable economically from any other section of the new middle class thrown up by recent developments.[2]

At the summit of the social pyramid was a small group who had entered into English society in a sense in which few City

---

[1] See *Bibl.* B.10. 33 for what is said to be the first sermon preached and published in English (Liverpool, 1819). In the same year English was first used for the official records of the Spanish and Portuguese Synagogue (Picciotto, *Sketches*, p. 320): it had already been adopted by the 'German' congregations.

[2] E. Halévy (*History of the English People in the Nineteenth Century*, London, 1924, i. 401) instances the growing prosperity by the construction, in the early years of the century, of new synagogues which he describes as 'sumptuous', in Liverpool, Birmingham, and Manchester. In fact the buildings were modest to a degree.

magnates were privileged to do. Almost from the moment of the Resettlement there had been wealthy Jews who had mixed in Court and government circles like the *Hofjuden* of contemporary Germany—Sir Augustine Coronel, Sir Solomon de Medina, or Samson Gideon. But it had been during the Napoleonic wars that this series reached its culminating point in the brothers Goldsmid, who were on terms of some intimacy with the sons of the reigning monarch, whom they not only entertained on many occasions in their houses, but even took with them to synagogue one Friday evening in 1809. Such intercourse inevitably opened many doors which would otherwise have remained closed; and Nelson's heirs were happy that his home passed on his death into the hands of a Goldsmid rather than those of a stranger. More prominent still, though less urbane, was Nathan Meyer Rothschild, whose activities during the closing stages of the war brought him into extremely close relations with the government, and whose family's legendary wealth caused him to be courted like an independent potentate. Apart from (though largely because of) their intimacy with the Goldsmid brothers, the Royal Dukes—who, with all their shortcomings, were, after all, the leaders of English society—showed the best side of their characters in the manner in which they rid themselves of anti-Jewish prejudices. There were Jewish musicians in their households and Jewish bon-vivants in their entourages: they gave their patronage to Jewish charities, and presided at Jewish public dinners. Above all, the Duke of Sussex was not only on friendly terms with many Jews, but also studied the Holy Tongue and built up a superb Hebrew library. However much the cynics might deride, all this could not fail to have a profound influence in completing the social emancipation which was the necessary prelude to the removal of political disabilities.

Jews were now increasingly prominent in many callings besides that of financier which brought them into the public eye. Since the days of Hannah Norsa and Giacomo Basevi Cervetto, they had figured more and more frequently on the stage. The sisters Abrams, long the delight of the concert-rooms; Myer Leoni, because of whose religious scruples the performances of Sheridan's *Duenna* were suspended on Friday evenings; John Braham, his protégé, the prodigious tenor, composer of *The*

*Death of Nelson*, and formerly a choir-boy in the Great Synagogue; Jacob de Castro, author of one of the earliest theatrical
autobiographies and the best known of the group of performers
who went by the name of 'Astley's Jews'; Philip Breslaw,
theoretician as well as practitioner of legerdemain; and very
many others entered into English life on the stage and could
hardly be excluded from it as individuals. Another profession
with which Jews were by now closely associated was that of
pugilism. From the penultimate decade of the eighteenth century
Daniel Mendoza, Samuel Elias, Isaac Bitton, and Abraham
Belasco familiarized countless persons throughout the country
with the actuality of the Jew, and convinced them that he could
excel in other capacities than as pedlar and old-clothes man.[1]

With the close of the eighteenth century, moreover, a new
spirit with regard to the Jews had come to manifest itself in
English literature. Whereas the stage had previously offered
its public for the most part resuscitations of Shakespeare's
*Shylock* or figures of fun such as 'Beau Mordecai' in Macklin's
*Love à la Mode* (1759), the publication of the first translation of
Lessing's *Nathan the Wise* in 1781 (followed by a new version
ten years later, similarly with apologetic intentions) marked the
beginning of a change in attitude. Richard Cumberland's *The
Jew*, first performed in 1794 and repeatedly published, anaemic
production though it was, marked an epoch in English literature in taking a Jew as its hero. He was followed by the play-
wright Thomas Dibdin (*The Jew and the Doctor*, 1789; *The
School for Prejudice*, 1801) and the novelists George Walker
(*Theodore Cyphon*, 1796, 1823) and Maria Edgeworth (*Harrington*, 1816—the first work to present the Jew not only in a favourable light, but as a gentleman). The new tendency was by no
means universal; but it was significant, and not without a lasting effect.[2]

Another powerful influence was that of the Evangelical move-
ment. This had resulted in the establishment in 1795 of the
London Society for the Promotion of Christianity among the
Jews, which at the beginning of the following century was given

---

[1] Cf. all these names and the publications by or associated with them in *Bibl.*,
index, and the biographical accounts in the *Jewish Encyclopaedia*, the *Dictionary of
National Biography*, and A. Rubens, *Anglo-Jewish Portraits* (London, 1935).
[2] See Note XI (*a*), p. 291.

fresh vitality by the enthusiasm of the philanthropist Lewis Way. In its immediate objects the society could not boast of much success. It was estimated that every convert cost the public between £500 and £600; and Jewish writers, no longer intimidated, replied to its polemics with a vigour which would have been impossible a generation earlier.[1] But there was now a new approach to the problem on the Christian side. Scholastic and benevolent institutions were established, which ultimately proved an example as well as incentive to the Jewish community. No longer were the unbelievers considered an object for insult and reviling; they were approached in a spirit not only of friendship but almost·of veneration, as the ancient people of God. Reasonable arguments were put forward in moderate language; it was freely admitted that Christendom owed a profound debt of shame in respect of the past centuries of persecution and maltreatment; some persons even maintained that the voice of reason could not make itself heard until the last relics of discrimination had been removed. Hence in Evangelical circles the movement resulted in the development of a spirit of friendliness, which insisted on the recognition of the Jews as members of English society.

Meanwhile the cataclysm of the French Revolution had given a great impetus to millenarian theorists, who believed that the second coming of the Lord, accompanied by the restoration of the Jews to their own land, was at hand. A number of writers foretold the approaching renewal of a Jewish state, and even urged the British government to take steps to further it; some (inspired by a naval pseudo-Messiah, Richard Brothers, who styled himself 'Nephew of the Almighty') went so far as to identify the English with the Lost Ten Tribes, and to associate them with the Palestinian revival.[2]

Hence there slowly developed an unmistakable current of opinion in favour of the removal of religious disabilities. In 1790 a pamphleteer who signed himself 'A Christian Politician' associated Jews, Catholics, and Dissenters together in a *Collection of Testimonies in Favour of Religious Liberty*. The Abbé Grégoire's epoch-making *Essay on the Physical, Moral, and Political Reformation of the Jews*, which had such influence on the Continent, was

---

[1] *Bibl.* A.7. 69, 76: cf. also the contemporary publications, B.6. 77 ff., B.8. 43 ff.  [2] See Note XI (*b*), pp. 291-2.

published in an English translation about 1791. In 1812 there appeared *An Appeal to the Humanity of the English People on Behalf of the Jews*.[1] By 1827 a secular pro-Jewish society, without any ostensible conversionist object, existed in London; and in the same year the *Quarterly Review* departed from its normal conservatism in an article which ascribed the degradation of the Jews to their age-long persecution, and appealed for a removal of restrictions so as to bring them up to the level of other human beings.[2]

By this time the question was no longer on a purely theoretical plane. Contemporary developments abroad presented it as a practical question. In the newly created United States of America (where many Jews had fought steadfastly on the patriotic side in the Revolutionary War, though some had supported the mother country with equal zeal) the constitution adopted in 1787 stipulated that no religious test should be required as qualification for any Federal office or post of trust. In the following year Latin logic forced upon the National Assembly of France, somewhat reluctantly, the conclusion that even Jews must enjoy benefit of the Rights of Man; and during the next decade the armies of the Revolution carried the same doctrine into Germany, Italy, and above all Holland, where Jews had not only proved useful citizens, but had distinguished themselves in offices of trust during these years. The grandiose Napoleonic 'Sanhedrin' which met in Paris in 1807, while of little practical importance, had been followed with the keenest interest by English observers[3] and seemed to demonstrate the rehabilitation of the Jews in the eyes of the world. The European settlement at Vienna left the Jews in full possession of their new-won rights in the Low Countries (they were internationally guaranteed in Belgium after she secured her independence in 1830) and, with a trivial reservation, in France. In Germany and Italy reaction was triumphant for the moment; yet even

---

[1] A conversionist publication, but unmistakably friendly in tone.
[2] The support of the London Society for the Promotion of Christianity among the Jews for the cause of Jewish emancipation was strenuously advocated by Thomas Thrush in his *Letters to Mr. Levy* (London, 1828). For the publications advocating or opposing Jewish emancipation see Bibl. B.1, *passim*; for Richard Brothers, the comprehensive bibliography, ibid. B.17. 14–71; and for the Palestinophile movement, ibid. B.16.
[3] *Bibl.* B.5. 24–25, B.18. 38–39.

English diplomats exerted themselves (though, as events proved, in vain) to perpetuate in Frankfort and the Hanseatic Towns the rights secured during the past few years, and nominally guaranteed by the Vienna Treaties.[1] Fifteen years before it became a question of practical politics in England, and half a century before it reached its culmination, Emancipation had passed elsewhere beyond the experimental stage.

## § 11

The position of the Jews in England had in fact been ameliorated insensibly during the previous generation, notwithstanding the absence of any legislative action. In 1770, for the first time, one had been admitted as solicitor (there had been Notaries Public even as early as 1731).[2] A little while after, in 1780, the annual gift to the Lord Mayor was summarily discontinued, a special grant being voted by the aldermen to compensate the Chief Magistrate for his loss. Though the maximum recorded price for the succession to a Jew Broker's medal was reached in 1826, two years later the limitation on their number was abandoned. In the same year the Court of Aldermen reluctantly admitted certain baptized Jews to the Freedom of London, from which persons in this category had been excluded since 1785. In 1805 Aaron Cardozo (a Gibraltar Jew whose probity was deeply appreciated by Nelson) was sent on an official mission to the Bey of Oran, with whom he concluded a treaty—a natural corollary of the procession of Jewish envoys in the reverse direction. During the recent West Indian campaigns, a certain Joshua Montefiore, a professing Jew, had received the king's commission;[3] and in 1826 Parliament passed a statute (6 George IV, cap. 67) abolishing in all cases the necessity for receiving the Sacrament according to the rites of

[1] L. Wolf, *The Diplomatic History of the Jewish Question* (London, 1919), pp. 12–16; *Pub. A.J.H.S.* xxvi. 33–125.

[2] Henriques, *Jews and English Law*, pp. 205–6; *Pub. A.J.H.S.* xix. 179–80. (From this it would seem that the candidate took the oath in the Christological form; but he remained a professing Jew.) For notaries cf. *Trs. J.H.S.E.* xvii. 113–59.

[3] Picciotto, *Sketches*, pp. 335–6, 386; A. B. M. Serfaty, *The Jews of Gibraltar*, pp. 14–15; Wolf, *Essays*, p. 221. There is no evidence to show how Joshua Montefiore (who with Moses [later Sir Maurice] Ximenes had led a band of adventurers to establish a colony in West Africa in 1791: *Bibl. B.20. 60*) evaded the statutory Christological oaths.

the Church of England before naturalization, thereby achieving incidentally—without so much as mentioning the Jews, and without attracting the slightest public attention—the object of the ill-fated 'Jew Bill' of seventy-three years before.

Apart from this gradual and spontaneous amelioration in practice, English law as interpreted in the courts of justice had begun to reflect the changed position of the Jew in society. In 1772, when the City authorities endeavoured to compel the Spanish and Portuguese Synagogue to support an incorrigible member (an annoyance which had not been uncommon a century before, even when persons who had abandoned Judaism were concerned), forensic opinion decided that no legal obligation existed. Five years after, an attempt to enforce the payment of Church rates by the same place of worship was successfully resisted. In 1788 the courts recognized the competence of a Rabbinical tribunal to regulate ritual 'kosher' food, and in 1793 to decide the validity of Jewish marriages (put on a legal basis by Lord Hardwicke's Marriage Act of 1753, which had treated Jews and Quakers more generously than other non-Anglicans). In 1818 a synagogue was recognized as a legal establishment, able to sue for withheld dues. Taken individually these isolated advances did not mean much; together they signified a good deal, implying that Jews enjoyed liberty in all things except where the law expressly prescribed the contrary.[1]

Hence the positive disabilities from which English Jews suffered were not considerable, as compared with those of their co-religionists in most parts of the continent of Europe. They could settle where they pleased throughout the kingdom, and in any part of the place of their choice. There was no legal bar to their employing non-Jewish labour, whether in their homes or businesses, to dealing in any commodity, to engaging in any business occupation or in any branch of manufacture. Though there was some doubt as to their legal ability to own freeholds, there was admittedly no obstacle to their acquiring land on lease on peppercorn rent for an indefinitely long period, which amounted to the same thing. In practice they were even allowed to vote in parliamentary elections (though the returning officer had the power, sometimes exercised, to demand from voters the Oath of Abjuration, which was phrased in a form repugnant to

[1] See Note XI (c), p. 292.

the Jewish conscience). In London, indeed, they still suffered from a serious economic disability owing to their exclusion from the Freedom; but the force of this had been mitigated by the expansion of the Metropolis in every direction, with the result that the bar was operative in only a relatively small area of the entirety, where, moreover, the difficulty was sometimes evaded by selling retail from warehouses ostensibly wholesale.[1]

Theoretically, however, the position was very different. The entire body of medieval legislation which reduced the Jew to the position of a yellow-badged pariah, without rights and without security other than by the goodwill of the sovereign, remained on the statute book, though remembered only by antiquarians. As late as 1818 it was possible to maintain in the courts Lord Coke's doctrine that the Jews were in law perpetual enemies, 'for between them, as with the devils, whose subjects they are, and the Christian there can be no peace'. Public life was, in law, entirely barred. Jews were excluded from any office under the Crown, any part in civic government, or any employment however modest in connexion with the administration of justice or even education, by the Test and Corporation Acts, passed at a period when the participation of Jews in such activities was inconceivable. These made it obligatory on all persons seeking such appointment to take the Sacrament in accordance with the rites of the Church of England, in addition to the statutory oaths of Supremacy (of the Crown over the Church of England), of Allegiance (to the sovereign, coupled with abhorrence of Papal pretensions), and of Abjuration (of the claims of the former Royal House of Stuart) —the last, 'on the true faith of a Christian'. Naturally these disqualifications included the right to membership of Parliament, for which the statutory oaths in the statutory form were a necessary preliminary. For the same reason the universities were closed, and, as a consequence of this, various professions.[2] But these political disabilities were shared with a large proportion of native-born British subjects of older lineage

---

[1] A. Pellatt, *Brief Memoir* (1829), p. 26.

[2] The disabilities from which the Jews suffered are stated in detail in J. E. Blunt, *A History of the Establishment and Residence of the Jews in England, with an inquiry into their civil disabilities* (London, 1830), pp. 110 ff., and various contemporary works: see *Bibl.* B.1. Cf. also Ursula Henriques, *Religious Toleration in England* (Oxford, 1961), pp. 175 ff.

—Roman Catholics and to a considerable extent (nominally at least) even Dissenters. Till the complaints of the latter had been satisfied it was out of the question to expect any appreciable alleviation of those of the Jews. Indeed, Jewish emancipation in its fullest sense had first been ventilated in various eighteenth-century pamphlets, re-adapted in some cases at the beginning of the nineteenth, as a *reductio ad absurdum* of the idea of emancipating Christian Nonconformists.[1]

## § III

The progress of the movement for the removal of the disabilities of the Dissenters and Roman Catholics logically implied a change of attitude towards the Jews. On 14 July 1820 the young Whig champion John Cam Hobhouse (later Lord Broughton de Gyffard) gave notice in the House of Commons of his intention to move a resolution that the condition of the Jews and the disabilities under which they laboured ('which would be hardly believed to exist in such an age as this') should be taken into immediate consideration.[2] For the moment this was little more than an academic demonstration. But, within ten years, intolerance had narrowed down so far that the reform came within the sphere of practical politics. The Repeal of the Test and Corporation Acts in 1828, as originally contemplated, would automatically have removed the political disabilities of the Jews; but, on the motion of the Bishop of Llandaff, the House of Lords insisted upon the insertion of the words 'on the true faith of a Christian' in the Declaration henceforth required on taking up a public office. (An amendment of Lord Holland's, that Jews should be permitted to omit the newly introduced phrase, was negatived.) In the Lower House, after the amended Bill had been read for the third time, Brougham made a spirited protest against the change, explaining that he had not expressed his disapprobation earlier for fear of endangering the

---

[1] Cf. *Bibl.* B.1, 50, 54, 155.

[2] *Parliamentary Debates*, 1820, ii. 475. The story that, when the removal of the disabilities of the Dissenters was first mooted, their leaders refused to accept the collaboration of the Jews with the same object because they were not subject to grace, is derived from the satirical *Lamentations of the Children of Israel* (1813), which in turn copies *The Complaint of the Children of Israel* (1746)—the most popular of the works referred to at the close of the previous paragraph.

It is said that Isaac Lyon Goldsmid began to work for Jewish emancipation after a memorable speech of Ricardo's in 1823 on Religious Liberty.

measure. Thus the incidental disqualification of former years was replaced by one directed in fact against the Jews alone.[1] For the moment Roman Catholics continued to be discriminated against, for reasons as much political as religious. Their emancipation in April 1829 left the Jews the only section of the English population which was excluded from political rights ostensibly because of their faith. It was no longer a mere disability: it was felt by some of their leaders, confident of their talents and proud of their English birthright, to be a slight.[2]

Particularly was this the case with Isaac Lyon Goldsmid, nephew of the famous financiers and well known in financial and philanthropic circles. In March 1829, while the Catholic Emancipation Bill was under discussion, the Board of Deputies of British Jews (by now a force in the community) was informed of the steps he had taken in the matter, and expressed itself in favour of action to secure the relief of the Jews from their political disabilities. The interest of Nathan Meyer Rothschild was enlisted (though being foreign-born he preferred to be represented on formal occasions by his son Lionel). After consultation as to procedure with the Duke of Wellington, then Prime Minister, the first practical steps were taken—the presentation of a Petition to Parliament praying for the removal of Jewish disabilities, and the preparation of a Bill for achieving that object. The government, though not unfriendly, considered that the turmoil created by the Catholic Emancipation Bill was so great that it was unwise to introduce another of a similar nature in the same session, and the formal opening of the campaign was accordingly deferred to the following year.[3]

On 5 April 1830 the Whig stalwart Sir Robert Grant introduced into the Commons a Bill 'to repeal the civil disabilities affecting British-born subjects professing the Jewish religion' whereby all 'civil rights, franchises and privileges . . . offices, places, employments, trusts and confidences' that had been made available to Catholics in the previous year should now be thrown open to them also. Leave to bring in the Bill was

---

[1] In one respect the repeal of the Test and Corporation Acts made the position of the Jews worse than it had been before, as an annual Indemnity Act had previously mitigated religious disabilities.

[2] See Note XI (d), p. 292.

[3] Emanuel, A Century and a Half, pp. 16–17; Trs. J.H.S.E. iv. 116 ff., vi. 240 ff.: U. Henriques, op. cit., p. 185.

granted by a majority of 18. The opposition proved stronger than had been anticipated, and appreciably hardened while the Bill was before Parliament—according to report, through the influence on the king of his cousin, the Duke of Gloucester, and his sister, the duchess. The second reading was therefore defeated by 228 votes to 165. In the same session Lord Bexley (who had worked with Rothschild when Chancellor of the Exchequer, as Nicholas Vansittart, at the time of Waterloo) made a similarly unsuccessful attempt in the Lords. The fall of Wellington's administration shortly after, and the concentration of the national energies on the Reform Bill controversy, prevented anything more from being done at the moment, though numerously signed petitions from London and the provinces showed that the general public was by no means indifferent.

The Reformed Parliament met early in 1833 imbued with a passionate desire to sweep away old abuses. On 17 April Grant moved that the House should resolve itself into a committee to consider the disabilities affecting Jewish subjects. Despite a protest from Sir Robert Inglis, the reactionary member for the University of Oxford, who was to maintain his uncompromising opposition for an entire generation, the motion was adopted without a division. In committee Grant moved 'that it is expedient to remove all civil disabilities at present existing affecting His Majesty's subjects of the Jewish religion, with the like exceptions as are provided with reference to His Majesty's subjects professing the Roman Catholic religion'. The debate that followed reached a high level, Hume, O'Connell, and Macaulay speaking strongly in favour of the motion (the speech of the last-named was to be a classic of English apologetics).[1] The minority did not challenge a division, and the resolution was adopted. The second and third readings of the Bill were carried by ample margins against an intractable minority of 52. On being sent to the Lords, however, it was thrown out on the second reading by 104 votes to 54, the Archbishop of Canterbury leading the opposition. The Duke of Sussex was characteristically vehement in his support, but his

---

[1] Cf. *Bibl.* A.7. 51. Of even greater importance than his speech was Macaulay's powerful *Essay* on the subject in the *Edinburgh Review* for January 1831, which was frequently republished in England and abroad. For the debates of 1833 see *Bibl.* B.1. 181. Hazlitt had also championed the Jewish cause in *The Tatler* in March 1831.

influence was counterbalanced by that of his brother, William IV, who got it into his head that it was his duty to oppose this innovation. 'My Lord', he said anxiously to a newly appointed bishop when he did homage, 'I do not mean to interfere in any way with your vote in Parliament except on one subject, *The Jews*, and I trust I may depend on your always voting against them.'

In the following year (24 April 1834) Grant reintroduced his Bill, which was easily carried, but rejected by the Lords by an increased majority. After Melbourne's Whig administration was reinstated the measure was taken under government auspices. But both support and opposition were by now lukewarm. The Commons mustered only 56 votes all told to pass the second reading (3 August 1836); and in the Lords, owing to the lateness of the session and the general apathy, the second reading was never moved. For the next eleven years the question was permitted to lapse.[1]

## § IV

The parliamentary debates of 1830 to 1836 made it patent that the now dominant middle class was antagonistic to the continuance of religious disabilities—a remarkable contrast to conditions at the time of the 'Jew Bill' of 1753, when this same element had been foremost in agitating against the derisory concessions then contemplated. Hence, during the ensuing period of delay, before political emancipation was achieved, it was relatively easy to secure the removal, little by little, of minor Jewish disabilities affecting civic life. The new tactics were in fact more in accordance with the English genius of building up a doctrine from practical details, as opposed to the continental fashion of imposing a general principle without working out its implications, which the advocates of emancipation had at first favoured. Moreover the opposition, with its indignant repudiation of medieval prejudice and its concentration on the doctrine that, in a Christian country, non-Christians should have no share in the government, implicitly admitted that Jewish disabilities short of exclusion from Parliament were an

---

[1] The most careful summary of the progress of Jewish emancipation in England is in Henriques, *The Jews and the English Law*. See also the list of contemporary publications and polemic literature in *Bibl.* B.1, and U. Henriques, as above.

anachronism. Thus in these years the various disabilities were swept away one by one, until in the end parliamentary emancipation only remained to be effected.[1]

The main campaign took place in the City of London. At the close of 1830, in accordance with the recommendations of a committee set up in the previous year, the Common Council enacted that henceforth any person who took up the freedom could make the necessary oath in a form agreeable to his religious convictions. This implied not only that Jews could now become freemen, but also that they could carry on trade in the City and be members of Livery Companies. David Salomons, a well-known City figure and one of the founders of the Westminster Bank, whose family had for three generations played their part in the affairs of the Anglo-Jewish community, had ambitions in public life. As soon as it became possible, he applied for membership of the Coopers' Company, and proceeded rapidly from one civic dignity to another. In 1835, in the teeth of some opposition on religious grounds, he was elected sheriff. The statutory declaration 'on the true faith of a Christian' (incumbent since the repeal of the Test and Corporation Acts) made it impossible for him to enter upon his functions. To solve the difficulty Parliament promptly passed the Sheriff's Declaration Act (5 & 6 William IV, cap. 28) making special provision for persons elected to this office. The measure applied, however, to no other dignity, and when in the following December Salomons was returned as alderman, he was refused admission by the Court of Aldermen and a new election was ordered.[2] In 1837 the Municipal Corporations Declarations Act gave relief to Quakers and Moravians, but Grote's amendment to extend it to all classes of Her Majesty's subjects was negatived, the government feeling that this would jeopardize the measure as a whole. But that same year Moses Montefiore, who had already made himself known as a philanthropist, became sheriff of London, and was knighted by Queen Victoria on the occasion of her state visit to the City after the coronation, being the first Jew since Sir Solomon de Medina to receive that distinction.

For some time to come the movement for the removal of

[1] See Note XI (e), pp. 292–3.
[2] See A. M. Hyamson, *David Salomons* (London, 1939). Alexander Raphael, sheriff in 1834 and M.P. in 1835, was a Persian-born ex-Jew, now Catholic.

civic as of parliamentary disabilities remained in a state of imperfectly suspended animation. But in other spheres there was gradual amelioration. In 1833 Francis Goldsmid, the son of Isaac Lyon Goldsmid, was called to the Bar, the first Jewish barrister. In 1835 an Act which incidentally relieved voters from the necessity of taking any oaths threw the franchise open *de jure* as well as *de facto* to professing Jews. On 17 November of the same year the earliest recorded Jewish juryman was sworn on the Pentateuch as a member of the Grand Jury at the Kirkdale Quarter Sessions. In 1836 the Board of Deputies (which had by now begun to extend representation to synagogues outside London) received statutory recognition in the Marriage Registration Act as a competent authority to certify Jewish places of worship. In 1837 the non-sectarian university of London, in the foundation of which Isaac Lyon Goldsmid had been one of the most active and most generous workers, was incorporated, enabling Jews to proceed to the degrees from which they were excluded by the older universities.[1] In 1841 Goldsmid was rewarded for his outstanding philanthropic services by being created baronet, being the first Jew to receive an hereditary English title.

The same year (1841), largely owing to Salomons's unflagging efforts, the government carried through the House of Commons a measure 'for the relief of persons of the Jewish religion elected to municipal office', but it was defeated on the second reading in the Lords. The struggle was then transferred from the Senate to the City. In 1844 Salomons was once more elected to the Court of Aldermen, and once more refused admission. His pertinacity had brought the problem to public attention, and it was considered preposterous for the wishes of the Liverymen to be persistently overridden in this fashion. In 1845 accordingly a Jewish Disabilities Removal Act, introduced by Lord Lyndhurst, enabled any member of the Jewish faith on admission to municipal office to substitute for the declaration laid down by law one in a form acceptable to his conscience (8 & 9 Victoria, cap. 52). Thus municipal offices of every description—including that of Recorder, with its judicial functions—were thrown open to Jews. Two years after, Salomons was at last admitted as alderman, and no further obstacle was put in his way when, in

[1] See Note XI (*f*), p. 293.

the normal course of succession, he was elected Lord Mayor
of London in 1855, thereby setting the seal on the municipal
emancipation of English Jews.[1]

Meanwhile, in the course of the general reforming movement
which was sweeping away old abuses, an Act of 1846 'to relieve
Her Majesty's subjects from certain penalties and disabilities in
regard to religious opinions' (9 & 10 Victoria, cap. 59) formally
repealed, among other legislation, the intolerant *statutum de
judeismo* of 1271 (still on the statute book) and the act of 1702
compelling Jews to maintain their Protestant children, and
placed English Jews in the same position as Protestant dissenters with respect to their schools, places of worship, and charitable foundations.

One disability only was now left—that they could not take part
in political life. A remote ideal twenty years before, it became
a common-place in Europe with the emancipation of the Jews
in ever-widening areas of the Continent in the middle decades
of the century. That full emancipation should have been so
long delayed in England, where the Jews were so mildly treated,
is perhaps not so remarkable as would appear. In those countries where important vestiges of the Ghetto system remained
until the nineteenth century, the granting of full legal equality
to the Jew had become a cardinal principle of constitutionalist
doctrine. In England, for the very reason that the disabilities
from which he suffered were comparatively slight, it was possible to withhold the final step so long.

§ v

In the interval of waiting, before they could achieve complete
integration in the English body politic, the Jews were setting
their own house in order. There was a section in the community
which imagined that the withholding of full emancipation was
due to the fact that the traditional forms of Judaism were, if
not foreign, at least non-English, and that an approximation in
externals between the Hebrew and Christian forms of worship
would convince the outside world at last that their Jewish neighbours were differentiated from them only in adherence to a
creed which was, at root, not so remote from that which they

[1] Meanwhile, in 1846, (Sir) B. S. Phillips had been elected to the Common
Council.

themselves professed. This reasoning had been the basis of the Reform Movement in Germany, which had come to a head with the opening of a reformed 'Temple' in Hamburg in 1818. In England rumblings of discontent with the established ecclesiastical order had made themselves heard from the beginning of the nineteenth century. The few minor reforms which were introduced did little to meet the criticisms, which in London were aggravated by the attempt of the existing synagogues to retain their dominance by allowing no Jewish place of worship to be opened outside the City area. The agitation grew; and in 1836 a number of members of the Spanish and Portuguese community presented a petition requesting the introduction into the service of 'such alterations and modifications as were in the line of the changes introduced in the reform synagogue of Hamburg and other places'. Counter-petitions and prolonged debates encouraged the governing body not to compromise; and in the spring of 1840 eighteen prominent and wealthy members of the community, in association with six members of other synagogues, resolved to establish a place of worship in West London which would be neither 'Ashkenazi' nor 'Sephardi', but 'British'. Thus, notwithstanding strenuous efforts on the part of the older bodies, culminating in an ecclesiastical ban, the first English Reformed Synagogue, the West London Synagogue of British Jews, was opened in 1842.[1]

To the credit of both factions the dissidents did not become a sect—not even in the following century, when the movement took a radical turn—the difference being one rather of presentation than of dogma. Nor, indeed, did the new movement, alien to the formal conservatism of the Englishman, achieve by any means so sweeping a success, or so far-reaching results, as was anticipated. Outside London it established a foothold in the course of the next generation only in Manchester and Bradford. But its influence on the conservative majority, though unacknowledged, was nevertheless considerable. Synagogue decorum improved, organized choirs were introduced, the vernacular sermon became the rule, education was reorganized, and ministers of religion began to replace the old type of synagogal factotum:

---

[1] D. Philipson, *The Reform Movement in Judaism* (New York, 1931), chapter v, Hyamson, *Sephardim*, chapter xv, and the controversial publications in *Bibl.* B.5. 30–37.

while, in London, geographical decentralization was no longer discouraged. In 1845, after an election in which for the first time some twenty communities throughout the country participated, the Chief Rabbinate was filled by a pastor, in the person of the Hanoverian Nathan Marcus Adler, who combined with his Talmudical training and orthodox principles a sound western education. Under his auspices a Jewish theological seminary on modern lines was established in London (1855), and the first steps were taken towards the unification of the London community, to culminate in the establishment of the United Synagogue in 1870. At the same time the organization of Jewish Boards of Guardians and similar institutions helped to cope with the problem of the indigent who, at the beginning of the century, had presented so serious a difficulty.[1]

In the historical evolution of the Anglo-Jewish community the year 1840 was of crucial importance. A charge of ritual murder which was brought up against the Jews of Damascus, accompanied by a particularly brutal persecution, stirred the English conscience to its depth. A protest meeting was held at the Mansion House; and when Sir Moses Montefiore proceeded to the East to champion the cause of his co-religionists, he enjoyed not only the sympathy of the English people, but the diplomatic support of the English government as well. (In this, his position was very different from that of his French colleague, Adolphe Crémieux, who had to contend with the prejudices and opposition of his compatriots.) When Montefiore came back in triumph from his mission, after securing the release and unconditional acquittal of the prisoners, he was received in audience by the queen and accorded supporters to his coat of arms—a recognition of the fact that this intervention on behalf of persecuted Jews was at the same time a service to the humanity of his fellow countrymen.[2]

---

[1] N. M. Adler (whose predecessor in office, from 1802 to 1842, Solomon Hirschell, had hardly been able to keep pace with the anglicization of the community during his pastorate) was succeeded by his son, Hermann Adler (1891–1911), and the latter by J. H. Hertz (1913–46) and I. Brodie. For the institutions mentioned in the text see *Bibl.* A.8. ii and iii. The United Synagogue, a union of the older London Ashkenazi congregations, was supplemented in 1887 by a Federation of Synagogues embracing the less highly organized foreign element.

[2] The selection of this slightly bizarre distinction was probably due to the fact that Montefiore was already a knight, and that there was as yet no precedent for a Jew becoming baronet.

This episode marked the meridian of the benevolent work of Montefiore, who, almost to the end of his long life, was engaged in journeys of intercession—to Russia, to Morocco, to Italy—on behalf of his persecuted co-religionists. This protracted activity, on the part of a personality of exceptional distinction and moral force, gave English Jewry a position of pre-eminence in political activities on behalf of the communities of backward states; while its representative institutions, hitherto concerned only with domestic matters, had their purview widened and began to think in international terms. The British government, too, maintained the benevolent attitude which it had taken up at the period of the Damascus Affair. From that time onwards, except when urgent political considerations made action inadvisable, it could generally be relied upon for diplomatic support if conditions for Jews abroad became intolerable.[1] The tendency culminated shortly after the Damascus Affair when Palmerston (anxious to obtain a *locus standi* in the Holy Land, equivalent to that enjoyed by Russia on behalf of the Orthodox Church, and by France on behalf of the Roman Catholics), attempted to take Palestinian Jewry in its entirety under British protection in a formal sense. This did not indeed materialize, but for some while England exercised the right on behalf of expatriated Russian Jews.[2] Such philosemitism abroad could hardly fail to influence events at home.

§ VI

When at the outset of the movement for Jewish emancipation Isaac Lyon Goldsmid had been in touch with Daniel O'Connell, the latter warmly advised him to force the claims of the Jews on Parliament, as he himself had the claims of the Catholics. Such methods accorded admirably with David Salomons's pugnacious temperament. Accordingly in 1837, 1841, and again 1847 he offered himself as a parliamentary candidate, but in each

---

[1] L. Wolf, *The Diplomatic History of the Jewish Question* (London, 1919). Cf., for a little-known instance of intervention in Syria, S. W. Baron, 'Great Britain and Damascus Jewry in 1860–1', in *Jewish Social Studies* (1940), ii. 179–208.

[2] A. M. Hyamson, *The British Consulate in Jerusalem* (London, 1939, &c.). The establishment in 1841 of the Anglican Bishopric in Jerusalem, with a converted Jew, Michael Solomon Alexander, as its first incumbent, was an outcome of this policy. The tendency was reflected in the interest shown by the British government in Zionism from its early days, culminating in the Balfour Declaration of 1917.

case unsuccessfully. In the last year, however, Baron Lionel de Rothschild, head of the famous banking-house, was nominated for the City of London, in conjunction with Lord John Russell, the Prime Minister. Success for one who fought here in the Liberal interest was almost a foregone conclusion, and he was elected by an adequate majority.

There was no statute that forbade a Jew to sit in Parliament; but (as has been indicated above) it was rendered impossible by reason of the form of the statutory oaths. It was not only that they were normally administered on the New Testament—this was a matter of usage only. The real obstacle was that, in addition to the Oaths of Allegiance and Supremacy, the conservatism of English institutions preserved also a third abjuring the right to the throne of the descendants of the Old Pretender, which concluded with the words 'on the true faith of a Christian'. The oath now had little significance in practice; but, its form having been laid down by Parliament, another Act of Parliament was necessary to modify it.[1]

When Parliament assembled in December 1847 Rothschild presented himself at the Table of the House and intimated his inability to take the oaths by reason of his religious beliefs. He was directed to withdraw, and as soon as possible the Prime Minister moved that the House should resolve itself into a Committee on the removal of the civil and religious disabilities affecting Her Majesty's Jewish subjects.[2] The resolution was agreed to by 257 votes to 186. The consequent Jewish Disabilities Bill, introduced early in the following year, which placed the Jews on the same footing as the Roman Catholics, was unlike those of the series introduced between 1830 and 1836 in that it involved in fact little more than admission to Parliament. For this very reason it provoked a greater measure of opposition. The debates were remarkable in the annals of parliamentary eloquence. Russell based his argument on the theory that every

---

[1] No provision was made to meet the difficulty of the Oath of Abjuration in the successive Emancipation Bills, and had any of them been carried an abbreviated tussle over the oath would presumably have taken place. Contemporary critics did not fail to point out that, though the statutory obligation excluded a conscientious Jew, it meant nothing to an insincere Christian.

[2] The precedent of the Quaker Joseph Place, who was allowed to affirm, on being returned for the first Reformed Parliament in 1833, had no bearing on this case, as an Act of Parliament specifically allowed Quakers to make an affirmation in all cases where an oath was normally necessary.

Englishman is entitled to all the honours and advantages of the British Constitution. The opposition was led by Sir Robert Inglis, who insisted on the vital necessity of preserving the Christian character of every person holding any share in the government, and Lord Ashley, the later Lord Shaftesbury, who elaborated Dr. Arnold's view (which carried considerable weight in Liberal circles) that the Jews were voluntary strangers who could have no claim to citizenship unless they conformed to the law of the Gospel. Peel and Gladstone, former opponents of Jewish emancipation, demonstrated their political progress by speaking and voting in favour of the measure—the latter in opposition to what he knew to be the views of his new constituents at the university of Oxford. Benjamin Disraeli (who, for all his ostentatiously Jewish name, appearance, and sympathies, had become a leading figure in the House since Jewish emancipation was last debated) showed courage as well as eloquence in his support of the measure, and carried with him his associate, Lord George Bentinck, the head of the Protectionist fraction. Their followers, however, voted against them to a man: Bentinck withdrew from his leadership: and the episode had the ultimate result of making a man who was a Jew by birth parliamentary leader of the party of the landed gentry, without admitting to his seat one who was a Jew by faith. For, though the Commons carried the second reading by 277 votes to 204, the peers were so aroused by the clerical agitation, to the effect that the measure would dechristianize the legislature and imperil the country's religion, that they rejected the Bill in an exceptionally full House by 163 votes to 125.[1]

In the following session (1849) a modified measure, the Parliamentary Oaths Bill, was steered successfully through the Commons, but again rejected almost mechanically though with a narrower margin by the Lords. Rothschild thereupon applied for the Chiltern Hundreds and vacated his seat, but offered himself for re-election and was once again returned. But the City electors were not disposed to submit to virtual disenfranchisement without protest, and instructed their nominee to

[1] The Parliamentary Debates of 1847–8 on Jewish Emancipation are conveniently reprinted in Margoliouth, *The Jews in Great Britain*, ii. 257–95, iii. 1–75, and in C. Egan, *Status of the Jews in England* (London, 1848), pp. 50–149. See also W. F. Monypenny and G. E. Buckle, *Life of Disraeli* (London, 1929), i. 882 ff.

demand the rights which the action of the Lords withheld. On
26 July 1850, accordingly, he again presented himself at
Westminster and requested to be sworn on the Old Testament.
After an adjournment and three divisions the House decided
to allow the applicant to take the oaths in a form binding upon
his conscience, but when he came to the Oath of Abjuration he
refused to pronounce the final words 'on the true faith of a
Christian' as stipulated. A motion that his seat should be
declared vacant was then proposed and rejected; others were,
however, carried declaring first that he was not entitled to vote
or sit in the House until he took the oath in the form appointed
by law, and secondly, that the form of the Oath of Abjuration
should be taken into consideration in the next session, with a
view to the relief of persons professing Judaism. In accordance
with this, in 1851 the government introduced its Oath of Abjuration Bill, which passed the second reading by 202 to 177—a
margin narrow enough to encourage the Lords to persist in
their usual line of conduct and reject it (17 July 1851).

While the Bill was under consideration David Salomons had
been elected, at his fourth attempt, at a by-election for Green-
wich. The action of the Lords convinced him that the constitutional method hitherto followed could lead to no useful result,
and that a different policy was required to force the problem
on public attention. Accordingly, the day after the rejection
of the Bill, he attended at the Table of the House of Commons
and asked to be sworn. Instead of giving up the battle when he
arrived at the Oath of Abjuration, as Rothschild had done, he
recited it without the words to which he objected, and then
took his seat on one of the ministerial benches, ignoring an
order to withdraw. The Speaker appealed to the House for
support. In the ensuing proceedings Salomons not only recorded his vote three times, but even took part in the debate
to explain his position.

The motion was, of course, carried, and the trespasser was
removed from his place by the sergeant-at-arms. By recording
his vote without taking the prescribed oath he had rendered
himself liable to a statutory fine of £500 for each occasion,
besides various civil penalties. Since the government had
announced that it would not initiate proceedings, a common
informer applied for a writ. The case was tried before the

Court of the Exchequer, where judgement was given for the plaintiff by three voices out of four, the chief baron expressing his regret that as an expounder of the law he was forced to come to this conclusion. Salomons thereupon appealed to the Exchequer Chamber, which unanimously confirmed the decision as well as the sentiments of the lower court. An appeal to the House of Lords was in preparation when a general election took place, and (though the City of London was faithful to its previous choice) Salomons lost his seat, making further legal proceedings pointless.[1]

After this spirited interlude there was a return to the slower, and now almost mechanical, method that had previously been followed. In 1853 Lord John Russell, now Foreign Secretary in Lord Aberdeen's Coalition government, carried a new Jewish Disabilities Bill through the Commons; but notwithstanding the fact that in the Lords it was in charge of the Prime Minister himself, a former opponent, it was automatically rejected. The following year Russell changed his tactics, attempting to secure his object in his Parliamentary Oaths Bill, which substituted a new single oath for the three formerly requisite. The measure did not mention the Jews, but as the words 'on the true faith of a Christian' did not figure in the proposed formula, the barrier which kept them out of Parliament would incidentally have been removed. But the Bill also abolished the special Roman Catholic oath which had been laid down by the Catholic Emancipation Act, and the opposition which this drew from the Conservative benches resulted in the rejection of the Bill in the Commons by a narrow margin.

The attempt, in one form or the other, was by now all but annual, the monotony being relieved only by slight variations in the procedure. In 1856 a private member, Milner Gibson, the free-trade champion, tried to achieve the object by a Bill to abolish the Oath of Abjuration itself. It received the support of Palmerston's government and passed the Commons, but was rejected as a matter of course in the Lords. After the general election of the following year, when Baron de Rothschild was

---

[1] A. M. Hyamson, *David Salomons*, pp. 74–84; Wolf, *Essays*, pp. 331–4; Henriques, *Jews and English Law*, pp. 270–7. An Act passed by the short-lived Conservative government relieved Salomons of the civil disabilities to which his action had exposed him.

returned for the fourth time by the City of London, Palmerston
introduced a new Oaths Bill similar to that of 1855, except that
it did not affect the oath to be taken by Catholics. In the
Report stage clauses were inserted excluding Jews from those
dignities closed to Roman Catholics[1] and from the exercise of
ecclesiastical patronage attached to any government offices to
which they might be appointed. Thus amended, the Bill passed
by a rather more ample majority than usual. In the Lords the
second reading was automatically refused. Lord John Russell
(now out of office) immediately introduced a fresh Bill empowering members of Parliament to take an oath in the form
binding on their own conscience; but the government was
unable to grant facilities to forward the measure and it was
abandoned. Meanwhile, Rothschild had once more applied for
the Chiltern Hundreds, but was re-elected by his London constituents, who deliberately perpetuated a partial disenfranchisement which had lasted for ten years.

Thus encouraged, Russell renewed his efforts, and secured
the appointment of a select committee to consider whether a
statutory declaration could legally be substituted for the Parliamentary oath, under the terms of an act of 1835 which
permitted it for corporate bodies. When the question was decided in the negative he brought in a new Oaths Bill which
met some of the objections to previous drafts by adding 'on the
true faith of a Christian' to the stipulated form (thereby preserving its basic religious nature), but providing that a Jew
might omit the final words. By the time it reached the House
of Lords Palmerston's government had fallen, and the opposition was led by the new Conservative Lord Chancellor, Lord
Chelmsford, who as Sir Frederic Thesiger had for many years
taken a prominent part in the debates in the Commons. On
his motion the clause affecting the Jews, which was the essence
of the Bill, was omitted. In the Commons Russell moved that
the House should disagree with the Lords' amendments, and
a committee was appointed to draw up the reasons. In this, by
an adroit stroke of political strategy, Baron de Rothschild was
included; for no law prevented any person duly elected by a
constituency from exercising the rights of a Member of Parliament other than voting or sitting in the House during a debate.

[1] See below, p. 265, n. 2.

A conference of both Houses which followed was unable to
come to an agreement.

Both sides were by now weary of the contest. Even the Conservative Prime Minister, Lord Derby, an old opponent of
Jewish emancipation, realized the harm this intransigence was
doing to his party, and was ready to accept any solution which
might bring the struggle to an end without giving the appearance of complete surrender. When therefore the report of the conference came up before the Lords for consideration, Lord Lucan,
who had consistently voted against the successive measures,
suggested as a compromise that each House of Parliament
should be allowed to determine by resolution the form of oath
administered to a Jew. The proposal was received with obvious
relief, and a Bill to give it effect was introduced in the following
week.[1] Despite the understanding that had been reached, it was
stubbornly contested, the second reading being carried by only
143 votes against 97. In the committee stage two additional clauses
debarred Jews from holding those high offices of state from which
Roman Catholics had been excluded by the Catholic Emancipation Act,[2] and conferred on the Archbishop of Canterbury the
right of presentation to ecclesiastical benefices which normally
belonged to any office of state during its occupancy by a Jew.

Thus amended, the Bill (21 & 22 Victoria, cap. 29)—the
fourteenth of that wearisome series that had occupied the
attention of Parliament for more than a quarter of a century—
passed through both Houses: the Lords on the third reading
by 33 votes to 12 (eight peers, stubborn to the last, recording
their solemn protest) and the Commons by 129 votes to 55.[3]

---

[1] Another Bill on the lines of that of 1853, substituting a single oath for the
three hitherto obligatory and making provision for Jewish religious scruples, was
simultaneously introduced by Lord Lyndhurst (an old champion of Jewish emancipation notwithstanding his stern Tory principles—perhaps because his wife was
a daughter of Lewis Goldsmith): but Lord Lucan's was preferred as being more
in accordance with parliamentary procedure.

[2] Regent of the Kingdom, Lord Chancellor or Lord Keeper, Lord Lieutenant
of Ireland or his Deputy, and High Commissioner to the General Assembly of the
Church of Scotland, as well as 'the office of Guardians and Justices of the United
Kingdom'.

[3] The amended Oaths Bill which had occasioned the altercation between the two
Houses, and on which the Jewish Relief Bill was based, was passed at the same time.

In 1847, when Lionel de Rothschild was first elected for the City of London,
five Jewish candidates had presented themselves in various constituencies, but all
the others were at the bottom of the poll.

On Monday, 26 July 1858, Baron de Rothschild at last took his seat in the House. Two hundred years after Cromwell's death the work that he had begun reached its culmination, and an English Jew was for the first time recognized as an equal citizen of his native land.

# EPILOGUE

IT is usual to regard this scene in the House of Commons as the culminating-point in the emancipation of English Jewry. In fact, this was not quite the case. The piecemeal removal of their grievances, after the failure of the first experiments, made symmetry impossible, and some disabilities still remained which affected Jews by reason of their faith. Indeed, the very nature of the compromise of 1858 was personal rather than general. The member for the City of London was admitted to take the oath in a form acceptable to him by a special resolution of the House of Commons, passed in the teeth of determined opposition on the part of the die-hard minority, which provided no precedent for any future occasion. When, however, in February 1859 Baron Lionel's brother, Mayer de Rothschild, was returned for Hythe at a by-election, not only was he empowered to take the oath in the fashion acceptable to him, but in addition it was resolved that henceforth any Jew duly elected might swear in the form then prescribed. A Resolution of the House remained in force only until the Prorogation, and would therefore have to be reintroduced at every succeeding session. The Resolution was, however, converted into a Standing Order by an Act of 1860 (23 & 24 Victoria, cap. 49). It was this which in fact set the seal on parliamentary emancipation in England, making the admission of Jews to the House of Commons a matter of right instead of privilege. The matter was finally consolidated by the Parliamentary Oaths Act of 1866 (29 & 30 Victoria, cap. 19) which prescribed a new and simplified oath for both Houses, omitting the phrase which had held up Jewish emancipation for so many years.

Up to this time the admission of a Jew to the House of Lords would have been dependent similarly on a special resolution, though refusal would have been difficult without personal affront to the sovereign. This was now no longer the case. In 1885, on the recommendation of Gladstone, who sixteen years before had been unable to overcome her objection to conferring the same honour on Baron Lionel de Rothschild, Queen Victoria raised his son Nathaniel to the peerage, and he took his seat in the Upper House in the normal fashion without difficulty.[1]

Meanwhile the Promissory Oaths Act of 1871 (34 & 35 Victoria, cap. 48) repealed the section in the Relief Act of 1858 which excluded Jews from various offices of state, and did away with all the old forms of oaths and declarations laid down by former statutes. With the passage of this Bill into law Jews were placed at last on precisely the same footing as regards political rights as their Christian fellow subjects with one or two insignificant qualifications.[2] In the same year (1871) a Jewish member of Parliament, Sir George Jessel (more effective in politics than Baron Lionel de Rothschild, who after all the effort of entering the House of Commons is never recorded to have made a speech), was appointed Solicitor-General, being the first Jew to become a Minister of the Crown.[3]

By the time Lionel de Rothschild took his seat in Parliament the 20,000 to 30,000 Jews who had been in England at the beginning of the nineteenth century were increased in number to some 35,000. The economic basis of their existence had widened. It was no longer possible to specify any callings which were in the fullest sense characteristic of them, nor was there any basic economic differentiation between them and other sections of the urban middle classes. The improvement in communications and the change in the balance of population were indeed hastening the decline of some of the old provincial communities, founded in market towns in the reign of George III. Their place was taken by new ones in the growing industrial centres, such as Nottingham (1822), Leeds (1823), Glasgow (1823), and so on. A majority of the Anglo-Jewish community

---

[1] Lord Shaftesbury (though once an opponent of Jewish emancipation) had previously urged Disraeli to recommend the elevation of Sir Moses Montefiore to the peerage, but the other, being of Jewish extraction, had not been able to comply.

[2] The one statutory restriction that still obtains is that, in virtue of the terms of the Act of 1858, Jews cannot exercise ecclesiastical patronage attached to any public office they may happen to hold. It is not altogether certain that a Jew may be 'keeper of the King's conscience'—i.e. Lord Chancellor; see Halsbury, *The Laws of England*, vii. 56, disputed, however, by H. S. Q. Henriques, in *Trs. J.H.S.E.* viii. 55–62.

[3] Since 1871 professing Jews have served as Judge (first appointed 1873), Privy Councillor (1873), Colonial Governor (1900), Cabinet Minister (1909), Lord Chief Justice (1913), Secretary of State (1916), Ambassador (1918), and Viceroy of India (1920).

was by now native born—a fact that had not been without its bearing on the successful issue of the struggle for emancipation. There had of course been some immigration during the past generation, but owing to the progress of assimilation on the Continent it was of a very different type from that of the previous century, being largely composed of members of middle-class families (frequently commercial agents or technical experts) who needed only linguistic adjustment in order to acclimatize themselves in England. They had settled not only in the capital but also in the new manufacturing centres in the provinces, to the cultural as well as the economic life of which they brought in some cases a new impetus; and though some of them collaborated in the activities of the Synagogue, a goodly proportion drifted insensibly in this tolerant climate into the religion or irreligion of the environment.

In addition, there were a number of immigrants of humbler social status from the reservoir of traditional Jewish life in eastern Europe, for whom the process of acclimatization was less simple. These remained relatively few in number until the penultimate decade of the century. In 1881, however, there began in Russia (under the inspiration of German anti-Semitism of a more academic type) a savage outbreak of persecution, which was to remain unabated so long as the rule of the Czars continued. This led to a terror-stricken wave of emigration, on a scale (owing to the improvement in communications) unexampled hitherto in all Jewish history. Within a single generation something like 2,500,000 eastern European Jews sought new homes overseas. The overwhelming proportion settled in the United States. A perceptible eddy, however, reached Great Britain, as well as other portions of the Empire, superimposing on the native communities a completely different element, in masses so compact that they were able to maintain unimpaired their characteristic way of life, their institutions, even their dialect. Circumstances led them in the first instance to a great extent into the tailoring and allied industries, which for some time became almost as characteristic of them as peddling and dealing in old clothes had been of their co-religionists a century before. The tendency was not without its importance for the country as a whole: for the development of the industry and the consequent lowering of prices brought facilities within the reach of the working man which initiated something in the nature of a revolution in social life.

A majority of the new arrivals settled in London, whose Jewish population increased between 1883 and 1905 from 47,000 to 150,000; but Leeds, Manchester, and Glasgow also acquired communities which exceeded in number the entire Anglo-Jewry of a century before. Elsewhere in the country old synagogues were revitalized and new ones established, the area of settlement being increased beyond anything known in the past. The number of Jews in England, estimated in 1880 at 65,000, more than tripled by 1905. The Aliens Immigration Act of that year—a product of the agitation which had come to a head at the beginning of the century—stemmed the influx, which thereafter was on a much smaller scale. But, during the quarter-century over which it had continued, the face of Anglo-Jewry had been changed.[1]

The alembic of English tolerance has operated by now on the newer arrivals as well. Their sons have taken part in English life, contributed to English achievement, striven for England's betterment, shed their blood in England's wars. In this happy land they have attained a measure of freedom (and thereby of collaboration) which has been the case in scarcely any other. That this has been possible is due in no slight measure to the process of Anglo-Jewish history—a gradual acceptance based on common sense rather than on doctrine, consolidating itself slowly but surely, and never outstripping public opinion. Hence it has been possible for the English Jews to exemplify how men can enter a society by methods other than descent, and to absorb traditions which are not those of their physical ancestors. If their reaction to privilege has been to deserve it, it is because they have the good fortune to possess as their inheritance two noble histories.

---

[1] The recent history of the Anglo-Jewish community is described, for the close of the reign of Queen Victoria, by Wolf, *Essays*, pp. 355–62; and for the reign of George V by the present writer in *The Jewish Year Book* (London, 1937), pp. 356–75. Cf. also most recently V. D. Lipman, *Social History of the Jews in England, 1850–1950* (London, 1954) and the same author's *A Century of Social Service, 1859–1959* (London, 1959); L. P. Gartner, *The Jewish Immigrant in England, 1870–1914* (London, 1960); [C. Roth], *The Jewish Chronicle, 1841–1941* (London, 1949); the supplementary sections to James Picciotto's *Sketches of Anglo-Jewish History*, ed. I. Finestein (London, 1956), and the ample bibliography comprised in *Nova Bibliotheca Anglo-Judaica*, ed. R. P. Lehmann (London, 1961).

# ADDITIONAL NOTES

*(The figures in parentheses are to the pages of the text.)*

## CHAPTER I

(*a*) The passages of the Penitential of Archbishop Theodore of Canterbury (d. 690) which seem to indicate the existence of Jews in England in the seventh century (cf. Jacobs, *J.A.E.*, pp. 1–2) are absent from the authentic text of that code as edited by P. W. Finsterwalder, *Die Canones Theodori Cantuarensis* (Weimar, 1929). The two allusions in the 'Excerptiones' ascribed to Archbishop Egbert of York (d. 766) are completely academic, and would signify nothing even if (as is improbable) that compilation were of English origin. A spurious charter of Witglaff of Mercia to the monks of Croyland (833), one of the fictitious 'Laws of Edward the Confessor', probably belonging to the reign of Stephen, and an unsubstantiated allusion by a sixteenth-century Hebrew chronicler, Joseph haCohen, to the immigration into England in 810 of Jewish refugees from Germany, need not be given serious consideration. There remains only a clause in the Latin paraphrase of a Law of Æthelred of *c.* 1010 which condemns the selling of Christians into slavery outside England, lest they fall into pagan or Jewish hands; but even this insignificant allusion is absent in the Anglo-Saxon original (see F. Liebermann, *Die Gesetze der Angelsachsen*, i. 251, ii. 527–8). Jacobs (*J.A.E.*, pp. 5 ff.) calls attention to various biblical names in the Domesday Book, but there is not the slightest reason to imagine that those who bore them were Jews. It may be mentioned that St. Florinus, who worked in Switzerland and the Tyrol some time between the seventh and ninth centuries, is said to have been the son of a Jewess married to an Englishman ('Vita S. Florini' in *Analecta Bollandiana*, xvii. 199 ff.). (2)

(*b*) William of Malmesbury, *Gesta Regum Anglorum*, iv. 317, states incidentally that the Jews of London had been brought thither by William the Conqueror. Since this author died *c.* 1146, this represents a very old tradition. So, too, in a recently discovered petition of 1275, the Commonalty of the Jews of England speak of their establishment in England 'pus le conquest de la terre' (*Select Cases in Court of King's Bench, Edward I* (Selden Society, 1939), iii. cxiv). An often-repeated statement of Anthony Wood (*Annals*, i. 129) fixes the settlement of the Jews at Oxford about 1075, but this is based on nothing more solid than a misinterpretation of the spurious charter now printed in the *Oseney Charters*, iv. 5. Fuller (*Church History of Britain*, 1655) states that they arrived in Cambridge two years earlier, but this too can hardly be more than approximate, and in his *History of Cambridge University* he gives the date as 1106. (4)

(*c*) See H. W. C. Davis, 'London Lands of St. Paul's, 1066–1135', in *Essays Presented to T. F. Tout*. The date 1115, to which this record was previously ascribed, is now abandoned, and the preliminary reference to the

Ward of Haco is recognized to have nothing to do with the *vicus judaeorum*, which was clearly in the neighbourhood of the later 'Old Jewry'. It appears that the Jewry was mainly, but not exclusively, inhabited by Jews at this period: the parcel of land described in the Terrier was in Christian hands. For grants of land in London in 1152 by the canons of St. Paul's to Benedict the Jew and Abraham fil' Simon, see M. Adler, *Jews of Medieval England* (= *J.M.E*)., pp. 255 ff. (The medieval term *fil'* will be used in these chapters in preference to the longer 'the son of' or the exotic Hebrew 'ben'. Abraham was probably spoken of in his day as 'Abraham fitz Simon'.)                                                                                  (7)

## CHAPTER II

(a) Ephraim of Bonn's Hebrew account of the York Massacre, published in Neubauer and Stern's *Hebräische Berichte über die Judenverfolgungen während der Kreuzzüge* (Berlin, 1898), and incorporated in Joseph haCohen's sixteenth-century chronicle *Emek haBakha* ('*Valley of Tears*'), has not yet been published in an accurate translation in English. One is therefore subjoined:

Afterwards, in the year 4551 (l. 4550 = 1190) the Wanderers came upon the people of the Lord in the city of Evoric in England, on the Great Sabbath [before Passover]: and the season of the miracle was changed to disaster and punishment. All fled to the house of prayer. Here Rabbi Yom-Tob stood and slaughtered sixty souls, and others also slaughtered. Some there were who commanded that they should slaughter their only sons, whose foot could not tread upon the ground from their delicacy and tender breeding. Some, moreover, were burned for the Unity of their Creator. The number of those slain and burned was one hundred and fifty souls, men and women, all holy bodies. Their houses moreover they destroyed, and they despoiled their gold and silver and the splendid books which they had written in great number, precious as gold and as much fine gold, there being none like them for their beauty and splendour. These they brought to Cologne and to other places, where they sold them to the Jews.

This is virtually the only episode in medieval Anglo-Jewish history recorded in detail in the contemporary Hebrew sources, with the exception of the garbled account of the Expulsion (divided into two stages, with a thirty-year interval between them!) referred to below, note *e* to Chapter IV (pp. 275–6). While there are three elegies referring to the York massacre, there is no mention of subsequent events in any other of the very many similar compositions that are known. The later martyrologies speak in general terms of the 'martyrs of England', and somewhat more specifically although very succinctly of the London massacre of 1263 (above, pp. 61–62). It is desirable to mention this in order to emphasize the very slight prominence of English affairs in the eyes of continental Jewry, at least after the massacres of 1189–90, which clearly had a permanent effect.                                      (24)

## CHAPTER III

(a) The following table (mainly from Patent and Close Rolls, with amplifications from lists published by Elman in *Economic History Review*, 1933, pp. 153–4, and by Jenkinson in *Trs. J.H.S.E.* viii. 32 ff.) summarizes the exactions of the reign so far as they can be ascertained; but it is not easy to trace in the Rolls some of the levies mentioned by the chroniclers, or to distinguish in some cases between arrears and new levies. The total between 1230 and 1255 seems to be at least one-quarter of the 950,000 marks which the king is said to have wasted in this period. After the middle of the century (by which time the worst spoliations were over) an annual tallage of 5,000 marks was regarded as moderate, that amount being paid by the Jews of the realm in 1253 on condition that they should be exempt from any fresh levy until the following Easter.

| Year | Amount (in marks) | Year | Amount (in marks) |
|---|---|---|---|
| 1219 | ? | 1249 | 760 |
| 1221 | 1,000 | ,, | 10,000 |
| 1223 | 3,000 | 1250 | 500 |
| 1224–5 | 5,000 | ,, | 1,500 |
| 1225 | 1,000 | 1251 | 5,000 |
| ,, | 3,500 | ,, | 10,000 |
| 1226 | 4,000 | ,, | 1,000 |
| ,, | 1,000 | 1252 | 3,500 |
| 1229–30 | 6,000 | ,, | 10,000 |
| 1230 | 8,000 | 1253 | 5,000 |
| ,, | 1,000 | ,, | 100 |
| 1231 (arrears?) | 8,000 | 1254 | 10,000* |
| ,, | 6,000 | ,, | 5,000 |
| ,, | 10,000 | 1255 | 2,000 |
| 1233 | 10,000 | ,, | 500 |
| 1233–9 | 25,000 | 1255–7 | 8,500 |
| 1234 | £500 | 1259 | 5,000 |
| 1236 | 10,000 | ,, | 500 |
| 1237 | 3,000 | 1260 | 500 |
| 1241 | 20,000 | 1261 | 3,000 |
| 1244 | 60,000 | ,, | 1,000 |
| ,, | 4,000 | 1267 | 500 |
| 1245 (arrears) | 8,000 | 1269 | 1,500 |
| ,, | 4,000 | 1272 | 5,000 |
| ,, | 10,000 | | |

* ? 1,000: cf. *Trs. J.H.S.E.* viii. 33. (45)

(b) Since the case at Winchester in 1192 there had been numerous indications that, in this city especially, the atmosphere was unchanged, but in each case hitherto a judicial inquiry averted serious consequences. In 1225, for example, a child whom the 'King's Jew', Deulesault fil' Soleus, was accused of murdering was discovered to be alive (C.R. 1225, p. 53*b*). That same year two other Winchester Jews were found guilty of the murder of a boy, but as three others implicated in the charge were acquitted, it is probable that no ritual object was alleged: ibid., pp. 50, 51). Seven years later another charge ended similarly, the mother of the alleged victim being imprisoned in place of the persons accused (C.R. 1232, p. 80). In

1236 many leading members of the Oxford community, imprisoned on a charge of forcibly 'rescuing' a boy who had been converted to Christianity, were released when the lost infant was traced at Exeter (C.R. 1232, p. 383; Roth, *Oxford*, pp. 24–25). About this time two persons were sent from England to attend the assembly of converts convened at Fulda by the Emperor Frederick II, which resulted in the publication of an imperial rescript exonerating the Jews from the Blood Accusation (cf. Henry III's letter of February 1235 in Huillard-Bréholles, *Historia Diplomatica*, IV. ii. 809).

(55)

(*c*) C.R. 1250, p. 263; P.R. 1250, p. 59. The subsequent career of Abraham of Berkhamsted (for whom see Caro, *Sozial- und Wirtschaftsgeschichte der Juden*, ii. 17, 282; *E.J.* i. 58, 60, 61, &c.; C.R. and P.R. for these years, *passim*) was chequered. Before many months were over he offended the king again in some way and was released from prison only on condition of forfeiting his entire property, and keeping out of the royal sight for a twelve-month (C.R. 1250, pp. 339, 375). In the following year he got into trouble, with Gamaliel of Oxford, on a charge of clipping the coinage (C.R. 1251, p. 418). In 1255, however, he was sufficiently re-established to be granted to Richard of Cornwall, and empowered to lend money under favourable conditions (P.R. 1255, p. 396), an *archa* being opened at Wallingford to register his transactions. After Richard's death the grant was confirmed to his son, Edmund of Almain, for two and a half years (P.R. 1272, p. 654).

(56)

## CHAPTER IV

(*a*) Cf. the lists of assets of English Jewry printed in *Trs. J.H.S.E.* ii. 87–105 and the documents in *E.J.* ii. 293, 299, 303, &c. Bonami fil' Josce of York, who was granted a licence to trade in 1278, similarly dealt in wool (*Bibl.* A.10. 28) and Jacob fil' Hagin of London, in cloth. It is, however, possible that at this period credits in terms of commodities often conceal clandestine money-lending operations, as the prices are so often in round figures, the quality is seldom specified and there is frequently an option for cash payment (Elman, *Hist. Jud.*, 1939, p. 97). No Jews are in fact included among those to whom licences for exporting wool were granted by Edward I, and the documents concerning the Expulsion specify as the main charge against the Jews the fact that they lent money, notwithstanding the prohibition, 'under colour of trading and good contracts and covenants'.

(73)

(*b*) It was presumably in response to the Papal appeal that the clergy of the diocese of York were instructed at this time (21 April 1287) to preach against the Jews, who were henceforth forbidden to set foot within the walls of certain monasteries—e.g. Bridlington (*Register of John le Romeyn*, Surtees Society, i. 22, 201). It is possible that the brutal imprisonment and tallaging of the Jews in May 1287 was a further consequence of the Papal intervention. The Northampton episode referred to in the text presents certain problems. The local historians speak of the outrage as having been perpetrated on Good Friday 1277 or 1279 in the churchyard of St. Sepulchre, where a tablet incorporating a crucifix long commemorated the event. In punishment, fifty Jews are said to have been drawn at horses' tails outside the walls and hanged, others being subsequently sent to London for punishment. There is, however, in the records no trace of this or reference either to the punishment or the property of the victims. It seems, therefore, that all this is the result of (i) a confusion of the *Dies Sanctae crucis exaltatae* of the contemporary Chroniclers (14 September) with Good Friday, (ii) a muddled attempt to explain the confiscations and executions known to have taken place at this period, actually the outcome of the allegations of clipping the coinage, this necessitating a change of date to 1277, and (iii) an endeavour to find some reason for the carving of the Crucifixion on a wall overlooking the churchyard of St. Sepulchre. The contemporary chroniclers make it clear that the alleged victim did not at all events die at once. (78)

(c) Cf. the Winchester inscription published by Selden, *De Jure Naturali*, p. 215, and by Schwab, *Inscriptions hébraïques de la France*, p. 162. The translation runs: 'On Friday, eve of the Sabbath in which the pericope *Emor* [*Leviticus, caps: xxi–xxiv*] is read, all the Jews of the Land of the Isle were imprisoned. I, Asher, inscribed this.' Selden's reading, notwithstanding a slight error in spacing, does not require emendation: the date corresponds with 2 May 1287, the day indicated by the English chroniclers, e.g., J. de Oxenedes, p. 268, or Wykes in *Ann. Mon.* iv. 308–9. The writer is presumably Asher, or Sweteman, of Winchester, son of Licoricia of Oxford. In view of this evidence Richardson's scepticism regarding the arrests (*J.A.K.*, p. 227) seems unjustified. (79)

(d) For the original Norman French text see Rigg, *P.E.J.*, pp. liv ff. Contrary to the general view, it does not seem that this measure was ever put into effect: for in his communication of 5 November 1290 to the Barons of the Exchequer (ibid., p. xli) Edward specifically stated that he had been compelled to banish the Jews from England because they persisted in levying clandestine usury, in contravention of his measure of fifteen years before. Moreover, fictitious loans in terms of commodities seem to have been continued until the Expulsion, and this would have been unnecessary had money-lending been reauthorized. The document represents therefore the draft of a law which was never enacted. Since it refers to the fact that the chirograph-chests 'have long been closed and sealed by command of our Lord the King' it is between 28 January 1284, on which date a royal mandate for the general closing of the *archae* was issued, and 28 February 1286, when commissioners were appointed to reopen that of London (ibid., p. lxi)—i.e. at the close of the ten-year experimental period envisaged in the Statute of 1275. (81)

(e) The Jewish sources, almost unanimously, place the expulsion of the Jews from England in the year 5020: so Ibn Verga, *Shebet Jehudah*, § xvii, who brings it into relation with the false accusation of clipping the coinage: Don Isaac Abrabanel, quoting from a lost work of Profiat Duran in his *Yeshuoth Meshiho* (p. 46); and others who derive from them. It is to be imagined that Samuel Usque in his *Consolaçam ás Tribulaçoens de Israel* (Ferrara, 1553) iii, § xii, concurs in this date, though through a misprint

5002 is given as the year instead of 5020. The reason for this equivocation is not easy to understand, unless exaggerated rumours of the persecutions at the time of the Barons Wars reached the ears of the continental communities. It has been plausibly suggested, however, that ⊃ (= [50]20, i.e. 1260) was read for ⊐ (= [50]50, i.e. 1290). In order to bring this date into accordance with the known historical facts it was necessary for Usque, Verga, and perhaps Duran to introduce a recall, and a final expulsion, in the reign of tne successor of the original monarch.

The ancient Jewish chroniclers associate the Expulsion with the conversion to Judaism of a certain friar. It has been thought that this was due to a confusion with the famous case of the converted Deacon, who was burned at Oxford in 1222. However, the Jewish account is confirmed by the continuer of Florence of Worcester, who gives a circumstantial report of the conversion of the Dominican, Robert of Reading, in 1275. It is obviously to this episode that the Hebrew chroniclers refer: thus Usque (loc. cit.) states specifically that the central figure in the episode was a *frade pregador*: i.e. a *Dominican* friar. This did not immediately precede the Expulsion; but it may well have been responsible in part for the reaction of 1275.

On the whole, therefore, the account of the Jewish chroniclers is not so fantastic as it seems. Even Usque's tale of the existence of crypto-Jews in England is paralleled by the complaints of contemporaries regarding the insincerity of the converts from Judaism. Certain of the old synagogues were in fact standing in his day, as he asserts. The story of the pavilion over the sea, into which those who adhered to the Law of Moses were enticed to be drowned, seems, however, to be based on an apocryphal story told by a Spanish anti-Jewish polemist: see below, p. 282.                    (87)

## CHAPTER V

(a) 15,060 (Walter of Hemingburgh, ii. 22); 17,511 (J. de Oxenedes, p. 277); 16,511 (*Flores Historiarum*, iii. 70). The close identity of these figures is persuasive. Nevertheless. though this would represent only 1 per cent. of the total population, it would be something nearer 10 per cent. of the urban population, which is manifestly excessive. The annual poll-tax was paid in 1280 on behalf of 1,179 persons above the age of twelve years, of 1,153 in 1281, of 1,133 in 1282, and of 1,151 in 1283: it is not certain, however, whether anything is to be deducted for the expenses of collection, or whether the pauper proletariat, now comparatively numerous, was actually included. On the other hand there are said to have been 680 Jewish householders in England in 1278. The figure given by the contemporary chroniclers may have been based on a rough computation on the basis of the grant of £202. 0s. 4d. to the *Domus Conversorum* by which the poll-tax of threepence per head was ultimately replaced, without taking into account the fact that it was not levied on children. Caro (*Sozial- und Wirtschaftsgeschichte der Juden*, ii. 63–64) maintains that the total Jewish population during the last phase (i.e. after the wholesale banishments, conversions, and executions [over 300] of Edward's reign) cannot have exceeded 2,500 or 3,000.

The following is a tolerably comprehensive list of all Anglo-Jewish

settlements of the medieval period, places where communities or *archae*
existed being printed in capitals: cf., however, additional names on p. 282.

| | | |
|---|---|---|
| Abingdon | Dunwich | Newmarket |
| Andover | Eden | Newport |
| Arundel | Evesham | NORTHAMPTON |
| Aylesbury | EXETER | NORWICH |
| Banbury | Eye | NOTTINGHAM |
| Basingstoke | Faversham | Ospringe |
| Bath | Finchingfield | OXFORD |
| BEDFORD | Frenningsham | Pinkeneye |
| Berdefield | Fressinton | Pontefract |
| Berham | Gillingham | Reading |
| BERKHAMSTED | GLOUCESTER | Rising |
| Beverley | Grimsby | Rochester |
| Bosham | Guildford | Romsey |
| Bottisham | Hampton | Royston |
| Bradesworth | Hastings | Rye |
| Brentford | Hatcham | Sandwich |
| Bridgnorth | Haverford | Seaford |
| BRISTOL | HEREFORD | Shoreham |
| Buckingham | Hertford | Sittingbourne |
| Bungay | Hitchin | Southampton |
| BURY ST. EDMUNDS | Holm | Southwark |
| CALNE | Hungerford | STAMFORD |
| CAMBRIDGE | HUNTINGDON | SUDBURY |
| Camden | Ilchester | Tewkesbury |
| CANTERBURY | IPSWICH | Thetford |
| Chepstow | Kendal | Thornbridge |
| Chichester | Kingston | Tickhill |
| Chippenham | LEICESTER | Tonbridge |
| Clare | Lewes | WALLINGFORD |
| COLCHESTER | LINCOLN | WARWICK |
| Colton | LONDON | WILTON |
| COVENTRY | Ludlow | Wells |
| Cricklade | LYNN | WEOBLEY |
| Derby | Malling | WINCHESTER |
| DEVIZES | MARLBOROUGH | Windsor |
| Doncaster | Merton | WORCESTER |
| Dorchester | Newbury | Wycombe |
| Dorking | Newcastle | Yarmouth |
| Dunstable | Newland | YORK (91) |

(*b*) The variety of the pledges specified in contemporary records is be-
wildering. Cf. *E.J.* iii. 42, where a Jew is sued for the return of a psalter,
a book of medicine, and a saddle: or *Oseney Cartulary*, i. 335, where an
Oxford financier records in Hebrew a loan in 1182 in terms of fourteen cows
and twelve *pisa* of suet. The London Jewry received in pledge even furs,
cushions, and silks from the royal wardrobe (Lib.R. 1250, p. 271). Mendaunt

of Bristol, hanged in 1278, seems to have specialized in jewellery and armour, according to the inventory of his property, which included four coats of mail and ninety-six silver brooches, in addition to two silk cushions and a Rheims carpet (Adler, *J.M.E.*, pp. 224–5). According to the 'Assize of Jewry', however, jewels of high value could not be accepted as pledges or purchased without royal licence (P.R. 1267, p. 154).         (105)

(*c*) The Chronicle of Meaux (i. 173–8) reports a typical transaction of the twelfth century. A son of one of the great benefactors of this Cistercian Abbey was ward of the Earl of Aumale, whose daughter he seduced. It thus became necessary for him to leave the country. Finding his affairs greatly embarrassed on his return, he borrowed some 1,800 marks on mortgage from various Jews. The Abbot of Meaux reluctantly consented to assume responsibility for these debts on good security, and applied to Aaron of Lincoln, 'the first and greatest of the Jews', for assistance. The latter assumed the entire obligation, cancelled 500 marks of the debt, and bought out the other creditors. When he died not long after, the Crown, a less obliging creditor, claimed immediate payment of the balance and even of the amount that had been remitted.

Only a small number of capitalists could engage in operations on this scale. It is estimated (*Trs. J.H.S.E.* ii. 82) that at the time of the Expulsion, in 11 out of 17 Anglo-Jewish communities, two-thirds of Jewish wealth was concentrated in the hands of 82 persons belonging to 18 families. One family in Oxford owned more than half, and one in Norwich two-thirds, of the entire capital of the community.         (106)

(*d*) See the excursus on Adam de Stratton by W. Page in *Starrs*, vol. ii. For instances of William of Valence's activities, cf. C.R. 1259, p. 446; P.R. 1257, p. 543, and for those of Gilbert Clare, Rigg, *P.E.J.*, p. 48; the latter's father Richard had been so little trusted by the Jews that when he went on his crusade in 1249 he could only borrow money from them through the medium of the monks of Tewkesbury (*Ann. Mon.* i. 137, 139: 50 per cent. interest was charged—whether by the Jews or the Abbey is not clear). Not all non-Jews, however, worked through Jewish intermediaries. At Lichfield, in 1254, the justices in Eyre were instructed to investigate what property had been left by Christian usurers, while in 1275 an inquiry was made in Norfolk concerning Christians who were acting as Jews (*judaizantes*) in lending money to the indigent (P.R. 1275, p. 172). Aaron of York (Adler, *J.M.E.*, p. 153) was certainly not the only medieval English Jew who borrowed from Gentiles.         (109)

(*e*) H. Jenkinson, in *Trs. J.H.S.E.* viii. 19 and elsewhere, showed that the revenue from Jewish sources was handled (contrary to what had hitherto been believed) through the ordinary machinery of the Exchequer, and drew the conclusion that the Exchequer of the Jews was primarily a judicial body. There are, however, many records of receipts at the *Scaccarium Judaeorum*; and under Henry III (above, p. 50) the justices at its head were able to deflect to their own pockets a considerable proportion of a tallage levied on the communities of the realm. A. C. Cramer, 'The Jewish Exchequer: an enquiry into its fiscal functions', in *Am. Hist. Rev.* xlv. 327–32 (cf. *Speculum*,

xvi. 226–9), has arrived independently at this conclusion, and shows that the Jewish Exchequer was regularly concerned with the various processes of receipt and audit involved in the handling of revenue from Jewish sources. (111)

(*f*) Above, pp. 48, 101. Cf. P.R. 1272, p. 606, where there are listed eleven properties of Jacob of Oxford (some consisting of more than one dwelling-house) in that city, York, and two different London parishes. Of these only two were apparently acquired from Christians, and might have been forfeited pledges: the rest passed into his hands from Jewish property-owners. The extent of the real estate held by Jews in the thirteenth century is vividly illustrated by the Norwich deeds published by Davis in his *Shetaroth* (and commented in the *East Anglian*, N.S., vols. iv and v) and by the long lists of escheated property in *Rot. Orig. in Scaccario*, pp. 73–76. Five centuries later, at the time of the 'Jew Bill' of 1753 (see pp. 214–23), a considerable body of material bearing upon this was brought together by 'A Gentleman of Lincoln's Inn' (P. C. Webb): '*The Question whether a Jew, born within the British Dominions, was, before the making of the late Act of Parliament, a Person Capable, by Law, to purchase and hold Lands*' (London, 1753). (114)

(*g*) For example, the 'School' of Peitevin the Great at Lincoln (*Trs. J.H.S.E.* ii. 99, 134: Jacobs is in error in interpreting the term literally); that of Mocke at Hereford (*Cal. Inq. Misc.* i. 62); of Abraham Pinch at Winchester (C.R. 1236, p. 271); of Elias at Warwick (*E.J.* i. 104). The principal London synagogue at one time belonged to Abraham fil' Rabbi (Richardson, *J.A.K.*, pp. 237–41) and was afterwards constructed on a parcel of land granted by Aaron fil' Vives (Charter Rolls, ii. 253); and when the community was reduced to a single place of worship it was in the house of the Arch-presbyter Cok Hagin (above, p. 77). The Cambridge synagogue was maintained by 'Magister' Benjamin. Hence, after it was made over to the Franciscans, the latter found themselves sharing a common entrance with the town jail, to which use Benjamin's private house had been turned, until they were permitted to incorporate this too in their friary (A. G. Little, *Studies in English Franciscan History*, p. 12). (117)

(*h*) G. Cambrensis, *Itin. Camb.* II, c. xiii. The passage is sufficiently illuminating to deserve quotation in full:

We set forth thence towards Wenloch through a narrow and steep way which they call *Malam plateam*. Here it happened in our days that a certain Jew was journeying towards Shrewsbury with the archdeacon of the same place, whose name was Peche, and the deacon whose name was Dayville. When he heard the archdeacon by chance saying that his deaconry began at this place, which is called *Malam plateam* and lasted till Bad-pass in Chester, considering and reflecting upon the name of the archdeacon and the name of the dean, he made rather a witty and neat remark. 'It will be a wonder', said he, 'if chance brings me back safe from this country whose archdeacon is sin, whose deacon is the Devil, which you enter by a Bad-Place and leave in a Bad-Pass.' (119)

(*i*) Adler, *J.M.E.*, pp. 34–36, 193–5, 209–10, 213, 223, cites some instances. Cf. also C.R. 1225, pp. 7*b*, 50*b*. Particularly graphic details are given of a case at Gloucester. One day in 1220 a group of persons approaching

the castle gate saw something fall from the top of the tower. The porter
went to investigate and found Solomon Turbe, a prisoner, terribly maimed.
He had enough strength left to affirm that he was tired of life and wished
to kill himself like King Saul. However, he was overhead to say to his wife,
Comtissa: 'Flee hence, for it is by thy plot that I am slain.' It was rumoured
afterwards that he had not fallen, but had been pushed, and Abraham
Gabbay was accused by her of having conspired with Andrew, a beer-server,
to bring about his death, in revenge for a former brawl in which he himself
had been wounded. For an unruly episode in London in 1278, graphic
details of which are given, see H. T. Riley, *Memorials of London* (London,
1868), pp. 15–16.                                                       (121)

(*j*) Cf. the account in Giraldus Cambrensis, *Opera*, viii. 65. 'Master
Robert, the Prior of St. Frideswide at Oxford . . . was a man of letters and
skilled in the Scriptures, nor was he ignorant of the Hebrew tongue. Now he
sent to diverse towns and cities of England in which Jews have dwelling, from
whom he collected many Josephuses written in Hebrew, gaining them with
difficulty, since they were acquainted with him because of his knowing the
Hebrew tongue. And in two of them he found this testimony about Christ
written fully and at length, but as if recently scratched out; but in all the
rest removed earlier, and as if never there. . . .' Robert Eisler, in his work
*The Messiah Jesus*, and Marmorstein, in *Trs. J.H.S.E.* xii. 106–7, attempt
to identify the passage in question and draw conclusions which, if substantiated, would be of great importance.                                   (125)

(*k*) The identity of the two (the names mean precisely the same) was
championed with characteristic vigour by Jacobs (*J.A.E.*, pp. 165–73,
196–9, 278–80), but strenuously contested by A. Neubauer. However, in
the addendum to his *Notes on the Jews in Oxford*, the latter admitted that
Berechiah visited England, and this would seem to vindicate Jacobs's conjecture in this case at least. The fact that Berechiah is cited by the English
scholar Moses ben Isaac (for whom see p. 127), that his Fox Fables follow
the lines of those of his contemporary Alfred Anglicus, and that he translated a work by Abelard of Bath, all go to support the theory. Alternative
explanations of 'Pointur' are (i) Point-maker—i.e. Tailor or Lace-maker;
(ii) Painter; (iii) Tax-collector—perhaps the most reasonable. Adler,
*J.M.E.*, p. 199, cites an unidentified Vives le Pointur of Bristol. The
problem is further discussed in my *Intellectual Activities* and *Oxford*. (126)

(*l*) Particularly Jacobs, in his *Jews of Angevin England*, and the articles
listed in *Bibl.* A.4. 43–50 and A.11. 59–61; later, he was able to secure
ostensible endorsement of his views in the *Jewish Encyclopaedia*, of which he
was an editor. Neubauer's case for the English origin of certain translations
of Abraham ibn Ezra's works (*Bibl.* A.11. 90 and *Romania*, 1876, pp. 129 ff.)
falls short of that rigidly scientific standard which he demanded from others:
cf. R. Levy, *The Astrological Works of Abraham ibn Ezra* (1927), p. 23.

There remain a few Anglo-Jewish scholars mentioned in the secular
records of whom no literary relics survive—e.g. Magister Josce fil' Magister
Hel' (*E.J.* i. 19), perhaps identical with Rabbi Joseph ben Elijah of Melun
(Gross, *Gallia Judaica*, p. 353); and Magister Samuel of Bolum (*l.* Lohun),

whose marriage was discussed before a rabbinical court in 1267 (*E.J.* i.
152). For the subject generally see now my *Intellectual Activities*.        (128)


New publications and research make it possible to correct and supplement
further the account of medieval English Jewry given above, apart from the
details incorporated in the text. It has been suggested (B. Blumenkranz,
*Altercatio Acclesiae contra Synagogam*, Paris, 1954) that this anti-Jewish polemic
possibly composed in England in the tenth century reflects the existence of
a Jewish community there at the time: most scholars, however, consider it
to be no more than an academic exercise, as is the case according to R. J. Z.
Werblowsky (*Journal of Jewish Studies*, xi. 69–77) even with the famous disputation of Gilbert Crispin (above, pp. 5–6). New details constantly accu-
mulate regarding the financial activities of the Jews in Angevin England.
It was, for example, from a London Jew that a loan was raised to cover
the expense of Thomas Becket's flight to France in 1164 (*Festschrift G.
Kisch*, 1955, p. 227). On the other hand, Richardson (*J.A.K.*, pp. 47–48)
has shown how in the twelfth century opulent London citizens borrowed
heavily from Aaron of Lincoln in order to develop real estate in the city:
the clients of the Jews were not by any means only the needy. Indeed, the
royal borrowings from Christians were on a larger scale than those from
the Jews, the amounts raised from whom did not represent in fact as Jacobs
believed a substantial proportion of the royal income. For the most part,
this was short-time anticipating of revenue, almost like modern Treasury
bills. This borrowing ceased after about 1180, when the king found that it
was easier and more lucrative to tax than to borrow.

F. M. Powicke (*Henry III and the Lord Edward*, Oxford, 1947) showed how
the reorganization of the administration of the Jewish Exchequer by Peter
des Rivaulx was part of a general scheme of administrative centraliza-
tion. He gives, moreover (pp. 310–13), a survey of the levies made on the
Jews during the reign: their careful planning is illustrated by the procedure
in 1240–1, when a census of the Jews and their debts by the royal clerks was
followed by the Worcester 'Parliament', the imposition of a fresh tallage,
the appointment of assessors, and stern measures against defaulters. For
some of the activities of Adam de Stratton, 'an early expert in financial
graft' (pp. 108–9), see N. Denholm-Young, *Seigneural Administration in England* (Oxford, 1937), and now also M. W. Farr, *Accounts . . . of the Wiltshire
Lands of Adam de Stratton* (Wiltshire Archaeological Society, 1959). He was
ultimately disgraced and suffered forfeiture (1289) when it was found that
he possessed £12,500 in cash—far more than any medieval English Jew is
known to have owned. But H. G. Richardson (*J.A.K.*, pp. 71–73) suggests
that his case was neither exceptional nor exceptionally bad: many others
worked along similar lines, including respected figures such as the royal
Chancellor, Walter de Merton (Roth, *Oxoniensia*, xxii. 63–67), who also
systematically exploited the favourable conditions resulting from the financial
stress after the Barons' Wars. For Richard of Cornwall's dealings with the
Jews see the biography by N. Denholm-Young (Oxford, 1947). Edward I's
prohibition of residence in places where there was no authorized Jewry

(p. 72) probably reflected the decision of the Council of Bourges in 1276 forbidding Jews to live in the countryside, lest they should exercise an undue religious influence on the peasantry. On some occasion apparently early in the reign of Edward I the Jews were either imprisoned, tried, or else sought refuge in the London Guildhall: cf. the repeated references to the time when the Jews were here in *A Letter Book . . . of the City of London*, ed. R. R. Sharpe, 26, 27, 225, and Price, *Historical Account of the Guildhall*, pp. 21, 79, 273. The earliest reference is in the spring of 1278, so that there is possibly some connexion with the coin-clipping charge in that year, though certainly not as formerly conjectured with the general arrest of 1287. The story of the tragedy enacted above the water at the time of the Expulsion (p. 86) is apparently an invention of the fifteenth-century Spanish Franciscan Alfonso de Spina, first figuring in his anti-semitic work *Fortalitium Fidei* (III. ix), from which it was taken over by the Jewish chroniclers: yet even so it might have some factual basis. The question of Jewish influence on English legal procedure has been dealt with more recently by J. J. Rabinowitz, perhaps overemphatically, in a series of studies, now collected in his *Jewish Law: its influence on the development of legal institutions* (New York, 1956).

Although the Jews were excluded from some towns by charter there is no evidence that they ever had a Jewish settlement: for example, Caernarvon, Conisford, Conway, Criccieth, and Flint in Wales (see p. 92). On the other hand, isolated Jews were to be found in a number of additional places—Bread Street (Glos.), Bridgwater, Burford, Chesterton, Graham, Hendon, Honiton, Rayleigh, Shaftesbury, Wolverhampton, &c.—bringing the total number of ascertainable medieval Anglo-Jewish settlements to approximately 200. It is out of the question, of course, that these isolated individuals can have spent their time lending money: they must certainly have had supplementary occupations, whether commercial, industrial, or even agricultural.

## CHAPTER VI

(a) *Annales Paulini* (Chronicles of Edward I and Edward II, vol. i), p. 269; also (from former Hargrave MS.) in preface to Johan. de Oxenedes, ed. Ellis, p. xiii, with the addition *unus eorum fuit medicus*. The view that this Master Elias is identical with the former Arch-presbyter Elias le Eveske is fantastic, in view of the fact that the latter was appointed in 1243, and had been converted to Christianity in 1257; nor can he be equated with the physician-scholar Elijah Menahem of London who was dead by the autumn of 1284. E. N. Adler, in his *History of the Jews in London*, p. 70, identifies him with the contemporary French financier Heliot of Vesoul, who had been forced to leave France with his co-religionists in 1306, though he was neither physician nor Rabbi. (132)

(b) For Master Dionysius see Sousa Viterbo, *Noticia sobre alguns medicos portugueses* (Lisbon, 1893), pp. 15 ff.: his identity with the physician of the same name who practised in England is clear from a comparison of the data. He left London for Antwerp before the break-up of the Marrano settlement and (according to Wolf: this does not tally with Sousa Viterbo's information) died in Ferrara in 1541. [See now also H. Friedenwald in *Bulletin of the*

*History of Medicine*, vii (1939), pp. 249–56.] His son, Manuel Brudo, is a more important figure in the history of medicine. His *Liber de ractione victus in singulis febribus* . . . *Ad anglos* (Venice, 1544), contains (pp. 8, 81, 92, 94, 97–100, 128, 148, 152) repeated references to his career and clientele in England, the latter including Sir Thomas Audley, Lord Chancellor, and Sir William Sidney, Lord Chamberlain; the importance of these allusions for the social history of the period is considerable. He subsequently settled in the Levant and wrote a Hebrew polemical tractate, now lost (*Tarbiz* vi. 162; *Trs. J.H.S.E.* xix. 5–6).                                    (137)

(c) Wolf's account of Nuñez's career, in *Trs. J.H.S.E.*, vol. xi, is to be supplemented from J. R. Dasent, *Acts of Privy Council*, viii (1571–5) and ix (1575–7), *passim*. The references are perhaps equalled in number in the case of no other London merchant of the period. His importance to the government was so great that the Privy Council intervened with his creditors when he found himself in difficulties (viii. 128), while in 1573 he was specially exempted from the reprisals against Spain (viii. 92). He had dealings with the Earl of Desmond in Ireland (viii. 20). In 1576 he was made a member of a special commission for the trial of insurance cases, in conjunction with Gresham, the Master of the Rolls, and a Spaniard named Spinola (ix. 168, 230). H. de Castries, *Sources inédites de l'histoire de Maroc: Angleterre*, i. 322–5, published his remarkable letter written from his house in Mark Lane to Burleigh on 25th September 1578 giving a detailed report of the Portuguese disaster in the previous month at the Battle of the Three Kings. At this time Henrique Rodriguez, also probably a Marrano, petitioned for a monopoly of brokerage insurances, promising to pay the Crown one-half of the penalties imposed on interlopers: *Select Pleas of Admiralty*, Selden Society, ii. xvi.)

'Corsina the Jew' referred to in a letter to Cecil of 1592 in *H.M.C., Cecil*, iv. 244, is clearly identical with Philip Corsini (*Acts of Privy Council*, 1591, pp. 125 ff.), his Judaism being a purely malicious attribute.          (140)

(d) This legend is recorded in De Barrios, *Casa de Jacob* (Amsterdam, c. 1683), pp. 5–6, and Uri Levi, *Memoria para os siglos futuros* (ibid., 1711). S. Seeligman, in his *Bibliographie en Historie* (Amsterdam, 1927), discredits the story entirely, but it probably embodies a certain element of truth.

Another Marrano notable in England at this period was a reputed descendant of Gonsalvo de Cordova named Alonso Nuñes de Herrera, who was captured by the Earl of Essex in 1596 at Cadiz (where he was acting as Moroccan resident). After being ransomed he retired to Amsterdam: here he spent his last years, under the name of Abraham Cohen de Herrera, in Cabbalistic study. But Barrios's account is reconcilable only with some difficulty with the official correspondence in *H.M.C., Hatfield*, vi. 536 and in Castries, op. cit. ii. 107–8, 99–100.                               (142)

(e) The full details of the expulsion of the Marranos from England in 1609 have never been published. On 20 August 1609 Marcantonio Correr, Venetian ambassador in London, wrote home to his government (R. Archivio di Stato di Venezia, Dispacci Ambasciatori, Inghilterra, busta viii: cf. the abstract in S.P.V. 1609, p. 320):

Sono stati scoperti molti mercanti Portoghesi, che vivevano in questa citta secretamente all' Hebraica, et però alcuni sono di già partiti, et gli altri hanno havuto qualcne commodo per riserar li loro negotii, non ostante le leggi molto severe in questo proposito. Mi viene affermato esser questi cosi scellerati che per meglio coprirsi non solo intervenivano molte volte alla messa nella Casa d'Amb.ri, ma che habbino anco ricevuta la santissima Eucaristia.

The parallel dispatch from the Tuscan envoy, Ottaviano Lotto, fo 12 August 1609 (Archivio di Stato di Firenze; Mediceo, Principato) adds further details:

Qui son molti portoghesi che negoziano, et essendo ultimamente venuti in discordia fra loro, una parte n'è stata accusata d'ebraismo, et è stata però comandata di sgombrare il Regno, et con molta agevolezza perche la legge di essa gli fa rei di morte.

In the *Nicholas Papers*, iii. 51, reference is made to the fact that King James granted a patent to the Earl of Suffolk (Lord Chamberlain 1603-14) for the discovery of the Jews 'which made the ablest of them fly out of England'. The allusion is plainly to the same event. [Cf. *Trs. J.H.S.E.* xix. 9-10.]

(144)

(*f*) Another means by which the Jew was familiarized to Englishmen at this period was through inquisitive, bible-loving travellers who did everything possible to become acquainted abroad with those whom they had such slight opportunity of observing at home. One Elizabethan traveller after another—Peter Wendy, Laurence Aldersey, William Lithgow, William Davies, Richard Torkington (and, later on, George Sandys, Philip Skippon, John Evelyn, Richard Lassels, &c.) gave their compatriots intimate glimpses of the Italian Ghettos or the teeming Jewries of the Levant. John Gordon, later dean of Salisbury, held a public disputation with the Rabbi of Avignon in 1574; Immanuel Aboab, a famous Marrano scholar and controversialist, entered into a theological discussion with an argumentative Englishman at Pisa in 1597; Francis Smith painted fair Jewesses from the life at Istanbul; and Thomas Coryat above all lost no opportunity of making Jewish contacts. At Venice, in 1608, the latter came across Rabbi Leone da Modena, upon whom he forced a discussion regarding the fundamental tenets of Christianity; and being hustled out of the Ghetto was rescued by the English ambassador, Sir Henry Wotton, who happened to be passing in his gondola. Subsequently Modena made the latter's acquaintance and compiled at his request, for presentation to James I, his famous treatise on the Rites and Ceremonies of the Jews. Modena's English correspondents ultimately included Sir William Boswell and John Selden (*Bibl.* A.11. 95: *Nov. Bibl.* A.11. 33).

Similarly, English sailors, merchants, and adventurers frequently came into contact with Jewish dragomen: thus the first English expedition to the East Indies in 1601 was accompanied by a Moroccan Jew, who knew Arabic and negotiated a satisfactory treaty with the Sultan of Achin (*Bibl.* A.5. 1-2). On the Dalmatian coast the local Jews were in close relations with English traders from the sixteenth century (Jorjo Tadic, *Jevrei u Dubrovniku*, Ragusa, 1938, pp. 149, 182-4 ff.), while those of Venice and Salonika dealt in English cloth. The merchants of London even exported Hebrew Bibles for the use of the Jews of Morocco, notwithstanding Portuguese protests (c. 1574: *Cambridge History of British Empire*, i. 42). In 1616 Jews were importing English cloth into Bohemia from Poland (? Danzig: Bondi, *Juden in Böhmen*, Prague 1906, § 1090). (148)

## CHAPTER VII

(a) In 1624 James Whitchall, of Christ Church, Oxford, was prosecuted for teaching 'Judaism' (S.P.D. 1624, p. 435). Eleven years later (ibid., 1635, pp. 111, 122, 132), Mary Chester, a prisoner at Bridewell, was ordered by the Court of High Commission to be set at liberty under bond upon acknowledgement of her errors in holding certain Judaical tenets, such as teaching the Sabbath and distinction of meats. Major Thomas Harrison, the regicide, publicly advocated government by a council of seventy members, in imitation of the Sanhedrin (E. Ludlow, *Memoirs*, London, 1751, p. 176). More than one Baptist minister (e.g. Sellers, Jessey, Tillan) observed the seventh-day Sabbath, and John Smyth led his secession from the main body partly through his conviction that the Hebrew text of the Old Testament should be used in worship. (149)

(b) The Jewish associations of the Traskites have been dealt with in *Trs. J.H.S.E.* xv. 53–62 by H. E. I. Phillips, who identifies the English proselyte to Judaism recorded in D. Henriques de Castro, *Keur van Grafsteenen . . . te Ouderkerk* (Leyden, 1883) with the Thraskite Hamlet Jackson (another of the body, Christopher Sands, became a demi-convert). Evelyn (*Diary* for 1641) mentions a proselyte Englishwoman whom he met at Amsterdam, and Sandys (*Purchas*, viii. 95) one at Zante: while a *Guer* from England was assisted by the Hamburg synagogue in 1653 (*Jahrbuch d. jüd.-lit. Gesellschaft*, Frankfort-on-Main, x. 248). Most significant of all was the case of Alexander Cooper, the very distinguished English miniaturist of the seventeenth century, who settled at Stockholm, and whose profession of Judaism there is clear from the documents published in G. C. Williamson, *History of Portrait Miniatures* (1904), vol. i, chapter 7. (Dr. Williamson, in a private communication, agreed with my interpretation, as it is out of the question that Cooper was born a Jew and there is no evidence that other members of the family shared his beliefs.) (149)

(c) Notwithstanding these negative results the readmission of the Jews to England was spoken of abroad at this time as an accomplished fact. Royalist publicists openly stated that the real aim of the Republicans was 'to plunder and disarme the City of London . . . and so sell it in bulk to the Jews, whom they have lately admitted to set up their banks and magazines of Trade amongst us contrary to an Act of Parliament for their Banishment'. It was alleged that the Jews had made an offer for St. Paul's Cathedral, which they desired to convert into a synagogue. A Marrano at Rouen, asked what he thought of the recent developments, diplomatically replied that he believed that 'none of his Religion would ever adventure themselves among such bloody traitors as had murdered their own King', but saw no reason to doubt the reports that were current.

The purchase by Parliament in 1647–8 of a collection of Hebrew book;
for the Library of the University of Cambridge (*Trs. J.H.S.E.* viii. 63–77)
illustrates the trend of public opinion at the time.                          (154)

(*d*) It is probable that Menasseh was influenced by Nicholas's *Apology for
the Noble Nation of the Jews*, which he, perhaps, translated into Spanish
('London', 1649), and the sentiments of which he sometimes echoes in his
book. The reception of this in Puritan circles is illustrated from the Rev.
Ralph Josselin's *Diary* (ed. E. Hockliffe, Camden Society, 1908), p. 95
(20 December 1650): 'Released from going to Halsted, saw Manasseh ben
Israel, on the hope of Israel. Lord, my heart questions not the calling home
the nation of the Jewes: thou wilt hasten it in its season, oh my God; oh,
thou God of the ends of the whole earth, hasten it, Amen.' From the entry
(p. 113) of 16 December 1654 (?5) it seems that the diarist's interest was
essentially conversionist: 'Great rumo^rs of the Jewes being admitted into
England; hopes thereby to convert them; the Lord hasten their conversion
and keep us from turning.'                                                     (155)

## CHAPTER VIII

(*a*) Sasportas, *Zizath Nobel Zevi* (Jerusalem, 1954), pp. 71 ff.; S.P.D.
1655–6, pp. 50 (letter from H. O.—presumably Henry Oldenburg), 232;
A. Wolf, *Correspondence of Spinoza*, p. 217; Pepys, *Diary*, 19 February 1666.
The invitation to New Christians to join the community is based on oral
information from the late Lucien Wolf, who derived it from an unpublished
Inquisitional denunciation. The curious aftermath, when devotees throughout the world persisted in belief in a False Messiah who had not only
failed, but also apostatized, had its echoes in London, where various pole-
mics on the subject were published (*Bibl.* B.5. 5*a*, 6, 7). Solomon Ayllon,
Rabbi to the community from 1689 to 1700, was heavily tinged with the
Sabbataean heresy, this causing serious dissension in the community and
hastening his resignation. (M. Gaster, *History of the Ancient Synagogue of the
Spanish and Portuguese Jews*, London, 1901, pp. 22 ff.; *B.M. Records*, i. 27–28).
                                                                               (176)

(*b*) *The Case of the Jews Stated*: Wolf, *Essays*, pp. 112–13. The account-
books of Alderman Backwell, the outstanding London goldsmith, with
whom the majority of the well-to-do members of the community banked,
vividly illustrate the extent of their commercial operations, the turnovers of
some amounting to tens of thousands of pounds each half-year. Fernando
Mendes da Costa had in 1664 four separate accounts, which give details of
many large-scale transactions and numerous items relating to bills of exchange and the import of bullion. Other important names are those of
Alfonso Mendes, João da Costa, Henrique Alvarez, and Alfonso Rodrigues
—probably the most affluent of all. The financial transactions of the London
Jews at this period were, however, completely eclipsed by those of the
English goldsmith-bankers. (R. D. Richards, *Early History of Banking in
England*, pp. 27–28.) In the evolution of English banking as such, indeed,
the Jews played no part.                                                       (193)

(c) Treasury Books, 1690, *passim*. It seems that this was in the nature of a forced loan: cf. C. Dodsworth's *Proceedings against the exportation of Silver by the Jews* (*Bibl.* B.1. 35): 'The Earl of Monmouth . . . told the said Mr. Levy . . . that their Majesties wanted Mony, and that he believed the Jews to be a wealthy people, and could lend them a considerable sum . . . and that if ever they expected Favour from the present Government, then was the time to deserve it. . . .' In reply, Levy (who apparently acted as official agent or 'solicitor' for his co-religionists in public affairs: *Bibl.* B.6. 39) stated that there were only seventeen or eighteen Jews of considerable estate in the country. In the same year six Jews contributed upwards of £3,000 to the loan on the 2s. aid (Treasury Books, ibid.). (193)

(d) The Barbados community had been established by refugees from Brazil *c.* 1650, this being the first English possession in which Jews were formally authorized to settle (Council Minutes of Barbados [Typescript in P.R.O., London], i. 46; *Bibl.* A.9. 115–18, 129). Jews are reported to have collaborated in the conquest of Jamaica, and had formed an open community there before 1671 (ibid., A.9. 120, &c.); there were small settlements in Nevis and Tobago also by the end of the seventeenth century. Surinam received Jewish settlers from Cayenne *c.* 1664. When it was attacked by the Dutch in 1668 the Jews rallied to the defence, and several lost their lives in the course of the operations (*H.M.C., Portland*, iii. 308); subsequently, when the colony was surrendered, the English authorities specifically reserved the right of removing with them to Jamaica those who desired (*Pub. A.J.H.S.* vi. 9–23). In New Amsterdam [New York] the settlement formed in 1654 was undisturbed after the English occupation, by which time a community had also been established at Newport, Rhode Island; and there were traces in other parts of the American plantations. Jews came under British rule in 1662, but were cruelly expelled by Colonel Kirke: cf. G.P., *The Present State of Tangiers* (London, 1676), pp. 42–51; Pepys, *Second Diary*, 23 October 1683; *Trs. J.H.S.E.* iv. 198–201; *Journal of J. Luke 1670–3*, ed. Kaufman (1958), *passim*. (194)

(e) This profession received its greatest development during the War of Spanish Succession, at the beginning of which Harley was accused of ruining the English in order to enrich Jews and other foreigners (*H.M.C., Portland*, viii. 96). During Peterborough's campaigns in the Peninsula the commissariat was in the hands of Joseph Cortissos, formerly of Amsterdam, claims by whom on the Treasury to the amount of £90,000 were argued interminably before the courts (MSS. in the Jewish Museum, London). John da Costa was one of the three London financiers who provided bills for £300,000 in a single transaction in 1710 to provide for the needs of the army in Flanders (Luttrell, *Brief Relation*, vi. 622). But the most important figure by far was Solomon de Medina, the military purveyor, whom William III visited and who was principal contractor to the forces under Marlborough. Like Rothschild a century later, he established a system of expresses, so that his agents were often in the possession of important news before it reached the Ministers of the Crown. He had been knighted in 1700 by William III, being the first professing English Jew to receive that distinction. He was,

however, implicated in the outcry against Marlborough, to whom he paid
by way of commission £5,000 annually, ostensibly for Secret Service purposes. Summoned to England for examination before the special commission
in 1711, he alleged that he had given the Captain-General in the last four
years nearly 350,000 guilders for his own use on the bread and various other
army contracts, besides providing him with twelve or fourteen wagons.
This evidence was partly responsible for Marlborough's disgrace, and occasioned the epigram:

> A Jew and a G-n-l both join'd a Trade,
> The Jew was a Baker, the G-n-l sold Bread.

Cf. *The Examiner*, 14 April 1712; *Bibl.* A.7. 85, B.3. 4; Luttrell, *Brief
Relation*, vi. 718; W. S. Churchill, *Marlborough*, iv (1938), pp. 483, 525–6;
S.P.D. 1696, p. 320. Later on, during the continental wars under George II,
Abraham Prado, of Twickenham, took a considerable part in the commissariat organization (cf. Roth, *Anglo-Jewish Letters*, pp. 136–40): the diary
and letter-book of one of his subordinates, David Mendes da Costa, is in
the British Museum, MS. Eg. 2227.                                    (194)


## CHAPTER IX

(*a*) This system was extended owing to the common use in Germany,
&c., of an animal 'agnomen', based upon the similes used in the Blessings
of Jacob and of Moses (Genesis xlix and Deuteronomy xxxiii). Naphtali
thus became Hart, and Naphtali's son would use that as his surname;
Benjamin was Wolf; Judah was Lyon, sometimes (through the German
Loewe) Levi; and so on. Of Hebraic surnames the tribal patronymics
Cohen and Levi persisted. Often surnames which were already in use on
the Continent were dropped when the bearers came to England: though a
few (e.g. Waag or Wagg, Heilbuth, Gompertz, &c.) persisted. But very
often more than one surname ran concurrently. Thus Ze'eb Wolf, son of
Isaac Margulies of Jungbunzlau, was known in the Hambro' Synagogue as
Wolf Prager, but figured to the outside world as 'Mr. Benjamin Isaac, Jew
merchant, of extensive charity' (*Gentleman's Magazine*, xx. 139).     (201)

(*b*) There was a case in 1726 which attracted attention even in the non-
Jewish world—that of José da Costa Villareal, formerly Comptroller-General
to the armies of the King of Portugal. In 1726 it came to his ears that his
arrest on a charge of Judaizing was imminent. Profiting by the confusion
caused by an outbreak of fire at Lisbon, he embarked for England on one
of his own ships, together with as much of his property as he could collect
and seventeen members of his family. The total value of the fortune which
they brought with them was said to exceed £300,000 (*Daily Journal*, 26 Aug.
1726; *Trs. J.H.S.E.* xiii. 271 ff.). Another noteworthy case was that of Diego
Lopez Pereira (d. 1759), who had farmed the tobacco revenue in Portugal,
established branches of his banking house in London and Amsterdam, and

after the War of the Spanish Succession followed Charles VI to Vienna to administer the tobacco *régie*. Immediately on his arrival he declared his allegiance to Judaism, adopting the name of Moses and proving a constant champion for his brothers in faith at any time when persecution threatened. The emperor created him Baron D'Aguilar; Maria Theresa made him a privy councillor; and he was responsible for the rebuilding of the imperial palace at Schönbrunn. Ultimately the Spanish government requested the extradition of this wealthy renegade for trial by the Holy Office. He then settled in London, with his fourteen children and his retinue of servants and slaves. His son, Ephraim Lopez Pereira (d. 1802), succeeded to his title and his fortune, and became notorious as the miserly proprietor of 'Starvation Farm' at Islington (*R.E.J.* xcvii. 115 ff.; Wilson, *Wonderful Characters*, ii. 92–97). (201)

(*c*) For the fullest accounts of the 'Jew Bill' see *Bibl.* A.7. 28, 31*a*, and 65; Henriques, *Jews and English Law*, pp. 240–5; and Picciotto, *Sketches*, chapters ix and x. Other details are added here from British Museum, Add. MSS. 33053, ff. 56, 69; L. Dickins and M. Stanton, *An Eighteenth Century Correspondence* (London, 1910), pp. 200, 227; *H.M.C.* viii, App. 219*b*, and vi, App. 207; *H.M.C., Carlisle*, p. 207; *B.M. Records*, i. 41 ff.; contemporary periodicals; and the pamphlets listed in *Bibl.* B.1. That the nervousness of the government was not unjustified is shown by the fact that General Oglethorpe, who had supported the Bill, was unseated at the general election, at Haslemere, although the solicitor for the Jews, P. C. Webb, was elected (*Misc. J.H.S.E.* i. ii–iii). In London, too, the anti-ministerial livery turned against Sir William Calvert for the same reason, in the most excited election in living memory (Maitland, *London*, ed. Entick, 1756, i. 703–7). (222)

(*d*) That the repeal of the Naturalization Act was responsible for a wave of conversions among the upper class of the Jewish community, as is generally stated, lacks foundation. These conversions had already been in progress for some time (an outstanding case was that of Moses Mendes, the poet), and they continued after 1753 without any perceptible increase in momentum other than what may be ascribed to the growing anglicization. That Samson Gideon's estrangement from Judaism was because of the failure of the 'Jew Bill' is incorrect. Being English-born it did not affect him: he had married outside the Jewish community long before, and his children were being brought up as Christians; and his quarrel with the Synagogue—not accompanied by conversion—was due not to the failure of the Bill, but took place before its repeal, owing to his disapproval of the steps which had been taken to procure it: see his letter of 5 September 1753, in *Anglo-Jewish Letters*, pp. 130–2.

The incidental question regarding the legality of land-owning by Jews continued to be discussed, notably in a celebrated work of P. C. Webb, writing under the name of 'A Gentleman of Lincoln's Inn' (*Bibl.* B.1. 114) replied to by Joseph Grove (ibid., 120). The legal ability of Jews to hold land in fee remained open to question as late as 1846, though generally admitted and acted upon (Henriques, op. cit., pp. 192–3). (223)

## CHAPTER X

(*a*) The Great Synagogue was reconstructed in 1766 (when Handel's music was used at the dedication) and again, drastically, in 1790. The first Hambro' Synagogue building was dedicated in 1725. In 1761 the so-called 'New Synagogue' was established, notwithstanding the opposition of the older congregations. These, with the Spanish and Portuguese synagogue in Bevis Marks, constituted the kernel of London synagogal organization until late in the nineteenth century: all, however, were independent, the most elementary rudiments of co-operative action appearing only at the close of the reign of George III. Apart from these bodies a small congregation was already in existence in Westminster at the beginning of the reign, and probably another in Rosemary Lane near the Tower of London, the nucleus of which went back to 1748. In the last decade of the century two minor congregations, following the Polish variation of the Ashkenazi rite, were founded in the East End. (227)

(*b*) The Jewish occupations are partially enumerated by M. D. George, *London Life in the 18th Century* (London, 1925), pp. 125–32, and by J. Rumney in *J.C. Supplement*, December 1935. The engraver, Abraham d'Oliveyra, was registered as silversmith in 1725, and from that date the record is continuous. Clockmakers occur from 1730 (C. E. Atkins, *Register of Apprentices, London Clockmakers Company*, London, 1931). As early as 1760 a London Jewish milkman is encountered (manuscript records of Great Synagogue) and a Jewish wine-merchant in fiction earlier still (*A Frolick to Horn Fair*, 1707). Jewish artists figure from 1720 (D'Oliveyra, followed in 1727 by David Estevens), and towards the end of the century they excelled in miniature-painting. The father of Hannah Norsa, the actress, kept the Punch-Bowl tavern in Drury Lane, *c.* 1732. Several printers emerge simultaneously (possibly in consequence of the abolition of some craft-restriction) in 1770. The lay head of the Bristol community in 1786 was the much-appreciated glass-worker, Lazarus Jacobs, who founded a dynasty. (227)

(*c*) It was naturally to the dealer in second-hand commodities that housebreakers and highwaymen turned to dispose of the proceeds of their crimes. Accordingly, as the century advanced, Jews began to figure as receivers. The abuse was no doubt exaggerated; and the community did its best to dissociate itself from the criminals, the Great Synagogue advertising a reward in 1766 for information which might result in the prosecution of the receivers of stolen goods.

Jews were also found in various border-line professions. They kept many of the sponging-houses, as the eighteenth-century novelists were abundantly aware; Abraham Mendes was the runner responsible for the arrest of Jack Sheppard in 1724; while a Mrs. Levy kept a Fleet Marriage Parlour. The phrase 'Cheap as Jew Bail', and the figure of 'Beau Mordecai' in Hogarth's *Harlot's Progress* and contemporary stage-pieces, suggest other eighteenth-century reproaches. The synagogues are said, however, to have formulated a scheme for checking the abuse of 'Jew Bail' also as part of their drive against criminality (*London Chronicle*, 21–23 Nov. 1771). The following additional eighteenth-century Jewish callings are to be noted: Abraham Francia (of Bordeaux), 'a Jew wine-merchant', d. 1749; Samuel Mendes, timber-merchant, d. 1759. A Jewish upholsterer is recorded c. 1738, a tea-merchant 1736, a 'penny barber' 1753, and an Anglo-Indian journalist, Emanuel Samuel, c. 1780 (cf. Goldsmith's *Haunch of Venison* for another). (228)

(d) The drive against criminality resulted in the re-emigration of a number of pauper Jews to the Continent (*London Chronicle*, 3–5 Dec. 1771 and 21–23 Jan. 1772). The results soon became apparent. The Plymouth Aliens Register shows that among Jews resident there at the time of the Napoleonic Wars twenty-four had landed at Harwich between 1758 and 1773, but only one after that date: while eight landed in London after 1773 as against only four before. It is clear from this both that the influx was stemmed and that the port (as well as the manner) of entry changed. (236)

(e) Emanuel, *A Century and a Half*, p. 7. Wills of Jewish sailors in the Navy are to be found from 1759. Soldiers can be traced only half a century later; but Jews figured in the Honourable Artillery Company—the oldest London volunteer organization—as early as the reign of Charles II, and the Spanish and Portuguese synagogue sent three persons to serve in the City Train-bands in and after 1684. In the roll of the White Regiment of the City Militia, in 1773, there are twelve Jewish names among a total of 200. At Waterloo, as Wellington admitted in the House of Lords in 1833, fifteen Jewish officers served under him. Apparently he meant persons of Jewish birth, as professing Jews could not obtain commissions until the repeal of the Test Act, and Judaism was not recognized by Army Regulations until 1886. (239)

## CHAPTER XI

(a) A comprehensive account is M. F. Modder, *The Jew in the Literature of England* (Philadelphia, 1939); see also *Bibl.* and *Nov. Bibl.* A.12, and the various works listed ibid. B.19. Before Cumberland (e.g. in Smollett's *Count Fathom* of 1753, the year of the 'Jew Bill') the Jew is occasionally depicted in a favourable light, but only as an incidental character. The change of attitude at the close of the century was probably due in some measure to personal intercourse with such persons as the art-patron David Alves Rebello, or Isaac Mocatta, the friend of Landor, as well as with the Jewish authors mentioned above. William Cobbett, writing in 1810, deplored the fact that on the contemporary stage the part of the moralist and virtuous sage was so often given to a Jew (*Political Register*, 1818, p. 522). (244)

(b) *Bibl.* A.10. 31–32, B.17. In one of these proto-Zionistic works, *An Attempt to remove prejudices concerning the Jewish Nation* (London, 1804), the enthusiastic Thomas Witherby pleaded that the sufferings of the Jews were the best evidence of their moral integrity, and that they should be honoured as the benefactors of mankind rather than persecuted on account of their opinions. Equally significant was the plea of the popular novelist who wrote under the name 'Deborah': 'the ardent wish of being in any degree useful to that sacred nation is constantly near to my heart'; while Anselm Bayly, sub-dean of the Chapel Royal, had declared in words which a generation before would have been considered preposterous: 'Jews and Christians should look on one another as brethren' (idem, *Vindication of Jews*, London, 1819: cf. further excerpts in A. Cohen, *Anglo-Jewish Scrap-Book*, pp. 334 ff.).     (245)

(*c*) This was explicitly laid down in a ruling of Lord Brougham in 1833: 'His Majesty's subjects professing the Jewish religion are born to all the rights, immunities and privileges of His Majesty's other subjects, excepting so far as positive enactments of law deprive them of those rights, immunities, and privileges.'

As against the advances mentioned in the text (for which see Henriques, op. cit., pp. 32–33; idem, *Jewish Marriages and English Law*, pp. 45–49; Picciotto, *Sketches*, pp. 108, 181–2, 214) is to be reckoned the decision in 1819, in connexion with Harper's Charity at Bedford, that Jews, though ratepayers, could not claim admission to parish schools. Yet seven years later Lord Chancellor Eldon admitted the abstract right of Jews to vote in the election of a vicar, while refusing it to Roman Catholics (Henriques, *Jews and English Law*, pp. 34–48, 247).

In 1818 a London vestry had admitted proxies in order to enable Jews to record their votes on their holydays. Already in 1783 the Lord Mayor had ordered the prosecution of a parish officer for refusing relief to a Jew (*London Chronicle*).
                                                                          (248)

(*d*) This feeling was accentuated by the fact that the presence in Parliament of persons of Jewish birth was now no longer exceptional. When a baptized member of the Villareal family had tried to become government candidate at Nottingham in 1758 his request had been ignominiously rejected (*Trs. J.H.S.E.* xiii. 285). But in 1802 Sir Manasseh Lopes (afterwards to be associated with a notorious scandal of the unreformed Parliament) was returned for Romney, remaining a member for one constituency or another for about a quarter of a century; while Ralph Bernal, whose father had left the synagogue out of pique, was returned for Lincoln in 1818, and David Ricardo, already famous as a political economist, for Portarlington in the following year. About 1830 Bernal, some of whose family were still contributing members of the synagogue, became Chairman of Committees. At least one half-Jew had preceded these—'Pitt's Jew', Samson Gideon the younger (later Lord Eardley), elected for Cambridge in 1770. The objection to the presence of Jews in the House at this time was thus frankly religious.
                                                                          (251)

(*e*) In the colonies emancipation proceeded more speedily than in the mother-country. Jamaica had been the most intolerant of British possessions. In the eighteenth century its numerous and prosperous Jewish community had been subjected to special taxation, excluded from public office and even from juries, forbidden to exercise the franchise, and heavily fined by their indignant fellow-residents of the Christian faith when they dared to request it. Civil restrictions went further still, preventing them under fantastically heavy penalties even from having Christians in their employment. But it was not easy to maintain this attitude after toleration had become firmly implanted on the mainland of North America, and in 1831 all Jewish disabilities were abolished, Jamaica leading the entire Empire in this respect. In Barbados the process followed rather different lines. Special taxation was abolished in 1761, and political disabilities were removed by an Act of the local government of 1802, confirmed by Parliament in 1820; but for some years to come the Jewish community enjoyed a special status, being entitled to elect five representatives to apportion their share of taxation. In Canada, where Jewish commissary officers had accompanied, and Jewish traders followed, the British conquest, a congregation had been established as early as 1768 at Montreal. In 1808 a Jew, Ezekiel Hart, was elected to the legislature, but was refused permission to take his seat. In 1831–2, however, a Bill was passed extending the same rights to Jews as to Christians. In the Antipodes the first community was established at Sydney in 1817, to be followed within a few years by others at Melbourne, Hobart, Auckland, and so on. In this new country the Jews were from the outset on terms of equality with their neighbours (Jacob Montefiore was one of the original commissioners for the colonization of South Australia), and religious discrimination could not very well find a place. The same was the case in South Africa, where scattered Jews had settled even before the British occupation, and a community was organized at Cape Town in 1841. The unquestioned success of the colonial precedent was frequently cited among the arguments for political emancipation at home.

It is curious that, while Jews were excluded from full rights in England, they were permitted to act on behalf of the government abroad: John Jacob Hart was Consul-General in Saxony, c. 1836–42. (254)

(f) As if to point the moral, in the same year James Joseph Sylvester had been placed second wrangler in the mathematical tripos at Cambridge, but was unable to graduate owing to the statutory declaration which had to be taken by every person on proceeding to his degree (at Oxford the declaration had to be made on matriculation, Jews being thus excluded from the university from the outset). The University of Edinburgh had, however, graduated a Jewish physician as early as 1779, and in 1836 Trinity College, Dublin, admitted a Jew to a degree for the first time, being the first Anglican university to do so. It was only in 1871 that the University Tests Act threw the universities open to all persons, including Jews, on equal terms; though contrary to what is generally believed Jews had been empowered to graduate in Oxford and Cambridge a few years earlier.

The process of civic emancipation outside the City of London had followed much the same lines as here but has attracted far less attention. In 1837 D. Levy refused to stand for election as City Councillor in Portsmouth, but E. Emanuel was duly elected there in 1841, Abraham Abrahams having been elected meanwhile (1838) at Southampton. David Barnett, together with the Quaker James Sturge, was elected similarly to the first Council after the incorporation of Birmingham in 1839 and both were allowed to sit, although the former refused to take the Christological oath and the latter any oath at all. The first provincial Jewish mayor was J. L. Levy (Rochester, 1857). Although a Jew could legally be Recorder after 1845, no Jew actually

was appointed until 1915 (S. H. Emanuel at Winchester; yet C. S. Samuel
had been Deputy Recorder of Liverpool in 1881).                    (255)

Towards the social history of the Jews in England in the Hanoverian
period much new information has accumulated, summarized by R. D.
Barnett in *Three Centuries*, ed. V. D. Lipman, pp. 45–64, and by A. Rubens,
'Portrait of Anglo-Jewry' in *Trs. J.H.S.E.* xix. 13–52. The immigration from
Portugal seems to have reached its climax in 1725–8, when the average
number of remarriages under the auspices of the London synagogue of
couples *vindos de Portugal* was 15; the last such case registered was in 1735
(possibly the result of a change of outlook in the Rabbinate) but the immigration continued long after—not only direct from the Peninsula, but also
via Bordeaux and in some cases proceeding to Dublin (cf. *Jewish Social
Studies*, xviii. 118–24). The role of the Sephardi element in London finance
in the eighteenth century is personified in Samson Gideon (for whom see
now also L. S. Sutherland in *Economic History Review*, xvi. 15–29, and *Trs.
J.H.S.E.* xvii. 79–90) and the less prominent, but religiously loyal, communal magnate Joseph Salvador or Jessurun Rodrigues, the only other
Jewish government underwriter, a Governor of the East India Company. He
also advised the Newcastle administration on financial matters and was responsible for issuing British government loans on the Amsterdam market: cf.
his correspondence in *The Jenkinson Papers*, ed. H. S. Tucker, London, 1949.

The commercial crisis and suspension of payments in Amsterdam in 1773
struck a very serious blow at the economic prosperity of the London
Sephardi Jews, many of whom were by now living on the income from in-
vestments: cf. for all this C. Wilson, *Anglo-Dutch Commerce and Finance in the
18th Century* (Cambridge, 1941), esp. pp. 116–18, 167. Meanwhile, the participation of Jews in general life had slowly expanded. By 1720 a Jewish
scholar who knew Arabic assisted Halley in making his translation of Mene-
laus' *Spherics*. In 1723 Dr. Isaac de Sequeira Samuda was elected a fellow
of the Royal Society, to be followed within the next generation by half a
dozen other Jews (*Misc. J.H.S.E.* v. 146–75) including Joseph Salvador and
Dr. Jacob de Castro Sarmento, who (and not his namesake Jacob de Castro)
was the advocate of variolation, as is proved by the fact that the name
figures in full on the title-page of the third (1731) edition of his work on the
subject. Jael, daughter of the Solomon Mendes who corresponded with
James Thomson (p. 209), became as Mrs. R. H. Pye the earliest Anglo-
Jewish poetess and novelist. Integration into London Society, good and bad,
proceeded simultaneously. Some families which played a prominent part in
the affairs of the synagogue—such as Lopes Suasso and Aguilar—flaunted
nobiliary titles, albeit only Baronies of the Empire. As early as 1768 Jews
were admitted to and ruined at the fashionable gaming clubs (cf. Hickey's
*Memoirs*, i. 79 ff.). The list of Moroccan envoys on p. 234 may be supplemented by the names of Hayim Toledano (1693), Moses ibn Attar (1721),
Masahod de la Mar (c. 1775), and Samuel Yulee (1820?). For the picture
of the Jew in English literature (above, p. 244) see now E. Rosenberg,
*From Shylock to Svengali*, London, 1961. The background of recent events is
outlined in H. M. Sachar, *The Course of Modern Jewish History* (London, 1958),
and S. Grayzel, *A History of the Contemporary Jews* (Philadelphia, 1960).

# INDEX

Aaron fil' Abraham (c. 1249), 112 n.
— of Canterbury, Rabbi (c. 1242), 128.
— of Colchester (c. 1277), 95, 96 n., 120.
— fil' Isaac of Oxford (c. 1141), 8.
— Joseph (Justice of Jews, 1198), 29.
— of Lincoln (d. 1186), 15–16, 17, 23, 109, 113, 278, 281.
— of London (c. 1223), 119 n.
— of Sittingbourne (c. 1266), 120 n.
— fil' Vives (c. 1270), 97 n., 279.
— of York (d. 1268: Archpresbyter 1236–43), 24 n., 31, 44 n., 48–49, 51, 102, 106, 113, 115 n., 125.
Abigail (Avegaye) of Norwich (c. 1233), 95 n.
Abingdon, 277: 'Jeweis' of, 133 n.
Abjuration, Oath, 214, 248, 249, 260 ff.
·Aboab, Rabbi Immanuel, 284.
Abrabanel, Don Isaac, 74.
Abraham of Berkhamsted (d. 1272), 46, 55–56, 274.
— fil' Deulecresse of Norwich (d. 1279), 73, 78 n.
— ibn Ezra (1093–1167), 12, 80 n., 126, 128, 280.
— of Felmingham, 15.
— Gubbay, of Gloucester (c. 1225), 279.
— Hasid (12th century), 119.
— Hayim b. Joseph, of Lincoln (c.1271), 118 n.
— of London, 118 n.
— fil' Muriel (c. 1203), 34 n.
— Pinch, of Winchester (d. 1235), 279.
— fil' Rabbi (c. 1175), 279.
— fil' Simon (c. 1152), 272.
— le Skirmiscur (c. 1250), 114.
Abrams sisters (Harriet, Theodosia, Eliza: c. 1760–c. 1830), 243.
Achin, sultan of, 284.
Acton Burnell, statute of (1283), 72.
Adler, Hermann (Chief Rabbi 1891–1911), 258 n.
— Nathan Marcus (Chief Rabbi 1845–90), 258.
Adolphus, John (1768–1845), 241.
Advowsons, 216, 221, 265, 268 n.
Aetheldred, law of, 211.
Agreement of the People (1648), 153–4.
Agriculture, 70 ff., 282.
Aguilar, Diego (Moses) Lopez Pereira, Baron d' (c. 1690–1759), 288–9, 294.
— Ephraim Lopez Pereira, Baron d' (1739–1802), 288–9.
Albigensians, 57.

Alcuin, 129 n.
Alexander III, Pope, 18.
— bishop of Lincoln, 130.
— le Convers (d. 1327), 134.
— Michael Solomon, Anglican Bishop in Jerusalem (1799–1845), 259 n.
Alfonsi, Petrus (c. 1062–1110), 6–7.
Alfred Anglicus, 280.
Algiers, 191.
Aliens Act (1793), 238.
— Immigration Act (1905), 270.
— Taxes, 195 n., 287.
Alsace, 200–1, 212.
Altercatio judaei cum christiano, 5, 129–30.
Alvares, Duarte Henriques (c. 1665), 282.
Amatus Lusitanus, 139.
America, 202–3, 287, 292–3: see Canada, New York, United States, West Indies.
Ames (Añes), Dunstan (c. 1521), 140.
— Francis (d. 1594), 140, 141.
— Jorge (c. 1584), 140.
Amidei, Alessandro (c. 1658), 147 n.
Amiens, 87.
Amsterdam, 142, 144, 149, 153, 154, 169, 173, 198, 232, 283.
Anesty, Richard of, 109.
Angevin (name), 94.
— of Canterbury, 94.
Anglesey, Lord, 181.
Anne, Queen, 185 n.
Anselm, St., 5–6.
Antwerp, 136 ff., 178, 282.
Apology for the Honourable Nation of the Jews (1648), 153.
Appeal to the Humanity of the English People (1812), 246.
Aquinas, Thomas, 69.
Archae (= Chirograph Chests), 29, 52, 61, 62–64, 65 n., 72, 73, 81, 92 n., 97, 100, 109 ff., 275.
Architecture, domestic, 11, 15, 123.
Archpresbyter, office of, 30–31, 51, 79–80, 112; see Aaron of York, Cok Hagin fil' Deulecresse, Elias le Eveske, Hagin fil' Magister Moses, Jacob of London, Josce fil' Isaac.
Aristobulus, first Bishop of Britain, 1.
Armada, Spanish, 140.
Army Contractors, 184, 185, 193, 209, 287–8.
Arnold, Dr. Thomas, 261.
Artists, Jews as, medieval, 115; eighteenth century, 202, 290.